INTERNATIONAL ECONOMIC

General Editor: John H. J

THE CONSTITUTIONALIZATION ~~~~ WORLD
TRADE ORGANIZATION

The Constitutionalization of the World Trade Organization

Legitimacy, Democracy, and Community in the International Trading System

DEBORAH Z. CASS

OXFORD
UNIVERSITY PRESS

OXFORD
UNIVERSITY PRESS

Great Clarendon Street, Oxford OX2 6DP

Oxford University Press is a department of the University of Oxford.
It furthers the University's objective of excellence in research, scholarship,
and education by publishing worldwide in

Oxford New York

Auckland Cape Town Dar es Salaam Hong Kong Karachi
Kuala Lumpur Madrid Melbourne Mexico City Nairobi
New Delhi Shanghai Taipei Toronto

With offices in

Argentina Austria Brazil Chile Czech Republic France Greece
Guatemala Hungary Italy Japan Poland Portugal Singapore
South Korea Switzerland Thailand Turkey Ukraine Vietnam

Oxford is a registered trade mark of Oxford University Press
in the UK and in certain other countries

Published in the United States
by Oxford University Press Inc., New York

British Library Cataloguing in Publication Data
Data available

Library of Congress Cataloging-in-Publication Data
Cass, Deborah Z.
The constitutionalization of the World Trade Organization : legitimacy,
democracy, and community in the international trading system / Deborah Z. Cass.
p. cm.
Includes index.
ISBN 0–19–928463–6 (alk. paper) — ISBN 0–19–928584–5 (alk. paper)
1. World Trade Organization. 2. Foreign trade regulation. 3. Commerce. I. Title.
K4610.C37 2005
382'.92—dc22

2005011138

Typeset by Newgen Imaging Systems (P) Ltd., Chennai, India
Printed in Great Britain
on acid-free paper by
Biddles Ltd., King's Lynn

ISBN 0–19–928463–6
ISBN 0–19–928584–5 (Pbk.)

1 3 5 7 9 10 8 6 4 2

To Eva and Ephraim, and Ben and Esther,
who came such a long way,

and to Hannah and Rosa, who are just starting out

General Editor's Preface

The Oxford University Press International Economic Law Series is designed to present works that deeply probe problems regarding the 'globalized' and 'interdependent' world in which we now live. As the series General Editor, I am honoured to present another distinguished work which develops material relevant to this subject. This latest volume in the International Economic Law Series, is a book about the 'constitutionalization of the WTO', authored by Dr Deborah Cass.

This extraordinary book probes the frontier of international economic law. The word 'constitutionalization' is a controversial word, when used in international relations, and indeed, the use of it in the context of institutions such as the WTO, has been criticized by diplomats and others who have a strong inclination to resist changes which involve departure from older ideas of 'sovereignty.' Thus, to use the nomenclature 'constitution' for a treaty-based institutional structure is threatening.

Dr Cass has done just this in an extraordinarily focused and well-developed analysis of 'constitutional principles' in connection with the WTO. The book is very stimulating and is clearly designed to force readers to think about a major international economic institution in a manner that is substantially different from many of the traditional approaches. It is thus an excellent contribution to the general literature of international economic law, and also specifically to thinking about the WTO, which has, itself, been the subject of considerable recent attention regarding its institutional structure.[1]

It is my pleasure to introduce this book, which will certainly enhance public and expert understanding of a number of complex topics concerning the 'globalized' world in which we live.

JOHN H. JACKSON[2]

---

[1] Peter Sutherland *et al*, *The Future of the WTO: Addressing Institutional Challenges in the New Millennium*, Report by the Consultative Board to the Director-General Supachai Panitchpakdi, available at <http://www.wto.org> last visited 9 February 2005.

[2] *University Professor of Law*, Georgetown University Law Center (GULC), Washington, D.C.; *Director*, Institute of International Economic Law, GULC; *General Editor*, International Economic Law Series, Oxford University Press; *Editor in Chief, Journal of International Economic Law*, Oxford University Press.

Preface

In December 2004, with war ongoing in Iraq, and the elections just over in Afghanistan following a lengthy conflict, the World Trade Organization opened accession talks with both countries. In the same year, the British Chancellor of the Exchequer, Gordon Brown, envisioned a 'new Marshall Plan' for the developing world, including increased aid targeting health, education, and infant mortality; continuing trade rule reform; and debt forgiveness. No less controversially, he called for 'increased trade and a globalization that also means both security and justice on a global scale'.[1] As the tenth anniversary year of the WTO approached, it seemed that policy-makers around the world had become convinced that, in a post 9/11 environment, international peace and security issues would only be tackled effectively if international trade, poverty reduction, health, and development could also be addressed.

The policies proposed were, of course, contentious. In 2001, Brazil had manufactured and supplied AIDS drugs free to people living with HIV, and India had threatened to sell drugs to an international medical organization for a fraction of the cost at which those drugs would have been supplied by a major pharmaceutical company. Both actions, potentially, were in contravention of WTO rules. Wherever one looked, it seemed as though international trade, once the domain of Geneva-based bureaucrats, had now become an issue of intense political interest. In 2004, Turkey was invited, subject to some strict conditions, to join the largest regional arrangement within the international trade system, the European Union, the first Muslim country to do so. The EU was enlarged, and with it came new questions about the type and level of compensation payable to states, under the GATT, for losses suffered as a result of the new accessions. In 2005, quotas in the textiles and clothing industry came to an end, marking not only the decline of developed state protectionism in this sector, but also the beginning of difficult South–South negotiations between China and less-developed states, the latter being vulnerable to China's comparative advantage in the textile and clothing market. Also in that year, China marked its first three years as a member of the formal trading system with a sometimes mixed, though mostly positive, report card.[2]

---

[1] Speech by the Chancellor of the Exchequer Gordon Brown at a conference on 'Making Globalisation Work For All—The Challenge Of Delivering The Monterrey Consensus', 16 February 2004, <http://www.hm-treasury.gov.uk/newsroom_and_speeches/press/2004/press_12_04.cfm>.
[2] Bridges Weekly Trade News Digest, Vol 8, Number 43, 15 December 2004.

Integral to all these transformations are questions about the so-called constitutionalization of the WTO. The accession of Iraq and Afghanistan, and the proposed new Marshall Plan, can be seen as raising questions about membership and participation in the international trade system, and the tendency of the WTO to position itself as an organization of international governance, rather than just trade. Brazil's health policy questions the scope of international patent protection sanctioned by the expansion of international trade rules into national regulatory domains. India's campaign to broaden WTO criteria for compulsory licensing and parallel importing is a response to perceived incursions by international trade rules on state sovereignty. EU enlargement highlights the precarious relationship between regional and multilateral trade. China's membership of the organization, as an economy-in-transition, opens the door to a discussion of WTO rule-making and application, especially in the sensitive area of dumping. And the elimination of textiles protection highlights the difficult problems of accommodating the developmental needs of different states within a trading system which purports to hold to the principle of non-discrimination. In short, constitutional questions about membership, governance, national regulatory control, state sovereignty, rule-making, and development policy are all implicated. Critical to these developments, then, is the claim that the WTO is 'constitutionalizing'.

This study seeks to understand what is meant by that claim and argues that the WTO is not constitutionalized, and nor, according to any current meanings of the term, should it be. Part I sets out the origins of the WTO constitutionalization debate. Chapter 1 begins by setting out a brief history of the contemporary development of institutional forms and democratic ideas associated with constitutionalism within the world trading system (1.2).[3] In the next section I set out the problem of constitutionalization (1.3), and, then provide a detailed outline of the argument of the book (1.4).

Chapter 2 turns to thinking about how to ask whether the WTO has been constitutionalized, and, having concluded that it is necessary to have some measure by which to address the question, I identify an account of constitutionalization which, traditionally, has been used to analyse changes in political and legal systems (2.4). This model, which I call the received account of constitutionalization, emphasizes the presence of six core elements: the emergence of constraints on social, political, and economic behaviour; a new *Grundnorm* or rule of recognition; political community; deliberative process; realignment of relationships within that community; and social legitimacy. Also in Chapter 2, I confront three preliminary objections to the constitutional analysis based on the view that, either constitutionalization applies only to national systems,

[3] Those familiar with the international trade system may wish to skim this section, or skip it altogether, and move directly to sections 1.3 and 1.4.

or the WTO is an international treaty, or the constitution of the WTO is general international law (2.5).

The study then goes on to describe how WTO constitutionalization models emerged from international economic law, and argues that the field is characterized by a number of tendencies that fuelled speculation about WTO constitutionalization (Chapter 3). These tendencies include an increasing conflation of institutions with constitutions; integration of world markets through globalization; a consensus on the benefits of liberalization; an expansion of law to take in new forms of regulation; and an anxiety about how to define and limit the field of economic law, and its role in transforming international order.

In the middle chapters of the study, in Part II, I analyse three models of WTO constitutionalization that emerged from this general international economic law landscape. *Institutional managerialism* focuses on management of international trade disputes using institutions and rules that are largely procedural in nature (Chapter 4). Its method is empirical and yet it contains a strong reformist element which yearns to show how this form of constitutionalization is conducive to improving international economic order. The second model, *rights-based*, is an explicitly prescriptive model whose purpose is to mould WTO law, using cosmopolitan theory, into a system of directly effective supra-constitutional law (Chapter 5). The third model, *judicial norm-generation*, claims that the WTO is constitutionalizing by virtue of the judicial work of the Appellate Body which is actively constructing norms and structures of a constitutional type (Chapter 6).

The study concludes on the basis of this analysis that none of these three models conform with the received account of constitutionalization drawn from domestic and international legal literature. While institutional managerialism addressed the problem of *Grundnorm* change, and to some extent legitimacy and deliberative process, it failed to satisfy the requirement of positing a community to authorize any constitution-making. Rights-based constitutionalization only in passing focuses on the nature of the community and its deliberative processes, and is more concerned with elaborations on constitutionalization, which are not part of the core model of the received account. Judicial norm-generation addresses realignment of relationships, and to some extent legitimacy, but is not sensitive to the requirements of community or deliberative process.

The argument continues, in Part III, to address the case against constitutionalization, and alternative conceptualizations. It argues that not only is constitutionalization descriptively inappropriate, but it is normatively undesirable. This position, which I term the *anti-constitutionalization* critique, contends that constitutionalization contracts the capacity of states to decide matters of national interest; is weakly deliberative in form; emphasizes economic goals at the expense of other values; ignores the important contribution of private law to any constitution of rules for international economic order; and is self-legitimating (Chapter 7).

The study concludes that WTO constitutionalization is dominated by these three models, which are neither descriptively accurate, nor prescriptively desirable. Moreover, I suggest that this ascendancy obscures the relationship between WTO constitutionalization discourse and issues of democracy, sovereignty, and economic and political organization in the international economic order (Chapter 8). Not only have the WTO models been shown to be deficient, but the received account has also been revealed as inadequate in the face of various changes to international society, including the decline of the state as the locus of constitutionalization, interdependence between states, and increasing varieties of governance.

I end by calling for trading *democracy* rather than trading constitutionalization. Trading democracy would consist of two elements. First, it would consist of procedural transformation in order to produce a more nuanced, open, and flexible model of constitutional change. A procedurally transformed constitutionalization would take into account the myriad ways in which trade is regulated and managed in the context of the changes wrought by globalization, where normative predictability in trade is generated not only by the state in the legal–political arena, but by a range of other actors located in sites beyond where law is traditionally crafted. But even this is not enough. In my view, a better account of constitutionalization would also address the difficult issues of substance raised by the anti-constitutionalization critique in relation to, for example, the overemphasis on economic over social goals, and inadequate attention to economic effects of the process. This could be achieved by refocusing the constitutionalization project on the primary goal of the WTO system, which, I suggest, is development rather than free trade. This interpretation is consistent with the treaty terms and context, and the intentions of the constitutional community as expressed through those modes, and is the only plausible reconciliation of divergent emphases within the agreements between the principles of non-discrimination, multilateralism, transparency, and liberalization in trade on the one hand, and economic and sustainable development on the other.

Finally, the problem of WTO constitutionalization, and indeed transnational constitutionalization generally, is of considerable importance in the current international order. Will a constitutionalized WTO help producers and manufacturers reduce discriminatory trade practices of foreign competitors? Will it open up market access for developing countries? Will it be participatory, transparent, and accountable enough to be called a constitution? Will states have sufficient political control over the judicial activity of the organization? Should it be able to decide questions of mixed trade and environmental or health policy? Will it turn, by stealth, into an institution of governance rather than trade? In short, is the World Trade Organization just another international institution or does it warrant the label 'constitution'? I do not claim to have all the answers, or even to know what the right questions are. The aim of this study is to begin unscrambling the various meanings of the term in order to think about their significance both for the WTO and for general international law conceptions of constitutionalization. To do that, I have relied on some very useful analyses of WTO constitutionalization already in the literature, and, to this extent, I owe an enormous debt to that work. This book seeks to capitalize on that very rich field of WTO constitutionalization analysis in such a way as to open up debate about the WTO and about constitutionalization itself.

Acknowledgements

This book has had a long gestation. It was conceived about the same time as my first daughter, Hannah, when I was studying at Harvard Law School in 1994, and the manuscript was completed ten years later, in London, in 2004. In the meantime I had moved through three continents, lived in five different houses, and had a second child, Rosa. Despite this peripatetic existence, and with much support from my husband and colleague, Gerry Simpson, and our two children, the project was completed. At Harvard I would like to thank my dissertation supervisor, Fred Schauer and my two doctoral committee members, Frank Michelman and Robert Howse. David Kennedy was a superb teacher of international law, and the creative intellectual environment in his class of 1995 has influenced my thinking over a long period of time. Conversations at that time with Kerry Rittich, Robert Wai, Treasa Dunworth, Patricia O'Donovan, and, in 1999, with Hani Sayed, Outi Korhonen, Fleur Johns, Amr Shalakany, John Ohnesorge, Jin Chen, Sunjoon Cho, and Mattias Kumm, were not only most enjoyable, but influential on my work.

Gerry Simpson and Susan Marks generously read, and reread, and critiqued, large parts of the manuscript. Joel Trachtman, Damian Chalmers, and Niki Lacey helpfully commented on chapters. Two anonymous reviewers provided detailed and incisive criticism, much of which has been taken into account in the final product. Tom Campbell, at the Australian National University, facilitated leave for me in 1995. Caltex Pty Ltd funded my period of study in the United States.

The London School of Economics Law Department has been supportive in a number of ways. The Department provided me with research leave for the period September to December 2002, sick leave from August 2003 to July 2004, and a further sabbatical in late 2004. As Convenors of the Law Department, Robert Reiner and Christopher Greenwood went to great lengths to assist me in completing the manuscript and their efforts are very much appreciated. Martin Loughlin has been enormously encouraging to me, by dint not only of his insightful and challenging observations on the manuscript, but also with his laughter and friendship.

Excellent research assistance was provided by LSE research students, Gus Van Harten and N'Gunu Tiny. I would also like to thank John Louth, Gwen Booth, Geraldine Mangley, and Jack Sinden at Oxford University Press. Mandy Tinnams at the LSE Law Department provided administrative assistance above and beyond the call of duty.

Earlier incarnations of chapters were presented at the London School of Economics Law Department; the Australian National University Law Faculty;

Harvard Law School; the British Institute of International and Comparative Law Annual WTO Meeting; the International Law Association Theory Conference; and at Birkbeck College Law Department. Some of the arguments in Chapter 6 are based on DZ Cass, 'The "Constitutionalization" of International Trade Law: Judicial Norm-Generation as the Engine of Constitutional Development in International Trade' (2001) 12 *European Journal of International Law* 39; and Chapter 3 draws on DZ Cass, 'International Business Law and Commerce', in P Cane and M Tushnet (eds), *The Oxford Handbook of Legal Studies* (2003).

The field of international trade is in a moment of great flux. I am fortunate to be writing at a time in which the parameters of the field are still being debated, and to have chosen a topic which is open to so many varied interpretations. These remarks would not be complete without mentioning the enormous debt I owe to the founding scholars of international economic law, and a far-sighted subset of authors who began tinkering with the idea of the WTO as a constitution some ten or so years ago. Ernst-Ulrich Petersmann wrote prolifically and provocatively on the subject. Robert Howse meticulously tracked and critiqued its development. John Jackson was hugely influential, both on WTO constitutionalization, and the field of international economic law from which it emerged. His seminal work, co-authored with William Davey and Alan Sykes, was, for many years, almost the only game in town. Later, Professor Jackson conceptualized the WTO as a constitution, and has, over the years, revisited and expanded upon that argument. The rich body of work produced by all these authors debunks the idea that there is an ivory tower and perfectly illustrates the important role of the academy in developing the theory and practice of law. I am also grateful to Professor Jackson not only for his scholarship but for the generous personal support he, and his wife Joan, have shown me over the years.

Many years ago, when I began my legal studies at the University of Melbourne Law School, Gillian Triggs taught me international law, and Cheryl Saunders taught me constitutional law. I did not realize then that the fields taught by these two inspirational women would ultimately converge for me and become the focus of my major research interest. I owe them a debt for that.

Finally, and again, I cannot overestimate the contribution to my ways of thinking, and being, that my parents, Moss and Shirley Cass, and my brother and sister, Daniel and Naomi Cass, have made. Without their ideas and love I could not have begun to achieve what I have.

Gerry Simpson has supported me in more ways than I could have imagined. He, like me, will be pleased to see the project come to fruition and this particular stage of our travels come to an end.

Contents

Tables of Cases

DOMESTIC

EUROPEAN COURT OF JUSTICE (ECJ)

GATT AND WTO REPORTS

GATT Decisions

WTO Decisions

PCIJ AND ICJ

Tables of International Instruments

Abbreviations

AB	Appellate Body
BISD	Basic Instruments and Selected Documents
BWI	Bretton Woods Institutions
CP	Contracting Parties
DSB	Dispute Settlement Body
DSU	Dispute Settlement Understanding
EC	European Communities
FSC	Foreign Sales Corporation
GATT	General Agreement on Tariffs and Trade
GMO	Genetically Modified Organism
ICSID	International Convention on the Settlement of Investment Disputes
IMF	International Monetary Fund
MS	Member States
NIEO	New International Economic Order
NGO	Nongovernmental Organization
SCM	Subsidies and Countervailing Measures Agreement
SPS	Sanitary and Phytosanitary Agreement
TBT	Technical Barriers to Trade Agreement
TRIMs	Trade-Related Investment Measures Agreement
TRIPs	Trade-Related Aspects of Intellectual Property Rights Agreement
US	United States
WB	World Bank
WIPO	World Intellectual Property Organization
WTO	World Trade Organization

PART I

THE ORIGINS OF THE WTO CONSTITUTIONALIZATION DEBATE

1

International Trade and Constitutionalization

1.1 INTRODUCTION

What *is* the World Trade Organization? Does it represent a new constitution for the international economic order? Should it? This is a book about the constitutionalization of the World Trade Organization, and the contemporary development of institutional forms and democratic ideas associated with constitutionalism within the world trading system. It is about constitutionalization enthusiasts who promote institutions, management techniques, rights discourse, and quasi-judicial power to construct a constitution for the WTO. It is about constitutional sceptics who fear the effect the phenomenon of constitutionalization is having on the autonomy of states, the capacity of the WTO to consider non-economic and non-free-trade goals, and on democratic processes at the WTO and within the nation state. The aim of the study, then, is to disentangle debates about the various meanings of the term 'constitution' when it is used to apply to the World Trade Organization, and to reflect upon the significance of those meanings for more general international law conceptions of constitutions.

I argue here that the WTO is not a constitution by the standards of any conventional, historical definition, nor should it be described as such. After setting out the international economic law context in which the constitutionalization debate has arisen, I begin by showing that the field is dominated by three conceptions of constitutionalization. In one, the WTO is a tool of institutional management to order trade disputes between states. In the second, the WTO is portrayed as a system of rights, somewhat akin to human rights, and this conception is combined with the suggestion that their enforcement should allow individuals to claim against governments, in domestic courts, for violations of international trade rules. In the third approach, constitutionalization is the result of judicialized rule-making by the WTO's dispute resolution body. The study juxtaposes these three models, which it calls institutional managerialism, rights-based constitutionalization, and judicial norm-generation, against a received account of constitutionalization, drawn from domestic and international legal theory and constitutionalization literature, and finds each of them deficient by the light of that account. In the next part of the book, I examine the normative implications of the term using a further school of arguments which I label anti-constitutionalization critique. On the basis of both sets of analyses, the study concludes that the idea of WTO constitutionalization is both descriptively inaccurate, because of the failure to comport with classical understandings of constitutionalization, and prescriptively undesirable, because the ascendancy of these models has so dominated the constitutionalization debate that they have retarded other ways of thinking about the WTO and its relationship with issues of democracy, sovereignty, and the association between economics, politics, and law in the international economic order.

Yet I will also suggest that, as well as there being good descriptive and normative reasons for rethinking the use of the term *constitutionalization*, a more profitable form of argument would be to think about the way its meaning has been transformed by the WTO experience, and, specifically, to consider the way democratization of the trading system, rather than constitutionalization in a formal sense, has emerged as the most important challenge facing the WTO. If a constitution is to be a measure by which an international institution is judged, then a new understanding of that term needs to be fostered, one that is sensitive to contemporary trends, such as globalization, and one that at least recognizes or treats with the absence of elements that have, traditionally, been perceived to be essential for a constitutional structure, such as the existence of a community to authorize constitution-making. A more nuanced, flexible, and open form of constitutional transformation is required, one that can take account of, for example, different levels and types of governance, public and private, state-centred, and non-state controlled, which influence the creation, management, operation, and regulation of international practices in particular sectors such as trade.

But even this is not enough. If all that emerges from this study is agreement that current WTO constitutionalization models are poorly defined, and that multi-level governance and flexibility should be built into any transnational constitutional theory, then an essentially formal model of non-state constitutionalization will still remain. I want to go further and suggest that concentrating merely on the form of constitutionalization runs the risk of losing sight of what sort of constitution people might want for an international trading system. Therefore, in addition to showing the unsuitability of WTO constitutionalization models, and the difficulty of applying general constitutional theory to contemporary international conditions, I will end by making a normative argument that democratized trade, incorporating a more substantive form of democratic entitlement, focusing on development, is what the WTO should be building. In my view, a constitutional model is needed that addresses not only the formal, procedural failures of a state-based constitutionalism, but, also its substantive deficiencies; deficiencies highlighted, very often, by those making the anti-constitutional critique. We need to develop an understanding of constitutionalism that considers, for example, the distributive consequences of WTO decision-making. We need to consider the public effects of private rights in constructing the playing field in which international trade is conducted. We need to question the self-legitimating nature of a project which uses constitutional language to authorize its very existence. We need to ask whether the WTO lives up to its promise of development for developed and developing states. In short, I propose a constitutionalism consisting of three attributes: a rejection of WTO constitutionalization models as currently defined; adoption of a transformed constitutionalism which confronts the globalized, multi-governed, deterritorialized world in which we live; and, the marrying of the latter with a more substantive, thicker, notion of trading democracy as economic development, applicable to WTO constitutionalization theory. A procedurally transformed, substantively democratic, argumentative form of WTO constitutionalization is what is warranted. Trading *democracy* not trading constitutionalization should be its goal. Before I begin, however, I want to introduce the problem by sketching an account of how ideas about institutions, democracy, and constitutionalization have informed international trade.

1.2 THE INSTITUTIONAL BACKGROUND TO THE WTO CONSTITUTIONALIZATION DEBATE

The story of WTO constitutionalization does not begin in the twentieth century. Its origins can be traced back through the history of Western interstate relations. From Thucydides to Paul Kennedy, interstate trade has been, if not synonymous, then closely associated, with the course of war and peace, and the construction of international order.

This coincidence is not surprising. International order has long been bound up with the practice of institutions and ideas about democracy and individual freedom,[1] and in many cases trade has been the key vehicle for these changes. Whether in the form of the Hanseatic League of trading states in the fourteenth century; or the fusing of ideas about free trade with constitutional progress in the eighteenth century; or the World Trade Organization of the twenty-first, international trade often has worn an institutional face and has been infused with ideas about democracy and constitutional progress in the name of international order.

Historically, the development of international law itself runs parallel with the growth of international trade and commerce. One of international law's most enduring instruments—the interstate treaty—arose from the desire of

[1] I Kant, *Perpetual Peace: A Philosophical Essay*, translated with introduction and notes by M Campbell Smith; with a preface by Professor Latta (London: Allen & Unwin, 1915).

states to make agreements to foster friendship, commerce, and navigation. Rules regulating international commerce evolved out of long-standing mercantile customs between buyers and sellers situated in different states. International rules on piracy developed because of the need to secure shipping routes for the pursuit of trade. The rules of international shipping coincided with the emergence of a colonial demand to purchase exotic spices and silks, and functional rubber and timber, from faraway colonies in the New World for use in the Old. In no small part then, trade—the desire to buy and sell, to exchange new products and ideas, and generally to open up intercourse with other countries—was the foundation upon which international law was constructed, and upon which the international order subsequently developed.[2]

Coincident with these changes, freedom of trade, as a branch of freedom of commerce, developed, and was also closely linked with liberal arguments about freeing individuals from the domination of religious or other hierarchical authorities. Freedom to trade was an important part of the Enlightenment project:[3] the repeal of the English Corn Laws, 1846, being a key historical example. At the same time, there arose tension between the desire to increase individual freedom, and the need to institutionalize public order. These two features of trade debate—the construction of order and the freedom of the interests within that order—influenced and opposed each other within the field of modern international trade, and continue to inform it even today.

It is not surprising, then, that the manner in which trading relationships were organized, both between states and with other entities, should have been a matter of political, and ultimately legal, concern. Nor was it surprising, given this tension, that interstate trade was characterized by both a desire to institutionalize these relationships and a resistance to their formalization.

Periodically, groups of Western countries formed unions or leagues in which preferences would be guaranteed between members. In the mid-fourteenth century, Northern Germanic towns banded together to create a political and commercial league, the Hanseatic League, which became one of the first formal institutions to create order in trade between groups of communities. Friendship, commerce, and navigation (FCN) treaties formalized bilateral agreements between states and allowed some goods to enter internal markets of trading partner states under favourable terms. But for the most part, the law of international trade was rudimentary at best.

---

[2] JH Jackson, *The World Trade Organization: Constitution and Jurisprudence* (London: Royal Institute of International Affairs, 1998) 9 [hereinafter Jackson, 'Constitution'] (arguing that the fields virtually overlap because all international law raises economic questions). See also JH Jackson, W Davey, and A Sykes, *Legal Problems of International Economic Relations*, 4th edn (St Paul, Minn: West Publishing, 2002) (citing George Schwarzenberger's claim that international law is the 'generalization' of rules which originally applied to foreign merchants).

[3] See, eg, E Rothschild, *Economic Sentiments: Adam Smith, Condorcet, and the Enlightenment* (Cambridge, Mass: Harvard University Press, 2001) 72–78.

Even in the absence of legal controls, trade was a valuable means to extend revenue and interests of both states and private entities. The colonial project was animated by the mutually compatible desires of imperial expansion and capital extension. England, Portugal, Holland, and France stripped their colonies of foodstuffs and raw materials such as cotton, rubber, and timber, manufactured them into new products and sold the manufactured goods back to the country of origin while not encouraging the supplier of resources develop any industrial capacity. Semi-governmental authorities, and large trading entities, such as the Dutch East Indies Company, were formed. These bodies operated in the non-industrialized regions of the world looking for goods and markets, buying up resources, and, in some cases, establishing themselves as quasi-governing bodies over the local communities.[4] England pressed trade in harmful materials, such as opium, in order to repair its massive trade deficit with China.[5] Trade was the vanguard for international material expansion, and more than occasionally the cause of war.

At home, the newly expanding industrial economies used trade rules, in a protectionist manner, to shore up internal economic development and thwart promotion of exports by countries which might have used their comparative advantage in resources and labour to improve their economies. The United States,[6] Germany, and Japan all grew economically by protecting their borders with tariffs and nurturing and subsidizing their infant industries. In short, the absence of mutually agreed rules to regulate international trade discrimination was one reason that, for the most part, interstate market access was limited, industrial capacities developed unevenly, and economic asymmetries characterized international economic relations.

The lack of a formal international trading regime, with regularized rules equally applicable to all states, was a factor in the disintegration of international order in the early part of the twentieth century. Depressed prices, profits, and interest rates, a resurgence of protectionism in commodities trade, and increased economic concentration led to intense economic competition and political rivalry between states.[7] Ultimately, strained interstate economic conditions contributed, in 1914, to the outbreak of world war.[8] Limited attempts were made to introduce economic order under the auspices of the League of

---

[4] For discussion of the domination of one such island in the Central Pacific, Nauru, see, eg, M Williams and B MacDonald, *The Phosphateers: A History of the British Phosphate Commissioners and the Christmas Island Phosphate Commission* (Melbourne: Melbourne University Press 1985), and N Viviani, Nauru: Phosphate and Political Progress (Canberra: 1970).

[5] John Newsinger, 'Elgin in China' (May/June 2002) 15 *New Left Review* 119.

[6] B Hoekman and M Kostecki, *The Political Economy of the World Trading System*, 2nd edn. (2001) 23.

[7] N Stone, *Europe Transformed 1878–1919*, 2nd edn (Oxford: Blackwell, 1999); E Hobsbawm, *Age of Empire, 1875–1914* (New York: Pantheon Books 1987).

[8] N Ferguson, *The Pity of War* (London: Penguin, 1998).

Nations, but when this organization began to collapse in the mid-1930s so did its international economic aspirations.

Little progress was made in the inter-war period.[9] States generally resumed protectionist trade and monetary policies which emphasized local interests at the expense of international cooperation. The US erected high tariffs, and in 1932 Britain abandoned one hundred years of free trade and entered into preferential trading arrangements with her imperial dependencies.[10] The gold standard was resurrected in the 1920s but almost immediately came under threat. The traditional belief that the standard would automatically maintain balance of payments equilibrium between states, by providing that domestic currencies were convertible into gold at a fixed price, was not tenable in the economic conditions of the new century. The main currencies were 'seriously misaligned'[11] including undervaluation of the franc and overvaluation of sterling. As a result, the US and French economies boomed at the expense of the British. In response Britain de-linked its currency from the gold standard, in the process taking twenty-five dependent countries with it. This precipitated deep hostility from the United States which then suspended its dollar convertibility into gold, despite the presence of ample reserves, immediately wiping out Britain's temporary competitive advantage. In Germany, the National Socialists' violent brand of fascism emerged largely on the back of a 'hash' of 'defective economic arrangements'[12] and was encouraged by widespread national discontent with an economy which had been bankrupted by a combination of poor national management, international demand for reparations after the First World War, and reluctance by other states to open their borders to German products.[13] States adopted 'beggar-thy-neighbour' policies towards other potential trading partners, which ultimately led to unemployment in those states, external debt crises, and currency devaluations. At the outbreak of the Second World War in 1939, any thoughts of international trade cooperation had vanished.

However, during the war, economic and political factors forced Britain and the United States to take the first tentative steps towards interstate economic cooperation. Britain needed money to fund its vast war effort. As Skidelsky argues, the United States, traditionally isolationist, but led by a President, Roosevelt, who was keen to support Britain while maintaining a façade of independence, concocted a plan to lend materials, munitions, and aircraft to Britain in exchange for consideration, the definition of which was kept intentionally vague. Britain's war expenditure was, therefore, largely underwritten by the United States, in a programme designated Lend–Lease, and the first stage of modern transatlantic economic cooperation had been launched.

---

[9] The following account of the inter-war period and international monetary cooperation during the Second World War is based on R Skidelsky, *John Maynard Keynes, Volume 3: Fighting for Britain, 1937–1946* (London; Papermac, 2001) 179–199.   [10] ibid 187–188.
[11] ibid 183.   [12] ibid 179.
[13] P Kennedy, *The Rise and Fall of the Great Powers* (New York: Vintage Books, 1989) 288–291.

Simultaneous with this development came the realization by the United States that its infant industries had grown into highly competitive industries, keen to exploit Britain's traditional export markets. Accordingly, it suddenly became strategic for the US to use Lend–Lease to pressure Britain to abandon its imperial preference system, and to promote a liberal trade agenda in which non-discrimination in trade was the order of the day. Thus the opportunity offered by the Lend–Lease plan, as well as the United States' eventual entry into the war following the attack on Pearl Harbor, put paid to its long-standing isolationism and ushered in a new era of international economic cooperation.

By the end of the war, Britain, and indeed most of Europe, maintained large external debts which hampered economic recovery, while the United States had large reserves to lend. Leading economists, John Maynard Keynes from Britain, and American Harry Dexter White, began to draw up plans for international monetary cooperation, the fruits of which became the template for the modern international monetary system. According to the proposal, first floated by Keynes, states in deficit could borrow from an international institution thereby avoiding the consequences of either running up huge trade imbalances or increasing tariffs. Rather than reducing the value of their currencies and introducing policies of adjustment, such as decreasing government spending and wages and so exacerbating internal economic instability, states would turn to the international body which would assist it to rebalance its payments. So instead of leaving balance of payments equilibrium to the vagaries of gold convertibility, international economic management was proposed.

On the trade side, the US began to pursue a more liberal trade policy and the US President, with authority vested in him by the US Congress, began entering into a series of bilateral trade agreements. By the end of the war, thirty-two such agreements to lower tariffs had been introduced.

Following the end of hostilities in 1945, the Allies began working on plans to establish a permanent system of international economic order through institutional management. Political and security issues would be managed by the new United Nations and economic order would be secured by the establishment of a group of institutions known collectively by reference to the hotel in the New England hills at which, in 1944, their creation was first mooted, Bretton Woods. The Bretton Woods Institutions (BWI) were to consist, in the first place, of an institution designed to control currency movements worldwide and help states avoid the destructive devaluations which precipitated economic crises in the past, the International Monetary Fund (IMF); and one to promote reconstruction and development of countries affected by war or lacking in industrialization, the International Bank for Reconstruction and Development (IBRD), or the World Bank. The need for a trade organization was also recognized at Bretton Woods and in a series of conferences held between 1946 and 1948, in New York, Geneva, and Havana, ideas were developed for an International Trade Organization (ITO) to promote non-discrimination and establish universal rules regulating international trade, and to oversee reduction of tariffs under the terms of an international treaty. In the event, the ITO did not come into existence, due largely to resistance in the US Congress toward any perceived diminution of US state sovereignty. But the other two institutions were created and, more importantly for our purposes, the seeds of the idea of an international trading organization based on non-discrimination, were planted. Despite US resistance, twenty-two contracting parties (CPs) agreed to sign up to a provisional agreement on trade known as the General Agreement on Tariffs and Trade (GATT 1947),[14] which came into force in January 1948.[15]

Although GATT 1947 made no provision for the creation of any formal organization, an institution of sorts did emerge, albeit without official imprimatur. According to the Agreement, states were to meet regularly in order to discuss and 'swap' trading concessions, with the goal being to reduce tariff barriers and avoid creation of new tariff measures. GATT was a bargaining forum if nothing else, and a highly successful one at that.[16] The new talks, which were held about once a decade and became known as liberalization 'rounds', took the name of either the city in which they took place (the Tokyo Round 1973–9) or the political figure in whose term they began (the Kennedy Round of 1962–7).

These liberalization rounds, negotiated under the auspices of the GATT and supported by a new, small, but influential trade elite in the GATT Secretariat, ultimately created a rudimentary form of institutional structure which was to prove significant in laying the groundwork for the emergence in the 1990s of the WTO. With a small executive in permanent location, a larger organization could be envisaged. Moreover, in addition to creating a simple political entity consisting of the membership negotiating at the rounds, and a basic administration in the GATT Secretariat, a precursor to a dispute settlement body emerged. Although judicial conflict resolution was far from the minds of the contracting parties, and, repeatedly, commentators emphasized that the agreement was about 'bargaining' not legalized decision-making, some notion of the latter began to foment. Articles XXII and XXIII of the Agreement provided sparse but critical scaffolding for the development of an elementary process of dispute resolution, and this indeed was what occurred. The process began with the formation of working parties in the 1950s to consider conflicts between contracting parties; it developed with the establishment of more formal structures of dispute resolution, which included members independent of the

[14] Protocol of Provisional Application of the General Agreement on Tariffs and Trade, 30 October 1947, 55 UNTS 308 [hereinafter GATT 1947].
[15] For a history of GATT, see, eg, JH Jackson, *World Trade and the Law of GATT* (Indianapolis: Bobbs-Merrill, 1969).
[16] Total trade in 2002 was twenty-two times the level it had been in 1950: *The WTO in Brief*, <www.wto.org>.

dispute, and excluded the member against whom the complaint was made; and was gradually refined and strengthened over the years.[17]

However, despite the increasing sophistication of the structures of dispute settlement, the process itself was hampered significantly by a GATT rule that all disputes had to be settled by consensus. Effectively, this rule allowed all states, including the party against whom the complaint was made, a veto against any decision which was not in that state's interest. This blocking veto was used repeatedly throughout the 1960s and 1970s, crippling any attempt by the organization as a whole to develop a coherent set of universally applicable trade rules, other than the basic prescriptions in the Agreement itself. The repeated use of the veto also led to criticism of the entire institution as politicized, ineffective, and beholden to a small group of powerful states, themselves in thrall to a Geneva-based, technocratic trade policy elite.[18] However, despite some dissatisfaction with the dispute settlement process, the system continued to grow in strength and complexity, as did the Agreement itself.

As well as creating a regular forum for conducting political negotiations— a loose legislative assembly of sorts—and, inadvertently, a dispute settlement system, the sphere of competences covered by the GATT began to expand. With the rise in power of the newly industrializing countries (NICs) in the 1970s and the increasing resort to new forms of protectionism by industrialized states under challenge from these newly burgeoning economies, contracting parties met under the auspices of the negotiating rounds, and agreed to increasingly sophisticated elaborations of the non-discrimination principle. These new elaborations gradually extended the ambit of GATT 'law' so that issues formerly within the domain of national control came to be seen as valid sites for international trading rules. Discussion moved beyond tariff barriers; non-tariff measures were also up for negotiation. New GATT codes were introduced aimed at reducing and eliminating subsidies, anti-dumping and countervailing duties were discussed, and technical product standards and health and safety regulations came to be perceived as de facto forms of discrimination and so ripe for GATT consideration.

The increasing sophistication of the legislative menu of the GATT system, combined with growing resort to the still-primitive, but operative, dispute settlement arm, finally led to pressure to renegotiate the entire package that constituted the international trading system. Over a period of six years between 1989 and 1994, in a round which began in Uruguay, contracting parties met and discussed, argued and compromised, in order to come up with a single set of agreements. In 1994 the final agreements were signed with agreement to establish a formal organization introduce dispute settlement, and extend disciplines

---

[17] Jackson, 'Constitution' (n 2 above) 64 *et seq.*
[18] R Howse, 'The Legitimacy of the World Trade Organization' in J Coicaud and V Heiskanen (eds), *The Legitimacy of International Organizations* (Tokyo; New York: United Nations Press, 2001).

on agriculture, textiles, subsidies, and anti-dumping, along with new issues such as services, intellectual property, and investment.[19]

The new institution of the WTO was, in some respects, grander than the one anticipated in the 1940s, and in others less ambitious. The WTO, unlike its earlier incarnation, the ITO, did not include within its scope controversial issues such as labour standards, or restrictive trade practices. However, its general organizational stance was bolder. The new organization made provision for a general decision-making body, the General Council (in addition to the infrequent ministerial meeting), which would consist of all Member States (the old term 'contracting parties' was discarded) and would have plenary authority over all matters. There would be a Secretariat to handle the day-to-day running of the affairs of the General Council and a Director General to supervise the Secretariat. Importantly, two-tiered dispute resolution was created with the ultimate arbiter, the Appellate Body, consisting of respected international legal personnel, with the aim of finally putting paid to the criticism of dispute settlement decisions as political. However, any misconception that this was a court was avoided by the fact that the Appellate Body (the AB) and its first instance Panels could issue only 'reports' and not judicial decisions. Moreover, the membership continued to act as a brake on that body by playing the role of Dispute Settlement Body (the DSB) which would authorize any report before it could take effect. The notorious blocking veto was also abolished; now reports could only be rejected by reverse consensus (states voting unanimously to reject), and the dispute settlement process itself was radically overhauled with the introduction of clearer, speedier, and less complex procedures.

On the political front, states made compromises, some of which paid off, and others of which did not. Developing countries agreed to the inclusion of new rules on intellectual property, largely to their organizational and sometimes financial detriment, on condition that longstanding protectionism of developed states' agricultural and textile markets would be reduced and ultimately abolished. Ultimately, although the new agreements were supposed to embody a new reciprocity between developing and developed states, in practice, this did not prevail. New, potentially anti-competitive[20] rules on intellectual property were introduced, the result of which was to extend monopolies in certain products by, for example, regularizing a lengthy period of patent protection and requiring states to introduce penalties to enforce the new rule. Although they were made under the auspices of a package of agreements professing to free up trade between states, it is generally accepted that the benefits of these

---

[19] Marrakesh Agreement Establishing the World Trade Organization, in *The Results of the Uruguay Round of Multilateral Trade Negotiations: The Legal Texts* (1994), [hereinafter WTO Agreement] GATT Doc No MTN/FA, 33 ILM (1994) 1125.

[20] JR Paul, 'Do International Trade Institutions Contribute to Economic Growth and Development' (2003) 44 *Virginia Journal of International Law* 285, 339.

rules have accrued, in the main, to largely Northern, pharmaceutical, industrial, and agricultural chemical manufacturers, which have regularly enforced their rights. On the other hand, (Southern) states which formerly produced drugs at prices below patented manufacturers' prices because of an absence of intellectual property protection in those states were forced to pass their losses on to the consumer. Meanwhile, the promised dismantling of farm support in the United States, European Union, and other parts of the developed world, although a priority for developing states in order that they integrate effectively into the world economy, has been long, slow, and bogged down in detail.[21] At the time of writing, agricultural producers were still waiting for a clear commitment to freeing up agricultural markets, let alone evidence that it is occurring.[22]

The political make-up and role of the new institution was also noteworthy. As with all new organizations which transcend state boundaries, the three issues of state autonomy, institutional transparency, and democratic participation became immediately prominent. At the time of writing, the WTO is composed of 148 Member States. Each member has signed up to a single package of agreements[23] agreed to at Uruguay (in contrast to the old GATT system which allowed states to pick and choose between agreements) and each has negotiated mutually agreed concessions with trading partners which, upon scheduling to the GATT, become applicable to all Member States.[24] The Ministerial Conference, the broad decision-making forum, comprised of all Member States, meets not less than every two years.[25] Between meetings, decisions are made by the General Council,[26] which also consists of all members, but is normally comprised of heads of delegations in Geneva. General Council, which has overall supervisory authority, meets monthly, and three other Councils (on trade in goods, trade in services, and trade-related aspects of intellectual property rights[27]) also meet regularly. Alongside General Council are two other Councils (also comprising of the membership), the Dispute Settlement Body,[28] which monitors disputes between members, and the Trade Policy Review Body,[29] whose job it is to monitor national trade policies of members.

Because of the delegation of power to an international institution, questions arose about how transparent the process of decision-making was likely to be, and how participatory it was. Decisions are made by consensus if possible.[30] Where consensus is impossible to achieve, majority voting is the rule.[31] Interpretations of the agreements and waivers are to be resolved on a three-quarter majority;[32] amendments, depending on their nature, can be made by

---

[21] See, for eg 'Agriculture: WTO Members Prepare for Extended Modalities Phase' (5 March 2003) 7:8 *Bridges Weekly Trade News Digest* 1.   [22] Paul (n 20 above) 315.
[23] WTO Agreement, Art II.2.   [24] GATT, Arts. I and II.
[25] WTO Agreement, Art IV.1.   [26] ibid, Art IV.2.   [27] ibid, Art IV.5.
[28] ibid, Art IV.3.   [29] ibid, Art IV.4.   [30] ibid, Art IX.   [31] ibid, Art IX.1.
[32] ibid, Art IX.2 and 3.

consensus[33] or a two-thirds majority (although only taking effect for consenting states[34]); and admissions questions can be resolved by a two-thirds majority.[35] As a matter of practical reality, the Secretariat takes the running on many issues and, *sotto voce*, exerts considerable control over decisions made by the membership, because it sets agendas; controls the manner, timing, and placing of matters that come up for discussion; composes background papers; and generally influences the process, if not the substance, of decision-making. This system is sometimes criticized for the obscurity of its technical trade law language, secrecy of the decision-making process, and jettisoning of democracy for the sake of efficiency. Moreover, as with all international institutions, voting patterns are dictated by a mixture of habit, exigency, or membership of one of the various informal groups. Politically, the WTO is said to be a 'medieval institution' more akin to the Roman Catholic church in the Middle Ages than a modern legal institution.[36] Decisions remain largely within the control of a small number of powerful Western states, and even during the more open period of the trade round meetings, only states with access to the informal talks prior to formal decision-making—the so-called 'green room' talks—have a strong influence on outcomes. Moreover, the criticism runs, those states controlling the WTO agenda disingenuously proclaim fealty to free trade while pursuing self-interested ends. They 'pay[] lip-service to free trade as they once did to Catholicism, but they spend most of the time at war with each other, seeking territorial advantage'.[37]

Nevertheless, the Uruguay Agreements also made provision for establishment of a number of technical committees on the various matters subject to the Agreements,[38] and at this level participation is open to all members. There is a committee system attached to the specialist councils on goods, services, and intellectual property. For example, the Trade in Goods Council has, attached to it, committees on particular issues such as agriculture, market access, and anti-dumping. Other committees report directly to General Council, including one on trade and the environment, another on trade and development, and one on regional trading arrangements. Membership of both sorts of committees is open to all Member States. In practice, membership of the various bodies depends on the type of issue under discussion and the seniority and expertise of the participant. For example, General Council would normally be constituted by heads of delegations in Geneva, whereas the Agriculture Committee under the Trade in Goods Council would include agricultural experts. These committees are consultative only and formal decisions affecting matters within their

---

[33] WTO Agreement, Art X.2. Included here is the amendment provision itself; Art IX of the WTO Agreement; Arts I and II of GATT 1994; Art II.1 GATS and Art 4 TRIPs.

[34] WTO Agreement, Art X.3 and 4.   [35] ibid, Art XII.2.

[36] *Guardian Weekly*, 6–12 August 2004, L Elliot, 'Geneva deal has more to do with intrigue than free trade'.   [37] ibid.

[38] WTO Agreement, Art IV.6.

purview must go to Ministerial Council or General Council for approval. Again, however, influence on issues can be hugely dependent on the resources, financial and otherwise, at the disposal of Member States. Smaller, developing countries rarely possess the wherewithal to participate regularly on such committees or to study the long policy papers produced with a view to making relevant comments in their interest. Technocratic procedure, the need for efficiency in decision-making, and the reality of economic inequality, stand, if not in opposition to, then certainly not in unison with, open, participatory, decision-making. Given that crucial controversial issues such as farm support have remained held up in negotiations for years now, these problems are acute. In recent discussions over intellectual property rights and public health, technical discussions in committee have had a huge bearing on policy outcomes. For example, the question of which diseases were to be listed as indicating a public health emergency, such that states might be entitled to authorize the manufacture of generic drugs in contravention of pre-existing patent rights,[39] was influenced by committee negotiations. States present at these discussions, and able to marshal resources to put their positions with force, obviously have a distinct advantage in terms of participation and contribution to outcomes. Being at the table is important if you want to be heard.

In sum, the Uruguay Round vastly extended and entrenched the international trade system opening it up for involvement by all members. Yet, at the same time, it heralded a new era of institutional domination with all its attendant problems of transparency, participation, and state autonomy, and cemented a shift in the nature of the organization from a clearly inter-governmental one to something more. The nature of that something more was, at the conclusion of the Round, not entirely clear, but it soon came to be viewed as something 'constitutional'.

1.3 CONSTITUTIONALIZATION, WHAT CONSTITUTIONALIZATION?

Structurally, after 1995, it was possible to discern in the WTO the beginnings of a system which, at base, seemed to have constitutional aspirations. There existed a loose assembly, a basic administration, and a form for settling disputes. People began using terms such as 'participation', 'transparency', 'state autonomy', and 'democracy' to critique the new institution. To North Americans at least, the WTO mimicked a familiar tripartite system of constitutional government, consisting of legislature, executive, and judicial branches.

---

[39] See generally F Abbott, 'The Doha Declaration on the TRIPs Agreement and Public Health: Lighting a Dark Corner at the WTO' (2002) 5 *Journal of International Economic Law* 469.

Substantively also, the spectre of constitutional development was present, because the new organization purported to include within its jurisdiction a raft of new issues which, to this point, had been entirely within the national legal domain.

It was at this moment then, at the conclusion of the Uruguay Round, with the attendant growth of the institution, its conceptual foundations, and its competences, that the idea that the WTO might be constitutionalizing began to take hold. And with it came fears about what that constitutionalization might mean. Thus almost since the precise moment of WTO establishment in 1995 the term 'constitutional' was used to describe ongoing transformations both within the WTO and caused by it.[40] To those who harboured the fantasy of building a system of binding international law above the particularism of the nation state, the constitutionalization of the WTO promised improved economic order. To others it was a threat, either to State sovereignty itself—the WTO is interfering with national policy choices—or, alternatively, to those within the State who wished to exert some control over decisions the State makes—the democratic community itself.

Despite these contradictory claims and the sometimes inflammatory connotations of the word,[41] constitutionalization, as a term of art, has remained fashionable with a small but influential subset of international trade law commentators. In 2004, the leading article in the pre-eminent journal in the field, discussing what the author referred to as the future of the trade constitution, read: 'The global trading system has thus far undergone two constitutional moments: the birth of GATT 1947 and the birth of the WTO'.[42] Moreover, the term's currency persisted in the face of considerable unease on the part of the trade law establishment, developing countries, and non-government organizations. Whether oriented towards government, business, environment, or labour, these groups found the use of the term provocative. Indeed, international protests in Singapore (1996), Seattle (1999), Genoa (2001), Johannesburg (2002), and Cancun (2003) were generated, largely, by a perception of constitutionalization: the WTO was an elite, non-national, unelected, and unrepresentative body, extending its power beyond its pure trade mandate and illegitimately influencing the democratic decisions of national governments.

What is immediately striking about these protests, and academic discussions of constitutionalization, is the level of disagreement about what the term

[40] See, eg, Jackson, 'Constitution' (n 2 above) 6, 14; and E-U Petersmann, *The GATT/WTO Dispute Settlement System* (London: Kluwer, 1997).

[41] A leading trade scholar, John Jackson, reported that his 'innocent' use of the term compelled the then head of the World Trade Organization to issue a press release retracting its use. JH Jackson, Lecture, John F Kennedy School of Government, Boston (3 November 1999).

[42] Sunjoon Cho, 'A Bridge Too Far: The Fall of the Fifth WTO Ministerial Conference in Cancun and the Future of the Trade Constitution' (2004) 7 *Journal of International Economic Law* 219, 244.

means,[43] and whether it applies to the WTO. Prior to the presentation of the European Constitution in 2004, a similar uncertainty pervaded discussions of European constitutionalization. Thus a classic text on constitutionalization in the European Community offered up a kaleidoscope of meanings, from abolition of monarchy, through a 'mutation in public ethos',[44] to 'an operating system' of governance.[45] Some international trade lawyers take constitutionalization of the WTO to refer to increasing strength of the institutional structure,[46] or deepening of rights penetration into national legal systems;[47] others claim that the term is used to vest WTO reform with a legitimacy it otherwise lacks.[48] Some distinguish between a 'structural' form focusing on matters such as division of powers, or establishment of institutions for representation, and between a 'material' form in which obstacles to trade are eliminated.[49] Some refer to European constitutionalization as 'the conversion into text of society',[50] or use the qualifier 'post-national'[51] constitutionalism in relation to the WTO and international law generally, and others to 'meta-constitutionalism'.[52] The list of elements or indices of each varies enormously[53] as do the sources upon

---

[43] For discussion of some of the multiple meanings of the term in the European context see, eg, G Frankenberg, 'The Return of the Contract: Problems and Pitfalls of European Constitutionalism' (2000) 6 *European Law Journal* 257 (arguing that the meaning varies depending on whether a constitution is perceived as contract, political manifesto, plan/program, or statute).

[44] JHH Weiler, 'Introduction: "We Will Do, and Hearken"' in *The Constitution of Europe* (Cambridge: Cambridge University Press, 1999) 3.

[45] JHH Weiler, 'The Transformation of Europe' in *The Constitution of Europe* (1999) 12.

[46] Jackson, 'Constitution' (n 2 above).

[47] Petersmann (n 40 above).

[48] R Howse and K Nicolaidis, 'Legitimacy and Global Governance: Why Constitutionalizing the WTO is a Step Too Far' in RB Porter *et al* (eds), *Efficiency, Equity, Legitimacy: The Multilateral Trading System at the Millennium* (2001).

[49] JHH Weiler, 'Epilogue: Towards a Common Law of International Trade' in JHH Weiler (ed), *The EU, The WTO and the NAFTA: Towards a Common Law of International Trade* (Oxford: Oxford University Press, 2000) 206.

[50] G Frankenberg, 'Tocqueville's Question—The Role of a Constitution in the Process of Integration' (2000) 13 *Ratio Juris* 1, 7.

[51] F Snyder, 'Governing Economic Globalization: Global Legal Pluralism and European Law' (1999) 5 *European Law Journal* 334.

[52] N Walker, 'Flexibility within a Metaconstitutional Frame: Reflections on the Future of Legal Authority in Europe' in G de Búrca and J Scott (eds), *Constitutional Change in the EU: From Uniformity to Flexibility* (Oxford: Hart Publishing, 2000) [hereinafter Walker, 'Flexibility within a Metaconstitutional Frame'].

[53] Compare, eg, N Walker, 'The EU and the WTO: Constitutionalism in a New Key' in G de Búrca and J Scott (eds), *The EU and the WTO: Legal and Constitutional Issues* (Oxford and Portland, Oregon: Hart Publishing, 2001), [hereinafter Walker, 'Constitutionalism in a New Key'] 35 (arguing that there are seven indices of constitutionalization: explicit constitutional discourse; a claim to foundational legal authority; jurisdictional scope; interpretative autonomy; institutional structure; specification of conditions and incidents of membership; and terms of representation of membership) with Frankenberg (n 50 above) (articulating a view of a constitution as: organization of communal life by rules, convention, a social contract, text, rights, sources of law, a complex of norms, an ideal-positive legal order, organizational statute, etc); and, Frankenberg (n 43 above) (listing what he calls a number of 'architectural components' of a constitution as including questions of justice, common good, political organization, validity and constitutional change).

which constitutionalization draws.[54] International relations scholars refer to transformations in the WTO as 'regime formation'[55] or the construction of a system of governance.[56] Some international lawyers seem to want to hold on to an image of the WTO as a simple treaty arrangement, albeit with a strong central dispute resolution mechanism.[57] Still others read constitutionalization to connote a kind of 'spirit' without which there can be no durable social contract within the authorizing constitutional community.[58]

It is not my goal to add to the confusion surrounding the term by trying to pin down its meaning in any rigid fashion, or to claim definitively that the WTO is, or is not, constitutionalizing. Indeed, in view of the many ways in which the term constitutionalization is used in the literature, and of the many meanings which attach to it in domestic legal theory, I believe that either objective would be virtually impossible. In the words of one writer, '[c]onstitutionalism and constitutionalization are...not...black-and-white, all-or-nothing terms but [are] question[s] of nuance and gradation.'[59] These nuances and gradations are the subject of my study. Nevertheless, it should be possible to analyse the problem of constitutionalization with more precision than has been used to date, and to this end this study attempts to formulate preliminary and negotiable answers to four questions:

1. What is constitutionalization in the non-state context?
2. Do any of the models of WTO constitutionalization accord with settled meanings of the term?
3. What critiques are there of constitutionalization?
4. Is there a 'better' form of constitutionalization than the ones contained in either pre-existing uses of the term, or WTO models of the phenomenon?

1.4 OUTLINE OF ARGUMENT

The goal of this book, then, is to try to unscramble what is meant by the claim that the WTO is constitutionalizing. The argument will begin by asking what

---

[54] eg, Neil Walker relies on political sources and differentiates his own work from Snyder's (n 51 above) on the basis that Snyder 'would extend the analysis of post-national sites further to include not only political sites but also [economic] sites....': Walker, 'Constitutionalism in a New Key' (n 53 above) 31 n 17.

[55] See, eg, discussion in M Levy, O Young and M Zurn, 'The Study of International Regimes' (1995) 1 *European Journal of International Relations* 267, 288.

[56] AS Sweet, 'Judicialization and the Construction of Governance' (1999) 32 *Comparative Political Studies* 147.

[57] Some writers do not mention the term constitutionalization whilst discussing factors that others classify in constitutional terms. See, eg, discussions of changed practice and procedure in DP Steger and PVD Bossche, 'WTO Dispute Settlement; Emerging Practice and Procedure' in (1998) *American Society of International Law: Proceedings of the 92nd Annual Meeting* 79.

[58] JHH Weiler, 'To Be a European citizen: Eros and Civilization' in *The Constitution of Europe* (1999).   [59] Walker, 'Constitutionalism in a New Key' (n 53 above) 33.

constitutionalization means when it is used, in the general literature, to refer to arrangements within and beyond the nation state. It will draw on sources from international, transnational, supranational, and domestic legal theory scholarship to build up a picture of the received account of the term (Chapter 2). I will show that, traditionally, constitutionalization consists of six elements. Constitutionalization entails a set of *social practices to constrain economic and political behaviour*. It includes a belief that a *new foundational device* or *Grundnorm* has emerged such that what was once merely a set of rules is transformed into a coherent and unified body of rules with the appearance of a new system of law. Constitutionalization occurs only where there is a *political community* to authorize its making and that community's interests are represented. A *process of deliberative law-making* is necessary in order for a constitutionalized entity to emerge and for the members of the community to be constituted as authors of its law. The standard version necessarily entails some *realignment of the relationship* between the sub-entities and the central, putatively constitutionalized entity. Finally, constitutionalization entails a level of *social acceptance, or legitimacy* of the process itself. In short, according to received wisdom, constitutionalization is associated with the emergence of a foundational device signalling a new, coherent system of social practices to constrain behaviour, whose authority is legitimized by a political community whose views are represented, and which, in turn, uses a deliberative process to make law and which has the effect of realigning traditional sovereign relations among constituent entities and between itself and those sub-parts.

Of course, this account of constitutionalization is not the only one available. Neither is it neutral in its origins, or objective in its prescriptions. It is an account that originated largely in a state context and has not, therefore, been shaped by international factors. It is an account which emphasizes the existence of facts as the foundation of legal change. It contains within it a normative predisposition, which, in this case, leans towards positive state-based theory. So, why have I chosen to begin with this account rather than others? First, as Chapter 2 will show, the received account has a long and authoritative legacy. Secondly, this particular model includes useful information about the genesis (*Grundnorm*), content (community, constraining social practice), and form (deliberation) of a new constitution. Thirdly, I believe the account represents a generally accepted view of what constitutes the constitutionalization process, and so provides a plausible starting point for discussion. It may be that other models are possible or desirable and, indeed, in our working through of the meanings and application of the term in the WTO context, the received account will itself be revealed as in need of renovation. The very concept of constitutionalization will be challenged when we ask whether the term applies to the transnational experiment that is the WTO. With this caveat in mind, I will return to the outline of argument.

In the next chapter (Chapter 3) I will show how this orthodox or received definition of constitutionalization emerged from general international economic law scholarship. So my aim here is to draw attention to some of the recurring themes in international economic law and WTO constitutionalization law, and to locate WTO constitutionalization debate within this broader context. I shall suggest that six themes of international economic law literature resonate with, and indeed were enormously influential in producing, a debate about WTO constitutionalization. Briefly, these themes are an institutional–constitutional conflation; globalization linkage; a liberalization consensus; procedural regulation; a fixation with self-definition; and a transformative urge to change world order. Specifically, I will argue here that international economic law has increasingly conflated institutions with constitutions, and has led to the former being vested with a legitimacy and authority that they would otherwise not possess. In tune with this conflation is an interdependence with globalization literature in which new sites of political authority are identified with the processes of economic change. This has led to a blurring of lines between economic, political, and legal authority with the result that the modification of an essentially economic treaty arrangement into a political/legal entity became suddenly more plausible. In this context, normative questions about the goals that might underpin any constitutional structure have been buried by a consensus that trade liberalization is a necessary good, and procedural-ization of law within the new institution/constitution has also muffled contests about free trade and rendered constitutionalization apparently uncontroversial. Yet controversy is exactly what has been generated, and this is reflected in the somewhat paradoxical twin desires of the field of international economic law and those advocating the use of the term constitutionalization in respect of the WTO, both to transform economic order, and to solve the identity crisis of the discipline.

Finally, before I leave this description, it should be noted that my aim in Chapter 3 is not to demonstrate that the themes of international economic law are identical to the received account of constitutionalization but to begin to think about the almost dialectical relationship between the two processes. International economic law produced the constitutionalization debate, and, the constitutionalization debate informed the general economic literature. Both fields influenced each other. In this sense WTO constitutionalization is not only a result of developments in the broader field. It is also a window on to more general issues concerning international economic order, and so the argument of the chapter lays the groundwork for the discussion in the penultimate chapter which addresses opposition to WTO constitutionalization in similar terms.

Having set out the background to our discussions, the study will identify three specific approaches to WTO constitutionalization. All three approaches are inspired by enthusiasm for the thesis that the WTO is constitutionalizing. These approaches are labelled *institutional managerial constitutionalization, rights-based constitutionalization*, and *constitutionalization by judicial norm-generation*. The discussion will analyse these WTO-specific constitutionalization models on their own terms, and evaluate the extent to which they reflect the received account. The point of this discussion is not to match the models against the received account in any rigid fashion. Some of the models will meet some of the requirements of the received account and some will not. But in each case the received account will act as a kind of rough template against which the analysis occurs. After noting the strengths and weaknesses of each in terms of the received account of constitutionalization, I conclude that none meets the standards of the received definition to any great extent.

Specifically, I will argue that constitutionalization in the form of *institutional managerialism* (Chapter 4) suggests that constitutionalization occurs by way of management of policy diversity between states by institutions and rules, which are given the imprimatur of a 'constitutional' character. It presents itself as a natural deduction from factual developments, which are presented as existing beyond the law, and yet proponents of this approach also aspire to change the WTO system and other facts of the wider economic order.

The critique of institutional managerialism suggests that although the model seems to have modest claims, its effects may be quite radical. Institutional managerialism conflates institutions with constitutions in an attempt to enhance the legitimacy of the former, and make the institution appear to be a coherent system of functions and rules resembling a constitution. The approach presents the process of 'management' as a foolproof method of dispute resolution. But it can mask inequalities between international trade law actors. It contains a tension between reinforcing and undermining sovereignty, and, it is incomplete because it excludes private law background rules of property and contract from the constitutional structure it claims exists. For the purposes of the received account of constitutionalization, therefore, institutional managerialism responds, to an extent, to the need to provide a process of deliberation (rules, institutions, and managerialism), but it is under-explanatory in relation to system legitimacy (conflation of institution with a constitution), and *Grundnorm* change (discovering the facts of a constitution), and ambiguous as to the extent and results of any realignment of relationships within the system (discussion of sovereignty).

By contrast with the empirical basis of the first approach, *rights-based constitutionalization* (Chapter 5) is aspirational in character—it is an argument for what the system should be, not what it is. Constitutionalization should, according to this view, be promoted and it should be a constitutionalization process in which a right to trade is recognized. According to this approach, the right to trade already has both substantive (intellectual property rights) and procedural (access to courts) manifestations, and its recognition as a plausible form of constitutionalization would lead to a strengthening of the effect of WTO law in domestic legal systems. This reinforcement of the effect of WTO rules could occur by way of direct effect, stronger judicial review, or interpretation of national law in conformity with WTO law. The virtues of this approach, according to its advocates, are that rights-based constitution-alization would strengthen the failing legitimacy of the WTO legal system, prevent governmental power abuse, and ensure equality between trade participants, namely producers and consumers.

Against these claims I argue that the approach is, overall, inconsistent with traditional methods for the incorporation and transformation of rules into international law. In any case, the right to trade is rarely protected domestically. Moreover, the notion of rights proposed lacks definition and the effect of such rules in domestic law is uncertain. The theory behind the model is based on an unnecessary and outdated opposition between State and individual, and it is an over-ambitious and evangelical model, which attempts to 'hijack' traditional human rights' legitimacy.[60] Rights-based constitutionalization seeks to address the received definition's concern with legitimacy, and the realignment of State decisional autonomy, but fails to confront adequately the elements of political community, deliberative process, and *Grundnorm* change.

The last model, *judicial norm-generation* (Chapter 6), which is based on my earlier work, seeks to escape from the problems of the first two approaches by distancing itself from any explicit normative claim. Instead it presents itself as simply describing the work of the Appellate Body of the WTO in creating structures of a constitutional type for the WTO legal system. So constitu-tionalization is said to be taking place, regardless of its desirability, through a variety of judicial techniques described as amalgamation of national consti-tutional doctrine and values into WTO law; constitution of a WTO system by adoption of particular constitutional procedural rules; and incorporation of domestic subject matters (health).

Against the claim for impartiality made by this technique is the criticism that, even by merely describing the WTO in this manner, the approach promotes the WTO as a constitutionalized entity. It fails to acknowledge the complex relationship between legitimacy and constitutionalization, or that the former can exist without the latter. It ignores the role of political constitutionalization by means of legislative or popular mechanisms, as opposed to judicial activity. Moreover, the techniques the approach identifies as constitutional could be merely procedural in nature, and applicable in other international legal contexts without implicating constitutionalization. In terms of the received account, judicial norm-generation is concerned with the realignment of relationships within the system, and to some extent legitimacy, but neglects political community, deliberative process, and *Grundnorm* change.

To this point the study will have shown that, to a limited extent, elements of the received account of constitutionalization are reflected in the constitu-tionalization literature of the WTO. However, it is also clear that none of the

[60] P Alston, 'Resisting the Merger and Acquisition of Human Rights by Trade Law: A Reply to Petersmann' (2002) 13 *European Journal of International Law* 815.

three approaches conforms satisfactorily to the standard account. This, then, partly explains the level of dissatisfaction, amongst observers and commentators, with the current constitutional discourse. Constitutional talk about the WTO, represented by these three dominant paradigms, fails to meet, let alone match, the criteria of familiar accounts of constitutionalization. From the perspective of a constitutional purist the WTO has some ground to make up before it deserves the label 'constitutional'. This is an important insight because while the WTO (and some of its advocates) may have constitutional aspirations or pretensions, the language of constitutionalization is likely to obfuscate the debate, diminish the more quotidian achievements of the WTO, and deflect scholarly attention from other, less glamorous aspects of its functioning.

But there is a deeper problem. Constitutional talk may well involve a category error or a linguistic mismatch, but more than this, it represents, for many, a normative failure or deficit of the imagination. What I call the *anti-constitutional critique* (Chapter 7) worries about the effects of constitutionalization and constitutional talk on the way in which the operation and possible reform of the WTO and international economic order is being imagined, understood, and oriented. Some anti-constitutionalists are hostile to the idea of constitutionalization (or at least, both the received account and imperfect reflections of that account found in the three models). For them, constitutional talk is a way of masking certain deformities in the international economic order, and the process of constitutionalization itself, albeit in its embryonic form, exacerbates problems of declining sovereignty, economic inequality, and legitimacy of the global order.

Specifically, the anti-constitutionalization critique makes a number of charges. First, it argues that constitutionalization is contracting the decisional capacity of states, thus causing a shift towards a stronger central entity and a weakened Member State. Secondly, WTO constitutionalization, it is argued, is only weakly deliberative in nature, indicated by the WTO's poor mechanisms for diverse participation, transparency, and accountability. Thirdly, the current decision-making process focuses almost exclusively on economic goals and free trade at the expense of other social goals and other economic choices, and, at the same time, fails to take sufficient account of the economic and distributive effects its decisions have on Member States. The combination of these latter two myopias (too narrowly economic in relation to goals, not economic enough in relation to consequences of its actions) means that the behavioural constraints of WTO constitutionalization are uneven across the range of economic and social behaviour, and are skewed toward a particular vision of economic life. In this restricted vision, governments make decisions primarily for economic reasons but also downplay the economic consequences of those decisions, and the choices of types of economic development available to states become more limited. Fourthly, the particular models of WTO constitutionalization currently in circulation are also incomplete in the sense that they claim the system is constituted only by the boundaries of public law and fail to regard private law and non-legal constraint as a part of the constitutionalization process. Fifthly, and finally, constitutionalization is dangerous because it is based on a self-fulfilling thesis whereby the language of constitutionalization is used as a means to create the very process it is supposed merely to be describing. In short, in terms of the received account then, the anti-constitutionalization critique challenges constitutionalization for its centralizing realignment of relationships between State and central entity, the weakness of its deliberative process, the uneven quality of the constraints it places on economic, social, and political behaviour, its failure to acknowledge private constraint as constituting a system for international trade, and the artificial nature of the legitimacy it promotes.

Despite the vehemence of the anti-constitutionalization critique, there are differences of emphasis. While the indirect result of the anti-constitutionalization critique may be to undermine the received account of constitutionalization, and to suggest that a more sophisticated model of constitutionalization is necessary, reform of this kind is not generally, the goal. The critique's focus is not to create a 'better' version of constitutionalization, but to challenge absolutely the application of constitutionalization terminology in relation to the WTO, and the effects this has on international economic order. By and large, these rejectionist voices are the loudest in anti-constitutionalization scholarship. They use that power to call for complete abandonment of the use of the term, and resistance to any of its attractions, legitimization for example. A small minority, whom I would still label 'anti-constitutional' because of their deep and fundamental criticisms of the project as a whole, nevertheless seem instead to want to harness its argumentative energy, albeit in radically modified ways.[61] My own current thinking would be located here with the latter anti-constitutional critique.

So, having analysed constitutionalization in the abstract, and in relation to the WTO, the book will conclude, in Chapter 8, that, despite the enthusiasm of some for the WTO constitutionalization process, deep doubts must remain about the viability of the project from both a descriptive and normative point of view.

Moreover, this conclusion is disturbing in view of the links I made in Chapter 3 between the received account, and, WTO constitutionalization models and international economic order. In that discussion I located constitutionalization and its WTO modelling within a skewed international economic law order,

---

[61] eg T Cottier and M Hertig, 'The Prospects of 21st Century Constitutionalism' in AV Bogdandy and R Wolfrum (eds), *Max Planck Yearbook of United Nations Law*, vol 7 (The Hague, London and New York: Kluwer, 2004) 261. For similar arguments in relation to European constitutionalism, see, eg, D Chalmers, 'Post-nationalism and the Quest for Constitutional Substitutes' (2000) 27 *Journal of Law and Society* 178; J Shaw, 'Process and Constitutional Discourse in the European Union' (2000) 27 *Journal of Law and Society* 4; Walker (nn 52 and 53 above).

and argued that the legitimacy of any constitutionalized WTO was open to serious challenge because it was based on a blurring of the division between economic, political, and legal authority with the result that the institutional structure of the WTO had been conflated with a constitution. I also claimed that, in the process, serious differences of value had been buried in a consensus about the benefits of trade liberalization, and a proceduralization of the mechanisms resolving disputes. I contended that the label 'constitutional' encapsulated an urge to transform the international order, but ended up masking its own anxiety about the identity and authority of the WTO. Far from leading toward greater legitimacy, the labelling of the WTO as constitutional has led it away from it.

In the penultimate chapter, similar patterns of argument were present in the anti-constitutionalist point of view. This critique derided the self-legitimating character of constitutional discourse, criticized the extent of constraint it created on sovereign decision-making, and questioned the explicitly economic, public law focus of the WTO, which, nevertheless, failed to take account of the economic effects of constitutionalization.

Taking these two sets of concerns together—the skewed nature of the international economic law order, and the self-legitimating, myopia of constitutionalization discussions—it will become clear that there is something deeply unsatisfying about the dominant models of constitutionalization of the WTO. First, the dominant models are unworkable, in the sense that they do not even meet the descriptive criteria for constitutionalization set out in the received, conventional account of the process. The WTO is not constitutionalized in these terms. Secondly, normatively speaking, the particular type of constitutionalization embodied by the models is undesirable, for the reasons set out in the anti-constitutional critique. Thirdly, the models are flawed because they read WTO transformations as if constitutionalization had occurred, and was necessarily desirable, and thereby obscure development of new modes of thinking about constitutionalization. Fourthly, the models make it seem natural for the WTO to undergo a metamorphosis from a trade treaty, into an economic organization, then a legal system, and ultimately a political instrument of international order, while bypassing concerns about legitimacy, economic and political ordering, and democracy. In short, the ascendancy of these WTO constitutionalization models has so dominated the constitutionalization debate that they have retarded other ways of thinking about the WTO and its relationship with issues of democracy, sovereignty, and the association between economics, politics, and law in the international economic order.

In the light of my analysis it will be clear that the very concept of international constitutionalization needs reconsideration. At the very least it might be prudent to resist using constitutionalization to describe the current WTO; the WTO does not meet the criteria of constitutionalization in any of the three incarnations popularized in the literature. But even if it did resemble the received account of constitutionalization, that account itself will have been revealed as no longer appropriate to describe situations beyond the nation state. I will end by arguing that the concept of constitutionalization has been transformed by the WTO transnational experiment. It is not just that the WTO does not meet the received model, but that the received model no longer constitutes an accurate or desirable model. So in order for discussions about non-state constitutionalization to be credible, and specifically constitutionalization of the WTO, the deficiencies in our ways of thinking about, talking about, and indeed doing, constitutionalization, must be addressed. For example, greater attention would need to be paid to thinking about how a non-national trade community—separated by borders, languages, resources, and political systems—can plausibly authorize the making of a constitutional system, above the domain of the State. Although options have been mooted, none are particularly convincing. From the strengthening of international civil society,[62] the encouragement of transnational networks or epistemic communities,[63] the creation of a public sphere,[64] an international assembly,[65] or a location for national parliaments to meet, there is something vaguely wishful about these ideas. The European experience is a very particular one, based on long-standing historical ties, and yet even in that arena constitutionalization has been, and remains, controversial. Europe aside, to date, no amount of internet communication, modern telecommunications, and cheap aviation would be able to overcome the fundamental obstacles noted above to the creation of an authorizing WTO constitutional community.

Finally, reconsideration of post-national constitutionalization, and its specific application to the WTO, should not be limited to procedural matters only, however important. Focus should expand to include not just questions of who is at the table, but also on what they want. A focus on what I call *trade democracy* rather than trade constitutionalization might begin to produce answers to the difficult economic questions that beset the international trade system, questions that were highlighted most effectively in the anti-constitutionalization critique. This could be done by making development the centrepiece of trade constitutionalization, in such a way that the democratic emphasis of the project would be highlighted. This might involve, for example, giving consideration to the distributive consequences of WTO decision-making so that the WTO can better fulfil GATT's preambular objective to 'rais[e] standards of living' especially in developing world. Social as well as economic values could be formally incorporated in interpretations of trade,

[62] B Einhorn, M Kaldor, and Z Kavan (eds), *Citizenship and Democratic Control in Contemporary Europe* (Aldershot: E Edgar, 1996).

[63] J Braithwaite and P Drahos, *Global Business Regulation* (Cambridge: Cambridge University Press, 2000) 29–31.

[64] J Habermas, 'A Constitution for Europe?' (2001) 11 *New Left Review* 5.

[65] T Franck, *Fairness in International Law and Institutions* (Oxford: Clarendon Press, 1995).

again fulfilling the GATT promise that trade is indeed about health, environment, and safety as well as economic policy. The slant of the trade playing-field caused by an underlying structure of private and public laws of contract, jurisdiction, companies, and, investment, for example, could be examined as an integral constructed part of the constitutional framework of the WTO, rather than facts beyond its reach. Instead of trading constitutionalization, trading democracy would be the aim, in a form that makes development central, rather than ancillary, to the constitutionalization project. Moreover this would render plausible reconciliation of the tension in the agreements between principles requiring more openness, from states and within markets, and those which maintain state control over trade policy.

In short the aim of the book is to reveal the meanings and shortcomings of the present discussion on constitutionalization of the WTO, so that we can clear the ground, and get on with the job of building a democratic development-oriented trade regime, rather than merely a constitutionalized trade regime. In so doing, I am not arguing for jettisoning all that has been written and discussed on constitutionalization and its reform, much of which is useful and important. But I am suggesting that it is time to move beyond the sometimes pallid contours of those discussions and turn to the key issue in the international trade system, development, and not concentrate merely on constitutional form. Otherwise we run the risk of being distracted by enthusiasm for constitutionalization and so lose sight of the disparities a non-discriminatory trade system was designed to address. By worrying incessantly about *whether and when the WTO will be constitutionalized* we have turned our attention from *what sort of trading system we might want*. It is this question, of international trade democratization through development, not constitutional form, which should be at the heart of our concerns.

2

Constitutionalization: The Received Account

2.1 INTRODUCTION

This section will draw on international supranational, and domestic legal theory with the aim of identifying what constitutionalization means, in general terms, before examining the term in the specific context of the WTO. However, it should be noted that this study is not about constitutionalization per se but about constitutionalization in relation to the WTO. I do not therefore present a comprehensive analysis and critique of the phenomenon of constitutionalization in the abstract. The purpose of this chapter is merely to outline a somewhat condensed and truncated account of constitutionalization, in order to analyse its application to the WTO.

At the outset, however, three premises of the received account of constitutionalization require explanation. First, although there is a distinction between constitution, constitutionalism, and constitutionalization, the terms are used interchangeably throughout much of the literature.[1] In my view the distinction corresponds, roughly speaking, to a division between

- the formal arrangements of government (the constitution proper);
- the set of values ordinarily associated with liberal constitutions such as rule of law and rights protection (constitutionalism); and
- the process of change by which those formal arrangements are made and the values of liberal constitutionalism are embedded in them (constitutionalization).

In this work, constitutionalization will be used to refer to the total of all three elements, namely the processes of making a constitution, the arrangements themselves, and embedding of constitutionalism within the formal structure.

---

[1] See, eg, the many forms the term takes in the work of one leading commentator: JHH Weiler, *The Constitution of Europe* (Cambridge: Cambridge University Press, 1999) [hereinafter Weiler, *Constitution*] viii (arguing that various dictionary definitions of *constitution* are all relevant to a discussion of Europe, including, *inter alia*, a process of *constituting*) and compare with JHH Weiler, 'Cain and Abel—Convergence and Divergence in International Trade Law' in JHH Weiler (ed), *The EU, the WTO and the NAFTA: Towards a Common Law of International Trade* (Oxford: Oxford University Press, 2000) [hereinafter Weiler, 'Cain and Abel'] 2 (referring to, what he calls 'the principal achievement of Europe' as *constitutionalization*). (My emphases in both references.)

Secondly, in the account I give of constitutionalization in this chapter, two forms of the phenomenon become visible, core constitutionalization and elaborated constitutionalization. The core elements of the received account will form the main subject of my discussion. The elaborated elements coincide roughly with the notion of constitutionalism noted above, and will not, in the main, be the focus of my discussions (although one aspect—rights—is an important part of one of the models discussed below). I do not, however, claim that all of these elements (core and elaborated) are present in all of the discussions of constitutionalization or that there is any hierarchy or sequence to their inclusion.[2] Moreover, as my discussion in Chapter 1 indicated, I do not present the received account of constitutionalization as an ideal type of constitution, the terms of which are incontestable. Indeed one theme of this study will be to examine the way in which this account, borne largely of the experience of the nation state, might be forced to change under pressure from exposure to the international system. Nevertheless, the aim of this chapter is to set out a working definition of constitutionalization to enable an analysis of its operation within the WTO to be carried out.

The third premise of my discussion is that these core elements are essential to my conception of the term; without a strong display of each of these it is implausible, in my view, to speak of a legal system as constitutionalized. The elaborated elements, by contrast, are neither necessary nor sufficient to ground a finding of constitutionalization. They are elaborations on the core concept. Although their presence indicates a process of constitutionalization in general, their absence is not determinative. A system may be constitutionalized without any of the elaborated elements.

2.2   THE BASIC STRUCTURE OF CONSTITUTIONALIZATION

Generally speaking, constitutionalization is the process of change by which a set of social practices defined as law (rules, principles, procedures, and institutions), and generally associated with Western industrialized democracies, emerge in a relatively coherent and unified arrangement, in relation to a particular community, and attain a level of social acceptance (defined as legitimacy). These practices structure and generate the division and exercise of public power within that community; determine the recognition of further practices within the system; modify social, economic, and political relationships between actors within it; and create a government, or, supranationally, a form of governance.

---

[2] Cf T Cottier and M Hertig, 'The Prospects of 21st Century Constitutionalism' in AV Bogdandy and R Wolfrum (eds), *Max Planck Yearbook of United Nations Law*, vol 7 (2004) 261, 280, (distinguishing between a constitution's 'basic or core functions', and 'additional qualifications').

The core elements of the received account of constitutionalization are, therefore, sixfold. First, constitutionalization assumes a set of social practices—whether they are rules or institutions—that regulate and constrain economic and political relationships among actors in the system. Secondly, it requires the emergence of a new higher order basic norm, containing authoritative criteria capable of recognizing whether a law belongs to the new legal system. Thirdly, constitutionalization involves the existence of a constitutional community to authorize the creation and continual remaking of a legal order. It is this community which is represented in the construction of the constitution. Fourthly, there must be a process of deliberation according to which members of the community contribute, directly or indirectly through their representatives, to the making of the laws of the system. Fifthly, a realignment of relationships between the states and the putative central constitutional entity is envisaged. Sixthly, legitimacy in the sense of social acceptance of the process is required.

There are other features of constitutionalization, such as rights, or rule of law, or particular purposes,[3] but, as noted above, these latter features are elaborations on the core concept of constitutionalization, and, although I will recount their function briefly below, I do not propose to focus on them in detail.

2.3 ELABORATED CONSTITUTIONALIZATION

As a tool of discussing legal systems, constitutionalization conveys a rich and variegated set of meanings,[4] over and above the slim basic account. In addition to the six core elements defined herein—social and political constraint, *Grundnorm* change, community, deliberation, realignment of relationships, and legitimacy—the process of constitutionalization connotes a variety of other features or elaborations. In constitutional literature from the UK, emphasis is placed on the notion of the rule of law, and features associated with democracy such as representation of a constituency by elected law-making representatives.[5] In US constitutional literature, emphasis is placed, in addition, upon the existence of separate executive, legislative, and adjudicative functions,

[3] To this extent I would follow the approach known as constitutional political economy which suggests that purposes are not part of the constitution itself and that members of the constitutional community decide which particular purposes their constitution will serve: G Brennan and JM Buchanan, *The Reasons of Rules: Constitutional Political Economy* (Cambridge: Cambridge University Press, 1985) 7 (arguing that 'the rules that constrain socio-political interactions—the economic and political relationships among persons—must be evaluated ultimately in terms of their capacity to promote the separate purposes of all persons in the polity').

[4] For a comparison of the features of constitutions, constitutionalism, and constitutionalization from a variety of jurisdictions, and discussion of methods of comparison, see VC Jackson and M Tushnet, *Comparative Constitutional Law* (New York: Foundation Press, 1999).

[5] For a classic account of the constitutional laws of the UK see I Jennings and CM Young, *Constitutional Laws of the British Empire* (Oxford: Clarendon Press, 1938).

protection of rights, and written-ness.[6] To others a constitution must have a *telos* or goal, or at least a set of agreed substantive values impelling its creation. The received account of constitutionalization therefore suggests that a constitution may consist of the core elements plus some constellation of other elaborations such as an institutional framework, possibly consisting of separate executive, legislative, and adjudicative functions, rule of law, protection of rights, written-ness, and a federalizing or unitary structure.

By labelling these latter elements 'elaborations' I am not suggesting that they are entirely absent from the core model. Indeed it would be impossible, for example, to have deliberation without some attention to rights to protect opportunities to participate and be heard, or, to have a system of legal rules without recognizing some notions of legality associated with the rule of law. But this chapter does not focus on the elaborated form of constitutionalization for a number of reasons. First, these forms are more likely to be contextually specific to the particular state in which they originated whereas the core elements are not. Secondly, the elements of an elaborated form of constitutionalization are primarily associated with a particular form of constitutionalization, common amongst Western states, normally referred to as liberal constitutionalism, and therefore do not represent the core elements of constitutionalization. Moreover, core constitutionalization is not dependent upon the inclusion of a complete set of fully articulated and realized constitutional rights, or a fully operational rule of law; the international system is peppered with examples of constitutions that lack these elements. Accordingly I will now return to focus on core constitutionalization.

2.4 CORE CONSTITUTIONALIZATION

2.4.1 Constraints on social, economic, and political behaviour

The received account is premised on the idea that constitutionalization, at its most fundamental level, consists of social practices to constrain economic and political behaviour.[7] Sometimes these practices are referred to as rules,[8] at other times they are called institutions,[9] or even principles.[10] The WTO 'trade

---

[6] For a classic account of constitutional law in the US see, eg, GR Stone, LM Seidman, CR Sunstein and MV Tushnet, *Constitutional Law*, 2nd edn (Boston: Little Brown, 1991).

[7] Brennan and Buchanan (n 3 above).

[8] Positive legal theory referred to the foundations of a legal system as consisting of rules: HLA Hart, *The Concept of Law* (Oxford: Clarendon Press, 1961).

[9] Economists claimed it was institutions that constrain behaviour: DC North, *Institutions, Institutional Change and Economic Performance* (Cambridge: Cambridge University Press, 1990). See also Brennan and Buchanan (n 3 above) 5 (noting that Adam Smith referred to rules as inclusive of law and institutions).

[10] R Dworkin, *Law's Empire* (London: Fontana Press 1986) 211 and *passim* (arguing for a model of constitutional community based on 'common principles, not just...rules hammered out in

constitution', for example, is said to 'represent a "very delicate mix of economic and governmental policies, political constraints, and above all an intricate set of constraints imposed by a variety of rules or legal norms in a particular institutional setting" '.[11] Whatever form they take, these practices perform the same function, which is to provide a mechanism for dealing with the 'central problem of social order', namely of 'reconciling the behaviour of separately motivated persons' so as to 'generate patterns of outcomes that are tolerable to all participants'.[12] They do this by pressuring, guiding, controlling, or changing behaviour of agents with decision-making capacities.[13] Whichever form they take, core constitutionalization cannot occur in the absence of such practices.

2.4.2   *Grundnorm* change: coherence, unity, and a rule of recognition

Although not always openly acknowledged in the literature, a further basic core element of constitutionalization is that it involves the emergence of a new higher order norm giving a set of otherwise disparate rules a unity and coherence sufficient to suppose that the rules constitute a new legal order, and, to set criteria by which to identify whether subsequent rules and institutions are valid within that legal system. According to positive legal theory, the emergence of a new basic norm signals historical discontinuity between the old, non-unified system, and the new order; the new system of law is identifiably separate from the pre-existing state of affairs, whether that previous state consists of another legal system, or a non-legalized arena. To Hans Kelsen, this process occurred when a new foundational concept emerged, in the form of a basic norm or *Grundnorm*, giving a validity and unity to the rules.[14] HLA Hart argued that a new legal system came into being when it was possible to detect a union of primary rules of obligation (rules on substantive matters such as contract, property, etc) and secondary rules (rules about making the rules) including a key secondary rule, the rule of recognition, the latter being the authoritative criterion with which to identify that a law belonged to a

political compromise'. These principles affect the view the community takes of justice, fairness, and due process. Political decisions taken by the community's institutions 'presuppose' these principles, the authority of which are not dependent on each member's consent to them, but 'arise from the historical fact that this community has adopted [them]').

[11] Sunjoon Cho, citing John Jackson, 'A Bridge Too Far: The Fall of the Fifth WTO Ministerial Conference in Cancun and the Future of the Trade Constitution' (2004) 7 *Journal of International Economic Law* 219, 220.   [12] Brennan and Buchanan (n 3 above) 5.

[13] F Schauer, *Playing by the Rules* (Oxford: Clarendon Press, 1991) 2.

[14] H Kelsen, *General Theory of Law and State*, trans Anders Wedberg (Russell and Russell edn, 1961) (Cambridge, Mass: Harvard University Press, c 1945) [hereinafter Kelsen, *General Theory*] 115. See also SL Paulson, 'Towards a Periodization of the Pure Theory of Law' in L Gianformaggio (ed), *Hans Kelsen Legal Theory: a Diachronic Point of View* (Turin: Giappichelli Editore, 1990) 34 (arguing that Kelsen's *Grundnorm* was derived from the work of Walter Jellinet).

system.[15] Common to both Hart's and Kelsen's formulations was the idea that the foundational concept (*Grundnorm* or rule of recognition) was a higher order norm which functioned to validate the system as a system,[16] and to identify the rules and practices that belong to that system. Absent such a foundational device, there can be no legal system. It is clear that, at the very least, in order to be constitutionalized a system would have to be based on the existence of a new basic norm.

So the finding of a new system of constitutionalized WTO law would be dependent upon the finding of a new *Grundnorm*, or rule of recognition, providing the authoritative criteria with which to recognize the existence of a new system. It would have to be shown that a new basic norm had developed in relation to the WTO and that this new norm inaugurated a new system of law, which was separate from national law, international law, and the previous GATT international legal system.

How, then, is it possible, according to positive theory, to know when a new system of law exists, or, for our purposes, a set of legal rules constitutionalize? According to Kelsen, under ordinary conditions a new legal order emerges when it can be said that the laws of the system are valid and effective,[17] and legitimate.[18] However, during what Kelsen calls a 'revolution' or when a new legal system breaks free from the previous system (as in the case of constitutionalization), the legitimacy of the norms is determined according to whether the revolution is successful or not, measured in terms of its

[15] Hart (n 8 above). The rule of recognition may take any number of forms including enactments and other texts, customs, and declarations of specified persons, but only this rule 'deserves, if anything does,' to be the foundation of a legal system.

[16] Other positive legal theorists have emphasized that validity of the system depends, in addition, upon judicial recognition and use of the foundational concept: on this point in relation to Kelsen see: J Raz, *The Concept of a Legal System* 2nd edn, (Oxford: Clarendon Press, 1980), 108; on Hart see: N MacCormick, *HLA Hart* (Stanford: Stanford University Press, 1981) 115.

[17] For Kelsen there is no necessary correspondence between efficacy, validity, and legitimacy. Efficacy refers to the idea that the norm does, as a matter of fact, constrain behaviour. The norm is effective, it *is* a law. Validity, by contrast, means that people ought to behave as the norm states, although this 'ought' does not entail a judgement about the justice of the measure. But the two are related because 'a coercive order, presenting itself as the law, is regarded as valid only if it is by and large effective.' H Kelsen, *Pure Theory of Law* (translated from the second revised and enlarged German edition edited by Max Knight, University of California Press edn, 1978) (c 1967) [hereinafter Kelsen, *Pure Theory*] 46–49. Nevertheless the relationship is complex because he later suggested that efficacy is necessary but not sufficient for validity. 'The validity of a legal order is thus dependent upon its agreement with reality, upon its "efficacy", and so efficacy refers to power whereas validity refers to law-ness and right', Kelsen, *General Theory* (n 14 above) 120–121.

[18] Legitimacy meant only that the rules have been made according to the method determined by the legal order. Legitimacy, in Kelsenian terms, does not refer to any value of justice. Kelsen, *General Theory* (n 14 above) 117. In international law, Thomas Franck has developed a similar argument that the legitimacy of a rule is indicated by: a clear and determinant meaning; its 'symbolic validation' or authority it carries; its coherence within a wider pattern of rules by treating like cases alike; and adherence of states to it: T Franck, *Fairness in International Law and Institutions* (Oxford: Clarendon Press, 1995) 30–42.

efficacy.[19] For Hart, no new legal system can emerge until the rules are both valid and effective, although effectiveness could follow after validity. Rules are valid from a viewpoint internal to the system because they satisfy the authoritative criteria provided for by the rule of recognition indicated by shared acceptance of the rule, on the part of officials in the system.[20] Effectiveness, in Hart's terms, refers to the efficacy of the system as a whole, from the external viewpoint.[21] If this is applied to the constitutionalization problem, the WTO could be said to be constitutionalized as a new system of law when its rules are effective in constraining behaviour, according to Kelsen, or when they are considered, internally, to have complied with a new rule of recognition, according to Hart.

The purpose of the new foundational device is to act as a hypothesis for a new system of law by giving a unity and coherence to an otherwise incoherent set of rules.[22] The *Grundnorm* provides the justification for seeing the rules as a system of law.[23] To Kelsen, the new *Grundnorm* justifies the rules as a system because it has a 'transcendental logical'[24] quality, outside of law.[25] By contrast, the rule of recognition lays no claim to transcendentalism. According to Hart, justification is provided by the fact that the rule of recognition is simply a 'complex social situation' or a 'general practice'[26] whereby officials and private persons identify legal rules. Moreover, its existence is 'shown'[27] by its use and 'is simply accepted as appropriate for use in this way'.[28] The same would have to be true for the WTO in the sense that it would be necessary

[19] If the revolution is effective, the norms of the new regime will be valid and therefore legitimate hence 'the principle of legitimacy is limited by the principle of effectiveness': Kelsen, *Pure Theory* (n 17 above) 211.   [20] Hart (n 8 above).

[21] A rule could be valid, from an internal perspective, without being effective. Although the efficacy of the entire system was normally presupposed in any statement about the validity of a rule: ibid 100.

[22] To Kelsen, the *Grundnorm* was a 'presupposition' about the way a legal system was constructed: Kelsen, *General Theory* (n 14 above) 116. See also JW Harris, 'When and Why Does the *Grundnorm* Change?' (1971) 29 *Cambridge Law Journal* 103 (arguing that Kelsen's *Grundnorm* 'closes up the arch of legal logic' (131) such that all valid legal norms could be interpreted as a 'noncontradictory field of meaning' (106)).

[23] Kelsen, *Pure Theory* (n 17 above) 46–50 (arguing that the *Grundnorm* is what distinguishes a command of a legal community, from a command of a gang of robbers). The *Grundnorm* has a self-fulfiling quality: although its verifiability is *not subject to testing* because it is a way of seeing and imposing order which must be presupposed if there is to be any order; the *Grundnorm* itself *must be presupposed* in the sense of being valid if the first constitution is to be seen as valid.

[24] ibid 202.

[25] The *Grundnorm* stands outside of law. But it is not a 'meta-legal authority' such as God or the state of nature: ibid. Nevertheless, there is no external referent for the *Grundnorm* because it is something which legal science simply does, albeit unconsciously, ibid 204.

[26] Hart (n 8 above) 98.   [27] ibid.

[28] ibid 106. When it is seen, used, and accepted by people within the system, it is valid from an internal point of *law*, and, has the character of *law*. When viewed from an external viewpoint, the validity of the rule of recognition is a question of *fact* because outsiders will recognize its existence, but only from beyond the borders of the legal system in question (104).

to show a new general practice, or unconscious assumption that the WTO constituted a new system of law, beyond a collection of rules.

In order for a system to constitutionalize, it must, clearly, be possible for a new *Grundnorm* to emerge. According to positive legal theory the *Grundnorm* can change,[29] because, as a matter of logic, if a *Grundnorm* is a presupposition which stands apart from law, then if the political or social presuppositions change then similarly the *Grundnorm* must change also.[30] So if it can be shown that the facts of international trade support the existence of a new presupposition then it would be possible to argue that the WTO has been constitutionalized.

Moreover, Kelsen himself argued that during a revolution, broadly defined,[31] a new *Grundnorm* may emerge from a triangulation of the political facts, the new system's instruments of change (the new 'constitution'), and the interpretation imposed upon both.[32] Unusually enough, this theory of constitutional change gained further political and legal recognition when it was expressly judicially approved and applied in a series of cases in the 1960s concerning the post-revolutionary legitimacy of new regimes in Uganda, Pakistan, and Southern Rhodesia.[33]

Hart also argued that a new system can arise by way of change in a basic norm, but he focused on the experience of the states of the Commonwealth for what he called the 'embryology of legal systems', when a new legal system 'emerges from the womb of an old one'.[34] He traced the way in which a state

---

[29] *Grundnorm* change occurs even though the constitution cannot change otherwise than in the manner set down by the drafters of the historically first constitution: Kelsen, *General Theory* (n 14 above) 116.

[30] F Schauer, 'Amending the Presuppositions of a Constitution' in S Levinson (ed), *Responding to Imperfection: The Theory and Practice of Constitutional Amendment* (Princeton: Princeton University Press, 1995).

[31] Revolution encompasses both forceful change in a legal situation and change achieved by peaceful means 'whether by a mass movement...or by a small group of individuals': Kelsen, *Pure Theory* (n 17 above) 209.   [32] ibid 210.

[33] *Uganda v Commissioner of Prisons, Ex parte Matovu* [1966] E Afr LR 514 (Uganda); *The State v Dosso* [1958] 2 PSCR 180, PLD S Ct 533 (Pakistan); and *Madzimbamuto v Lardner-Burke* [1968] 2 S Afr LR 284, 315 (Rhodesia App Div) (Beadle, CJ). The judgments quoted at length from Kelsen's *General Theory of Law and State* (n 14 above) referring to his arguments on the principle of legitimacy, change in the basic norm, and birth and death of the state, eg, in the Ugandan case Chief Justice Udo Udoma at 535 concluded '[o]n the theory of law and state propounded by the positivist school of jurisprudence represented by the famous Professor Kelsen' it was 'beyond question' that the events surrounding the abolition of the constitution were a revolution. At 537 Justice Udoma held that the new constitution, which was produced, had an extra legal origin and that it created a new legal order. This trio of cases were subsequently read as affirming the correctness of Kelsen's theory of *Grundnorm* change: Harris (n 22 above). This view was repeated in the Privy Council's overruling of the Southern Rhodesia Supreme Court decision, *Madzimbamuto v Lardner-Burke* [1969] 1 AC 645, 723 (PC), where the Privy Council, (ineffectually) denied the legitimacy of the Southern Rhodesian revolution: ibid, 29. Any criticisms of the courts' applications of Kelsen were limited to denying that the *particular conditions or criteria* for showing *Grundnorm* change had been satisfied, not to rejection of the change thesis itself.

[34] Hart (n 8 above) 116.

whose legal system has been dependent for its validity upon the legal practices of the colonizing state will, at some point, find that its legal system has taken 'local root'.[35] Whenever this process occurs, (and it may occur over a long and indefinable period), a new rule of recognition was created, a new system of law emerged, and this was simply a matter of law following the facts.[36] Similarly some contemporary WTO scholars have argued against the 'big bang' theory of constitutional change in favour of a more graduated, long term, processual conception,[37] while still retaining commitment to the idea of transition occurring.

From the perspective of legal positivism, it seems clear that the basic norm of international trade law could change so that a new system of constitutionalized law could come into existence. This could occur either by acceptance and use of a new rule of recognition (in Hart's terms) or by revolution, or gradual legal change (in Kelsen's terms). Moreover, rejection of that change by states will not preclude the reality of a new constitution emerging for the WTO because ultimately the question of its emergence is a question of fact, (although what constitutes a 'fact' may be subject to disagreement between states in the international system). The important point here, for our purposes, is that, according to the received account of constitutionalization, the new system must be valid from an internal point of view, whether or not it is recognized as a new system from an external point of view.[38] Although external recognition is important, its absence is not fatal. Moreover, the situation is complicated by the presence of two external points of view, or two parent systems, from which to assess whether a new system of WTO law has emerged—national law and international law. Nevertheless, following positive theory, strictly speaking it will only be necessary to show that it is valid *from an internal viewpoint*. In order to prove the claim of WTO constitutionalization, it must be possible to achieve a reconciliation along Hart's lines, that from an internal point of view, as a matter of fact, a new rule of recognition has arisen, and this differs from the viewpoint of either or both of the international or the previous national law regimes.

---

[35] Hart (n 8 above) 117.

[36] Hart emphasized that however the separation occurs, it is a matter of *fact* that an independent legal system has emerged. This fact may not be recognized by the legal system of the parent state, and it may even lead to disunity amongst officials in the parent state, but it is nevertheless a factual statement: ibid 118.   [37] Cottier and Hertig (n 2 above) 295–298.

[38] Shared internal acceptance of a new rule of recognition is what is important: *Madzimbamuto v Lardner-Burke* [1968] 2 S Afr LR 284, 319 (Rhodesia App Div) (Beadle, CJ), following Wheaton, suggested that a sovereign can exercise full powers internally, which are not dependent upon external recognition. He makes this argument in order to show that efficacy of internal control is the test for validity of the new constitutional structure stating: 'It cannot therefore be assumed that the ultimate success of the present revolution must necessarily depend on some express or implied acquiescence by Great Britain or on recognition of the present Government by other states'. See also: Harris (n 22 above) 103–104: 'Even the Privy Council, in holding that the laws and administrative acts of the Smith regime were completely without legal effect in Southern Rhodesia, does not appear to have dissented from the general principle that successful revolutions create new legal orders whose validity may be adjudged by courts within the territory subject to the revolution.'

So how do we know when a new foundational device has emerged? What are the specific criteria of constitutional change according to this approach?[39] Positive legal theory does not elaborate a set of criteria by which it would be possible precisely to identify when a new constitutional system has emerged, other than to refer to the principle of effectiveness, or to the idea that citizens obey the primary rules and officials display a shared acceptance towards the secondary rules. In order to discover the criteria of *Grundnorm* change we could look to judicial interpretations of the revolutionary situations of East Africa (Uganda), Southern Rhodesia, and Pakistan.[40] Reiterating Kelsen, it is clear, first, that factual evidence of a social and economic nature, not law, was creative of the new *Grundnorm*.[41] Secondly, the key factor was whether the revolution was successful or not,[42] in terms of effectiveness. Effectiveness itself was assessed according to various factors including whether, for example, government continued as usual;[43] the new regime was recognized by foreign governments;[44] it was economically viable;[45] it collected taxes;[46] the business of the courts continued;[47] there was an absence of protest from the population;[48] and there

---

[39] It is worth noting that the criteria might vary, or overlap, between international law and national law. International law contains an elaborate set of criteria for recognition of new constitutions, governments and states: see J Crawford, *The Creation of States in International Law* (1979). Sometimes these international criteria are relied upon in national law: see, eg, *Madzimbamuto v Lardner-Burke* [1968] 2 S Afr LR 284, 315 (Rhodesia App Div) (Beadle, CJ), where the international law distinction between recognition of *de facto* and *de jure* governments was one basis upon which the Supreme Court of Southern Rhodesia decided that constitutional change in that state was valid. However, on appeal, the Privy Council rejected the applicability of these principles dismissing them as 'conceptions of international law', which were 'inappropriate in dealing with the legal position of a usurper within the territory of which he has acquired control': *Madzimbamuto v Lardner-Burke* [1969] 1 AC 645, 723 (PC).

[40] It should be noted that the main concern in these cases was with the validity of the legislative or administrative acts (often detention orders) of the new regime, and not with the validity of the constitution itself, or with the existence of any *Grundnorm*. Indirectly these latter issues were raised, but the discussion here must be seen as merely drawing certain inferences about constitutional validity and *Grundnorm* existence from the more specific discussions of legislative/administrative validity. For example, in the Privy Council decision concerning Southern Rhodesia, the Board was at pains to point out that it was only the validity of the acts of the usurping government that it was assessing. Neither of the courts of lower instance recognized the validity of the revolutionary constitution, even if they did recognize the validity of the legislative/administrative acts of the revolutionary regime: *Madzimbamuto v Lardner*-Burke [1969] 1 AC 645, 717–718 (PC).

[41] *Uganda v Commissioner of Prisons, Ex parte Matovu* [1966] E Afr LR 514, 538 (Uganda).

[42] An extensive list of authorities for this proposition are set out in detail: *Madzimbamuto v Lardner-Burke* [1968] 2 S Afr LR 284, 318 (Rhodesia App Div) (Beadle, CJ). On appeal to the Privy Council the proposition is not challenged; the cases which challenge the proposition are distinguished on the basis that efficacy of the change cannot be adjudged whilst two contending rivals for power exist: *Madzimbamuto v Lardner-Burke* [1969] 1 AC 645, 725 (PC).

[43] *Madzimbamuto v Lardner-Burke* [1968] 2 S Afr LR 284, 321 (Rhodesia App Div) (Beadle, CJ).

[44] ibid.   [45] ibid.

[46] *Uganda v Commissioner of Prisons, Ex parte Matovu* [1966] E Afr LR 514, 535 (Uganda).

[47] *Madzimbamuto v Lardner-Burke* [1968] 2 S Afr LR 284, 321 (Rhodesia App Div) (Beadle, CJ).

[48] *Uganda v Commissioner of Prisons, Ex parte Matovu* [1966] E Afr LR 514, 535 (Uganda).

no longer existed a contending rival.[49] Not all these elements would be applicable to the WTO but it could be argued that effectiveness is satisfied by, for example, state recognition of the organization evidenced by their membership of it; state acceptance of its effectiveness indicated by high levels of participation in the organization's activities and financial support from states; acknowledgement of WTO tribunal decisions in national courts; and compliance with WTO rulings by Member State governments.

A further feature of effectiveness, according to the 1960s cases, was the separation of the new system from the expected ways of legal change. The more illegitimate the change[50] in terms of not conforming with the method of change prescribed by the pre-existing constitution, the more extra-legal change was in its origins,[51] the more likely that a new system of law had evolved. Evidence of such separation included the abruptness of the change; the fact that it was not within the contemplation of the existing constitution; and that it caused the destruction of the entire existing legal order.[52] In short, change at the WTO showing success and effectiveness of a new regime, and historical discontinuity with the past, would provide a basis for finding that a new legal order has been brought into being. In relation to the requirement of de-linkage from the old regime, it might be suggested that the WTO did not usurp the GATT, but develop from it. Indeed the AB 1996 tribunal decision in *Japan—Taxes on Alcoholic Beverages* suggests that the WTO system is merely a continuation of the old. However, the notion that remains apposite is the idea that the new regime must represent a break with the old regime, whether gradual in Hart's terms, or more abrupt in Kelsen's terms. In either case it would be possible to suggest that the criteria of *Grundnorm* change have been satisfied.

In sum then, in order to be constitutionalized, according to positive legal theory, it would have to be shown that a new foundational device was present in relation to the WTO, either in the form of a new *Grundnorm*, or new rule of recognition, providing the authoritative criteria for that legal system, and thereby providing it with a coherence and unity that it would otherwise lack. This new rule of recognition would have to be shown to have been in existence from a viewpoint internal to the WTO system, by officials within the system, as well as the subjects of the system accepting the primary rules of obligation contained in the covered agreements. The emergence of a new *Grundnorm*, will be shown, as a matter of fact, if it can be shown that the WTO system is effective, and that it origins are de-linked from the parent system, whether that be the GATT, the national legal systems, or international law. Moreover, in order to be constitutionalized, the WTO system must be effective.

---

[49] *Madzimbamuto v Lardner-Burke* [1969] 1 AC 645, 725 (PC).
[50] *Uganda v Commissioner of Prisons, Ex parte Matovu* [1966] E Afr LR 514, 535 (Uganda).
[51] ibid.   [52] *Madzimbamuto v Lardner-Burke* [1969] 1 AC 645, 725 (PC).

2.4.3 Community

The third core element of constitutionalization is the existence of a community that can authorize the making, and continual remaking, of a constitution. So in relation to international law it has been suggested that it is only the existence of a community that creates the 'existential moment' in which the legitimacy of the system can be assessed.[53] In relation to Europe a similar argument is made. The constitutionalization of Europe depends upon authorization by a polity, or a demos: 'In Western liberal democracy public authority requires legitimating through one principal source: the citizens of the polity.'[54] A system without an authorizing community can never be democratic, or, it is implied, constitutionalized:

> Citizens constitute the demos of the polity....Demos provides another way of expressing the link between citizenship and democracy. Demcracy does not exist in a vacuum. It is premised on the existence of a polity with members—the demos—by whom and for whom democratic discourse with its many variants takes place. The authority and legitimacy of a majority to compel a minority exists only with political boundaries defined by a demos. Simply put, if there is no demos, there can be no democracy.[55]

The requirement of community does not mean that the community has to be a fully-fledged democratic body with full rights of voting and participation, for in most circumstances it is assumed that, in the deliberative process discussed below, the community is represented by some other entity, be it individual or group (in this case the State), and that the community's desires are conveyed through these representatives. Alternatively, a Hartian view of constitutionalization suggests that a community of trade officials could form the necessary community to authorize the making of a trade constitution. Others suggest that publics in different states sharing a set of understandings about international trade could be the constituting community of the WTO,[56] or that the WTO should create a 'necessary agora where transnational politics could flourish'.[57] It is clear, therefore, that even within the received account of community there exist two different notions of community and so two different notions of constitutionalization. In one, constitutionalization can be authorized merely by a small trade elite, and the necessity of having

[53] Franck (n 18 above) 10 (arguing that the existence of a community is what makes it possible to consider whether a legal system is fair, and it is only in the face of the latter that a system can be deemed legitimate. In chapter 13 Franck presents international trade law as an example of a system in which fairness can be discussed, thereby implying that the existential moment in relation to creation of an international trade community may have arrived.)

[54] JHH Weiler, 'To Be a European Citizen: Eros, and Civilization' in Weiler, *Constitution* (n 1 above) [hereinafter Weiler, 'To Be a European Citizen'] 336.   [55] ibid 337.

[56] S Charnovitz, 'WTO Cosmopolitics' (2002) 34 *New York University Journal of International Law and Politics* 299 [hereinafter Charnovitz, 'WTO Cosmopolitics'] 326.

[57] AB Zampetti, 'Democratic Legitimacy in the World Trade Organization: The Justice Dimension' (2003) 37 *Journal of World Trade* 105, 125.

representatives to represent the interests of that elite is diminished. In the other, the public at large is the authorizing community and its wishes must be conveyed and conducted through the medium of representation. While it is the latter that is conventionally assumed by democratic theory, we shall see that the various models of WTO constitutionalization identified in this study do not make explicit the nature of the community that supports their view of WTO constitutionalization, nor how representation theory operates in that context.

Some hold to a 'statist'[58] view of community and constitutionalization and reject the possibility of community in a polity other than the nation state; to them the community is a homogenous, culturally and geographically contained unit. Others favour a more porous conception of community claiming that a collectivity can reflect multiple identities, and is, in any case, shaped by social forces rather than state boundaries.[59]

Another approach to this problem rejects altogether the notion that constitutionalization is dependent upon the existence of a community prior to a constitution being formed[60] and suggests that the community itself might emerge from the process of constitutionalization; the community does not precede constitutionalization but is, in part, constituted by it. Walker, for example, argues that the 'no demos' critique noted above, is 'overstated', 'essentialist', and 'unsustainable'.[61] He says instead that constitutional community can emerge as a mutually constitutive process in which constitutional structures arise and reproduce the community, and argues that political community, in a complete homogenous sense, does not pre-exist the graduated emergence of a constitution. 'Constitutional law and discourse, thus should be understood not, or not just as an external map of the polity, but as one of the polity's key defining and constitutive features'.[62] He goes on:

the mutual constitution of law and politics [is] a dynamic and ongoing process... In this process of mutual constitution and containment, therefore, constitutional law is recursively involved in both the *presentation* and the *representation* of the polity—both seeking to reflect the prior political state and in that process simultaneously translating and redefining that prior political state in legal-constitutional terms.[63]

Regardless of whether a community creates a constitution or a constitution creates a community, the literature suggests that a community is only constitutionalizing when it takes collective action, in the belief that what it is doing

---

[58] See description of international trade 'statism' in Cottier and Hertig (n 2 above) 283–293.

[59] ibid 290–293.

[60] Charnovitz, 'WTO Cosmopolitics' (n 56 above) 325 (arguing that consolidation of a global demos is not necessary in order for the WTO to develop a 'firmer political base', which is defined, at 299, as one in which 'global political action transcend[s] a strict state-to-state, or multilateral basis').

[61] N Walker, 'The EU and the WTO: Constitutionalism in a New Key' in G de Búrca and J Scott (eds), *The EU and the WTO: Legal and Constitutional Issues* (Oxford: Hart Publishing, 2001) 31, 49.   [62] ibid 34.

[63] ibid.

is creating a community. A community exists sufficient to ground a new system of law when there is an 'ongoing structured relationship between sets of actors', creative of a 'common, conscious system of reciprocity between its constituents'.[64] A constitutional community comes into being not only because the community thinks it is one but also because the community acts to create one. 'It is only through the "doing" that the true meaning of the covenant will be borne out'.[65]

But the community must not only act as a community, in the belief that it is a community, according to some, the constitution of a constitutional community is a metaphysical act as well. It is about creating an 'international social consciousness' engaging the 'public mind of international society'.[66] In order for a community, and hence a constitution, to emerge a certain 'faith' is required 'in one's self, in one's co-constituents, faith in one's institutions and their ability, in good faith, to "discover," to constitute the meaning of the constitution through its praxis'.[67] On this view, constitutionalization generally, and community in particular, is an existential, not just institutional accomplishment.[68] And, it is unlikely to be the product of a small trade elite.

Moreover, the concept of constitutionalization is presented by some as a saviour from the depredations of the conditions of postmodern life. It is vested with an almost spiritual capacity to rescue the community. Joseph Weiler argues that the constitutionalization process is said to satisfy the combination of, what he labels, humanity's urge for *eros* (embodied in the nation state with its emphasis on fixity, history, and stability), with its desire for civilization (embodied in the urge toward the modern, the rational, the humanistic).[69] The constitutionalization process is valorized because it possesses the potential to speak to people's deep-seated fears about the commodification of values, the depersonalization of the market, and the replacement of the authority of science with competing social narratives.[70] Weiler's constitutionalization process is no

---

[64] Franck (n 18 above) 10.

[65] JHH Weiler, 'Introduction: "We will do and Hearken"' in Weiler, *Constitution* (n 1 above) [hereinafter Weiler, 'We will do and Hearken'] 6–7.

[66] P Allott, *Eunomia: New Order for a New World* (Oxford: Oxford University Press, paperback edn, 2001, first published 1990) xx.

[67] Weiler, 'We Will Do and Hearken' (n 65 above) 6. See also G Frankenberg, 'Tocqueville's Question—The Role of a Constitution in the Process of Integration' (2000) 13 *Ratio Juris* 1, 7 (referring to Schneider's comment that constitutional theory is '[w]here mystery reigns, [and] faith rules').

[68] JHH Weiler's work is infused with biblical references and spiritual manifestations. See, eg, Weiler, 'We Will Do and Hearken' (n 65 above) 5, the introduction to his seminal collection of essays on Europe, which leads with the story of Exodus where Moses reads the Covenant between God and the Jewish people in order to illustrate that a community is created by acting as a community and this is then reinforced by a change in the mental conception of the community to a people. See also the title of work emphasizing the relationship between the EU and the WTO as like that between Cain and Abel: Weiler, 'Cain and Abel' (n 1 above).

[69] Weiler, 'To Be a European Citizen' (n 54 above) 347.

[70] Weiler, ibid 346–356. Note, although Weiler is aware of the role the constitution of Europe played in creating some of these conditions, he is hopeful that a meaningful European citizenship could combat the worst excesses of such conditions. So constitutionalization is both cause and cure.

mere construction of a new legal system; it has deep resonating consequences for the spirit, psyche, and soul of the constitutional community.

This process peaks, according to Weiler, when members of the community 'do and hearken' and thereby produce a feature critical to the creation of community and constitutionalization proper—the citizen. Moreover this actor must not be based around a banal notion of citizenship[71] but a meaningful notion of citizenship that 'goes to the very foundations of political legitimacy'.[72]

Nevertheless, constitutionalized citizenship does not mean the eradication of difference between constituent parts of the system.[73] '[M]anaging diversity and integrating different groups within one polity is an essential task of modern constitutionalism.'[74] The citizen of the State is not jettisoned in favour of a citizen of a new legal system.[75] Instead constitutionalization occurs when nationality is decoupled from citizenship and re-coupled in a new (constitutional) geometry.[76] The citizens of the new constitutionalized system retain their national identity, and remain situated within multiple demoi, both within the State and within the new system.[77]

In sum, constitutionalization requires the emergence of a community, which acts as a body to authorize the making of the constitution of the new system. It could be formed by a small community of officials, but is more often assumed to be comprised of the broader population. The community constitutes itself by acting as a community and believing that it is so doing, and by expressing a faith in the process of creating a constitution. Any such community will be composed of citizens, defined politically as such as well as economically. Finally, the citizenship of the constitutionalized entity does not replace the citizenry of the constituent parts of the constitutional community, and recognition of difference between the parts is retained.

2.4.4   Deliberation

The fourth core element of constitutionalization involves a process of deliberation. In order to be constitutionalized, a legal system must include processes

---

[71] Weiler, 'To Be a European Citizen' (n 54 above) at 335 (discussing the citizenship provisions of the Maastricht Treaty, which, he claims, should be jettisoned because they create a 'Saatchi and Saatchi' version in which the political process has been degraded, image has trumped substance, deliberative governance is replaced by commodification of the political process, and consumer has replaced citizen). [72] ibid at 336.

[73] ibid at 329 (arguing that European citizenship should be a 'hallmark of differentity').

[74] Cottier and Hertig (n 2 above) 292.

[75] Weiler, 'To Be a European Citizen' (n 54 above) at 338–339 (arguing that despite the dangers of nationhood, nationality remains important because it is 'a shield against existential aloneness' 338; it calls for 'loyalty...beyond...the self-interested social unit'; it celebrates 'the virtues of autochthony—the nexus to place and land'; and is a 'vehicle for realizing human potentialities in original ways'). [76] ibid at 337.

[77] ibid (arguing that nationality and central constitutional citizenship are 'interdependent' both 'conceptually and psychologically').

of deliberation and communication the purposes of which are to facilitate dialogue about the particular system in question, its values, practices, and procedures. In the process, members of the community make and remake the constitution of the community directly or through representation, but the key to a constitutionalization project, on this view, is communication facilitating civic participation in the making of law. According to this conception, Jürgen Habermas argues that '[deliberative] law emerges from and reproduces itself only in the forms of a constitutionally regulated circulation of power, which should be nourished by the communications of an unsubverted public sphere that in turn is rooted in the associational network of a liberal civil society and gains support from the core private spheres of the lifeworld'.[78] In relation to the WTO specifically, it is argued that the development of deliberative democracy and its techniques of reasoned argument, rationality, and persuasion would improve the democratic legitimacy of the institution.[79] For example, some suggest the WTO establish an advisory assembly which could supervise appointments at Director General and Appellate Body level, and consult in relation to budgets and new rules.[80]

The point of the communicative process is to create a deliberative structure in which private autonomy can be linked with the public sphere of 'informal and non-institutionalized opinion and will formation',[81] and with institutional decision-making. In the process, citizens are constituted as authors of law as well as its addressees.

Critics of the deliberative process aspect of constitutionalization have suggested that its claims are exaggerated. Richard Posner, for example, rejoins that any deliberative process will be undermined by the usual 'legal compromise between unequal power, or ignorance or confusion, or opportunistic coalition'.[82] Moreover, deliberative decision-making is not without flaws because 'stakes are high, emotion engaged, information sparse, criteria contested and expertise untrustworthy'.[83] Others argue that deliberative process will do nothing to cure the lacuna of legitimacy in modern legal systems because the 'flight to procedure' can never completely transcend contestable substantive normative assumptions.[84] Moreover, it is said that the deliberative process itself, while open to a wider range of values and interests, nevertheless excludes certain

---

[78] J Habermas, 'Paradigms of Law' (1996) 17 *Cardozo Law Review* 771, 777. A related argument is made in the domestic sphere by those arguing that constitutional interpretation should be the province not just of judges but other political institutions: on 'popular constitutionalism' see, eg, LD Kramer, 'The Supreme Court 2000 Term' (2001) 115 *Harvard Law Review* 4, 15 (stating that constitutional democracy requires non-judicial 'processes, formal and informal, by which our constitutional understandings and commitments can be challenged, reinterpreted, and renewed').
[79] Zampetti (n 57 above) 121.   [80] ibid 124–125.   [81] Habermas (n 78 above) 777.
[82] RA Posner, *The Problematics of Moral and Legal Theory* (Cambridge: Beltnap Press, 1999).
[83] ibid.
[84] M Rosenfeld, 'Can Rights, Democracy, and Justice be Reconciled through Discourse Theory? Reflections on Habermas's Proceduralist Paradigm of Law' (1996) 17 *Cardozo Law Review* 791, at 794–796.

norms[85] and fails to take account of genuine difference.[86] One aim of this study is to examine the extent to which the WTO models meet this criterion, and the ways in which the flaws in the deliberative process argument are also reflected.

2.4.5 Realignment of relationships

Another central element of the constitutionalization process is that it necessarily entails a rearrangement of the relationship between the states and the central putative constitutionalized entity. 'In a multilayered system, defining the relationship and the boundaries between the different levels of governance are essential constitutional functions.'[87] This rearrangement of the various actors of the regime is generally also assumed in the literature, rather than put forward as a requirement, but its importance to the overall schema of the received account is clear. In the absence of any positive rule to the contrary, states retain full decisional capacity, within the limits of international law generally,[88] but once a new constitutionalized entity emerges then the states' decisional capacity is altered. This element is most famously reflected in the dictum of the European Court of Justice in the *Van Gend en Loos* decision when it said that the Treaty of Rome heralded a 'new legal order of international law for the benefit of which the states have limited their sovereign rights, albeit within limited fields, and the subjects of which comprise not only Member States but also their nationals'.[89] In one sense, all the literature on constitutionalization in Europe, which followed from this landmark decision, is about the extent of the realignment of relationships between the states and the central entity.

This is not to say that any realignment necessarily involves a loss of decisional capacity. Some commentators claim that states within any new constitutionalization process retain the capacity to withdraw from the arrangements of constitutionalization and so revert to a pre-constitutionalized set of relationships.[90] Others claim that no sovereignty is 'lost', in any event, when states become a part of a constitutionalized arrangement,[91] that the two capacities or constitutional structures do not have to be mutually exclusive,[92] or that

---

[85] M Rosenfeld, 'Can Rights, Democracy, and Justice be Reconciled through Discourse Theory? Reflections on Habermas's Proceduralist Paradigm of Law' (1996) 17 *Cardozo Law Review* 791, at 811–812 (arguing that deliberative process excludes values such as religion and non-adherence to the principle of equality).   [86] ibid 798.

[87] Cottier and Hertig (n 2 above) 317.

[88] *The Lotus Case (France v Turkey)* 1927 PCIJ (Ser A) No 10.

[89] Case 26/62, *NV Algemene Transporten Expeditie Onderneming van Gend en Loos v Nederlandse Administratie der Belastingen* [1963] ECR 1.

[90] See, eg, P Eleftheriadis, 'Aspects of European Constitutionalism' (1996) 21 *European Law Review* 32.

[91] N MacCormick, 'The Maastricht–Urteil: Sovereignty Now' (1995) 1 *European Law Journal* 259.

[92] JHH Weiler and J Trachtman, 'European Constitutionalism and its Discontents' (1997) 17 *Northwestern Journal of International Law and Business* 354 (arguing that it is necessary to think

what is transferred is competence, not sovereignty.[93] Regardless of which position is taken, it is clear that constitutionalization entails a modification of relationships, the extent and nature of which may be open to question. Again, any discussion of WTO constitutionalization will therefore address this element as well.

2.4.6 Social legitimacy

The sixth core element of constitutionalization is legitimacy, defined here not as the making of law according to the correct processes[94] but as law commanding sufficient normative authority for the community to accept it as a constitution, what some have referred to as substantive or social legitimacy.[95] This is to be contrasted with what Scharpf refers to as effectiveness legitimacy, in which a system is judged legitimate according to its delivery of certain outcomes in an efficient manner.[96] The inclusion of this element of social acceptance legitimacy does not mean that agreement amongst scholars exists as to the level of legitimacy to be achieved, or indeed even on how to measure it, in either domestic or supranational systems. Indeed legal theory and sociology have long grappled with the difficulty of defining and measuring the term, as has international legal literature. A classical legal position is outlined in Kelsen, *General Theory* discussed above. A social theory of legitimacy is famously identified by Max Weber who argued that three types of legitimate authority could be identified, rational, traditional, or charismatic, and that rational legitimacy itself could be founded on the basis of either an ideological system such as religion, science, or technical expertise (substantive rationality) or formal–legal rationality.[97] A contemporary legal theory attempt to classify different legal theoretical approaches to the source of law's legitimacy is made by Richard Posner[98] who argues that that legitimacy has a number of sources depending on the theoretical outlook taken. Posner claims that positivists derive law's legitimacy from its emanation as a set of rules made by a sovereign authority, one of

about the creation of new 'constitutional' entities in such a way that they can be mutually interdependent with existing structures of sovereignty).

[93] M Loughlin, 'Ten Tenets of Sovereignty' in N Walker (ed), *Sovereignty in Transition* (Oxford; Portland, Oregon: Hart Publishing, 2003).

[94] This is legitimacy according to Kelsen, *General Theory* (n 14 above). Kelsen differentiated between legitimacy, effectiveness, and validity, arguing that in order to be legitimate rules had to be both (politically) effective and (legally) valid.

[95] R Howse, 'Adjudicative Legitimacy and Treaty Interpretation in International Trade Law: The Early Years of WTO Jurisprudence' in JHH Weiler (ed), *The EU, the WTO and the NAFTA: Towards a Common Law of International Trade* (2000) (arguing that the WTO is in the process of achieving a level of 'adjudicative legitimacy' which he distinguishes from social legitimacy referred to by Weiler). See JHH Weiler, 'The Transformation of Europe' in Weiler, *Constitution* (n 1 above) 80 (arguing that social legitimacy is a form of broad, empirically determined societal acceptance of the system) [hereinafter Weiler, 'Transformation'].

[96] F Scharpf, *Governing in Europe: Effective and Democratic?* (Oxford: Oxford University Press, 1999) ch 1.

[97] W Heydebrand (ed) *Max Weber: Sociological Writings* (London: Continuum, 1994).

[98] Posner (n 82 above) 90, 101.

which is a rule to recognize what is a rule. To Dworkin, law is a set of rules supplemented, and hence legitimized, by deep fundamental principles and the mythical figure of a judge, constantly weighing up the rules and principles to arrive at 'better' outcomes which best fit the constitutional story as told in earlier cases. To pragmatists, like Posner, law derives its legitimacy from a mixture of social science observation and hard-nosed political choice. To Habermas and communicative discourse theorists, the legitimacy of law lies in the democratic process by which it is made, so that law exists between social reality and normative behaviour and is authorized by a democratic process of participation, communication, and rational decision-making between citizens. In European constitutionalization literature Joseph Weiler comments that Thomas Franck provides a useful distinction between legitimacy as process, which Franck associates with the work of Max Weber; legitimacy as a mixture of process and substance, which he associates with Jürgen Habermas; and legitimacy focused on outcomes, which he associates with a neo-Marxist tradition.[99]

One international trade commentator has remarked that, whereas the system's legitimacy was once derived from a 'twentieth century commitment to technocratic decisionmaking', it is now in 'crisis' and must be met by an 'alternative model'.[100] As a result, some have sought to address the crisis of legitimacy in systems of international law by gauging it according to procedural measures, both old and new. So the legitimacy of supranational adjudication is said to be best assessed by measuring its effectiveness[101] (recalling positivism again), or by using the tools of principal and agency relations,[102] by the incorporation of constitutional principles such as subsidiarity, and cost-sharing,[103] or by assessing the fairness of the system's judicial procedure, the coherence and integrity of its legal interpretation, and its institutional sensitivity.[104]

Others, such as Zampetti, assert that legitimacy is not merely a matter of 'trying to fix procedural issues' because 'justice-related issues lie at the core of the democratic legitimacy deficit claim'.[105] In relation to the WTO, he claims that democratic legitimacy could only be aspired to if consideration was given to substantive issues such as market access and the compliance costs

[99] Weiler, 'Transformation' (n 95 above) 80, n 187.

[100] D Esty, 'The World Trade Organization's Legitimacy Crisis' (2002) 1 *World Trade Review* 7, 10.

[101] LR Helfer and A-M Slaughter, 'Toward a Theory of Effective Supranational Adjudication' (1997) 107 *Yale Law Journal* 273 (arguing that effectiveness is what is critical and suggesting a 'checklist' by which such effectiveness can be assessed including: at page 300 composition of tribunal; at page 308 awareness of audience and, at page 329 nature of violations).

[102] C Coglianese and K Nicolaidis, 'Securing Subsidiarity: The Institutional Design of Federalism in the United States and Europe' in K Nicolaidis and R Howse (eds), *The Federal Vision* (Oxford: Oxford University Press, 2001).

[103] R Howse, 'Association Identity and Federal Community', paper prepared for symposium on *Rethinking Federalism in the EU and US: The Challenge of Legitimacy*, Kennedy School of Government, Boston, 19 April 1999, <http://www.ksg.harvard.edu/visions/federalism/howse.doc>.

[104] Howse (n 95 above).   [105] Zampetti (n 57 above) 106.

of adjusting legal systems to, for example, sanction breaches of intellectual property rights.

Whatever form legitimacy takes it is clear that a system may be judged legitimate for a number of reasons. As one commentator observes, to those interested in welfare enhancement a system may appear legitimate if more countries achieve greater growth. To those promoting the so-called 'Washington consensus,' a system may be legitimate if it succeeds in encouraging states to adjust their microeconomic policies to meet macroeconomic demands of international institutions.[106] To others still, a system is legitimate if it disciplines the excessive use of discriminatory trade policies by states whilst deferring to national democratic outcomes which result from fully participatory decisions over regulatory policy.[107]

Moreover, the type of legitimacy sought depends, in part, on the democratic model ascribed to by the viewer. To those concerned to retain the power of a national interest perspective on international affairs, the state-centric approach of the WTO is a plus for legitimacy; for the cosmopolitan democracy approach, greater attention would be need to given to individual participation in order to call the system legitimate; from a communitarian perspective, an emphasis on local affairs and civic duty would signal democratic legitimacy.[108] Whichever stance is taken, and whatever form of legitimacy is promoted, legitimacy, however defined, measured, or justified, is a critical element in the constitutionalization process, and so will be central to discussions of WTO transformations.

2.4.7 Summary of the core elements of constitutionalization

According to received understandings of constitutionalization, the process of making a constitution consists of a set of core elements. On this account, then, constitutionalization occurs only in the presence of these elements. Constitutionalization is premised on the existence of rules or institutions constraining economic and political behaviour. It requires a showing of a break between a pre-existing legal system and a new system indicated by a change in the basic norm of the new system. The new norm consists of a rule to recognize other rules as belonging to the new system and gives the system coherence. Constitutionalization assumes the prior existence or simultaneous construction of a political community, with representation, to authorize constitution-making. Constitutionalization entails a process of deliberation, which facilitates communication, transparency, and a strong public sphere in order to ensure that the citizens of the community are the authors (directly or indirectly through representation) as well as subjects of the law of the system. Finally, it is only when the constitutionalization process has achieved a level of social acceptance

---

[106] R Howse, 'The Legitimacy of the World Trade Organization' in J Coicaud and V Heiskanen (eds), *The Legitimacy of International Organizations* (Tokyo; New York: United Nations Press, 2001) 355, 364–366.   [107] ibid 370.

[108] Zampetti (n 57 above) 120.

or social legitimacy, the specific quantity and quality of which remains undefined, that one can say a system has been constitutionalized.

Other elements such as rule of law, constitutional adjudication, or separation of powers may also form part of the constitutionalization process but they are not essential in the same manner as the core elements above. The former aspects are embellishments on the basic model, embroidery, so to speak, on a basic pattern of constitutionalization consisting of practices that constrain social and political interaction, *Grundnorm* change, community, deliberation, relationship realignment, and social legitimacy.

Before I leave the received account of constitutionalization, I would like to repeat that I am not positing here an ideal type of constitutionalization. The elements I have chosen to emphasize comprise a representative distillation of the literature on the constitutional process, most, but not all, of which describes a process occurring within the nation state. But even within that distilled core of ideas there may be omissions or differences of emphases. Some would focus more on representation rather than deliberation; some might interpret the form of legitimacy I propose as too subjective in nature; others would place rights at the centre, not the margins, of their constitutional analysis. Choices have clearly been made, and, to the extent that it is possible, I have tried to make the reasons for those choices visible. Moreover, as we proceed with the discussion, the limitations of the received account will be exposed and, ultimately, I will conclude that not only does the WTO not meet the received account, but that the account itself has been transformed, by virtue of the transnational experiment in constitutionalization occurring at the WTO.

2.5   THREE PRELIMINARY OBJECTIONS

The next chapter, Chapter 3, will explore the relationship between the international economic law background and the constitutionalization debate in order to show how the received account evolved, at a transnational level, and how the WTO constitutionalization story began to be told. Before I do this, I want to address three preliminary objections that are regularly made against the use of the term to describe the transformations in WTO law. The first is that constitutionalization, as a technical term, can only be applied to national legal systems. The second is that the WTO system is not constitutionalized because it is like any other international treaty arrangement. The third is that the constitution of the WTO legal system is international law itself.

2.5.1   Constitutionalization applies only to national legal systems

The first objection is simply that constitutionalization is not an appropriate term to use in relation to the transformations at the WTO because the term only applies to national legal systems; whatever occurs at the international level cannot accurately be called constitutional because it can never include all the elements which a national constitution contains including, for example, democratic legitimacy. This argument is circular; the WTO cannot be a constitution because a constitution only exists at national level, and the thing that exists at national level is a constitution, in part because it is at national level. Indeed one inference from this study is to highlight the deficiencies with the traditional account of what is a constitution, and to suggest changes to it. But putting this circularity aside, there are two responses which should be made.

First, there is a long history of use of the term 'constitutional' to describe transformations in power relationships at the international level, beginning with Kant, and continuing to the present day.[109] The current work on constitutionalization is therefore part of a long tradition of thinking about international legal systems in a constitutional mode. To borrow the words of one prominent international constitutionalization scholar, the work studied here and the study itself, is part of that tradition, part of a body of literature that fuses disparate legal events and 'baptize[s]' them as constitutional in the service of an argument that 'the whole is greater than the sum of the parts'.[110]

Secondly, none of the writers who claim the WTO is constitutionalizing also claim that the WTO legal system *is* a constitution, in the same sense as a national constitution. National constitutional law possesses a battery of doctrinal and institutional devices to divide public power, including the principles of judicial review (the vesting of power in a central court to decide the constitutionality of legislation), federalism (the vertical distribution of legislative power), and the separation of powers doctrine (the horizontal distribution of legislative, executive, and judicial power).[111] At the international level, the

---

[109] In international law, an intellectually rich example of recent years is Allott (n 66 above). Allott's aim was to write a 'general theory of law and society' (xlviii) in order to address the 'problem of international constitutionalism' (xxii) and goes so far as to draft an international constitutional treaty to implement his general theory (xxxv). In international trade law the tradition of literature with a normative agenda to promote constitutionalization is best exemplified by the work of Ernst-Ulrich Petersmann, see, eg: E-U Petersmann, 'Constitutionalism and International Adjudication: How to Constitutionalize the UN Dispute Settlement System?' (1999) 31 *New York University Journal of International Law and Politics* 753; and E-U Petersmann, 'How to Constitutionalize International Law and Foreign Policy for the Benefit of Civil Society?' (1998) 20 *Michigan Journal of International Law* 1.

[110] These characterizations are borrowed and adapted from JHH Weiler's discussion of similar trends in European Community literature: JHH Weiler, 'The Reformation of European Constitutionalism' in Weiler, *Constitution* (n 1 above) 225.

[111] The decisions illustrating these principles are legion in the case law of national legal systems. Landmark decisions in two federal constitutional systems are: in the United States, *McCulloch v Maryland* 17 US (4 Wheat) 36, 1819 WL 2135 (US Md), 4 L Ed 579 (1819) on federal distribution of power; *Marbury v Madison* 5 US (1 Cranch) 137, 1803 WL 893 (US Dist Col), 2 L Ed 60 (1803) on judicial review; *Youngstown Sheet & Tube Co v Sawyer* 343 US 579, 72 S Ct 863, 96 L Ed 1153 (1952) on separation of executive power from legislative and judicial power; and, in Australia, *Australian Communist Party v Commonwealth* (1951) 83 CLR 1 (Australia) on judicial

picture is much more malleable. States commit themselves to ways of managing divisions of power if those mechanisms suit their national interests and
are necessary to obtain agreement to the treaty in question. Ultimately, states
retain the capacity to withdraw from these arrangements, although the legal,
economic, and political costs of doing so may be high. Internationally, power
distribution is a much more flexible issue not determined by any rigid set of
constitutional techniques.

Moreover, national constitutional principles of power division are not replic-
ated in the WTO itself. States which are signatory to the WTO agreements
are not part of any federal system. There is no central executive other than a
very rough approximation in the Ministerial Conference which meets at least
every two years and the General Council which oversees the daily running of
the organization,[112] along with the administrative arm of that executive, the
WTO Secretariat.[113] There is no clear delineation of branches of government,
and so, strictly speaking, there are no entities to which the separation of powers
doctrine could apply, and a mix of functions are, in any case, exercised in one
body.[114] Moreover no WTO legislature exists, in the traditional sense. The
only body with a resemblance to a rule-making body, the Ministerial Conference,
meets infrequently, and is not representative in the sense of being elected by an
international trade constituency to fulfil the function of representing that
constituency on trade matters,[115] although it does consist of all Member States.
Moreover its authority is not plenary in the conventional constitutional sense.[116]
No division of legislative power analogous to a federal power distribution
(either domestic or supranational, such as Europe) has taken place within
international trade law. No regulatory powers have been explicitly transferred
to any central body. Strictly speaking, the only power possessed by the central
body is the power of treaty interpretation vested in the WTO central

---

review; *Commonwealth v Cigamatic Pty Ltd* (1962) 108 CLR 372 (Australia) on federalism; *R v
Kirby: Ex parte Boilermakers' Society of Australia* (1956) 94 CLR 254 (Australia) on the separation of powers.

[112] The Ministerial Conference is established under Article IV.1 of the Marrakesh Agreement
Establishing the World Trade Organization, the General Council under Article IV.2 [hereinafter
WTO Agreement], *The Results of the Uruguay Round of Multilateral Trade Negotiations: The
Legal Texts* (1994).   [113] WTO Agreement, Art VI.

[114] For example, the membership of the WTO functions both as a body of a legislative type
when it decides to extend the scope of the agreements to a new issue, and as a body of a judicial
type body when it acts as the Dispute Settlement Body with the authority to adopt reports of the
panels and Appellate Body.

[115] Contrast the situation at the WTO with the European Parliament, where the representatives
of are elected by a European constituency for the purpose of representing that constituency on
European matters.

[116] Although the Ministerial Conference is the highest law-making body within the trade structure for matters within its domain, that domain is, necessarily, limited by the extent to which
national governments are prepared to grant it authority over matters traditionally within national
control: WTO Agreement, Art IV:1.

adjudicatory system. No democratic constituency similar to a national body politic authorized creation of any constitution, nor is the WTO accountable to any such community. In the classic picture then, the WTO system is clearly not constitutional in any conventional sense as understood by national legal constitutional theory.

However, the lack of absolute identity between the WTO and a national constitutional system does not preclude discussion of a constitutionalization process within the WTO as something more than mere treaty interpretation, but less than full-scale constitutionalization. At the very least, as discussed below in Chapter 6, the transformations at the WTO have contributed to one of the elements of the core description, a realignment of the relationship between the centre and the constituent parts. Secondly, some of the features which are said to be absent (such as rights) are not part of the core definition defined above, but are part of what we have called elaborations on the core concept of constitutionalization. Thirdly, to some, the development of the core elements of constitutionalization is, in any case, a matter of degree. Indeed some writers discussed in this study suggest that the WTO system shares sufficiently similar characteristics with national constitutional law to characterize it, at least, undergoing a process of constitutionalization, or even possibly as conforming to a quasi-constitutional stereotype. So, for example, one model argues that the jurisprudence of the WTO is developing constitutional principles about the division of power which are akin to a national constitution, although not identical to it. Another relies on the comprehensive institutional structure, including its strong dispute settlement mechanism and broad range of principles and practices, to think about the WTO in constitutional terms. Others desist from calling the outcome at the WTO a constitution as such and instead stress the graduated, evolving nature of the constitutionalizing process. As one commentator has remarked:

There is no unitary template in terms of which constitutional status is either achieved or not achieved, but rather a set of loosely and variously coupled factors which serve both as *criteria* in terms of which forms of constitutionalism can be distinguished and as *indices* in terms of which degrees of constitutionalization can be measured.[117]

The use of the verb form rather than the noun indicates that what is being discussed is a process of change, rather than a particular static outcome, and that the process is an ongoing one. Accordingly, argue Thomas Cottier and Maya Hertig, the statist conception of constitutionalization needs to be discarded and replaced with a model of constitutionalization as process, in order to address a world in which boundaries between legal systems are 'blurred' and 'new polities have emerged which challenge the states' exclusive legal and political authority'.[118]

---

[117] Walker (n 61 above) 33.   [118] Cottier and Hertig (n 2 above) 32.

Finally, some might agree with the critics who wish to reject or subvert the constitutionalization model but who nevertheless use the language of constitutionalization in order to engage with the debate. These are critics concerned with, for example, the legitimacy of the authorization process or the institution's accountability. To these critics, the language of debate may be undesirable, and the outcomes unclear, but constitutionalization must be assumed at least to an extent necessary for the purpose of critiquing it.

In short, despite the lack of identical fit between the WTO and national constitutional law, constitutionalization can plausibly be used to describe ongoing changes in the WTO system. The term has a historical legacy, the WTO shares superficial and hybrid resemblances with both national and supranational forms of the phenomenon, and, in any event, the terminology is used in the service of both description and critique.

2.5.2 The WTO is an international treaty arrangement

The most awkward objection to refute is the argument that the WTO system is no different from international treaty law generally. Like WTO law, general international law bears many of the characteristics of a constitutional structure, as is witnessed by the writers referred to above who have indeed argued in similar terms for international law generally.[119] Moreover, international law exhibits many of the same features which WTO constitutionalization writers claim distinguishes the WTO system. For example, international law is also concerned with the delineation of state power;[120] it balances competences between states and other states, and states and the international law system.[121] International law relies for its sources on municipal law;[122] international law has a centralized dispute settlement mechanism in the form of the World Court; and, like WTO law, international law yearns for the legitimacy of national law. Moreover, some would suggest that the rules referred to here as constitutional are merely ordinary rules of practice and procedure in relation to treaty interpretation.[123] So in what respects is the transformation of the WTO

---

[119] For example, Allott (n 66 above).

[120] See, eg, rules on state responsibility outlined in DJ Harris, *Cases and Materials on International Law*, 4th edn (London: Sweet & Maxwell, 1991) 460–599.

[121] See, eg, rules on jurisdiction outlined in ibid 250–346.

[122] Article 38(1) of the Statute of the International Court of Justice provides that the court shall apply, *inter alia*, 'general principles of law recognised by civilized nations'.

[123] Note, no consensus exists within the international trade law community that the issues described herein are particularly constitutional in nature. Some commentators have described some of the matters under discussion here under the heading of 'practice and procedure' of the WTO Appellate Body; the word 'constitution' does not rate a mention: D Steger and PVD Bossche, 'WTO Dispute Settlement: Emerging Practice and Procedure' in (1998) *American Society of International Law: Proceedings of the 92nd Annual Meeting* 79. The Appellate Body itself does not necessarily mention that these matters have implications beyond that of simply being useful judicial techniques to help decide the cases before them. I do not dispute that the features I have identified are simple questions of practice and procedure, or that they arise from the mundane reality of having to resolve

different from international treaty law, such that it warrants the label constitutionalized law?

Intuitively it would seem that WTO law differs from an ordinary treaty arrangement under international law in three respects, although these claims could only be proved by socio-legal research. The first intuition is that the *content* of WTO law includes a higher density of doctrinal techniques, associated in national legal systems with constitutional law, than does international law. WTO law does, for example, frequently rely on doctrines such as proportionality, and jurisdictional competence. By contrast, international law favours reliance on its own highly specialized doctrinal rules (state responsibility, acquisition, jurisdiction). Even if the nature of the doctrines is similar in that they perform similar functions, the WTO doctrines are framed in the language of a constitutional type whereas the international doctrine is not.

The second intuition is that, because international trade law consists of a smaller, and therefore closer knit, *community* than does international law, treaty interpretation in relation to trade assumes a shared set of understandings, in a manner that is absent when the international court interprets a treaty, for example, on non-proliferation. So, the diffuse nature of interests in the international community as a whole militates against recognition of any international *polis*, and against an easily identifiable set of shared interpretations. This absence further distinguishes the international community from the international trade law community. By contrast, WTO law seems to have developed its own constituency, however narrowly it is defined to include, for example, trade law officials and trading states, or more broadly to encompass a wider set of trading interests including civil society, NGOs, and other communities in related fields such as environmental and health. Even if the authorizing community of the WTO constitution is the public at large, it is a specialized public with a set of shared concerns about trade and not international law in general.

Thirdly, the constitutionalization discussion is based on the intuition that WTO law is not a simple treaty arrangement because the level of *acceptance* of WTO decisions is stronger than ordinarily exists in relation to international law. Again, bearing in mind the rider that research would be needed to prove this claim, it would seem that a habit of obedience to the WTO system is developing, illustrated by the high number of ratifications of the agreements,[124]

---

a particular trade dispute. But what I do want to suggest is that whatever else they are, they may also be constitutional, in some of the senses that this study will define. For example, they raise matters relating to how the WTO system is constituted, the limits of its jurisdictional competence, and standing. These issues have one thing in common: they exist, within national legal systems, within a body of doctrine referred to as constitutional law. So however practical or procedural they may be, they are also constitutional and their appearance in the case law of the WTO will be taken as one indication that international trade law may be undergoing a process of constitutionalization.

[124] As at 18 October 2004, the WTO had 148 members: <www.wto.org>.

the regular use of the dispute settlement system,[125] and reasonable levels of settlement and compliance under dispute settlement.[126] In addition, the threat of WTO dispute settlement is more regularly invoked than say threat of action at the World Court. Finally, there is no doubt that the system of 'swapping' trade concessions mandated under the WTO Agreements constitutes one of the strongest, and most regularly honoured, obligations in international law, illustrated by liberalization negotiations in a variety of sectors from goods, to agricultural products, to services.

In short, a more specific, localized, process of constitutional interpretation and constitution-making seems to be occurring within the international trade sphere than that occurring in general international law; a primitive form of distinguishable WTO community exists; and the level of acceptance of WTO law and system is widespread. In this context the label constitutionalization may be warranted, above and beyond WTO law being an international treaty arrangement.

2.5.3   The constitution of the WTO is general international law

The third argument against the use of the term constitutionalization in relation to the WTO is not really a rejection of the constitutionalization hypothesis (as is the case with the national law and international treaty arguments) but

---

[125] As at 1 January 2003, 276 complaints had been filed: K Leitner and S Lester, 'WTO Dispute Settlement 1995–2002: A Statistical Analysis' (2003) 6 *Journal of International Economic Law* 251. This compares with 300 disputes within the entire life of the GATT between 1947 and 1994: *The World Trade Organization: In Brief* <www.wto.org>.

[126] Although settlement and compliance issues remain controversial, the general tenor of the scholarship is that the dispute settlement system has been largely successful. In relation to GATT, it was famously argued that states generally demonstrated a high level of compliance with reports, running at about 90% settlement: R Hudec, *Enforcing International Trade Law: The Evolution of the Modern GATT Legal System* (Salem, NH: Butterworths, 1993). Recent WTO scholarship suggests that optimism about the success rate of the system measured in terms of settlement and compliance has continued. See, eg, C Carmody, 'Remedies and Conformity under the WTO Agreement' (2002) 5 *Journal of International Economic Law* 307, 309 (arguing that remedies have 'done a reasonable job of providing security and predictability to individual traders and countries alike'); BM Hoekman and MM Kostecki (eds), *The Political Economy of the World Trading System* 2nd edn (Oxford: Oxford University Press, 2001) 79 (arguing that 'notwithstanding some significant flaws ... [dispute settlement] works quite well'); R Hudec, 'Review article' (2002) 1 *World Trade Review* 211, reviewing C Barfield, *Free Trade, Sovereignty, Democracy: The Future of the World Trade Organization* (2001) (stating '[d]espite some notorious examples of foot dragging, I know of no case in which a government has failed to promise compliance'). However, doubts remain as to the interpretation of the statistics: see, eg, Leitner and Lester (n 125 above) 261 (arguing that the high number of Panels called on to decide whether a respondent has correctly implemented the initial recommendation of a Panel could indicate, either, that Members are not implementing adverse decisions properly, or that such complaints are being 'routed through the proper procedures'). Controversy exists also over whether success can be measured in the same terms for all states: see, eg, Hoekman and Kostecki, ibid 78 (arguing that developing countries have benefited from the new dispute settlement system) and compare with Leitner and Lester, ibid 259 (arguing that the mechanism is 'still largely the province of the rich, industrialized countries').

a presentation of an alternative, or coincident, basis for constitutionalization. Here the argument is that general international law itself, and the Vienna Convention on the Law of Treaties in particular, is the constitutional framework of WTO law.

In response to this it is clear that the Vienna Convention is an important part of the framework for WTO law.[127] However, the only customary rules of international law incorporated explicitly into WTO law by the WTO Agreements are the Vienna Convention's rules of interpretation. It has therefore been pointed out that the Convention's rules do not include any 'substantive non-WTO international law'.[128] If this line of thought is followed, unless constitutionalization is conceived of as a purely procedural matter then the use of the Vienna Convention cannot be a complete constitution for WTO law, although it might provide some of the scaffolding for a broader constitutional structure.

However, it is also apparent from the case law of the WTO that general principles of international law, such as state responsibility, proportionality, and countermeasures, are a key part of the fabric of WTO judicial decision-making,[129] even if the particular character of those principles may become distinct from their international counterparts when interpreted within WTO law.[130] Indeed most authors, including those who posit the constitutionalization hypothesis, accept that WTO is not, what Joost Pauwelyn has called, a 'closed legal circuit'[131] and is part of international law as a whole. So the systems debate and the constitutionalization debate are not identical; the WTO could

---

[127] See Understanding on Rules and Procedures Governing the Settlement of Disputes, WTO Agreement, Annex 2, *The Results of the Uruguay Round of Multilateral Trade Negotiations: The Legal Texts*, (1994) [hereinafter the DSU Agreement]. Pursuant to Article 3.2 of the DSU Agreement, which requires clarification of the covered agreements to take account of 'customary rules of interpretation of public international law', Panels must follow the general rule of interpretation codified in Article 31 of the Vienna Convention: World Trade Organization, Report of the Appellate Body, *United States—Standards for Reformulated and Conventional Gasoline*, WT/DS2/AB/R (29 April 1996), DSR 1996:I, 3 at 15–16. The general rule requires Panels to discern the ordinary meaning of a text in the light of its context, inclusive of the object and purpose of the treaty. World Trade Organization, Report of the Appellate Body, *Japan—Taxes on Alcoholic Beverages*, WT/DS8/AB/R, WT/DS10/AB/R, WT/DS11/AB/R (4 October 1996) DSR 1996:I, 97 at 104–108, the Appellate Body again referred to the Vienna Convention when it stressed the importance of the effectiveness principle of treaty interpretation, and found that prior adopted Panel reports were part of the 'GATT *acquis*' and hence created 'legitimate expectations' that they would be taken into account in future disputes.

[128] J Trachtman, 'The Domain of WTO Dispute Resolution' (1999) 40 *Harvard International Law Journal* 333, 343.

[129] See, eg, World Trade Organization, Report of the Appellate Body, *United States—Transitional Safeguard Measure on Combed Cotton Yarn from Pakistan*, WT/D192/AB/R (8 October 2001) at paras 119–125 (holding that the US could not attribute 'serious damage' to Pakistan, for the purpose of imposing a safeguard to protect its cotton yarn industry, without conducting a comparative analysis with other Members, and involving a variety of factors including level of imports, market share and price).

[130] J Pauwelyn, *Conflict of Norms in Public International Law: How WTO Law Relates to other Rules of International Law* (Cambridge: Cambridge University Press, 2003) 39.

[131] ibid 35.

be constitutionalized and still remain part of the general international legal system. Constitutionalization is one step removed conceptually from questions about the relationship between the systems of international law and WTO law. As Pauwelyn has shown, the latter debate is concerned with the question of the extent to which states have or have not contracted out of the international legal system in relation to matters of trade and formed a separate system of law.[132] And, as he argues, even though in certain aspects the WTO may be self-contained, international law remains the 'fallback' onto which WTO treaty interpretation must revert.[133]

Nevertheless, even if general international law is the framework for WTO law, this does not negate the possibility that a secondary constitutionalization process is in train. This secondary constitutionalization may either, consistent with the argument that international law is the constitution for trade, coexist with the international legal constitution,[134] or, in a matter of time it may flourish to the point where the WTO constitution breaks off from the parent constitutional system of international law. If this were to occur we might see a closer convergence of the two discussions, about separate systems and constitutionalization. The separation of a new system would, of course, be simply an application of positive theory's approach to the embryology of new legal systems.[135] In either scenario it is perfectly possible to conceive of WTO law as undergoing a process of constitutionalization defined above, simultaneous with accepting that international law provides the foundational constitutional framework for WTO law.

2.6　Conclusion

In short then, this work dismisses the preliminary objections to WTO constitutionalization and assumes that, *descriptively* at least, constitutionalization is a plausible explanation for the transformations of the WTO system, and so now seeks to understand what is meant by the term. This assumption does not, of course, dispense with the many *normative* objections to the use of the

---

[132] J Pauwelyn, *Conflict of Norms in Public International Law: How WTO Law Relates to other Rules of International Law* (Cambridge: Cambridge University Press, 2003) 38.

[133] ibid 428.

[134] This seems to be the logic of the argument put by Weiler and Trachtman in relation to Europe: Weiler and Trachtman (n 92 above). They argue, at 359, that the constitutional premise of Europe is no longer doubted, at the same time as claiming, at 373, that the 'normative authority [of Europe] would be international law'. There is therefore no 'single constituent power or institutional fount of sovereignty' but only 'multiple allegiances and therefore multiple centers of power', 373. If this is correct, then international law can provide a constitutional framework for WTO law, but this does not preclude conceiving of WTO law as also possessing its own internal constitutional framework in the same double sense that Europe is constitutionalized and yet exists within an international legal constitution.

[135] See discussion of *Grundnorm* change at Section 2.4.2 above.

word constitutionalization but these will be dealt with later. At this stage of the discussion it is only necessary to show that something is going on within the WTO that, more or less, meets the descriptive criteria of constitutionalization[136] and therefore warrants exploration. This study is dedicated towards developing an understanding of what that something is.

---

[136] The constitutional lens is only one of many perspectives. Other equally plausible analytical tools exist including law and economics, see, eg, J Dunoff and J Trachtman, 'Economic Analysis of International Law' (1999) 24 *Yale Journal of International Law* 1 (arguing that law and economics has been underused in international law and showing how concepts of price theory, transaction costs, and game theory could be applied to international law, including the international trading system).

3

The International Economic Law Background

3.1 Introduction and definitions

The Constitutionalization debate did not occur in a vacuum; it arose in the context of general international economic law scholarship.[1] The purpose of this chapter is to situate the question of constitutionalization within a broader canvas of international economic law scholarship, and both to highlight shared themes between the general scholarship and constitutionalization scholarship and to foreshadow some of the critiques of the latter. I will describe six themes current in international economic law scholarship and identify where these themes intersect with the core elements of constitutionalization described in the previous chapter. The six features discussed are

- a focus on *institutions and constitutions*, and a *conflation* of the concept of an institution with a constitution;
- an interdependence with wider scholarship about *globalization*;
- a general consensus about the benefits of *liberalization* and the international economic law framework which supports it, punctuated by occasional critique;
- a concentration on *regulation rather than 'law'* in the traditional sense;
- a fixation with the problem of *defining the field*; and
- a belief in the *transformative* nature of international economic law.

---

[1] The law relating to international economic law generally is a vast field. For discussion of traditional rules about international trade in its public aspect (GATT and WTO law) see, eg, MJ Trebilcock and R Howse, *The Regulation of International Trade*, 2nd edn (London and New York: Routledge, 1999). For discussion of private international law rules, or conflicts of laws, see, eg, PM North and JJ Fawcett, *Cheshire and North's Private International Law* 13th edn (London: Butterworths, 1999). For laws governing international business transactions and commerce generally (including rules regarding the international sales contract; insurance; freight; insolvency; and payment) see, eg, IF Fletcher, L Mistelis and M Cremona (eds), *Foundations and Perspectives on International Trade Law* (London: Sweet & Maxwell, 2001). Plus there is a large literature on national rules in relation to similar subjects. Moreover, as the subject of international economic law is economics, it cannot fail to intersect with that field. This chapter focuses on a discrete part of the large literature governing international economic affairs. It addresses only the public international law structures that regulate economic relations and exchange between states, and have a primary emphasis upon trade. The chapter draws on: DZ Cass, 'International Business Law and Commerce' in P Cane and M Tushnet (eds), *The Oxford Handbook of Legal Studies* (Oxford: Oxford University Press, 2003).

Before I begin to make my arguments I want to provide some working definitions of key terms I will be using.

3.1.1 Institutions and constitutions

This study depends on a definition of *institutions* that blends a number of theories of institutions but places particular emphasis on the insights of sociological and historical institutionalism.[2] So the term institutions will be used primarily in the sense of sociological institutionalism to refer to a cultural phenomenon that is created not solely by rational actors seeking to maximize wealth in the most effective (regime theory[3]) or efficient (institutional economics[4]) manner, but also by a range of self-reinforcing and mutually constitutive cultural influences. Institutions consist of the range of elements anticipated by both of the latter two schools, including formal and informal constraints on human behaviour,[5] and component organizations and rules, of a formal and informal kind,[6] as well as the actors, processes of formation, and social forces motivating such.[7] But institutions are not limited to these: they are embedded in a range of broader cultural factors,[8] including, for example, interpretations of the goal of free trade. I will assume also that the growth of institutions is path-dependent, and therefore will be influenced by pre-existing distributions of power, and competition and coalitions amongst states.[9] In short, for the purposes of this

---

[2] This definition and the discussion which follows relies on PM Nichols, 'Forgotten Linkages—Historical Institutionalism and Sociological Institutionalism and Analysis of the World Trade Organization' (1998) 19 *University of Pennsylvania Journal of International Economic Law* 461.

[3] Regime theory presents itself in opposition to realist theory according to which states seeking power are the primary forces of international relations. By contrast, regime theory holds that it is not just states that define outcomes but also rules and procedures of regimes or institutions. The function of these institutions or regimes are to reduce transaction costs, facilitate information exchange, legitimize and delegitimize actions of states, and facilitate reciprocity: Robert Keohane in Nichols, ibid 465.

[4] Closely related to regime theory is the institutional economics school of institutionalism. According to this theory, international relations outcomes are the product of members of the society, whether individuals or states, seeking rationally to maximize their wealth, but limited by the availability and cost of information. Therefore institutions are important because they facilitate information gathering and reduce transaction costs for members of the society. The theory predicts that members will seek out and utilize institutions that minimize transaction costs, and will create alternative institutions as required: Douglass North in Nichols, ibid 472.

[5] DC North, *Institutions, Institutional Change and Economic Performance* (Cambridge: Cambridge University Press, 1990) 4.

[6] JP Trachtman, 'The Theory of the Firm and the Theory of the International Economic Organization: Toward Comparative Institutional Analysis' (1997) 17 *Northwestern Journal of International Law and Business* 470, 473 n 18 (arguing that institutions consist of '(i) formal organizational institutions such as legislative, executive and judicial bodies and the organizations they comprise, (ii) formal rules from constitutional rules down to normal legislation, and (iii) informal (non-legal) institutions comprised of organizations or rules that lack legal effect').

[7] M Levy, O Young and M Zurn, 'The Study of International Regimes' (1995) 1 *European Journal of International Relations* 267.

[8] Nichols, (n 2 above) 482–483. Nichols suggests, at 483, that sociological institutionalism explicitly questions the distinction between 'culture' and 'institution'.   [9] ibid 475–480.

study, an institution comprises rules, organizations, and procedures, of a formal and informal nature, the cultural factors that influenced them, and pre-existing paths such as distributions of power among states.

A *constitution*, by contrast, is an institution consisting of the various features described in this definition, but exhibiting also the six particular attributes of constitutionalization described above in Chapter 2, namely economic and political constraints, a higher order norm, an authorizing community, deliberation, realignment of relationships, and social legitimacy. So the difference between an institution and a constitution is that whereas an institution is a schematic concept consisting of organizations, rules, actors, processes, and social and cultural forces, a constitution has a different weight, or valency, derived from the intersection of these six additional factors and their manifestation as a higher order institution. It should be apparent therefore that an institution cannot simply metamorphose into a constitution without exhibiting these core features.

3.1.2   Rules and regulation

Rules will be used, following Fred Schauer, to refer to non-discretionary acts used in legal decision-making[10] that guide, pressure, control, and change the behaviour of agents with decision-making capacities.[11] Rules have general application, and provide certainty and predictability to individuals in their interactions both between themselves and between individuals and the state. The function of rules is to provide a mechanism for dealing with the 'central problem of social order', namely of 'reconciling the behavior of separately motivated persons' so as to 'generate patterns of outcomes that are tolerable to all participants'.[12] Familiar examples, according to Schauer, include rules of the game, of the road, of markets, and of political processes. It is the last two categories that are the focus of this work. It will be obvious therefore that there is no bright line between what is a rule[13] and what is an institution.[14] The symbiotic relationship between the two concepts does not obscure the fact that the literature on WTO constitutionalization refers to both as separate but related concepts, as will this work.

Regulation, by contrast, has many of the characteristics of rules in that it guides and pressures the behaviour of actors but its sources are broader and include both public and private institutions, and, accordingly, the implementation and

---

[10] F Schauer, *Playing by the Rules* (Oxford: Clarendon Press, 1991) 11. Schauer notes that rules take many forms and may be mandatory or instructional (2), constitutive or regulative (7), contingent, non-specific (13) or open-textured (36).   [11] ibid 2.

[12] G Brennan and JM Buchanan, *The Reasons of Rules: Constitutional Political Economy* (Cambridge: Cambridge University Press, 1985) 5.

[13] Rules can be made up of institutions. Brennan and Buchanan describe rules as inclusive of Adam Smith's category of laws as institutions: ibid 2.

[14] Note that Trachtman refers to institutions as containing rules: Trachtman (n 6 above) 473 n 18.

enforcement of regulation falls to a wider range of actors than merely the state's legal mechanisms.[15] So, for example, Ayres and Braithwaite show that an industry association might 'regulate' environmental impact through the formulation of a set of environmental principles that it then uses to monitor firms within its membership. Or individual companies may be called upon to self-regulate by applying an internal code of conduct. The advantages of regulation over rules, according to the commentators, are their flexibility: 'Legal institutions are designed to be stable and predictable, while economic entities ideally are rapidly adjusting to changing commercial and technological environments.'[16] So, regulation, as opposed to rules, is preferred because regulation can be tailored to the particular needs of the regulated actors; adjusted more quickly to changed commercial and technological environments; and itself can foster regulatory innovation. In addition, businesses can bear the costs of regulation; offenders can be disciplined in larger proportion; and companies can be more committed to the regulations which they participated in making.[17] In short, for our purposes, regulation will be taken to refer to a more flexible form of behavioural constraint, the sources of which may be non-legal or private.

3.1.3 Globalization and liberalization

Globalization is a contentious and contested concept. Early in the development of the field, one commentator characterized the global system as being in the grip of a 'capitalist globalization' in which the international system was 'structured around the transnational corporations, a transnational capitalist class and the culture-ideology of consumerism'.[18] Others argued that global social movements were, by engaging with multilateral economic institutions, 'contesting global governance'.[19] Held, McGrew, Goldblatt, and Perraton identify three schools of thought: hyperglobalists, sceptics, and transformationalists.[20] To hyperglobalists, the nation state has become virtually redundant other than as a conduit for global capital, and, in the new conditions of the single global marketplace and global competition, new forms of social organization will arise with great benefits to humanity.[21] In the view of the sceptics, globalization is a myth; the thesis is exaggerated, flawed, and politically naïve. Historically, the international movement of capital, goods, and labour has far exceeded current flows. Indeed, according to the sceptics, contemporary society

---

[15] I Ayres and J Braithwaite, *Responsive Regulation: Transcending the Deregulation Debate* (New York: Oxford University Press, 1992) 4–5. [16] ibid 110.

[17] ibid 110–114.

[18] L Sklair, *Globalization: Capitalism and its Alternatives* (Oxford: Oxford University Press, 1990).

[19] R O'Brien, AM Goetz, J Scholte, and M Williams, *Contesting Global Governance* (Cambridge: Cambridge University Press, 2000).

[20] D Held, A McGrew, D Goldblatt, and J Perraton, *Global Transformations: Politics, Economics and Culture* [hereinafter *Transformations*] (Cambridge: Polity Press, 1999).

[21] Held *et al*, *Transformations* 3–5.

is characterized by increasing regionalization and nation state retention of power, as well as heightened inequality and fragmentation.[22] By contrast, transformationalist theory perceives the current period of change as unprecedented in scale and intensification, but claims the consequences are uncertain. What is certain, according to Held's characterization of this argument, is that globalization challenges traditional assumptions about the distinctions between, and consequences of, categorization such as North/South, First/Third, core/periphery. Even if sovereignty remains a force, globalization is reshaping the power, functions, and authority of national governments.[23] Accordingly, the concept triggers 'multiple conversations' and 'no singular account is possible.'[24] In Held and McGrew's view, it has a material, spatial, and cognitive aspect and, at base, refers to the 'expanding scale, growing magnitude, speeding up and deepening impact of integrated flows and patterns of social interaction'.[25]

In this book, *globalization* will be taken to mean the global integration and fragmentation of markets in goods, services, capital, and to a lesser extent labour, induced by changes in technology, communication, and transport; combined with the changing nature and number of sites of political and legal authority, and the social effects and institutional changes which attend that process.[26] *Liberalization*, by contrast, consists more simply in the opening up of trade, capital, and financial markets by a variety of means including reduction of tariffs, privatization, and deregulation.[27]

3.1.4   Summary of argument

So having set out working definitions of key terms I will now return to my argument. In summary, the claim of this chapter is that international economic law scholarship fuelled the promotion of constitutionalization of the WTO in variety of ways, each of which intersected with the description of core constitutionalization made in the previous chapter. First, international economic law increasingly focused on institutions and constitutions, rather than mere rules, and conflated the two concepts. This led to a sense that a new *Grundnorm*, one of the core elements of the received account of constitutionalization, was emerging because the new system possessed a coherence and unity associated

---

[22] Held *et al, Transformations* 5–7.   [23] Held *et al, Transformations* 7–9.
[24] D Held and A McGrew, *The Global Transformations Reader: An Introduction to the Globalization Debate*, 2nd edn (Malden, Mass: Polity Press, 2003).   [25] ibid 4.
[26] This definition draws on Held *et al* (n 20 and 24 above); D Rodrik, *Has Globalisation Gone Too Far?* (1997) 1–9; and JE Stiglitz, *Globalisation and its Discontents* (London: Penguin Books, 2002) 9–10.
[27] Stiglitz, ibid 59–67, and S Picciotto and R Mayne (eds), *Regulating International Business: Beyond Liberalization* (Basingstoke: Macmillan, 1999) 1 (describing liberalization as the progressive removal of restrictions on the international flow of money and goods). Note that the definitions of globalization and liberalization have much in common with conventional notions of 'interdependence': compare, eg, especially, Stiglitz, ibid, with JH Jackson, *The World Trading System: Law and Policy of International Economic Relations* 2nd edn (Cambridge, Mass and London, England: MIT Press, 1997) [hereinafter, Jackson, *The World*] 6–7.

with the development of a new legal order. Moreover, the conflation of the concept of an institution with the concept of a constitution enhanced another of the core elements of constitutionalization, legitimacy. The old GATT, which was conceptualized as an institution, came to be distinguished from the new WTO, portrayed as a constitution. The latter was therefore vested with a legitimacy and authority it might not otherwise possess.

Secondly, international economic law, globalization, and constitutionalization literature began to feed off each other, and this interdependence caused each field to identify new sites of political authority (a constitution) arising out of essentially economic change. This led to a blurring of lines between economic, political, and legal authority with the result that the modification of an essentially economic treaty arrangement of the GATT into a political–legal entity, or a constitutional arrangement of the WTO, suddenly became more plausible, even though the legitimacy of the supposed transformation remained contested. Indeed a tension arose between constitutionalization being a source of legitimacy for the WTO, and being one of the challenges to that legitimacy: while some international economic lawyers adopted the term with the effect of legitimizing the claim that it had occurred international protest movements simultaneously questioned it.

Thirdly, a consensus about the benefits of trade liberalization was fortified in the international economic literature with the result that the notion arose that a community (another of the core elements of constitutionalization) existed with shared values about the benefits of trade liberalization. Fourthly, an emphasis on regulation emerged in international economic law literature, focused particularly on the merits of procedure as a way of protecting diverse interests. The procedural solution had echoes with another of the core elements of constitutionalization, deliberative process. Fifthly, international economic law's propensity to be concerned about its own identity was reflected also in the discussions about the boundaries of any constitutional community of the WTO. Sixthly, the transformative urge of the discipline and the discipline's belief in the link between trade and democracy led authors to construe the WTO as a new order, and a constitutional one at that. This chapter will describe these currents in detail and the way that they made the WTO constitutionalization debate seem propitious.

3.2 FACTORS TRIGGERING THE EMERGENCE OF THE CONSTITUTIONALIZATION DEBATE

3.2.1 Institutions and constitutions: enhancing the legitimacy of the trade order

This section will argue that international economic law scholarship is characterized by both an interest in institutions, and a conflation of the concept of institution with a constitution. Moreover, it will show that the pattern created by the overlapping of these concepts intersects with two of the elements of constitutionalization defined in Chapter 2, a new *Grundnorm* and legitimacy. The gist of the argument is that the focus of the literature on these concepts rather than on strict rules led naturally to the view that the WTO as an institution had a unity and coherence which is normally associated with the emergence of a new legal order. Moreover, the emphasis on the two types of phenomena—institution and constitution—enabled a distinction to be drawn between the old regime, the institutional GATT, and the new regime of the constitutionalized WTO. The WTO was represented as a historical break with the previous regime, encapsulating a new *Grundnorm*, one of the essential elements in the constitutionalization process. At the same time the concept of an institution was conflated with the concept of a constitution and this had the effect of laying the groundwork for the emergence of another of the core elements: the conferral of legitimacy and authority to its structures. The combined effect of giving coherence to the institution, portraying it as a new system, and blending the idea of an institution and a constitution was to trigger discussion, and indeed promotion, of the WTO as a constitutionalized entity.

To begin the argument then in tune with developments in law and legal theory, international economic law commentators, and trade scholars specifically, have long moved beyond the study of rules alone and emphasized the importance of other mechanisms of obligation, such as institutions. Almost from its genesis, international economic law had been aware of the existence, beyond rules, of broader social forces moulding and determining obeisance to its authority. Later, the field drew extensively on the work of economic historians such as Douglass North,[28] who proposed that the evolution and success of divergent economies could be best understood by studying formal and informal constraints on human behaviour as incentives for economic activity, as opposed to technical constraints in the form of technological change, prices, or income.[29] The leading casebook in the field signalled its departure from a specifically rules-based focus by framing its subject not in terms of 'the law of' the field but instead as legal 'problems' of international economic 'relations'.[30] Institutional models were used regularly: the trade regime was described as an example of the international relations theory of institutions or regimes as 'sets of implicit or explicit principles, norms, rules and decision

[28] North (n 5 above).

[29] John Jackson regularly invokes North's work, ibid. See, eg, JH Jackson, 'The WTO "Constitution" and Proposed Reforms: Seven "Mantras" Revisited' (2001) 4 *Journal of International Economic Law* 67 [hereinafter Jackson, 'Mantras'] 70; and JH Jackson, 'International Economic Law in Times that are Interesting' (2000) 3 *Journal of International Economic Law* 3 [hereinafter Jackson, 'Interesting Times'] 5.

[30] JH Jackson, WJ Davey and AO Sykes, *Legal Problems of International Economic Relations*, 4th edn (St Paul, Minn: West, 2002). Note that the fourth edition, which is the current edition, has been altered, in ways relevant to my discussion. I will, therefore, refer to the specific edition I am relying on as evidence for each point.

making processes around which expectations converge'.[31] Others emphasized the role of the diplomacy, as an institution.[32] More recently, it has been argued that what are critical in international business regulation are not legal rules alone but principles, mechanisms, and actors, and contests between these elements.[33]

In the first place, this trend toward studying international trade as an institution meant that it could be presented as something beyond a mere set of legal rules, possessing the qualities of unity and coherence associated with the emergence of a new legal order. The scholarship seemed to imply that international trade law was not just an old-fashioned treaty made up of particular legal rules establishing various entities and vesting them and the parties to the agreement with functions and obligations. Instead international trade came to be viewed as a modern institution, with a capital 'I', composed of an increasingly large number of structures,[34] substantive matters,[35] procedures,

---

[31] See, eg, S Krasner cited in BM Hoekman and MM Kostecki (eds), *The Political Economy of the World Trading System* 2nd edn (Oxford: Oxford University Press, 2001).

[32] RE Hudec, *Essays on the Nature of International Trade Law* (London: Cameron May, 1999) [hereinafter Hudec, *Essays*].

[33] J Braithwaite and P Drahos, *Global Business Regulation* (Cambridge: Cambridge University Press, 2000).

[34] The WTO structure includes a Ministerial Conference; a General Council; a Dispute Settlement Body; a Trade Policy Review Body; a Council for Trade in Goods; a Council for Trade in Services; a Council for Trade-Related Aspects of Intellectual Property Rights; a Committee on Trade and Development; a Committee on Balance-of-Payments Restrictions; and a Committee on Budget, Finance, and Administration; as well as a Secretariat and a Director General: Articles IV and VI, Marrakesh Agreement Establishing the World Trade Organization in *The Results of the Uruguay Round Of Multilateral Trade Negotiations: The Legal Texts* 5 (1994); GATT Doc No MTN/FA; 33 ILM 1125 (1994) [hereinafter WTO Agreement]. In addition, a Committee on Trade and Environment has been established: Decision on Trade and Environment, Ministerial Decision adopted by Ministers at the meeting of the Trade Negotiations Committee in Marrakesh on 14 April 1994, *The Results of the Uruguay Round Of Multilateral Trade Negotiations: The Legal Texts* 469 (1994); GATT Doc No MTN/FA; 33 ILM 1125 (1994). For a full diagrammatic description of the WTO structure see Jackson, *The World Trading System* (n 27 above) 67 Figure 2.1.

[35] The range of substantive matters included within the ambit of the WTO has been expanded with each round of trade negotiations in: Geneva, Switzerland 1947; Annecy, France 1948; Torquay, England 1950; Geneva 1956; 'Dillon Round' 1960–1961; 'Kennedy Round' 1964–1967; 'Tokyo Round' 1973–1979; 'Uruguay Round', 1986–1994 JH Jackson, WJ Davey and AO Sykes, *Legal Problems of International Economic Relations* 3rd edn (1995) 227; and, currently the Doha Round 2001. In the first five of these rounds, tariffs were the main subject of negotiation. In the Tokyo Round, the ambit of negotiations expanded to include non-tariff barriers such as subsidies, at Uruguay this was further extended to include intellectual property, services, and investment. The latest Ministerial Conference held at Doha in November 2001 adopted a work programme aimed at negotiating implementation issues; agriculture; services; market access; intellectual property; the relationship between trade and investment; competition policy; transparency; trade facilitation rules on subsidies, and regional trade agreements; dispute settlement; environment; electronic commerce; small economies; trade, debt and finance; technology transfer, technical cooperation and capacity building, least-developed countries; and special and differential treatment: Ministerial Declaration, Ministerial Conference Fourth Session, Doha 9–14 November 2001, WT/MIN(01)DEC/W/1 at <www.wto.org>. In July 2004 the General Council decided that investment, competition, and transparency in government procurement would not form any part of the Doha work programme: <http://www.wto.org/english/tratop_e/dda_e/draft_text_gc_dg_31july04_e.htm>.

actors, and expansively interpreted principles.[36] The breadth of these changes, and re-inscription of the subject as an institution, laid the groundwork for reconceptualizing the WTO as a constitution[37] because international trade, like a constitution, was much more than a simple, narrowly defined, system of law. In addition it facilitated the separation of the old institutional GATT from the new constitutional WTO. Under these conditions it was easier to suggest that the new system ushered in a new set of authoritative criteria for recognizing the obligations of international trade, a new *Grundnorm* no less, and a breaking off from the past. A core element of constitutionalization, in the form of *Grundnorm* change, is also embodied here.

The focus of international economic law and trade scholarship on the institutional nature of the regime, accompanied by a conflation of institutional developments with the idea of a constitution, had other effects in the field generally. So the term 'constitution' was used *descriptively* to depict the internal workings of particular legal arrangements in the field such as the WTO,[38] or the European Union,[39] or to compare these two major international organizations.[40] *Prescriptively*, also, writers talked about institutions being like constitutions in order to make a normative claim about the need for a constitution. Europe was said to need a constitution not only in order to instantiate a new form of political–economic relationship midway between a confederation and a federation, but also in order to conserve a distinctly European way of life based on basic human rights, social welfare, and minimal economic redistribution.[41] Or,

---

[36] The principle of non-discrimination contained in Article III national treatment has been interpreted broadly such that it mandates equality of competitive conditions between domestic and imported products, not just simple formal non-discrimination. See, eg, GATT, Report of the Panel, *United States—Section 337 of the Tariff Act 1930*, BISD 36S/345 (adopted 7 November 1989), GATT BISD (36th Supp) at 345 (1990) (the principle of non-discrimination contained in Article III is aimed at *protecting expectations on competitive relationships* between imports and domestic products and therefore this means *effective equality* of opportunities for imported products); and, World Trade Organization, Report of the Appellate Body, *Japan—Taxes on Alcoholic Beverages*, WT/DS8/AB/R, WT/DS10/AB/R, WT/DS11/AB/R (4 October 1996) DSR 1996:I, 97 (the purpose of the national treatment rule in Article III is to avoid protectionism between imported and domestic product and to *create equality of competitive conditions* between domestic and imports such that there is no need for legislation to cause actual harm to be prohibited by the rule). See also discussion of the principle of substantive discrimination in Chapter 6 below.

[37] John Jackson has been the scholar most instrumental in using the terminology of constitutionalization to create a system of law. See R Howse, 'Tribute—The House that Jackson Built: Restructuring the GATT' (1999) 20 *Michigan Journal of International Law* 107, 108 (arguing that it was Jackson's report to the Canadian government in 1990 which laid the groundwork for inclusion of a constitutional structure within the Uruguay negotiations); and, D Kennedy, 'The International Style in Postwar Law and Policy' (1994) *Utah Law Review* 7, 102 (arguing that it is largely owing to Jackson's work that changes to the trading system have been conceptualized as an 'imaginary trade constitution'. Indeed Kennedy goes further and claims, at 59, that Jackson 'largely invented the field [of international trade law]').

[38] E-U Petersmann (ed), *International Trade Law and GATT/WTO Dispute Settlement System* (London: Kluwer; London: Royal Institute of International Affairs, 1997); Jackson, Davey and Sykes (n 30 above) 5; JH Jackson, *The World Trade Organization: Constitution and Jurisprudence* (1998).

[39] JHH Weiler, *The Constitution of Europe* (Cambridge: Cambridge University Press, 1999).

[40] G de Búrca and J Scott (eds), *The EU and the WTO: Legal and Constitutional Issues* (2001).

[41] J Habermas, 'A Constitution for Europe?' (2001) 11 *New Left Review* 5.

international trade law should be constitutionalized so that states recognize the economic right of non-discrimination encapsulated in international trade agreements as a human right, domestic courts can apply it, and citizens can rely on it to challenge state action.[42] Or, indeed, liberal international trade rules serve a constitutional function in restraining powers of national governments, and so basic constitutional principles such as transparency, non-discriminatory market access, competition and property rights should be extended to apply to the foreign trade powers of states.[43]

Moreover, this emphasis upon a broad range of mechanisms of obligation (institutions), and on the creation of a legal system which realigned public power (constitutions), had important consequences for the nature of scholarship in the field as a whole. As noted above, the term 'institution' was used to signal that an almost open-ended range of public, private, legal, and quasi-legal mechanisms created obligations for actors and this realization prompted questions about the legitimacy of those new forms.[44] Constitutional language was used both to signal the development of a system of law and to distinguish it from a set of loosely associated rules and practices. Yet this use of language also triggered an inquiry into the authority of the law-making source, and to question the system's legitimacy, its levels of participation, representativeness, transparency, and even its democratic credentials.[45] In short, this trend toward conflating institutions and constitutions in turn generated a way of talking about international economic law, and the WTO, in which a key question was why states cooperated in the absence of a central legal authority. Legitimacy, and the question of law's authority, a further core element of constitutionalization, therefore featured strongly in this field of scholarship. The use of constitutional language both fed the legitimacy of the new WTO and undermined it.

The conflation of the two concepts was, therefore, not without its critics. Some argued that the emphasis on institutions and constitutionalization internationally led to a failure adequately to interrogate the particular nature of the legitimacy afforded by these forms. Focusing on 'good governance' as a foundational policy for the granting of IMF loans and World Bank development assistance has, they argued, instead of promoting democracy nationally, weakened it,[46] and this has had a flow-on effect of fracturing the legitimacy

---

[42] Petersmann (n 38 above).

[43] E-U Petersmann, *Constitutional Functions and Constitutional Problems of International Economic Law* (Fribourg, Switz: University Press, 1991).

[44] See, eg, G Teubner, 'Global Private Regimes: Neospontaneous Law and Dual Constitution of Autonomous Sectors?' (on file with author).

[45] R Howse and K Nicolaidis, 'Legitimacy and Global Governance: Why Constitutionalizing the WTO is a Step Too Far' in RB Porter, *et al* (eds), *Efficiency, Equity, Legitimacy: The Multilateral Trading System at the Millennium* (Washington DC: Brookings Institution Press, 2001) (arguing that the language of constitutionalization should not be drafted in to the service of legitimizing the transformations it purports to describe).

[46] JT Gathii, 'Good Governance as a Counter Insurgency Agenda to Oppositional and Transformative Social Projects in International Law' (1999) 5 *Buffalo Human Rights Law Review* 107.

that constitutionalization was supposed to bring to the international system. James Gathii argues that the very measures and reductions in government spending required to meet the standards of 'good governance' imposed by the international constitutional process (privatization, tariff reduction, financial sector restructuring) force governments to reduce spending in areas fundamental to the exercise of democratic rights at the national level, such as health, education, and employee benefits. Or the claim was made that the expansion of Bretton Woods institutions into poverty alleviation and environment management, and the increased legitimacy which accompanied that expansion, resulted not from any natural increase of the ambit of the institutions' jurisdiction, but from direct resistance to the institutions by social movements, especially from the Third World.[47] Any resulting legitimacy, according to Balakrishnan Rajagopal, was a by-product not of internal and graduated institutional reform, but of conflict between institutional international economic law and social movements. It is the resolution of these conflicts, often by incorporation of some demands of the social movements, for example in relation to assimilation of a human rights agenda into World Bank policies, that enhances the institutions' social legitimacy. On this reading, the social legitimacy of the institutions necessary for the constitutionalization process comes not from the process itself, but from an external source: social movement agitation. Paradoxically, perhaps protest strengthens rather than fractures the new institutions/constitutions.

Others focused on the use of the language of constitutionalization in conferring a legitimacy on the organization, which had not, in some respects, been sufficiently 'earned', so to speak, by any democratic authorization. The labelling of an institutional structure a 'constitution' carries dangers because it implies a form of government, and yet the WTO remained largely unhindered by the usual mechanisms of accountability imposed on national constitutional regimes. No elections were required for state representatives at the WTO; indeed no representation as such existed. No elected body sat in supervision of new rule-making, and no national monitoring was possible, except perhaps by that very generalized concept of supervision, the punitive power of publicity. The WTO has a 'deficient legislative function' when compared with its adjudicative function, and the 'missing legislator' cannot be replaced by any 'functional equivalents'.[48] In reality, national governments have, by and large, kept a fairly close watch on the WTO—witness public debate in the United States about cases concerning the use of beef hormones, or GMOs—although this can never substitute for institutionalized political accountability. International protest movements have also exercised considerable power to hold up negotiations and, in one case at Seattle, resulted in their abandonment. Nevertheless, despite the strength of

---

[47] B Rajagopal, 'From Resistance to Renewal: The Third World, Social Movements, and the Expansion of International Institutions' (2000) 41 *Harvard International Law Journal* 529.

[48] A von Bogdandy, 'Law and Politics in the WTO—Strategies to Cope with a Deficient Relationship' in JA Frowein and R Wolfrum (eds), *Max Planck Yearbook of United Nations Law*, vol 5 (2001) 609.

these informal mechanisms of keeping the WTO to account, no institutional means of doing so are built in to the system, and so the use of the language of constitutionalization, in the absence of formal accountability, is misleading.

Moreover, it is argued that the use of the term insulates the WTO from critique by serving, what Robert Howse and Kalypso Nicolaidis have called, a 'door-closing function'[49] that stops people questioning the extension of WTO competences into new fields. Again this is because the term constitution carries the implication that the institution has emerged as a result of a new *Grundnorm* giving it coherence, and has achieved social legitimacy; in the words of this critique the term 'reified' the WTO agreements.[50]

Most importantly, the use of the language of constitutionalization is a form of wish-fulfilment,[51] which attempts to 'bootstrap' a system into being.[52] If the WTO is just a set of rules, or even an institution, these forms are singular, diverse, disparate, and not necessarily part of any overriding logic. A constitution, on the other hand, suggests a logic, a system, and, of course, a legitimacy. And if it contains these three elements (coherence, systemization, and legitimacy) it has power: power to act, to command respect, and expect its decisions to be honoured. International law does not generally conceive of itself as a constitution,[53] partly because, as we saw above in Chapter 2, it lacks the notion of coherent community that characterizes other constitutional systems, and consequently states' obeisance to it is much less certain, more fractured, and inflected with national interest, and questions about the status of its laws.

In short, international economic law scholarship is characterized by an emphasis on institutions and constitutions, and a conflation between the two concepts. The emphasis on institutions initially distanced the international trade law system from a simple treaty arrangement and made it plausible to discuss it as a coherent new legal order. Later the focus on institutions and constitutions functioned to distinguish the institution of the GATT from the constitution of the WTO by suggesting that the latter marked a new *Grundnorm* in international trade and thus a separation of the past from the present. Moreover, the accompanying conflation of the terms institution and constitution signalled the presence of a further element of constitutionalization, legitimacy, because the conflation was accompanied by enhancement of authority of the institutions of trade, according to some, and concern about that increased authority,

---

[49] Howse and Nicolaidis (n 45 above) 228.　　[50] ibid.

[51] N Walker, 'The EU and the WTO: Constitutionalism in a New Key' in G de Búrca and J Scott (eds), *The EU and the WTO: Legal and Constitutional Issues* (Oxford: Hart Publishing, 2001) 38.

[52] A variant of this argument that focuses on enforcement as an outcome rather than constitutionalization can be found in: CR Kelly, 'The Value Vacuum: Self-Enforcing Regimes and the Dilution of the Normative Feedback Loop' (2001) 22 *Michigan Journal of International Law* 673, 701 (arguing that the WTO has become a 'self-enforcing regime' in the sense that it secures a high level of compliance by means of coercion, independent of any hegemonic influences, and in addition to pre-existing compliance mechanisms').

[53] Cf P Allott, *Eunomia: New Order for a New World* (Oxford: Oxford University Press, paperback edn, 2001, first published 1990).

according to others. The melding of the institutional–constitutional axis in international economic law fuelled speculation that the WTO, a new institution of international economic order, may have constitutional credentials.

3.2.2 Linking globalization scholarship to international economic law

This section will suggest that the interlinking of the globalization debate with international economic law literature fuelled an assumption within the latter that increasingly blurred lines existed between sites of political, economic, and legal authority. This blurring of boundaries suggested that economic and political constraints (part of the equation of the received account of constitutionalization) were increasing. Moreover, it enhanced the likelihood of thinking about the WTO in a constitutional manner, as a political–legal structure instead of a merely economic–legal form related purely to trade.

The second characteristic of international economic law scholarship relevant to our study is a marked interdependence between international economic law scholarship and globalization scholarship. Like general globalization studies which focus on the activities of the WTO, the IMF, and the World Bank,[54] international economic law also links itself explicitly with the globalization phenomena.[55] Business regulation is deemed 'utterly global'.[56] For this reason whole studies are christened as being about 'global business regulation'[57] or 'global legal pluralism'.[58]

Moreover, like globalization debate, international economic law studies are replete with discussion of the inherent uncertainty of the concept of globalization, which is conceived of as a porous, complex concept with an uncertain landscape. It is described as 'messy'[59] and 'non-linear',[60] in an echo of a view beyond legal scholarship that describes the contemporary international arena as governed by a 'decentred and deterritorializing apparatus of rule that progressively incorporates the entire global realm within its open, expanding frontiers'.[61] Power in a globalized world is conceptualized less as a matter of domination than as a complex and contingent process, a matter of 'webs of influence'[62] or 'global business and regulatory networks'.[63] US power is a result

---

[54] Stiglitz (n 26 above).

[55] See, eg, JW Head, 'Throwing Eggs at Windows: Legal and Institutional Globalization in the 21st Century Economy' (2002) 50 *University of Kansas Law Review* 731 (examining 'economic globalization' by focusing on the WTO, IMF, and World Bank); and MH Davis and D Neacsu, 'Legitimacy, Globally: The Incoherence of Free Trade Practice, Global Economics and their Governing Principles of Political Economy' (2001) 69 *UMKC Law Review* 733, 762 (claiming that GATT is the 'template for globalization').   [56] Braithwaite and Drahos (n 33 above) 3.

[57] ibid, n 8.

[58] F Snyder, 'Governing Economic Globalisation: Global Legal Pluralism and European Law' (1999) 5 *European Law Journal* 334.   [59] Braithwaite and Drahos (n 33 above) 5.

[60] ibid 15.

[61] M Hardt and A Negri, *Empire* (Cambridge, Mass: Harvard University Press, 2000) xiii.

[62] Braithwaite and Drahos (n 33 above) 30.   [63] Picciotto and Mayne (n 27 above) 6.

of the triumph of this mode of network power.[64] Or a strong strand of anti-capitalist scholarship, discussed below at 3.2.3, continues to utilize a domination model of globalization, pointing to and criticizing the continuing increase in the size, economic power, and political influence of transnational corporations.[65]

The emphasis on globalization naturally coincides with an interest in constitutions in international trade, in part because globalization focuses upon the changing nature of law. As a result of the instability of globalization, the law bred in its wake is a diffuse, fragmented creature. Global economic relations are governed by global legal pluralism, which Francis Snyder defines as the 'totality of strategically determined, situationally specific and often episodic conjunctions of a multiplicity of institutional, normative, and processual sites throughout the world'.[66] The state public law domain should be understood, according to Neil Walker, in a 'different key',[67] a key which captures the 'explicitly relational...the complexly layered character of the new post-Westphalia pluralism'.[68] Gunther Teubner argues that globalization has led to the development of regulation that is labelled as 'neo-spontaneous'[69] because it derives not from the ordinary processes of legislative development but instead appears to emerge, semi-autonomously, from new sources, commercial, institutional, and non-public. These various forms of regulation and law are 'peripheral', characterized by the location of their making, in private fora, and at the 'edge' of law, where law intersects with other social sectors such as science, media, or transport.

Characteristic also of the fuzziness of globalization, and the law that both produces it and is produced by it, is the breakdown of the traditional separation between economics and politics. The various 'sites' which produce law can be market or polity based.[70] Indeed globalization itself is new to the extent that the power it produces is a conflation of economic and political power[71] although this is contested within the literature.[72] The emergence of a constitution, a thing which is normally primarily a political entity, from the framework of trade, is not unexpected then where the line between economics and politics has become blurred.

Paradoxically perhaps, the inherently unstable nature of globalization and globalized economic law is presented in the international economic law literature as neither good nor bad and consequently there are not good or bad

---

[64] Hardt and Negri (n 61 above) 161–163.

[65] S George, 'Corporate Globalisation' in E Bircham and J Charlton (eds), *Anti-Capitalism: A Guide to the Movement* (London: Bookmarks, 2001). [66] Snyder (n 58 above) 371.

[67] Walker (n 51 above). [68] ibid 37. [69] Teubner (n 44 above).

[70] Snyder (n 58 above) 372.

[71] Hardt and Negri (n 61 above) 9 (arguing that the 'capitalist project' of 'bringing together economic power and political power' is being realized in the processes of globalization).

[72] Walker (n 51 above) 37 n 17 (arguing that the economic sphere should not be a 'generative context for constitutional discourse' although it is relevant to an analysis of constitutionalization).

outcomes; scholars are generally agnostic about the benefits or otherwise of globalization—even amongst those whose other work impliedly questioned this premise. Good institutions and more regulation can temper the harsher effects of liberalization.[73] Globalization alone cannot be 'blamed for appalling under-regulation';[74] the weak can prevail in a globalized world and citizen sovereignty may emerge.[75] The very fluidity of the process provides grounds for optimism about the possibilities offered by globalization for the making of positive linkages similar to those that have been made between trade and intellectual property; perhaps trade and the environment will be the next.[76] Ultimately, the picture is one of neither absolute improvement in general welfare brought about by increased flows of trade, transport, communication, investment, and information, nor rampant destruction of national sovereignty over economic policy making. Globalization is a question of degree and intensification.

Others outside law remain sceptical of the benefits of globalization and of law's role in furthering its aims. Globalization, in the form of international economic integration, is leading to domestic social *dis*integration,[77] it is not reducing poverty, or facilitating international economic stability, and it is seriously harming the environment.[78]

In sum, the loosening of the parameters of international economic law referred to above has made the scholarship amenable to linkage with much broader debates about globalization, and has coincided with an interest in institutions and constitutions. Institutional discourse functioned as a precursor of sorts to the globalization debate, in its emphasis on non-legal mechanisms of behaviour, and interstate and non-state forms of cooperation. Constitutional discourse was a natural companion of the globalization debate because it sought to describe the deep underlying structure of interdependence between states, allowed the conflation of economic and political mechanisms, introduced a certain legitimacy quotient, and focused attention on the changed nature of law. My second point, then, is that the inheritance by international economic law of a complex template of globalization in which the lines between economics, politics, and law are increasingly blurred, and the emergence of new sites of authority is contemplated, leads naturally to development of interest in a trade constitution, the classical expression of which represents the interplay between law, politics, and economics.[79] If globalization is, in part,

---

[73] Picciotto and Mayne (n 27 above) 5.   [74] Braithwaite and Drahos (n 33 above) 5.

[75] ibid 34–36; Hardt and Negri (n 61 above) 357–363.

[76] Picciotto and Mayne (n 27 above) 221; J Pauwelyn, *Conflict of Norms in Public International Law: How WTO Law Relates to other Rules of International Law* (Cambridge: CUP, 2003), 2.

[77] Rodrik (n 26 above) 2 [emphasis in original].

[78] Stiglitz (n 26 above) 214. See also the classification of globalization scholars as hypenglobalists, sceptics, on transformationalists by Held *et al* above (nn 20–23 and accompanying text).

[79] One example would be the combination of economic, political, and legal arrangements inscribed in the constitution of Australia: Commonwealth of Australia Constitution Act 1900 (UK). Australia's constitution began its life in negotiations aimed at combating interstate protectionism

the increasing integration of economic markets, and this has effects on political and economic behaviour, and constitutionalization is about constructing rules for social and political interaction, then globalization highlights another question raised by the received account of constitutionalization about the types of constraint that make up a constitutional system.

3.2.3 A consensus about trade liberalization

This section will argue that, in contrast to the past, international economic law scholarship currently exhibits a general consensus about the benefits of trade liberalization for overall economic welfare and the specific welfare of states. The consensus promotes constitutionalization because, the chapter argues, it suggests the existence of a further core element of constitutionalization—a constitutional community of shared values capable of authorizing the making and maintenance of a constitutional system. Nevertheless, the existence of a community of agreement sufficient to authorize a trade constitutional system continues to be challenged, particularly by those concerned that the trade liberalization consensus masks serious disagreements within any putative trade community. The discussion proceeds in three stages. In the early phase a consensus on liberalization existed; in the middle phase this consensus was challenged; in the late-middle phase the challenge declined but some of its main tenets were incorporated in a new consensus; and in the current phase a modified consensus continues, with only occasional contestation.

Let us begin with the early stage then. As discussed in Chapter 1, international economic law, as a field of law, developed at the same time as agreement by states to GATT, which had set as its goals the raising of standards of living, income, production, and demand through trade liberalization. General agreement therefore existed that trade liberalization was a necessary good. However, fairly soon after, states formerly acquiescent in a system of international law largely written by Western states, gained confidence and agitated for political and economic independence. With this new political balance the brief consensus on the best way to organize international economic life (through trade liberalization) was shaken. Instead, during the decolonization period of the 1960s and 1970s, international economic law scholarship, and practice was, generally, characterized by controversy. In international relations scholarship, dependency theory arose, and in law, a challenge from developing states

---

and facilitating free trade arrangements. Later it shed this solely economic justification and became a tool of combined political and economic organization. For discussion of the history of the Australian constitution see M Coper, *Encounters with the Australian Constitution* (North Ryde, NSW: CCH Publishing, 1987) chapters 2, 5 and 7 especially. For a discussion of the current law in relation to key elements of economic organization encapsulated in the Australian constitutional arrangements, including the distribution of fiscal power and control of economic and commercial activity, see, eg, P Hanks and DZ Cass, *Australian Constitutional Law, Materials and Commentary*, 6th edn (Sydney: Butterworths, 1999) chapters 9 and 10.

emerged that became known as the New International Economic Order (NIEO) critique.

This critique was aimed not only at particular rules of international economic law, but also at the very field itself, its place within public international law, its legitimacy, and its constitution. One of the most influential of the NIEO authors was Mohammed Bedjaoui, later judge of the International Court of Justice, whose views were summarized in a volume written at the end of the 1970s entitled *Towards a New International Economic Order*.[80] Bedjaoui challenged traditional principles of international economic law, and indeed international law generally, as pro-Western and biased in relation to their formation, content, and practical application.

As part of this general debate and controversy, legal structures changed. Judicial decisions were taken which reflected the influence of the NIEO critique including arguments about sovereignty and acquisition of territory[81] and expropriation.[82] Sources doctrine in public international law was modified (albeit minimally) to take account of new actors and forms of participation in law-making.[83] A new principle proclaiming states' permanent sovereignty over natural resources was declared.[84] Controversial legal instruments were passed by the General Assembly including one which, arguably, modified the standard of compensation for expropriation of foreign assets.[85] A right to development emerged[86] and, interpreted by the Southern states, this right imposed some legal responsibility upon Northern states to compensate them for the former's lack of wealth.[87] Most noteworthy of all, the GATT 1947 was amended by the inclusion of Part IV, which provided for special and differential treatment for developing countries in trading matters. Therefore, unlike the period of relative consensus from the introduction of GATT in 1947 and through the 1950s, this time was characterized by strong debate about the nature of international economic law, about the types of rights it should protect, and the types of obligations it recognized.

The interplay between economic fact, legal scholarship, and law-creation, was particularly vigorous during the period with visible consequences for economic policy as well as law. In the wake of the intellectual foment of the NIEO, developing countries adopted policies of import substitution and infant industry protection, both of which aimed to extend their economies beyond

---

[80] M Bedjaoui, *Towards a New International Economic Order* (New York: Holmes & Meier, 1979).

[81] Western Sahara, Advisory Opinion 1975 ICJ 12 (16 October).

[82] *Texaco v Libyan Arab Republic* (*US v Libya*) 53 ILR 389 (1979) (Dupuy, Arb).

[83] Military and Paramilitary Activities in and against Nicaragua (*Nicaragua v US*) 1984 ICJ 392 (27 June).

[84] See Resolution on Permanent Sovereignty over Natural Resources, G.A. Res. 1803 (XVII), UN GAOR, 17th Session, Supp 17, p 15, A/5217 (1962), 2:1 ILM 223 (1963).

[85] See Charter of Economic Rights and Duties of States, GA Res 3281 (XXIX), UN GAOR, 29th Sess, Supp 31, 50 (1974); 14 ILM 251 (1975).

[86] See Right to Development, GA Res 41/128, UN GAOR, 41st Sess, Supp 53, 186 (1986).

[87] I Seidl-Hohenveldern, *International Economic Law*, 3rd edn (The Hague: Kluwer, 1999) 5.

traditional primary production toward the building of stronger manufacturing bases. In the light of our definition in Chapter 2 as including a notion of community of shared understandings, it is hard to imagine how, in this period, a system of trade law could have been described as constitutionalized in an environment where so many of the basic premises of the background field of international economic law were being scrutinized.

Despite the relative success of the NIEO critique, ultimately it fell into decline in the late-middle period. The United Nations Conference on Trade and Development (UNCTAD), which had been formed in 1964, drafted Part IV of the GATT, and was strongly associated with ideas of the NIEO, lost much of its power. Economically significant subjects such as intellectual property were transferred from UNCTAD to The World Intellectual Property Organization (WIPO), an organization dominated by producer interests, and not explicitly concerned with the relationship between trade and development. East Asian countries, such as South Korea and Singapore, successfully pursued export-led growth after abandoning policies of import substitution, albeit while retaining strongly interventionist governments. And development economists began to argue against the intellectual tradition of the NIEO, and the insights of earlier import-substitution-promoting literature. According to Balasubramanyam they moved away from the position that gains from international trade and foreign investment accrued mainly to developed countries. They began to question the view that foreign investment in developing states, which occurred in primary production and minerals, lacked multiplier effects. They challenged arguments that free trade diverted domestic resources from other areas of economic development leading to an increase in the import of manufactures and, ultimately, to an imbalance in terms of trade. Now, instead, economists such as Jagdish Bhagwati calculated the high cost for developing countries of protectionism and, bringing a political economy perspective to the debate, demonstrated that vested interests sought to entrench protectionism despite evidence of its economic inefficiency. The intellectual and factual power of these arguments was such that India moved from a policy of import substitution toward export promotion.[88]

Allied to the economic arguments that trade protectionism reduced economic welfare were the legal critiques. These argued that the differential status accorded to developing countries, especially in the form of non-reciprocity and preferential treatment in trade concessions, was a one-sided system. It was impractical to implement, and would cause more harm than good to the domestic economies of developing countries.[89] Even though developing states

---

[88] VN Balasubramanyam (ed), *Jagdish Bhagwati—Writing of International Economics* (Delhi: Oxford University Press, 1997) 27–28 (stating that Bhagwati contributed to 'intense discussion' in India's planning commission during this period).
[89] R Hudec, *Developing Countries in the GATT Legal System* (London: Gower Publishing, 1987) [hereinafter Hudec, *Developing*], 4–5.

might be able to increase some exports to developed states, in the long run increased exports in these sectors would be offset by increased non-tariff measures in others. Moreover, the failure of domestic producers to restructure in order that they compete successfully with foreign rivals would, overall, reduce internal welfare. Also, international economic law rejected the insights of the NIEO critique because of the suspicion, deeply held by the North, that the goal of compensating inequality would necessitate the very thing which international economic law sought to protect against, namely it would require a planned economy and a world organization to plan it, rather than the relatively free flow of market forces.[90]

What is interesting about the victory of the free-trade counter-critique (to the NIEO) is that it returned the field to a state of *relative* stasis where the consensus about the benefit of liberalization was revived. In the main, the counter-critique quietened the voices calling for dismantling, or wholesale rewriting, of the international economic law, and it reinforced the original insights of the field, namely that liberalization could lead to an increase in general welfare. The economic and legal environment became more hospitable to international business and international commercial transactions generally. Importantly, the re-emergence of a consensus about the benefits of trade liberalization created the conditions in which it was possible to contemplate the idea of constitutional community.

Yet the new environment was now conditioned in subtle ways. Whilst favouring deeper liberalization and international economic integration, it did so in a different register. In this new register two strands of thinking are clear. First, the *legacy of the NIEO* became deeply embedded in the scholarship and in the law; secondly, the *anti-liberal impulses of developed states* came in for increasing criticism. By suggesting ways to bridge the gap between concerns of developing and developed states, both trends further increased the likelihood that a new consensus on values could emerge, and with it a community capable of founding the basis of a movement towards constitutionalization.

The first trend of the late-middle phase then was that the NIEO argument for differential status for developing states was incorporated into the new liberalization agenda. Hence the legacy of the NIEO persists today, even if it is sometimes unacknowledged and unrealized. The 'special status' approach persisted in key principles of the GATT–WTO system. It was enshrined as a non-binding principle in Part IV of the GATT. It later re-emerged with even more vigour during the Uruguay Round of trade negotiations, where, for the first time, in 1994, a large number of states signed a single package of trade agreements, covering a broad range of subjects including subsidies, dumping, health-related measures, agriculture, intellectual property, and dispute resolution. Included in most of these 'covered' agreements were special rules for

---

[90] Seidl-Hohenveldern (n 87 above) 6.

developing states. But special and differential treatment was present not just in the agreements themselves. It became more evident in almost every policy discussion within the key public institutions of international economic order, the WTO, IMF, and World Bank. Key institutions focused more and more on development, as an end itself. The World Bank shifted its objective from one of specific lending for reconstruction after the Second World War to one of development. Its project lending changed from 'hard' projects, such as transport or electricity, to 'soft', more generalized purposes of development, including legal reform, infrastructure, and even political development. IMF lending also reflected, to an extent, the insight that structural inequalities persisted between economies and it was the responsibility of the international economic institutions to assist with the alleviation of those inequalities. The Doha Round of trade negotiations launched in 2001 continued the NIEO tradition by carrying the mantle of fostering development.

Secondly, as well as this legacy, scholarship in the 1980s became more concerned with the anti-liberal impulses of developed states. The counter critique to the NIEO may have refuted some of the latter's claims. But it had also unsettled the earlier consensus on liberalization in one further aspect. The old consensus on liberalization largely assumed that it was developing states that had the most work to do in relation to achieving that goal. While exploding the myth of developing country special status, the NIEO counter-critique also exposed the hypocrisy and double standards inherent in developed states' attitudes to liberalization. The developed states may have been committed to liberalization, but, according to the counter-critique, they were equally committed to the 'practice of imposing new restrictions that limit developing exports once they begin to cause discomfort'.[91] The cumulative effect of the NIEO critique and its counter-critique punctuated the old consensus on liberalization, and laid the groundwork for the assault on the 'new protectionism' of developed states.[92] This led to an attack on a new set of policies which had arisen in the 1970s, partly in response to the success of export-led growth in South East Asia, which was characterized by an increased use, by developed states mainly, of non-trade barriers and trade remedies such as anti-dumping, and countervailing duties. Scholarship now focused on the new protectionist methods and criticized the heavy use of anti-dumping law, and the use of safeguards against competitive import surges. Later it condemned the 'dressing up' of the new intellectual property regime of the WTO as trade liberalizing when in practice it constituted a strongly protectionist regime which extended monopoly rights throughout the trading world. Other authors focused on granting greater access to markets in which developing states should have had a comparative advantage, namely agriculture, textiles and clothing, and steel. In short, international economic law sharpened its

---

[91] Hudec, *Developing* (n 89 above) 227.   [92] Hudec, *Essays* (n 32 above).

anti-protectionist credentials and took on board many of the insights of the NIEO critique.

The temper of the current phase of legal scholarship then, as it moved into the new century, became more optimistic, both about trade liberalization and about the potential for international economic law to act as a vehicle to improve world order generally. Pauwelyn, writing in 2003, nicely expressed this optimism and faith: 'The statistics show that trade liberalisation, the WTO's leitmotif, does increase welfare. The WTO is "good for you".'[93] Importantly, the new consensus about the benefits of free trade had made it more likely that a constitutional community could emerge. And, in this new register, constitutionalization scholarship began to take root and flourish, in part because questions about the values that might inform any new constitutional order are not agitated as vigorously as they were in an earlier period, and the idea of a community can now be envisaged. International legal scholarship in the twenty-first century instead takes a pragmatic approach to globalization, counsels the benefits of liberalization, and criticizes departures, by both North and South, from that goal.

So, in addition to agnosticism about globalization, international economic law scholarship, and WTO constitutionalization literature in particular, share a consensus about the benefits of trade liberalization, a consensus that led some to suggest that community existed with shared values sufficient to constitute a constitution for the WTO. International economic law is portrayed as a vehicle for liberalization and, when subject to appropriate limits, liberalization (and so international economic law) will contribute to an overall increase in economic welfare. The challenge is for international economic institutions and law, therefore, to improve international institutions; tame financial flows and volatility; create better mechanisms of accountability by managing the interaction between layers of regulation; and strengthen state regulation through flexible linkage to internationally agreed standards.[94] The literature therefore presents numerous strategies for improvement of global business regulation and indeed for constitutionalization itself, all of which are avowedly pragmatic.[95] These include harnessing management philosophies such as 'continuous improvement' and 'best practice'; strengthening competition law; increasing health and environmental standards; building 'global epistemic communities' to assist in competition enforcement; and transforming the consumer movement into a watchdog of monopolies.[96] In a constitutional voice, WTO law is a vehicle, according to some, for human rights because the latter can be harnessed to the promotion

---

[93] Pauwelyn (n 76 above) xi.   [94] Picciotto and Mayne (n 27 above) 5–7 and 22–23.

[95] Kennedy (n 37 above) 87–102 (arguing that one of the key players in the constitutional debates, John Jackson, has a vision of the constitutionalization of the WTO which is, at 62, 'pragmatic and realist'. It does not aim to achieve any particular goals, but instead operates according to, at 92, a policy of 'benign neglect' whereby trade disputes can be accommodated by techniques of management).   [96] Braithwaite and Drahos (n 33 above) 612–628.

of economic welfare through international trade law exploiting 'synergies' between the fields.[97] As noted in Section 3.2.5 below, 'pure' free trade is off the agenda (if it was ever there at all).

As a consequence of this pervasive consensus about the benefits of trade liberalization by both international economic law scholarship and constitutionalization literature, general critiques of liberalization, international economic law, and WTO constitutionalization are rare, and the idea of a community is promoted. This is not to say that there is not a wide and vigorous debate about specific aspects of the field, or about how constitutionalization should proceed. Arguments about what subjects to include within the ambit of the WTO; how to constitutionalize the field; or how to improve the voting structure of the IMF all contribute to a rich and vigorous discussion about improving international economic law. But voices that challenge the underlying structure of the fields are few and far between because they all essentially share the same premise.

Nevertheless, sustained criticism of this consensus comes from two or three quarters, which also question the assumption about the existence of any community capable of authorizing a new constitution of international trade. Disagreement comes from critiques variously labelled as social activist, anti-capitalist, or anti-globalization,[98] which are largely located outside legal scholarship, and a small branch of legal, post-colonial, and Third World scholarship. So the critiques are situated at the intersection with other disciplines such as economics, anthropology, and international relations, and, apart from occasional internal contributions,[99] none are central interlocutors with international economic law scholarship in the same way that the NIEO critique was. A brief account of some of their key arguments follows.

Beyond law, the social activist or anti-capitalist position is often aimed at what it refers to as 'corporate globalization'. One branch suggests that the international financial system is dominated by industrial and financial transnational corporations which make enormous profit at the expense of others, through, for example, demands for complete freedom of investment, capital, goods and services, including intellectual property, and education. The antidote

---

[97] E-U Petersmann, 'Time for a United Nations "Global Compact" for Integrating Human Rights into the Law of Worldwide Organizations' (2002) 13 *European Journal of International Law* 621.

[98] Some of the proponents of the critique are included in a collection organized as 'anti-capitalist', above n 65. Note however, some of the same writers object to their characterization as 'anti-globalization' which is described as 'at best a contradiction, at worst a slander': S George, 'The Global Citizens Movement. A New Actor For a New Politics', Paper completed 30 August 2001 presented at the Conference on *Reshaping Globalisation: Multilateral Dialogues and New Policy Initiatives* Sponsored by the Central European University, a project of George Soros's Open Society Foundation at <www.tni.org/archives/george/budapest.html>.

[99] JR Paul, 'Do International Trade Institutions Contribute to Economic Growth and Development' (2003) 44 *Virginia Journal of International Law* 285; J Trachtman, 'Legal Aspects of a Poverty Agenda at the WTO: Trade Law and "Global Apartheid"' (2003) 6 *Journal of International Economic Law* 3.

to this state of affairs includes 'fair trade' incorporating recognition of social and environmental concerns; taxing of international capital movements, and of mergers and acquisitions; corporate responsibility for environmental and other social damage; and cancellation of developing country debt.[100] Another variant of this argument claims that there has been a 'silent takeover'[101] of democracy by global capitalism with the result that 'the corporation is king, the state its subject, and its citizens consumers.'[102] The WTO is complicit in the 'take-over' because economic interests, on behalf of corporations not states, have prevailed in that forum,[103] often at the cost of other social concerns;[104] sovereignty has been weakened (again on behalf of corporations);[105] and developing countries sidelined in negotiation and decision-making.[106] In short, the WTO is unaccountable, non-transparent, and corporate interests have shaped its rules.[107]

A further branch of this social activist/anti-capitalist scholarship focuses upon the broader effects of new corporate strategies, such as increased use of brand recognition to increase sales. In respect of these methods, it is suggested that their aim has been to create the illusion of increasing consumer choice while at the same time severely limiting opportunities for the development of new culture and for the enjoyment of public space.[108] These strategies, supported by institutions such as the WTO, have also undermined free speech[109] and diversity[110] and 'degraded production'[111] by lowering wages, insulating

---

[100] George (n 65 above).

[101] N Hertz, *The Silent Takeover* (London: Heinemann, 2001) 8 (arguing that although there have been benefits to capitalism, the overall price has been too high in terms of an increase in poverty and overall inequality, corporate welfare in the form of low tax, governments turning a blind eye to corporate facilitated human-rights abuse, and cultural restriction. For a telling example of Hertz's notion of 'takeover' see discussion at p. 7 of refusal by multinational owned US broadcasters of a funded anti-consumerist advertisement urging people not to buy for a single day).

[102] ibid 5.   [103] ibid 103.   [104] ibid 105.   [105] ibid 106.   [106] ibid 107.

[107] ibid 108.

[108] ibid (arguing, at 130, that this has led to a 'double vision of vast consumer choice' coupled with 'Orwellian restrictions on cultural production and public space', which has been achieved primarily through converting advertising from a publicity function to a branding function in which the concept associated with the product is more important to increasing sales than the quality of the product. Moreover, she argues, at p. 89 *et seq*, that 'branding' has extended into heretofore untouched areas of culture such as sport, and importantly, education, with detrimental effects such as the MacDonalds corporation being permitted to build school-kiosks in which federal food vouchers are not accepted, and the school canteen being prohibited from selling products of 'competitors').

[109] ibid 117 (arguing that corporations seeking to invest in China self-censored reports critical of China's human rights record).

[110] ibid (arguing, at 117, that diversity, another shibboleth of participatory democratic theory, is simultaneously undermined and exploited as a strategy for increasing markets. So in the hands of global capitalism, diversity becomes a marketing device for creation of a 'One-World placelessness'. Moreover, Klein argues at page 130, that the creation of a borderless marketplace for the sale of goods and services occurs at the same time as consumer choice has been severely curtailed by corporate strategies such as mergers, buyouts, domination by superbrands, and aggressive assertion of intellectual property rights.)   [111] ibid 195.

corporations from local regulation, and leading to 'factory flight'.[112] Thus international economic arrangements which facilitate these new corporate tactics, and the international financial system, are not as benign as the consensus would have us believe.

Within law, critical scholars are small in number and low in profile, but their strongly argued positions suggest that any community of international law contains some deep and significant fractures. Rare voices contend that the WTO has not lived up to its promise for developing states and should now institute a 'poverty agenda',[113] or that trade, and the WTO in particular, does not lead to economic development or growth, and instead prevents states from reducing market distortions or correcting market failures.[114] Some critical authors are, variously, associated with Third World scholarship, and post-colonial critique, and they challenge the institutional arrangements, coverage, and outcomes of international economic law. The role and functions of the international economic law institutions such as the World Bank have been shaped by resistance between those institutions and Third World social movements and not by gradual legal change.[115] Examples given include the extension of the World Bank's mandate to cover environmental regulation and poverty alleviation. The new international economic law rule of good governance, with its emphasis on human rights and democracy combined with liberal economic solutions, undermines the achievement of social justice because it forces states to limit and reduce delivery of public goods such as education and health. The real agenda of good governance is to facilitate repayment of sovereign debts to institutional lenders and secure unhindered influx of foreign capital into developing states.[116] The World Bank encourages promotion of only those human rights that are consistent with increasing corporate investment, growth, and profit and neglects the social welfare aspects of human rights. Attempts to expunge corruption from developing states legitimizes a

---

[112] ibid 207 (arguing that much production now takes place, in areas designated as export processing zones, which are, 'bracketed' from local conditions. Within these zones, conditions for working people are drastically poorer than those in the North (at 204–216), corporations are insulated from local conditions, as well as from legal requirements of tax or regulation, for example, paying no import or export duties, income or property taxes (at 204–207), and benefits for local development are few. Owing to the insulation of corporations, little or no contribution is made to local infrastructure and, for countries in which the zones are created, the trickle down effect has proved to be ephemeral especially in the light of the currency crises of the 1980s in which workers' wages were, in some cases, halved (210, 218). Foreign investors have not, in practice, stayed to develop their investments and have fled countries where conditions are no longer conducive to high profit margins (at 197). Instead, what has been termed 'factory flight' (at 211) has occurred with corporations relocating from deprived countries such as Philippines towards China where wages are even lower and, 'wage cheating', among leading multinational corporations, is common.)

[113] J Trachtman, 'Legal Aspects of a Poverty Agenda at the WTO: Trade Law and "Global Apartheid"' (2003) 6 *Journal of International Economic Law* 3.

[114] JR Paul, 'Do International Trade Institutions Contribute to Economic Growth and Development' (2003) 44 *Virginia Journal of International Law* 285.

[115] Rajagopal (n 47 above) 259.　　[116] Gathii (n 46 above) 107.

strong police power of the state, and emphasizes market economic reforms such as privatization and tariff reduction, which were precisely the reforms which caused the corruption and social dislocation in the first place.[117] Finally, and relatedly, in political science a vast field of cultural studies scholarship intersects with the exact same interests of international economic law, and questions its basic assumptions. The global cultural economy is characterized by 'disjuncture and difference' in which markets in money, commodities, and people are 'deterritorialized', and so it can no longer be understood in terms of existing models of centre and periphery, surplus and deficit, consumers and producers.[118]

Finally comes the critique about issues which are categorized as 'trade and', such as labour and the environment. One trade and labour scholar suggests that international trade law will inevitably have to extend its reach to matters of internal regulation, such as labour, as explicit trade barriers have now largely been dismantled; '[f]air trade is free trade's destiny.'[119] This leads to a need to confront the issue of what is the optimal baseline for social policy concerning labour.[120] In the absence of agreement about what is 'normal' labour regulation, and given the increase in regulatory competition between states putting downward pressure on labour standards,[121] it may be necessary to step 'outside'[122] classical economic theory in order to consider how to resolve the trade–labour dilemma. So critiques from anti-globalization/anti-capitalism, post-colonial theory, and 'trade and' perspectives continue to question the consensus that unrestricted freer trade is a necessary good.

In sum then, in contrast to an earlier period, international economic law scholarship is currently characterized by a general consensus on the benefits of liberalization, which suggests that it is possible to envisage a further element of constitutionalization, namely authorizing community. This consensus has had the effect, in the early stages of WTO constitutionalization discussion, of muffling debate about the supposed new order. However, more recently, the so-called consensus and the community borne of it have been subject to occasional sustained contestation and strong critique. While most critique is located outside the legal field, it nevertheless suggests that the community of WTO constitutionalization may not be quite as coherent as some might imagine.

3.2.4 Regulation not 'law'

This section will revisit the argument made in the first section of the chapter that international economic law scholarship has increasingly focused on things

---

[117] B Rajagopal, 'Corruption, Legitimacy and Human Rights: The Dialectic of the Relationship' (1999) 14 *Connecticut Journal of International Law* 495.

[118] A Appadurai, 'Disjuncture and Difference in the Global Cultural Economy' (1990) 2 *Public Culture* 1.

[119] B Langille, 'General Reflections on the Relationship of Trade and Labor (Or: Fair Trade is Free Trade's Destiny)' in R Howse (ed), *The World Trading System: Critical Perspectives on the World Economy* (London: Routledge, 1998) 305.   [120] ibid 325.

[121] ibid 317.   [122] ibid 312.

other than strict law (namely institutions), but this time I want to suggest that the international economic law scholarship has concentrated on something called 'regulation' rather than law in a traditional sense. Moreover, this emphasis on regulation has led international economic law to focus on procedural methods of achieving agreement between states in preference to trying to attain agreement on substantive matters. The effect of this concentration on proceduralism has been to put another of the core elements of constitutionalization, deliberative process, into the frame.

The fourth theme of international economic law scholarship which is relevant to the WTO constitutionalization debate is the field's increasing emphasis on non-traditional law in the form of different kinds of regulation. The idea of regulation has truly taken hold of the academic consciousness of the twenty-first-century international economic lawyer. It is the central organizing principle of many texts;[123] academic courses make regulation their centrepiece, and entire academic centres of research specialize in it.[124] As the current catchword of the field, regulation is perceived of as *the* critical phenomenon of study. The international body that oversees trade rules, the WTO, is said to be the 'regulator of regulatory action by governments'.[125] Modernity itself cannot be understood without understanding regulation.[126]

An equally potent alternative to law as rules is the idea of legalization,[127] with the suggestion that the concept represents a move away from any 'rigid dichotomy between "legalization" and "world politics"'[128] and shows (unsurprisingly) that the fields of law and politics are 'intertwined at all levels of legalization' and that 'legal and political considerations combine to influence behaviour.'[129]

For international economic law and constitutionalization, the rejection of traditional concepts of law as rules and its substitution or supplementation with other conceptual devices has the effect of moving the focus away from the substance of particular rules towards the process by which they are made. This focus on procedure occurs partly because, although the range of forms of obligation are greater (as noted above in relation to institutions also), the forms of regulation, or legalization, affecting economic actors are often 'softer' than rigid rules, or even voluntary in the case of codes of conduct and guiding principles. Enforcement is presented as being less important than in strict legal systems: the concept of legalization is presented as drawn along three broad axes consisting of obligation, delegation, and precision, the point being

---

[123] See, eg, Trebilcock and Howse (n 1 above); Braithwaite and Drahos (n 33 above); Picciotto and Mayne (n 27 above).

[124] See, eg, Centre for Risk and Regulation at the London School of Economics and Political Science, and RegNet at the Australian National University.

[125] Hoekman and Kostecki (n 31 above).   [126] Braithwaite and Drahos (n 33 above) 9.

[127] KW Abbott, RO Keohane, A Moravcsik, A-M Slaughter, and D Snidal, 'The Concept of Legalization' (2000) 54 *International Organization* 401.   [128] ibid 419.

[129] ibid.

to reject the centrality of legal enforcement in a traditional sense.[130] Therefore, according to this approach, the WTO is a prominent example of an institution with a high level of legalization.[131]

The emphasis on regulation, as a process, rather than on law as a matter of substantive goals, has two significant consequences. First, this shift in focus to process has also allowed writers to recognize *non-state* forms of regulation, and *non-law* forms of obligation, as key components of the field. Major (US) corporations are portrayed as highly influential in formation of new international agreements and indeed in persuading public officials to link aspects of international economic law such as trade and intellectual property.[132] State regulation itself is, literally, written by private interests, usually in their capacity as participants in key standard-setting organizations in areas such as air transport and telecommunications.[133]

Secondly, it focuses attention upon the *way* in which things are done rather than on *what* is being done. So the focus on regulation, over law, is accompanied by a focus on procedural solutions rather than particular outcomes. How states 'manage' the 'interface' between national and international regulation will be the key to the success of the GATT–WTO system.[134] 'Accommodation' of competing interests will resolve the 'trade and labour', environment, or competition debates.[135] GATT has been successful in offering inducements to lower tariffs because a rule based system is superior to a results based one.[136]

European constitutionalists have explored proceduralism as a means of creating a more malleable, dialogic form of European constitutionalism. Some have suggested that, although the old mechanisms of achieving constitutional functions of recognizing and coordinating legal and political activity are less successful than they were in the past, newer, procedural 'constitutional substitutes' have been formulated which may yet lead to the same goals.[137] Others have sought to move beyond defining constitutionalization in terms of fixed legal doctrine and instead argued for a reconceptualization of constitutionalization as a flexible, non-static mode of communication, in which it becomes a language for accommodating a diversity of state and non-state interests.[138]

---

[130] Abbott and Keohane, *et al* (n 127 above) 418.

[131] ibid 406, the WTO is situated close to the 'ideal type' of legalized body, scoring well on the three axes of obligation, precision, and delegation.

[132] Braithwaite and Drahos (n 33 above) 218.   [133] ibid 218, 488–491.

[134] Jackson, Davey and Sykes (n 35 above) 1227. Note that the extract in which the terms 'management' and 'interface' were coined does not appear in the current 4th edition, n 30 above, published in 2002.

[135] JN Bhagwati and RE Hudec (eds), *Fair Trade and Harmonization: Prerequisites for Free Trade? Vol 2: Legal Analysis* (Cambridge, Mass: MIT Press, 2nd printing 1996) 13.

[136] Hoekman and Kostecki (n 31 above) 39–42.

[137] D Chalmers, 'Post-nationalism and the Quest for Constitutional Substitutes' (2000) 27 *Journal of Law and Society* 178.

[138] J Shaw, 'Relating Constitutionalism and Flexibility' in G de Búrca and J Scott (eds), *Constitutional Change in the EU: From Uniformity to Flexibility* (Oxford: Hart Publishing, 2000) (arguing that the

On this view, the somewhat negative associations of proceduralism with technocratic and lowest-common-denominator decision-making are replaced instead with a plus for constitutional development because, according to Jo Shaw, proceduralism leads states to recognize they have a duty to negotiate and listen, to forgo fixed outcomes, and to engage in a deliberative process.

Here we can see clearly that this trend away from law and towards regulation has affiliations with the procedural school of liberal democratic theory and, hence, facilitates discussion of a further core element of the received account, deliberative process. Regulation thus brings the constitutionalization question centre stage, although paradoxically it facilitates the avoidance of questions about the type of substantive goals that might underpin any constitution of international trade. International economic law is thus connected through proceduralism to wider concerns about the nature of democracy, but side-steps a discussion of particular goals or purposes. Instead, in the face of increasing variety between states, and diversity of interests within them, international economic law scholarship emphasizes the procedurally democratic aspects of regulation. The themes of the new international economic law become openness, transparency, public communication, and participation. In the context of the European Community, what is most important in deciding whether a national rule is valid, according to Miguel Poiares Maduro, is not whether freedom of goods is supposed merely to limit states' protectionist impulses or whether it was intended to give inter-state economic operators complete freedom to trade without any regulation; what is important is not the resolution of that particular polarity, but whether the state imposing a potentially discriminatory measure took sufficient account of interests beyond the state when doing so.[139] What is important is who is at the table, not what they decide.

So instead of tackling the question of links between trade and other issues such as environment in terms of a discussion of what is 'fair',[140] scholarship focuses on procedural solutions, on the 'interface' between national economies—in part because earlier studies had recognized the difficulties of identifying a normative baseline for what constitutes 'fairness'. Agreement being impossible on the particular outcomes or even starting points,[141] focus moved to method. Instead, improvements in participation (for other states and non-state groups); increases in the representative nature of the body making decisions whether it be the WTO, the IMF or the World Bank; and improved communication and transparency will improve and safeguard the legitimacy and authority of international economic law regulation and decision-making.

---

flexibility of enhanced cooperation can be complementary with constitutionalism defined procedurally, because cooperation allows states to combine on particular matters of interest, and at different speeds).

[139] MP Maduro, 'Reforming the Market or the State? Article 30 and the European Constitution: Economic Freedom and Political Rights' (1997) 3 *European Law Journal* 55.

[140] Bhagwati and Hudec (n 135 above) 13.   [141] Hudec, *Developing* (n 89 above).

Here we can also see how the notion of regulation, through subtle alterations to the idea of what is being studied (process not outcome), and links with other areas of scholarship (democratic theory), foregrounds a core constitutional element of the received account, deliberative process. If regulation entails changes in participation, representativeness, and other aspects of the language of democratic theory, then regulation becomes associated with notions of governance.[142] The move to constitutionalization is closer at hand. If the particular form of regulation substituting for the state is international economic law regulation then the structures of international economic law are seen by some as constituting new structures of international governance, a new constitution even. This link between international economic legal regulation and ideas about international governance has led to an increasing focus on constitutions, and has been met by strong public demonstrations at international economic institution meetings, beginning with the World Trade Organization's failed launch of a new trade round in Seattle in 1999. Public concern about international economic legal regulation reflects, in part, the field's shift toward regulation, and the association of regulation with notions of constitutionalization and governance.

In short, the trend in international economic law towards regulation presaged WTO constitutionalization by focusing on discussion of deliberative process. In the face of increasing variety between states, and diversity of interests within them, international economic law scholarship emphasized broader, softer, and more participatory forms of regulation. Regulation was linked to process, thus making it easier to think about the WTO as a constitution because states do not have to decide what are the fundamental constitutional goals that might underpin it. The shift to regulation has led also to questions perhaps not of government but of governance, and in this context the field was ripe for the emergence of the constitutionalization issue. This left open the question whether the shift to regulation facilitated the portrayal of WTO constitutionalization as a relatively uncontroversial, procedural solution to reasonable disagreement between states, or, indeed, whether it marked a trend toward what one commentator called, the 'evisceration of the political'.[143]

3.2.5   A fixation with definition of the field

This section will argue that discussion of the constitutionalization of the WTO was likely to emerge from international economic law because the field was increasingly fixated with how to define its own boundaries. In various ways this recalls the received account of constitutionalization because it raised questions about the geographical boundaries of community, its subject matter parameters, and, its legitimacy.

---

[142] Picciotto and Mayne (n 27 above) 4; Braithwaite and Drahos (n 33 above) 475.
[143] Kennedy (n 37 above) 15.

The next characteristic of the field of international economic law, which has had the effect of encouraging the emergence of WTO constitutionalization debate, is a fixation in the field of international economic law with the problem of defining its own scope. The problem of definition is present in relation to how to conceptualize a broad field provisionally labelled international economic law. What should be its name? What topics should fall within its range? How should we decide what is within and what is without? Is it a part of a broader field of public international law, or does it exist as its own discipline? Answers to these questions trigger discussion of two of the other core elements of constitutionalization by bringing into focus what are the boundaries of the community of international trade, and thinking about how these relate to its legitimacy.

Early scholars using the term 'international economic law' distinguished it from another growth area of 'transnational' law, and described it as 'embedded' within public international law, albeit with a broader range of subjects (multi-national enterprises) and sources (for example, the law merchant, which consisted of international commercial customs as recognized and applied between states).[144] Later, others made a distinction between the private *transactional* aspects, which included matters such as private contract law, customs law, and law relating to shipping, and *regulatory* aspects,[145] which involved government regulation at the national (import and export controls) and international (WTO, IMF, and WB rules and policies) levels and focused primarily on the latter.[146] To others still, public international law was not central to the examination and instead they mixed a number of topics under the label 'international trade law' where these include some from the transactional and some from the regulatory categories.[147] Particular examinations of, say, GATT dispute resolution were prepared under the heading 'transnational economic law'.[148] Other studies organized the field under the subject of international business transactions, or, as discussed above, they bundled together a collection of instruments, trends, and acts, which were labelled as 'regulation'. Clearly the self-image of the discipline is uncertain. (Witness the complex ongoing debate about whether WTO law is separate from, or part of, international law proper.[149]) In part, this self-doubt is a product of the discipline's (relative) novelty compared to public international law proper, or particular aspects of international legal studies. But the problem of definition is also a result of the inherent implausibility of separating economic and business transactions from

---

[144] Seidl-Hohenveldern (n 87 above) 1–2.

[145] For a critique of the distinction between public law as regulatory, and private international law as non-regulatory see R Wai, 'Transnational Liftoff and Juridical Touchdown: The Regulatory Function of Private International Law in an Era of Globalization' (2002) 40 *Columbia Journal of Transnational Law* 209 (arguing that the regulatory function of private international law has been ignored). [146] Jackson, Davey and Sykes (n 35 above) 3.

[147] Fletcher, Mistelis and Cremona (n 1 above). [148] Petersmann (n 38 above).

[149] Pauwelyn (n 76 above).

other aspects of social life, and is a product of the proliferation of new mechanisms of obligation generally (see above at Section 3.2.1). Nowhere are these three factors of novelty, economic and social separation, and extension of forms of control, more apparent, and therefore the problem of self-definition more acute, than in relation to the correct ambit of the field of WTO law.

The problem of definition in relation to specific sub-parts of the field, such as the law of the IMF and WTO, is born, in part, of a need to respond to the challenge to its authority. This problem of what is the correct and authorized scope of international economic law in relation to institutions such as the WTO or the IMF takes two forms—one related to the geographical jurisdiction of these bodies and the other to the subject matter of their jurisdiction. Both raise questions about the community and legitimacy of the system. First, what is the appropriate geographical scope of the field? Is its authority confined solely to economic behaviour on the international plane? Does it extend into the nation state, and if so to what extent, or is the intersection of national and international the correct focus for international economic law. Much of the literature is written with this underlying problem of self-definition at its core.

Some scholarship begins from a narrow point of departure but leads to a similar question of how to define the field, from a geographical perspective. Writers may discuss what the correct role of the World Bank is in determining national policy; how interventionist should the IMF be in setting conditions for loans?; what standard of review should the WTO Appellate Body adopt in reviewing national agency decisions in relation to, say, health, or environment matters?; how should this differ from the standard of review of national agencies in relation to dumping decisions?; what should be the respective powers of the WTO's 'legislative' arm (the Ministerial Conference–General Council) as opposed to its 'judicial' arm (the Dispute Settlement Body)?; what authority does the WTO's superior tribunal (the Appellate Body) have to accept *amicus* briefs, as compared to the authority of its legislative body (the General Council) to decide when to accept briefs? In each of these discussions the key underlying issue, behind the question of the extent of competence and power of the body in question, is the question of geographical jurisdiction, namely what is the correct and authorized definition of the field? How far into national state competence can the field of international economic law intrude?

The second and related aspect of the definitional problem concerns the scope of subject matters covered by international economic law, and in particular the law of the World Trade Organization. What subjects should fall within its field of regulation?

One obvious starting point would be to assume that international trade law should be about free trade. But this turns out not to be the case.[150] As one noted commentator remarked, it is doubtful whether 'a perfectly free market

---

[150] von Bogdandy (n 48 above) 659.

economy existed anywhere else than in the minds of some liberal philosophers'.[151]
The Havana Charter, the original constitutional agreement of the first international trade organization, which was never adopted by the international
community after rejection by the US Congress, was not restricted to purely
free-trade issues and included chapters on restrictive business practices, and
even international labour standards. The founding legal instrument of the discipline, GATT 1947, includes many departures from the basic principle of
non-discrimination including allowance for duties on dumping of products and
in response to state subsidization; permission for adjustments to protect a
state's balance-of-payments situation; conditional licence to impose safeguard
measures in the event of import surges causing injury to domestic industry;
and general exceptions to non-discrimination for health, environment, and
national security reasons. Indeed the form of liberal free trade embodied by the
GATT was not classical free-market liberalism in any pure sense[152] but 'embedded liberalism' to use John Ruggie's term.[153] In this modified form of free
trade, or managed trade, an international regime for liberalization was mandated in the form of compulsory tariffication and the imposition of binding
levels of tariffs, but modified or conditioned by allowance for state intervention where necessary to protect critical national interests. Nevertheless, in subsequent years economists and lawyers argued about the details of the trading
system (should dumping duties be prohibited or not; what level of subsidies
are acceptable) but the basic paradigm[154] was assumed to encapsulate the goal
of free trade, even though the practice consists of numerous sanctioned departures from that premise.[155]

The tension between the assumption of free trade and practice of something
less meant that the history of the discipline has been one of incremental expansion of subject matter of GATT–WTO law. The system began by focusing on
tariff barriers in 1947. It gradually accommodated new issues, most notably
non-tariff barriers and subsidies in the 1979 Tokyo Round of negotiations.
The subject matters continued to extend in the 1995 Uruguay Round, explicitly

---

[151] Seidl-Hohenveldern (n 87 above) 4.

[152] JT Gathii, 'Re-Characterizing the Social in the Constitutionalization of the WTO:
A Preliminary Analysis' (2001) 7 *Widener Law Symposium Journal* 137, 138 and 149.

[153] For a discussion of the tension in GATT–WTO between embedded liberalism and neo-
liberalism see ibid, at 148–153. See also R Howse, 'From Politics to Technocracy—and Back Again:
The Fate of the Multilateral Trading Regime' (2002) 96 *American Journal of International Law*
94, 112 (presenting an account of embedded liberalism, at 96–98, and arguing, at 99, that although
originally conceived by states after the Second World War is an as a political bargain, within the
hands of an 'insider network' of GATT trade policy elites, embedded liberalism was reinterpreted
primarily in economic terms and was infused with an ideology of free trade).

[154] For an intellectual history of international trade theory and policy see Trebilcock and Howse
(n 1 above) chapter 1.

[155] For a summary of the 'legal exceptions to the obligations' see Jackson, *The World* (n 27 above)
54–55 (including waivers; exceptions for balance-of-payments; developing countries; customs union
and free trade areas; the escape clause; general exceptions for *inter alia*, health, environment and
cultural heritage; national security; renegotiation of tariff procedures, and other opt-outs).

linking non-trade issues such as intellectual property to the trade regime. Current candidates for inclusion in the WTO agreements are environment, labour, investment, competition, and trade facilitation.

In the light of this variegated and expanding background, it is not surprising that a key concern of the scholarship is what should be within and what should be outside its subject matter ambit. Sometimes this question takes the form of the 'fair trade and harmonization' debate.[156] To what extent can states impose trade measures for actions they perceive to be 'unfair' because the comparative advantage of the other state is based on weak labour, environment, or competition policies and standards? To what extent should the international community be attempting to harmonize these matters? Is it possible, in any case, to decide matters of 'fairness' in relation to international trade, when there are so many competing conceptions of appropriate models for economic development nationally, and when no normative baseline can be identified,[157] or, as one commentator puts it, 'there is no transpolitical orthodoxy that can universally validate any particular relationship between domestic policies and trade liberalization'.[158] More recently, writers have characterized this problem as one of 'linkage' and have come up with a variety of methods for deciding how, when, and what should be linked to trade.[159] Others challenge conventional wisdom which assumes there is a necessity to ask which social issues should now be 'added on' to the mandate of international trade, by arguing that social issues have always been inextricably linked with the GATT system.[160]

The problem of linkage raises the crucial question of what level of integration is embodied in any legal arrangements in international economic matters. In European law the question of integration has long been a topic of discussion. In relation to the GATT–WTO system, and particularly since the agreement on intellectual property initiated introduction of particular internationally set legal standards into domestic systems rather than just the rule against non-discrimination, the question of integration has become more prominent. Does the system mandate negative integration, encapsulated by the non-discrimination principle—states should not do certain things—or is it better represented as promoting positive integration—states should introduce these particular standards into their domestic legal systems?[161]

Allied to the integration debate is the question of harmonization, and whether or not the GATT–WTO system should facilitate the production of global norms, or protect nation state norm diversity.[162] It has always been an article

---

[156] Bhagwati and Hudec (n 135 above) 13.   [157] Hudec, *Essays* (n 32 above).
[158] Howse (n 153 above).
[159] JE Alvarez, 'Symposium: The Boundaries of the WTO' (2002) 96 *American Journal of International Law* 1.   [160] Gathii (n 152 above).
[161] Hoekman and Kostecki (n 31 above) 413.
[162] See also Pauwelyn (n 76 above) (arguing that WTO law should be seen as part of a unified system of international law, but that other more specific law should, at times, protect national diversity).

of faith of the field that nation states retain full autonomy to regulate domestic issues in whichever way they deem appropriate.[163] This view is, of course, carefully hedged with the condition that states lose national power if their actions result in interstate discrimination in trade. Moreover, the autonomy of the position about retention of the full complement of national competence is subject to encroachment from a variety of angles discussed in section 7.2.1, including the expansion of the field into areas formerly within the domestic domain, such as health; adoption of more stringent standards of review; discussion of extension of existing agreements on services; and expansion into new areas, such as investment and competition.

Once again we can see how a feature of the international economic Law discipline in general had an effect on the development of WTO constitutionalization literature in particular. Identity anxiety within international economic law led to a similar concern for the limits of the WTO both in terms of where the geographical boundaries of the community lay, and how its subject-matter limits were related to its legitimacy.

3.2.6   The urge to transformation

The final section of this chapter will argue that international economic law scholarship has long displayed a belief in its capacity to facilitate transformations in world order, and that this urge led inevitably to thinking about the WTO as representing the emergence of a new *Grundnorm*. Hence another element of constitutionalization was present in discussions of the reformed trading system as a constitutional entity.

The characteristic I want to discuss concerns the transformative nature of international economic law scholarship and the clear link between this urge and a desire to conceptualize WTO system as a constitution. The equation of international trade harmony with peace and prosperity has a long intellectual tradition going back at least as far as Kant in the seventeenth century. Modern authors saw the field as having transformative potential and argued that it was able to assist in understanding economic change and thus improving social life. Douglass North argued that the institutional theory of economics made it easier to understand 'the endless struggle of human beings to solve the problems of cooperation so that they may reap the advantages not only of technology, but also of all the other facets of human endeavor that constitute civilization'.[164]

The transformative urge of international economic law has led WTO lawyers to think about their system in heroic terms also: 'trade is but an instrument

---

[163] F Roessler, 'Diverging Domestic Policies and Multilateral Trade Integration' in JN Bhagwati and RE Hudec (eds), *Fair Trade and Harmonization: Prerequisites for Free Trade Vol 2: Legal Analysis* (2nd printing 1996) 21.   [164] North (n 5 above) 133.

to achieve nobler goals: the prevention of war; raising standards of living and the creations of jobs, not just in the rich countries but also in the developing world; political freedom and respect for human rights; social protection and equitable distribution of wealth; the fight against environmental degradation and the protection of public health; etc.'[165]

The WTO is seen by some as a step on the road towards world peace.[166] The improved institutional arrangements of WTO law, post Uruguay, could be used as a model for international order more generally.[167] On the basis of the WTO experience, the UN could link human rights to security matters and establish a stronger centralized and binding dispute resolution system. WTO law is also linked to general rights protection and increased welfare: 'The worldwide trend towards deregulation, market economies, protection of human rights and democracies reflects also an increasing recognition that individual freedom, non-discrimination and rule of law are the best conditions for promoting individual and collective self-determination and social welfare.'[168]

In between understanding and modelling, the transformative urge of international economic law scholarship takes the form of an equation between international trade harmony and international peace and security. Simply put, states that trade together rarely, if ever, go to war against each other. Linked to this is the view that *democratic* states rarely, if ever, go to war with each other. Hence the conflation of the three ideals of free market, democracy, and peace,[169] and the return to our recurring theme about the constitutional issues implicated in international economic law change. International trade rights may even be re-characterized as human rights with all the conceptual baggage that the latter connotes.[170]

In short, the transformative agenda of international economic law triggered assumptions that the WTO represented a break with the past, in the form of a new constitutionalized system. Moreover, this belief was consistent with the idea that international trade law was linked to peace and democracy. Thinking about trade as a constitutional system suddenly seemed plausible.

---

[165] Pauwelyn (n 76 above) xi.

[166] HL Schloemann and S Ohlhoff, ' "Constitutionalization" and Dispute Settlement in the WTO: National Security as an Issue of Competence' (1999) 93 *American Journal of International Law* 424, 451.

[167] E-U Petersmann, 'Constitutionalism and International Adjudication: How to Constitutionalize the UN Dispute Settlement System?' (1999) 31 *New York Journal of International Law and Politics* 753.

[168] E-U Petersmann, *The GATT/WTO Dispute Settlement System: International Law, International Organizations and Dispute Settlement* (London: Kluwer, 1997).

[169] The obverse argument minus the peace aspect is made in: Davis and Neacsu, n 55 above, (arguing, at 762, that GATT is the template for globalization, and, at 734, that globalization is a political strategy to 'internationalize capitalism through legalization'). See also Amy Chua, *World on Fire* (London: Heinemann, 2003) (arguing that export of free market democracy has intensified ethnic tension and global violence).   [170] Petersmann (n 97 above).

3.3 CONCLUSION

In this chapter I have situated the WTO constitutionalization debate within the framework of international economic law. I have suggested that six features of the general field resonate with the WTO constitutionalization debate and fuelled speculation that constitutionalization was occurring. First, international economic law loosened its parameters, beyond rules to institutions, lending credence to the idea that the trade system possessed a unity and coherence associated with the emergence of a new *Grundnorm* for a new legal order. Moreover, these institutions began to be seen as rudimentary constitutions—with all the problems of legitimacy that are conveyed by that shift. Secondly, constitutional language for the WTO arose as a natural companion to linkage of international economic law with globalization, because globalization debate assumed the conflation of economic and political mechanisms, and focused attention on the new sites of authority, specifically in law. Thirdly, the trade liberalization consensus in the general literature gave rise to speculation that a community of trade may exist sufficient to constitute a new legal order. Fourthly, the focus on regulation in international economic law encouraged discussion of procedure and deliberative process, another key element of constitutionalization. Moreover, it inhibited discussion of particular goals and allowed WTO constitutionalization to be portrayed, initially at least, as a relatively uncontroversial, procedural solution to reasonable disagreement between states: a constitution without politics perhaps. Fifthly, the fixation of international economic law with its identity provoked anxiety within WTO scholarship about its definition. This led to discussion of its geographical competence and subject-matter authority—again constitutional concepts were on the table. Sixthly, the transformative agenda of international economic law has fuelled similar assumptions that the WTO marked a break in the old trading order and inaugurated a new constitutional system. Additionally, the transformative belief of the discipline led free trade to be necessarily linked with democracy, and the idea of speaking about international trade in a constitutional register seemed natural in this context.

PART II

THREE VISIONS OF WTO CONSTITUTIONALIZATION

4

Institutional Managerialism

4.1 INTRODUCTION

Drawing on the discussions in Part I, this part of the book will analyse three models of WTO constitutionalization. The aims of these three central chapters are to scrutinize the WTO models, and to use them to think about the template of constitutionalization we began with in the first place: what is 'constitutional' about the WTO models of constitutionalization, and what do the WTO versions tell us about our original conception of what constitutes constitutionalization outside the context of the nation state?

The first model discussed in this chapter will be labelled institutional managerialism. The model is based largely upon the writings of Professor John Jackson, whose seminal work, *The World Trade Organization: Constitution and Jurisprudence*, published in 1998,[1] set the agenda and tone for the WTO constitutionalization debate.

Jackson's project was a far-sighted one. It was radical to the extent that it conceptualized the trading system in an entirely new way, clothing it with legitimacy, and suggesting a new legal basis for what had previously been seen as a simple international treaty arrangement. It was prescient in its focus on finding a means to negotiate differences between states in a context where they were becoming profoundly interdependent; to this extent it prefigured the globalization debate. Yet institutional managerialism claimed modesty, too, in that it sought simply to describe, albeit in new terms, the nature of the changes in international trade, which, many already felt, were leading to a different sort of international orientation. Without the vision and conviction

---

[1] JH Jackson, *The World Trade Organization: Constitution and Jurisprudence* (London: Royal Institute of International Affairs, 1998) [hereinafter Jackson, *WTO Constitution*]. Other work in the institutional mould includes: D Esty, 'The World Trade Organization's Legitimacy Crisis' (2002) 1 *World Trade Review* 7; A von Bogdandy, 'Law and Politics in the WTO—Strategies to Cope with a Deficient Relationship' in JA Frowein and R Wolfrum (eds), *Max Planck Yearbook of United Nations Law*, Vol 5 (2001); JP Trachtman, 'The Theory of the Firm and the Theory of the International Economic Organization: Toward Comparative Institutional Analysis' (1997) 17 *Northwestern Journal of International Law and Business* 470; CE Barfield, *Free Trade, Sovereignty, Democracy: The Future of the World Trade Organization* (Washington DC: American Enterprise Institute, 2001); and, D Steger and PVD Bossche, 'WTO Dispute Settlement: Emerging Practice and Procedure' in (1998) *American Society of International Law: Proceedings of the 92nd Annual Meeting* 79.

of Professor Jackson's institutional managerialism, the WTO constitutional project would never have got off the ground. Nevertheless the approach has problems.

The general argument of the chapter is that institutional managerialism is characterized by three tensions.

- The first of these concerns the model's focus on *institutions*, which are represented as the *constitution* of international trade law. The problem here is that the use of the language of constitutionalism to unify and legitimize changes in the WTO contains some uncertainties, absences, and contradictions. Uncertainty exists about its content: does it include features ordinarily conceived of as constitutional? By whose authority were these features created? Absent also are some of the principles of elaborated constitutionalization such as institutional balance, and the ability to determine competence between constitutional organs, although these are not essential to our received account. Moreover, the approach is ambiguous because it tells a number of conflicting histories about the role institutions played in the development of constitutionalization. Facts about those institutions, which are said to justify constitutionalization, are uncontested.

- The second tension in the model is characterized by a desire to *manage* international trade relations by way of a system of *rules*. Again, there are difficulties. Rules alone do not ensure a system's legitimacy. Rules, especially where in the service of management, may be applied by bureaucrats, schooled in technical expertise, rather than lawyers applying law. These rules may be applied in a political and discretionary manner, rather than an apparently objective legal fashion. Moreover, management may lead to open-ended results which cannot be relied upon in future situations, or which favour a more (economically) powerful actor over a less powerful actor. This form of constitutionalization also assumes a set of classical economic values which privilege notions of trade liberalization and free trade over other social, political, and economic goals. Management constitutionalization could lead to a greater penetration of WTO law into national legal systems, sometimes at the expense of national policies; a drift toward uniformity of national law; and the classic legislative 'race to the bottom', especially in relation to environmental and social laws.

- The third and final tension in the approach is its use of an *empirical* method for deriving the existence of a constitution for the WTO, coupled with a desire to *transform* the international economic order. This feature, though, has a number of deficiencies. Most significant is the difficulty of separating the facts, upon which constitutionalization was supposed to be based, from the constitutionalization process itself. The separation of the pre-constitutional from the constitutional is artificial, and neglects the reflexive relationship between law and facts in forming a constitutional process. Also left out of the account are private laws structuring the entities that operate in the WTO, such as domestic property and contract law, and related international laws, such as conflicts laws, commercial law, and corporation law. The absence of these pre-constitutional facts produces an inchoate and under-inclusive picture of WTO constitutionalization.

In short, what is distinctive about this particular combination of management, institutions, rules, facts, and desires is that it creates the illusion of being a flexible, neutral, technocratic constitution while running the risk of becoming a self-legitimating, bureaucratic, insufficiently deliberative, and legalistic constitution which appeals to a predominantly classical economic *telos* and, indirectly, intrudes on national regulatory function and diversity.

Finally, the chapter will show the way in which discussion of each of these three tensions intersects with the elements of the received account of constitutionalization and raises questions about the accuracy and suitability of that account. So the first tension alerts us to the problem of *Grundnorm* change and legitimacy; the second brings into focus deliberative process, and to a lesser extent community; and the third gives rise again to discussion of *Grundnorm* change. The critique is set out in detail as follows.

4.2   FEATURES OF INSTITUTIONAL MANAGERIAL CONSTITUTIONALIZATION

4.2.1   Institutions and constitutions

Institutional managerialism, is, as the name suggests, based on the idea that institutions constitute the international trading system. Institutions are broadly defined[2] to take in a wide range of structures and entities including, the treaty arrangements of the WTO, dispute settlement processes, actors and organization, and a range of other informal features.[3] The point is that rules alone

---

[2] It should be recalled that institutions comprise formal and informal rules and formation processes, actors, and organizations that seek to maximize wealth by minimizing transaction costs, but the actions of those elements are path-dependent to the extent that they are influenced by pre-existing power distributions, and are also influenced by a broader set of cultural factors: see definition in Chapter 3, especially nn 2–9 and accompanying text. WTO constitutionalists who see the WTO in terms of institutionalism largely follow international relations conceptions of an institution either in the form of 'regime theory' or institutional economics. See also MA Levy, OR Young and M Zurn, 'The Study of International Regimes' (1995) 1 *European Journal of International Relations* 267 [hereinafter Levy, *et al*, 'International Regimes'] (stating that GATT and WTO international relations scholars adopt 'new institutionalism', which the authors define as the examination of the behaviour of actors in regime formation, the process of formation of regimes, and the social forces driving it).

[3] JH Jackson, WJ Davey and AO Sykes, *Legal Problems of International Economic Relations* 3rd edn (St Paul, Minn: West, 1995) [hereinafter Jackson, Davey and Sykes, *Legal Problems*, 3rd edn] see chapter headings and content of chapters 5–7; Jackson, *WTO Constitution*, (n 1 above) 6; and JH Jackson, *The World Trading System: Law and Policy of International Economic Relations* 2nd edn (Cambridge, Mass and London: MIT Press, 1997) [hereinafter Jackson, *The World Trading System*] chapter 2.

cannot construct an international trading system, and that governments ought to be aware of the new currency, so to speak, of trade.[4] From this perspective, then, institutions are promoted as a panacea for international trading problems[5] and institutions are the key to the constitutionalization of the WTO.[6]

The conceptualization of the WTO as an institutional system, and not a rules-only system, has important consequences, especially in relation to the received account of constitutionalization. The institutional conception vests WTO law with a unity and coherence. This coherence, according to its adherents, indicates that WTO law has been transformed from a simple set of rules into a new legal order: a new foundational device or *Grundnorm* has emerged sufficient to ground a new system of law. From here it is a relatively short step to the claim that WTO constitutionalization is occurring.

The focus on institutions matters for other reasons as well. First, institutionalism enables the model to distinguish itself from a realist approach according to which international relations are conducted on the basis, primarily, of states seeking to expand their power in a world of insecurity.[7] At the same time it distinguishes itself from a liberal approach according to which the members of the society, whether individual or collective, are the fundamental actors of international relations, and the state represents those members, and acts in accordance with their preferences, and not as a result of institutional pressures.[8] The institutional emphasis of this mode of constitutionalization makes the primary subject of analysis the WTO, rather than the state (realism) or its citizens (liberalism). It focuses on what the institution does,[9] not what the state or other members of society, whether individual or collective, desire. Accordingly, institutionalism is important because it deflects attention

---

[4] Jackson, Davey, and Sykes, *Legal Problems*, 3rd edn.

[5] AV Deardorff, 'Market Access for Developing Countries' in RB Porter, *et al*, (eds), *Efficiency, Equity, and Legitimacy: The Multilateral Trading System at the Millennium* (Washington DC: Brookings Institution Press, 2001) 167 (arguing that institutional mechanisms are the only way to escape the problem that 'attempts by the poor countries of the world to escape poverty will stimulate protection in the rich countries, and this protection makes the escape from poverty more difficult').

[6] See eg Jackson (n 1 above) and Jackson, *The World Trading System* (n 3 above) 49 (stating that 'one of the most important problems facing the world today is institutional'); von Bogdandy (n 1 above); Trachtman (n 1 above); Barfield (n 1 above); Steger and Bossche (n 1 above). For an explicit adoption of the institutional approach see P Holmes, 'The WTO and the EU: Some Constitutional Comparisons' in G de Búrca and J Scott (eds), *The EU and the WTO: Legal and Constitutional Issues* (2001) (contrasting what he refers to as the 'institutional "constitutions" of the EU and the WTO').

[7] For a description of realism in the context of the WTO see for eg, PM Nichols, 'Forgotten Linkages—Historical Institutionalism and Sociological Institutionalism and Analysis of the World Trade Organization' (1998) 19 *University of Pennsylvania Journal of International Economic Law* 461, 465.

[8] For a description of liberalism in the context of the WTO see, eg, ibid 466–467 n 27.

[9] One commentator of this school describes his approach as avowedly 'functionalist': Jackson, *The World Trading System* (n 3 above) 27.

away from the particular questions of state interest and preferences—for example, whether states want to conceive of world trade as consisting of a constitution—encourages us to look beyond the WTO's intergovernmental nature, and focuses thinking on the WTO as a thing-in-itself, a regime, a concept which is more than the sum of its parts.

In addition to it being premised upon institutions, institutional managerialism is based upon a blending of the concept of institution with the concept of a constitution, often without explanation of how this occurred, what similarities and differences there are between the two ideas, or the consequences of such a melding. John Jackson has long focused 'on the institutional side, on what I call the "constitution" of the world trading system'.[10] Indeed the centrality of institutions and their association with a constitution of world trade pervades his entire body of work. According to Robert Howse, in 1990, Jackson was the first person to propose that any new GATT structure be in the form of 'a "constitution" for global trade'.[11] The third edition of his jointly authored casebook, published four years later, continued to will the idea into being when it referred to a need to understand 'the "international constitution" of the world trading system'.[12] In 1997, the pattern is repeated when the new WTO Agreement is embraced as a 'new institutional charter for an organisation'.[13] A year later, Jackson produced what became a key text in the constitutionalization debate: *The World Trade Organization: Constitution and Jurisprudence*, and the symbiotic relationship between institutions and constitutions was cemented once and for all.[14]

In terms of the received account of constitutionalization, this conflation had the added effect of enhancing the institution's legitimacy in two ways. First, the description of the institution as a constitution caused ideas ordinarily associated with democracy to be grafted on to the WTO project. So, for example, the WTO was described in institutional terms as a 'Club Model' which facilitated democratic cooperation.[15] Or the current round of trade negotiations

---

[10] JH Jackson, 'The WTO "Constitution" and Proposed Reforms: Seven "Mantras" Revisited' (2001) 4 *Journal of International Economic Law* 67 [hereinafter Jackson, 'Seven Mantras'] 70.

[11] R Howse, 'Tribute—The House that Jackson Built: Restructuring the GATT' (1999) 20 *Michigan Journal of International Law* 107, 108 (arguing that Jackson's proposal for the Canadian government during the Uruguay round instigated the discussion of the new institution as a 'charter' or 'constitution').   [12] Jackson, Davey and Sykes, *Legal Problems*, 3rd edn (n 3 above) 3.

[13] Jackson, *The World Trading System* (n 3 above) 4.

[14] Jackson, *WTO Constitution* (n 1 above) 5. See also JT Gathii, 'Re-Characterizing the Social in the Constitutionalization of the WTO: A Preliminary Analysis' (2001) 7 *Widener Law Symposium Journal* 137, 137 n 4 (quoting John Jackson arguing that 'one common focus for the discussions... deal[s] with a form of "constitutional law"...embracing a variety of interconnected governmental institutions as well as evolving practice [sic] of many such institutions. The focus is truly the "world trading system", and its legal framework—that which we can here call the "constitution"'.).

[15] R Keohane and J Nye, 'The Club Model of Multilateral Cooperation and Problems of Democratic Legitimacy' in RB Porter, *et al* (eds), *Efficiency, Equity, and Legitimacy: The Multilateral Trading System at the Millennium* (2001).

was referred to as a 'Global Constitutional Convention' that will define 'core principles, establish...international standards, and creat[e] institutions'.[16]

Secondly, the WTO's legitimacy quotient was extended by the very breadth of the term 'constitution'. WTO scholars focused on 'the constitution of the WTO in the broad meaning of the word "constitution"', and stated that this included not only the organization itself but a 'larger landscape that forms the "constitution of the world's trading system"'.[17] This landscape extended to the structure of the organization, its treaty base, its dispute resolution procedures, and the relationship between each of these and the GATT, including the practices and procedures of the earlier organization—its *acquis* in European terms.[18] By moving beyond the narrow study of formal rules to study 'informal mechanisms and practice' as well as organizations,[19] institutional managerial constitutionalization shored up the project by implying that it had already achieved a certain amount of legitimacy.

The institutional model of constitutionalization, conceived of as institutional managerialism, also expanded the WTO constitutionalization project in a spatial sense. The WTO was portrayed as encompassing both internal and external constitutional dimensions. The external dimension referred to its over-arching rules and institutions and their effect in managing economic interdependence. The relationship between the WTO and Member States would be one example. The relationship between various institutions of the international order, including international law itself, existing organizations, such as the ILO, and perhaps even new ones, such as a putative global environmental organization, were all embraced as part of a 'global constitutionalism'.[20]

But the watershed constitutional moment in the development of the institutional constitutional perspective was the emergence of the internal constitutional dimension to the WTO; it is this dimension which forever transformed the system from one of management or diplomacy into a rules-based constitution. The internal constitution[21] was said to consist of the internal workings of the WTO itself, the structure of its internal organization, the functions of each part of the organization, the particular rules that are made under its auspices, and the underlying principles that inform their operation. According to the institutional managerial model, the international trade law system could not be described as 'constitutionalized' prior to 1995 because it did not possess such an internal order. Indeed, the original GATT suffered from numerous

---

[16] D Esty, 'The World Trade Organization's Legitimacy Crisis' (2002) 1 *World Trade Review* 7, 12.

[17] Jackson, *WTO Constitution* (n 1 above) 14.

[18] ibid 6. This broad definition has much in common with international relations regime theories noted above, n 2.   [19] Jackson, 'Seven Mantras' (n 10 above) 71.

[20] Esty (n 16 above) 19 (arguing that the WTO should be 'seen as a crucial element of the emerging international governance system'). Note that institutionalists explicitly include international law as one of the components of the emerging 'constitution' of international trade: see Jackson, Davey and Sykes, *Legal Problems*, 3rd edn (n 3 above) 244.

[21] Jackson, 'Seven Mantras' (n 10 above) 71.

'birth defects' that militated against its acceptance as a constitutional order.[22] These defects included the power of an individual state to block adoption by the GATT governing body of a dispute settlement report inimical to that state's interests. As a result, the non-constitutionalized GATT 1947 simply 'limped along', and it is a 'tribute to the pragmatism and ingenuity of many of its leaders' that it managed to function so effectively.[23] In a somewhat more optimistic assessment, some claimed that the 'Club Model' of the WTO and its technocratic decision-making process were highly successful in opening markets, liberalizing trade, and reducing protectionism, but were not ultimately suited for contemporary conditions which demanded less emphasis on technical expertise and more emphasis on institutional legitimacy.[24] With the conclusion of the Uruguay Round in 1995, all institutional constitutionalists agreed that a new structure was born. Important deficiencies were overcome, and a constitution came into being. Before that date, management by diplomatic means alone was the order of the day, and the rules were merely an unconstitutionalized melange of laws. This interpretation is reminiscent of that aspect of the received account of constitutionalization that emphasizes the importance of *Grundnorm* change. The sudden change of a set of legal arrangements into an internally sophisticated organization was symptomatic of a larger break between the former unconstitutionalized system and the present constitutionalized system.

So what other legitimating functions are served by suggesting that institutions are the basis for a constitutionalization process? In the view of some international relations theorists, institutions such as the GATT and the WTO thrive because of their practical functions: they stabilize mutual expectations, and reduce transaction and information costs.[25] They enhance cooperation, bestow authority, facilitate learning, redistribute domestic resources, lead to internal political change, and contribute to the rise of transnational issue networks.[26]

Legal scholars with a preference for this form of institutional constitutionalization note that institutions perform a number of other useful roles. Institutions *temper the harshness of markets*. Economics should not operate in the absence of 'human institutions',[27] because, as Douglass North argues, institutions can act as constraints on the excesses of the market and the strictness of classical economic theory. During the international financial crises of 1997 and 1998,[28] a 'potential meltdown of the economic system' was avoided because institutions constrained the market and limited welfare-harming state behaviour.[29] The implication is that without institutions, free markets would run roughshod

---

[22] Jackson, *The World Trading System* (n 3 above).
[23] Jackson, *WTO Constitution* (n 1 above) 19.   [24] Esty (n 16 above) 10–12.
[25] Levy, Young and Zurn (n 2 above) 287.   [26] ibid 304–306.
[27] JH Jackson, 'International Economic Law in Times that are Interesting' (2000) 3 *Journal of International Economic Law* 3 [hereinafter Jackson, 'Interesting Times'] 4.   [28] ibid 5.
[29] ibid 3–5.

over welfare concerns, and the corollary is that with institutions markets can be controlled. The legitimacy of a system that includes institutions is enhanced, and the constitutionalization process, conceived of in an institutional form, is rendered a benign welfare-increasing force.

Additionally, institutional managerialism follows Douglass North, who used institutional history as a means to tell the story of why some economies evolved while others did not, to vest institutions with great *explanatory* power in telling the story of the history of constitutionalized international trade. The early origins of constitutionalization are represented as coincident with the emergence of the institutions of free trade. First there was the Hanseatic League. Then came the law merchant and its subsequent incorporation into English law. The unilateral free-trade experience of Great Britain in the nineteenth century followed and was formative in the creation of the origins of a constitutionalized trade system. The Great Depression, the collapse of the League of Nations, and the inter-war period encouraged the view that countries which trade freely are less inclined to go to war with each other. Then came the establishment of the Bretton Woods institutions, and the rise of the provisionally applied GATT 1947. This was followed by a series of trading rounds which gradually liberalized the tariff system and eventually led to the establishment of a new organization. The new entity had a diverse membership, institutional formality, procedures for binding dispute settlement, and hence, in the view of Jackson, Davey, and Sykes, the organization—the institution—was transformed into one with a constitutional nature.[30]

Yet institutions do more than enhance the legitimacy of the WTO constitutionalization story by linking it to a credible developmental history and constraining markets. According to the institutional managerialist view of constitutionalization, they also *provide the means to distribute goods* accrued from increased trade. Institutions 'spread the benefits of prosperity of world trade'.[31] If constitutionalization is to live up to its reputation for enhancing fairness, then institutions are a means to facilitate fairness because they are a vehicle for the redistribution of public goods. Negotiations to open up agricultural markets of the developed countries, though notoriously slow, would be one example of the fairness-enhancing role of the institutions of the WTO. Without the institutional developments of the GATT, agricultural markets would have remained forever closed. Improving market access for developing states' textiles and clothing is another example of the way institutions secure a modicum of fairness in the market. Institutional managerialism suggests that, although

---

[30] Various versions of these events are familiar to many narratives of the constitutionalization process. See eg, Jackson, Davey and Sykes, *Legal Problems*, 3rd edn (n 3 above) 4–5, and 293–298; Jackson, *The World Trading System* (n 3 above) 35–44. This book relates a similar story in chapter 1 to explain the genesis of the connection between constitutionalization and trade.

[31] ibid; and see Kofi Annan in JH Jackson, WJ Davey and AO Sykes, *Legal Problems of International Economic Relations*, 4th edn (St Paul, Minn: West, 2002) 1214 stating that the WTO's 'vital task' is 'extending the benefits of free trade' to the developing world.

neither set of negotiations has yet resulted in a redistribution that many would classify as just, there have been improvements, and the potential for fairer distribution remains. In sum, institutional managerialism purports to include a core component of legitimacy because the model enhances welfare, explains history, and distributes goods.

Alternatively, some argue that the purpose of conceptualizing trade as an institution is not to serve these ends, but instead simply to analyse trade using the tools of institutional theory. For example, Joel Trachtman argues that 'business firms and [international economic organizations] have some characteristics in common'[32] and so can both be examined by focusing on their institutional face. Accordingly, he takes the insights of transaction-cost analysis and applies them to the 'linked problems of competence and governance of such organizations'.[33] Trachtman's application of a (law and economics) institutional approach to trade leads him to the view that, for example, power allocation between international economic institutions and states is similar to intra-firm centralization and decentralization, and so both problems could be analysed usefully through the same institutional approach.[34] Similarly, one could view international dispute resolution as one way to 'complete the contract', or the treaty as the case may be, in much the same way that domestic law and dispute resolution provides the 'thick context' for completion of domestic contracts.[35]

To summarize, the institutional aspect of the majority approach is based on fostering a relationship between institutions and constitutions, and this reflects aspects of the received account of constitutionalization in a number of ways. The focus on institutions, not rules, suggests that an otherwise disparate system of rules is unified and coherent, and that a new *Grundnorm* has emerged. The approach assumes that institutions can be equated with, or at least are compatible with, constitutions, and so promotes the legitimacy of WTO constitutionalization characterized in this form. The institutional basis of WTO constitutionalization has an external dimension, which includes relationships of power-sharing between WTO bodies, and between the WTO and states. The institutional–constitutional structure also possesses an internal dimension, consisting of the internal structures of the WTO, and it is this dimension which, it is claimed, inaugurated the constitutionalization of the WTO and overcame the defects of the previous GATT system. Institutional managerialism portrays the constitution of the WTO beginning in 1995 with a clear

---

[32] JP Trachtman, 'The Theory of the Firm and the Theory of the International Economic Organization: Toward Comparative Institutional Analysis' (1997) 17 *Northwestern Journal of International Law and Business* 470, 472.

[33] ibid 471. Trachtman draws on the literature of new institutional economics, law and economics and industrial organizations to develop his analysis.

[34] According to Trachtman the same approach applies to such issues as adaptation to changed local circumstances; costs of information transfer; and effective use of scarce central management time, ibid 534.   [35] ibid 525–528.

break between legal systems suggestive of *Grundnorm* change. Finally, the approach suggests that institutionalism is justified because institutions temper markets, distribute public goods, and provide the best evidence of the constitutional development of international trade.

Against these claims of compatibility, scope, and justification, a number of criticisms can be levelled. First, the approach fails to distinguish between an institution and a constitution. As discussed above,[36] an institution is a bundle of formal and informal rules, organizations, procedures and actors, and cultural factors influencing their formation. By contrast, and as also discussed above,[37] a constitution is a sub-category of an institution; it is a higher order set of social practices possessing coherence and including a rule of recognition for identifying practices belonging to the order, which is authorized by a community involved in its creation and deliberation, and, which enjoys a widespread level of social acceptance. It is not clear, on the evidence, that the WTO has, as yet, met these higher order demands. It is, of course, an international institution of some importance, but to label it constitutional confuses the definition of an institution with a constitution.

Secondly, and relatedly, the conflation of institutions with constitutions has the effect of formally legitimizing institutional developments at the WTO, without the institution having to go through the process of democratic authorization by a defined constitutional community, an element normally associated with core constitutionalization. By virtue of the very invocation of the term 'constitutional', the developments which are institutional by nature are vested with other connotations of social acceptance, political legitimacy, and perhaps also with the inference that they contain elements of elaborated constitutionalization such as separation of powers and rule of law.

Moreover, this conflation of the two concepts ignores the constitutive role international legal commentators have on transforming an institution into a constitution,[38] a role more readily acknowledged by scholars of European constitutionalization[39] than WTO constitutionalization. So while an institution ordinarily refers to a structural framework for a related group of organizations, ideas, principles, actors, and processes, and a constitution carries with it some notion of legitimacy, the institutional managerialist approach to

---

[36] See Chapter 3 at section 3.1.1 for a definition of institution.

[37] See Chapter 2 *passim* and Chapter 3 at section 3.1.1 for a definitional distinction between institution and constitution.

[38] Nichols claims that it was John Jackson's study of the international trade regime commissioned by the Royal Institute of International Affairs at the commencement of the Uruguay Round, which was endorsed by the European Commission, that helped create the World Trade Organization: Nichols (n 7 above) 504 n 183. A similar story is told by Howse (n 11 above).

[39] See for eg JHH Weiler and JP Trachtman, 'European Constitutionalism and its Discontents' (1997) 17 *Northwestern Journal of International Law and Business* 354 (acknowledging that one of the three 'substrata' of constitutionalization was the work of legal academics, the other two being doctrine and social science).

constitutionalization of the WTO, rooted, as it is, in institutional economics, can appear oblivious to such differences.[40]

Thirdly, by broadening the field of study to take in a wide variety of institutional developments and then naming it constitutionalization, this approach lends the field a coherence it might otherwise have lacked. This in turn reinforces the view that the WTO has undergone *Grundnorm* change although no new hypothesis exists to found a new legal system. Instead, many disparate developments have been interpreted as evidence of a constitutionalization process, because the parameters of study have been so broadened. Otherwise related but relatively discrete events are interpreted to fit within a broad notion of what an institution is and this idea is elided with the term constitution. The result is that the developments are conceptualized as belonging to the same system, and one which has a certain logic or coherence. The developments are invested with constitutional significance, when they may be merely examples of healthy institutional growth.

Fourthly, support for the claim that the establishment of the WTO signalled the emergence of a new *Grundnorm* is not clearly visible on the basis of the text of the agreements. The authoritative criteria for identifying the rules of obligation under the pre-constitutionalized GATT legal system were the general rules of international law, including those of custom, treaty (the GATT itself), general principles, and judicial decisions.[41] So in order for a new WTO system to emerge as a system separate from general international law, it would have to establish a different authoritative criterion, a different rule of recognition, perhaps one that could be located in the new treaty arrangements. It might be argued, then, that the new entity is 'legally distinct'[42] from the GATT,[43] because it is binding in character,[44] it includes a new organizational structure, a new amendment procedure,[45] new decision-making methods,[46] and new dispute settlement procedures.[47] Moreover, what counts as law for the purposes

---

[40] An alternative institutional approach would be to acknowledge, as does sociological institutionalism, that cultural factors, such as a desire to confer social legitimacy on the organization, play a role in institutional development, and that institutions are not just the product of entrepreneurs deciding that the benefits outweigh the costs of its creation: Nichols (n 7 above) 485.

[41] The sources of international law are defined in the Statute of the International Court of Justice, Article 38.

[42] Art II.3 Agreement Establishing the World Trade Organization, *The Results of the Uruguay Round of Multilateral Trade Negotiations: The Legal Texts* (1994); GATT Doc No MTN/FA, 33 ILM (1994) 1125. [hereinafter WTO Agreement].

[43] Nichols (n 7 above) 490 n 123 especially. Nichols notes also, at 491, that an institutionalist approach grounded in historical institutionalism would suit this viewpoint because it could be used to argue that Uruguay signified a critical juncture or historical cleavage in the path dependency of the international trade system.   [44] WTO Agreement, Art II.2.

[45] ibid, Art X.   [46] ibid, Art IX.

[47] Understanding on Rules and Procedures Governing the Settlement of Disputes, Annex 2, WTO Agreement [hereinafter DSU] 404.

of the new system is newly defined by the new Agreement,[48] and includes a range of new subject matters within its jurisdiction.[49] Finally, the all-or-nothing nature of the new system is indicated by the fact that the new system permits of no reservations.[50]

Nevertheless, strong arguments can be mounted that no new system has emerged, and the current system is merely a continuation of the old GATT, and, at the most, a sub-system of international law proper.[51] The WTO system conserves and continues GATT decision-making practice,[52] affirms the relevance of GATT principles of management of disputes,[53] and the AB refers to GATT panel reports in its reasoning. Acceptance of the WTO was limited, initially at least, to GATT contracting parties,[54] indicating that the Members themselves did not perceive themselves as inaugurating a new global trade system. Moreover, the text explicitly situates WTO dispute settlement within the framework of international law,[55] indicating that the system is seamlessly connected to international law and does not stand on its own. In short, textual evidence does not clearly indicate that a new *Grundnorm* has emerged, establishing a separate WTO legal order.

Fifthly, this putative process of constitutionalization is fraught with uncertainty as to its content. It is not always possible to know exactly what it is that is being constitutionalized or to judge either the accuracy of the claim to constitutionalization or the desirability of that development. Beyond identifying the broad contours of the constitutional vision of the approach, it is not apparent what it contains. Instead, the approach simply posits a 'constitution', and then goes on to describe it by listing an expansive category of things (organization, treaty, dispute resolution, relationship between each of the aforementioned, *acquis*) with no defining feature other than the fact that they are

---

[48] WTO Agreement Article II.4 provides that the law of the WTO comprises 'agreements and associated legal instruments' included in the Annexes to the WTO Charter. These Annexes include not only the agreements on substantive matters such as sanitary and phytosanitary issues, anti-dumping, and safeguards, but, the GATT 1994, which itself consists of GATT 1947, the pre-1995 tariff concessions, protocols of accessions, waivers, decisions, and understandings of particular articles.

[49] These include the elaboration of GATT principles on product standards and health in agreements on technical barriers to trade (Agreement on Technical Barriers to Trade, Annex 1A, WTO Agreement), and sanitary and phytosanitary protection (Agreement on the Application of Sanitary and Phytosanitary Measures, Annex 1A, WTO Agreement) respectively, and the extension of WTO into intellectual property (Agreement on Trade-Related Aspects of Intellectual Property Rights, Annex 1C, WTO Agreement) and services (General Agreement on Trade in Services, Annex 1B, WTO Agreement).   [50] WTO Agreement, Art XVI.

[51] J Pauwelyn, *Conflict of Norms in Public International Law: How WTO Law Relates to other Rules of International Law* (Cambridge: CUP, 2003).   [52] WTO Agreement, Art IX.1

[53] DSU, Art 3.1.

[54] Decision on the Acceptance of and Accession to the Agreement Establishing the World Trade Organization, *The Results of the Uruguay Round of Multilateral Trade Negotiations: The Legal Texts* 466 (1994).

[55] DSU 3.2 provides that the dispute settlement system is to 'clarify the existing provisions of [the] agreements in accordance with customary rules of interpretation of public international law'.

WTO-related. The institutional managerial definition of what is a constitution, is, ultimately, circular: the WTO is a constitution because it includes these things which are constitutional, and these things are constitutional because they are part of the WTO constitution.

This is not an argument for dreaming up a rigorous list of constitutional indices and matching it to the WTO. But in order for the claim of WTO constitutionalization to be convincing, it is necessary to attempt to identify and problematize the defining features of any supposed constitutionalization process, as has been done in this study and in other work,[56] even if the definition is provisional in nature. Without this, there is uncertainty as to whether what is being described is a constitution, or, for example, just another international treaty arrangement, or indeed an 'imaginary' constitution.[57] By not delineating what it is that binds these seemingly unrelated elements into a constitution, the approach cannot clarify its terms, or convince us that the sum of the things described is a constitution.

Sixthly, for an institution with constitutional aspirations, it is also odd that the WTO does not include any principles to govern the relationships between its various parts. Although a strict separation of powers doctrine is not essential to the core constitutionalization model, some notion of delineation of tasks between entities, and respect for the jurisdiction of each other, is likely to be presumed in a constitutional body. Yet, the AB has, in *dicta*, rejected the existence within the WTO of any principle of what it calls, institutional balance,[58] according to which each organ would pay due regard to the competence of another. Moreover, it has allowed uncertainty to persist about the conditions under which an adjudicative organ of the WTO will have the competence to decide a matter which could plausibly also be decided by another (political) organ. This problem has particular piquancy in relation to states seeking to rely on two of the more controversial exceptions to non-discrimination permitted under GATT, trade restrictions imposed for balance-of-payments reasons,[59] and restrictions imposed upon formation of a customs union.[60] Under the Agreements, these matters may be considered before either the adjudicative organs or the relevant political committee, namely the Committee on Balance of Payments, or the Committee on Regional Trade Agreements (RTAs). In relation to RTAs, the AB has expressed ambivalence about whether panels

---

[56] A number of writers have developed constitutional templates and attempted to apply them, with more or less success, to the WTO. See, eg, N Walker, 'The EU and the WTO: Constitutionalism in a New Key' in G de Búrca and J Scott (eds), *The EU and the WTO: Legal and Constitutional Issues* (Oxford and Portland, Oregon: Hart Publishing, 2001).

[57] D Kennedy, 'The International Style in Postwar Law and Policy' (1994) 1 *Utah Law Review* 7, 102.

[58] WTO, Report of the Appellate Body, *India—Quantitative Restrictions on Imports of Agricultural, Textile and Industrial Products*, WT/DS90/AB/R (23 August 1999), DSR 1999:IV, 1763 at para 105. [59] GATT 1947, Art XVIII:B

[60] ibid, Art XXIV.

possess the competence to decide if a particular free-trade agreement is compatible with the relevant GATT provision,[61] declining to answer the question on the grounds of judicial economy.[62] Moreover, when it came to addressing whether the AB had such a power, the AB again evaded the question on prudential grounds,[63] and left the issue unresolved.[64] This is despite the fact that the RTA Committee is considered by many to be a weak institution and has never found any regional trade agreement to be incompatible with Article XXIV.[65] The relative competence of political and adjudicative bodies over decisions in respect of balance-of-payments is a little clearer. The AB has stated that seizure of the issue by the relevant political organ (the Committee on Balance of Payments) does not detract from a panel's competence in dealing with the matter;[66] thereby permitting a 'dual track approach'.[67] In short, there is no clear map of inter-institutional relationships, consistent with a constitutional body, within the WTO.

Seventhly, in respect of the claim that constitutionalization simply evolved out of institutional development, this serves to naturalize the thesis. The history of constitutionalization is presented, in this account, as a history of institutions, with the result that constitutionalization is absorbed into a story about the establishment, development, and growth of institutions. This has mutual benefits for constitutionalization and for institutions. The institutions are vested with the normative cachet of being part of a constitutional project, and the constitutional project garners some of the respectability and solidity associated with institutional growth. So constitutionalization, in this model, does not appear only (if at all) at the level of ideas; it is a natural outgrowth of real, concrete, institutional change. Institutions vest the history of constitutionalization with plausible explanatory power. From this perspective, the legitimacy of constitutionalization process is enhanced because it is linked to institutions.

---

[61] GATT 1947, Art XXIV.

[62] The tribunal has said that it was 'not called upon to answer' the question. It did, however, offer some support for the Panel's competence by 'noting' that the Panel had such power in respect of restrictions imposed for balance-of-payments reasons WTO, Report of the Appellate Body, *Turkey—Restrictions on Imports of Textile and Clothing Products*, WT/DS34/AB/R (22 October 1999), [1999] 6 DSR 2345, DSR 1999:VI, 2345 at para 60.

[63] The matter was not appealed: WTO, Report of the Appellate Body, *Turkey—Restrictions on Imports of Textile and Clothing Products*, WT/DS34/AB/R (22 October 1999), [1999] 6 DSR 2345 at para 60.

[64] The lack of resolution on this issue seemed to be acknowledged as a problem in the penultimate paragraph of the decisions, which stated that the tribunal had made 'no finding on many other issues that may arise': WTO, Report of the Appellate Body, *Turkey—Restrictions on Imports of Textile and Clothing Products*, WT/DS34/AB/R (22 October 1999), [1999] 6 DSR 2345 at para 65.

[65] RE Hudec and JD Southwick, 'Regionalism and WTO Rules: Problems in the Fine Art of Discriminating Fairly' in M Mendoza, P Low and B Kotschar (eds), *Trade Rules in the Making: Challenges in Regional and Multilateral Negotiations* (Washington: Brookings Institution Press, 1999) 52.

[66] WTO, Report of the Appellate Body, *India—Quantitative Restrictions on Imports of Agricultural, Textile and Industrial Products*, WT/DS90/AB/R (23 August 1999), DSR 1999:IV, 1763.

[67] ibid at para 94.

The claim that institutions in the constitutional mould better distribute public goods also is open to question, even from within the institutional approach itself. For example, the institutional approach tells an alternative story in which the old institutions of world trade participated in creating the conditions which precipitated a need to constitutionalize. Indeed institutionalized liberalized trade had both welfare-creating and welfare-reducing effects. From an economic perspective, some claim that the WTO has been a failure; it has not led to economic growth or development and has prevented states from removing market distortions or correcting market failures.[68] Yet the actions of institutions are presented as one-sided facts outside the boundaries of the constitutionalization debate. Moreover, the negative consequences of interdependence (around which institutional management is built) are presented as events, facts, over which states have little control. Constitutionalization as institutional management is presented as a necessary antidote to the discovery that post-war optimism about interdependence and the rising tide of market liberalization was somewhat misplaced and that 'not all boats [were] lifted'.[69] There has been a realization that interdependence has led to, or exacerbated, the existence of winners and losers,[70] contrary to the predictions of classical economics that freer and more open markets would necessarily enhance overall economic welfare. As a result of the unintended, uneven distribution of the benefits of interdependence, institutional managerialism claims that a greater need for international cooperation arises and hence the need for constitutionalization as the management of interdependence by institutional means. In short, the story of institutions and their role in redistribution contains contradictory strands, and, facts are detached from the context in which they operate.

Eighthly, another shortcoming of this approach is that it contains a limited view of the type of institutions available for international trade. Some argue that other models of institutionalism might lead to different outcomes.[71] For example, sociological institutionalism, with its emphasis on cultural factors in creating institutions, might 'provide a theoretical justification' to include human rights, or environmental concerns, within the WTO,[72] rather than focusing, as do regime theory and institutional economics, on questions of whether such linkage is effective or efficient.[73] In a similar vein, Langille[74] claims that new institutions are needed, institutions which are capable of resolving the vexed relationship between

---

[68] JR Paul, 'Do International Trade Institutions Contribute to Economic Growth and Development' (2003) 44 *Virginia Journal of International Law* 285.

[69] Jackson, 'Seven Mantras' (n 10 above) 67, 69.

[70] See, eg, N Hertz, *The Silent Takeover* (London: Heinemann, 2001) 55 (arguing that the effects of WTO-prompted trade liberalization have been devastating: 'rather than the rising tide of the market lifting all boats, structural adjustment and liberalisation policies with no concomitant obligations on redistribution appear to have sunk some social groups, especially the vulnerable and the poor').

[71] Nichols (n 7 above) 491–499.   [72] ibid 507–508.   [73] ibid 510.

[74] B Langille, 'General Reflections on the Relationship of Trade and Labor (Or: Fair Trade is Free Trade's Destiny)' in R Howse (ed), *The World Trading System: Critical Perspectives on the World Economy* (London: Routledge, 1998).

labour and trade. From this perspective, a radical restructuring of the trade–labour debate is required, not just management of existing issues, an attitude that implies acceptance of the basic structure of the current relationship. Nevertheless, Langille does not support the use of unilateral action to protect labour interests or withdrawal from trade and labour negotiations altogether. Ultimately Langille is an institutionalist also, but his is a different kind of institutionalism, in which the issues of trade and labour are linked through joint participation by labour, business, and government. He states, '[t]he resolution of our dilemma must be based in multilateral negotiation, agreement and enforcement which aims at securing the gains from trade while permitting political negotiation of the proper scope of the market in labour.' The idea is to re-establish the conditions of political equality. The institutional process must be 'tripartite one.'[75]

Not all institutionalists are sanguine about the potential of the institutional managerial constitutional approach. Joel Paul argues that although the WTO is an unmitigated failure as an economic institution for increasing growth and development, as a 'political policymaking institution' it succeeds 'brilliantly'.[76] Trachtman's view of institutions is quite different from other approaches in that it is accompanied by a cautionary tone about their potential. His concern is not to improve trade by strengthening institutions, but to study trade using a form of 'comparative institutional analysis' in which trade institutions are compared with other forms of economic organization. Although Trachtman believes institutions perform valuable power-constraining functions,[77] he is, decidedly, not an advocate for them. His is not a 'blanket call...for "strong institutions"', but rather for close, contextual analysis of particular institutions and particular institutional functions.[78] Indeed, comparative institutional analysis is needed precisely because the sort of assumptions about, for example, the concern about market and government 'failures', which motivates other writers, does not inform Trachtman's model.

> there is no nirvana. Neither market failure not government failure alone has policy ramifications. Nor is there, in truth, a default option: an institution that should retain power unless it is affirmatively shown that another institution is more efficient. Neither the market nor the state can claim this advantage. Each is on an equal footing with the firm and international organizations as candidates for allocations of authority.[79]

So, according to the Trachtman view, institutions are primarily important, not as a focus for constitutionalization, but as a mode of analysis, because they share attributes with firms, and because cost-based analyses of firms have been

---

[75] B Langille, 'General Reflections on the Relationship of Trade and Labor (Or: Fair Trade is Free Trade's Destiny)' in R Howse (ed), *The World Trading System: Critical Perspectives on the World Economy* (1998) 327.   [76] Paul (n 70 above) 339.

[77] Trachtman (n 32 above) 482 (arguing that institutions 'constrain the naked exercise of power, serve as a conduit for power from an initial time to a later time, and result in states sacrificing later-held interests in order to comply').   [78] ibid 475.

[79] ibid 489.

particularly useful in order to identify both opportunities and costs of their ways of operating.[80] Institutions, in Trachtman's hands, become a useful descriptive mechanism for studying changes in world trade, rather than a prescriptive model of constitutionalization.

In sum, the institutional–constitutional preoccupation of the majority approach bolsters WTO legitimacy without undertaking or undergoing the usual legitimization process. Furthermore, this approach requires further definition, and performs ambiguous functions because it serves both as a pretext for constitutionalization and a solution to the conditions which those very same predecessor institutions created in the first place. Moreover, it is not clearly demonstrated that a new *Grundnorm* emerged in 1995 with all the coherence and unity required of a constitution.

4.2.2 Management and rules

The second aspect of the institutional managerial constitutionalist approach is its focus on management as a technique of trade decision-making. 'The process of global constitutionalism . . . [involves] defining core principles, establishing international standards and creating institutions to manage interdependence.'[81] Thus, according to this account, the primary role of institutions is to manage trade relations,[82] through a number of techniques of management including the balancing of competing values,[83] regime maintenance,[84] harmonization, reciprocity, and use of the WTO as, what is referred to as, an 'interface'.[85]

---

[80] One of Trachtman's main criticisms of neo-classical economics, as it applies to trade, is that it does not examine the costs for states in losing autonomy in order to make gains in trade: ibid 477.

[81] Esty (n 16 above) 12.

[82] Jackson, *The World Trading System* (n 3 above) 8 ('the problem of international economics today, then, is largely a problem of "managing" interdependence'); and for comment see Kennedy (n 57 above) 100.

[83] See eg, T Cottier, 'Limits to International Trade: The Constitutional Challenge' (2000) *Proceedings of the American Society of International Law, 94th Annual Meeting* 220 (arguing that the visibility of 'fundamental and ethical divergencies' between states, and the belief that the trade system is 'biased in favour of market access', makes the old 'functionalist' model redundant and calls for 'constitutionalism in a modest sense', the weighing of different and 'equally legitimate' policy goals). Howse and Nicolaidis call Cottier's approach a 'federal type model': R Howse and K Nicolaidis, 'Legitimacy and Global Governance: Why Constitutionalizing the WTO is a Step Too Far' in RB Porter, *et al* (eds), *Efficiency, Equity, and Legitimacy: The Multilateral Trading System at the Millennium* (Washington DC: Brookings Institution Press, 2001) 228. Neil Walker also evokes an image of the WTO conducting 'balance' and 'management' of competing values: Walker (n 56 above).

[84] GR Shell, 'Trade Legalism and International Relations Theory: An Analysis of the World Trade Organization' (1995) 44 *Duke Law Journal* 829 (arguing that Regime Maintenance is one of three models for the WTO, the others being a Trade Stakeholders Model and an Efficiency Model, and describing how adherents to Regime Maintenance draw on international relations theory to show that management by institutions is the only effective solution to the prisoner's dilemma of independent states with different policy perspectives, needing to capture the gains from increased trade. Although not an advocate of Regime Maintenance, Shell argues that it dominates the other models.)

[85] Jackson, Davey and Sykes, *Legal Problems*, 3rd edn (n 3 above) 1226–1227. Note that the passage in which the term 'interface' was coined, and linked to 'management' does not appear in the current 4th edition published in 2002.

Harmonization refers to agreement by states on international standards or, in the absence of this, agreement to recognize each other's standards if they comply with the principle of non-discrimination. (This latter method of harmonization is sometimes referred to as mutual recognition because, instead of adopting the same standard, states avoid discriminating against trading partners by recognizing the validity of each other's laws.) Reciprocity refers to a system of bargaining and agreement over liberalization measures, conducted on a 'give and take' basis. Interface is used as an all-encompassing conceptual term to refer to any institutional means, including organizations, and rules,[86] for defusing tensions that arise from states having different economic policies, goals, and techniques.

The TRIPs agreement is an example of three of the techniques of managerial institutionalism at work—reciprocity, harmonization, and 'interface'. Widely regarded now as a gain for industrialized country negotiators in the Uruguay Round at the expense of developing countries, the agreement was, nevertheless, at the time, agreed to by developing countries on the basis of the reciprocity principle: protection of intellectual property rights was seen as a *quid pro quo* for developing states gaining better market access in relation to agriculture and textiles. Within the agreement itself, reciprocity was also present. On the one hand, TRIPs gave intellectual-property-rich states the right to protect their inventions. At the same time, TRIPs contains provisions favourable to states lacking in intellectual property, such as permission for states to issue licences for the production of medicines without the authorization of the right holder, or permission for parallel importing of pharmaceutical products. TRIPs also is a classic example of 'interface' management, with the GATT negotiating rounds providing the necessary means of finding agreement between different states on matters of trade controversy. Harmonization also is present in the sense that the agreement requires states to adhere to international standards of patent and copyright protection.

So, why management? What function does it perform? One important feature of all management techniques, according to its proponents, is that management maintains the status quo, rather than creates new interests, new areas of competence, or new law. So management is promoted as a moderating, stable method of deciding issues. Indeed, in some respects, this modest vision of managerialism is reflected in the text of the WTO agreements. States negotiate tariff concessions and bind themselves to those agreements in reciprocal fashion.[87] Dispute resolution is a matter of achieving 'satisfactory adjustment'

---

[86] The exact nature of the interface is not clearly defined, but Jackson does provide an example of it in the form of the escape clause mechanism of the GATT (GATT 1947 Art XIX), which allows states to impose measures against imports when sufficient evidence exists that those imports are causing substantial injury to domestic industry of the importing state.

[87] GATT 1947, Art II.

between disputants,[88] and retaliation is a matter of 'last resort'.[89] Security and predictability in the multilateral trade system[90] are fundamental goals. Most important of all, adjudicative bodies must only clarify provisions of agreements and must not make law by adding to or diminishing rights.[91] These provisions all serve a similar function of stabilizing expectations rather than changing them.

Similarly, institutional managerial constitutionalism suggests that the techniques of management are to be preferred because they can be applied in a neutral fashion as between parties to a dispute. Institutional managerialism does not choose between different national policies. The only requirement is that states do not discriminate. So institutional managerialism resolves national policy differences between states, without prescribing a particular international standard. To this extent, it reflects one of the key components of a constitutional community, the capacity to accommodate different interests. By developing a technique which claims to ensure respect for national difference, this approach tries to negotiate the difficulties highlighted in Chapter 2 concerning the creation of multiple *demoi*, in which citizens of the new constitutionalized community retain their national citizenship, while assuming also a new form of supranational citizenship and thus creating a new form of supranational community.[92] Constitutionalization, on this model, is not the eradication of difference but the recognition of it.

Faith in technical expertise is also implicit in the management approach, and this faith encapsulates another of constitutionalization's core elements, legitimacy. The GATT regime marked the 'high water mark of the twentieth century commitment to technocratic decisionmaking',[93] and faith in technocracy is what gave the organization its status. 'Historically, the trade regime has not been managed by elected officials accountable to a defined public. Instead, its legitimacy derived almost entirely from its perceived efficacy and value as part of the international economic management structure.'[94] So management is good because decisions are made on technical rather than political grounds. Instead of diplomacy and politics, with all the difficulties they pose of accommodating different views, we have experts managing trade problems on the basis of technical (non-political) knowledge.

---

[88] Management is the foundation of the original provisions of GATT 1947 Articles XXII and XXIII which aimed to secure 'satisfactory adjustment' between the disputing parties.
[89] DSU, Art 3.7.   [90] ibid, Art 3.2.
[91] ibid, Art 3.2. Note the Appellate Body's insistence on the principle of judicial economy, and with it, a denial of any law-*making* function. So, eg, in *United States—Shirts and Blouses* the tribunal refused to inquire into matters which the appellant sought to raise, on the basis that they were not necessary to the decision, and because the tribunal was not entitled to 'make law' but only to clarify it: WTO, Report of the Appellate Body, *United States—Measures Affecting Imports of Woven Wool Shirts and Blouses from India*, WT/DS33/AB/R (25 April 1997) DSR 1997:I, 323. A constitutional system based on institutional management is dependent on stability and the application of rules, rather than the making of new ones, is a vital part of that image.
[92] See discussion above at Chapter 2, section 2.4.3.   [93] Esty (n 16 above) 10.   [94] ibid.

In short, the claim of institutional managerialism is that the job of constitutionalized WTO law is not to impose particular substantive values on states but to manage disputes by institutional means. In the process, institutional managerialism substitutes management for a form of deliberative process and thereby stabilizes expectations, avoids expansion of WTO competence into new areas of law-making, is neutral as between different interests, and promotes legitimacy.

Consistent with this view of constitutionalization as institutional managerialism is the suggestion that rules are also important, but they are rules at only the most general level. Jackson presents the constitutional rules as consisting of only a skeletal form of an institution:

> the objective...will be to focus on the 'constitution' of the WTO in the broad meaning of the word 'constitution'. That is it will consider the institutional structure of the WTO including the structure of the organization, its treaty base, its very important procedures for dispute settlement and the relation of these to GATT.... It will not be feasible here to go into the many substantive issues of international trade policy and regulation.... Instead the intent is to present an overview of the institutional and 'constitutional' aspects of the WTO.[95]

Rules are stated at a high level of generality: non-discrimination, multilateralism, transparency, reciprocity, and liberalization. Apart from these, the WTO Charter does not contain any substantive rules, but merely incorporates the other agreements which contain the substantive rules.[96] Particular regulatory aspects are separated from the constitutional features.[97] It is therefore a constitution concerned with institutional structure and management technique rather than substantive rules.

Nevertheless, rules are critical to this approach; otherwise, according to its advocates, the system would slide back toward a pre-legal power-based system. Institutions themselves include rules,[98] and rules are integral to an effective international trade law system.[99] However, it is a dedication to rules inflected

---

[95] Jackson, *WTO Constitution* (n 1 above) 6.   [96] ibid 6–8.

[97] Moreover, the separation of the 'constitutional' from the 'substantive' is indicated by the way material is divided in writings illustrative of institutional managerialism. eg, in Jackson, Davey and Sykes, *Legal Problems*, 3rd edn (n 3 above), the matters referred to as 'constitutional' on page 3 are dealt with in chapters on, for example, the policies underlying international economic law, the legal structure of the GATT–WTO system, and dispute settlement. The chapters described, at page 3, as dealing with 'core subjects involved in the regulation of imports' include such issues as dumping and subsidies, sanitary and phytosanitary measures, intellectual property, and agriculture. The same structure is maintained in the fourth edition. Similarly in Jackson, *The World Trading System* (n 3 above) 11 Jackson refers to chapters which outline the 'basic "constitutional structure" of the world trading system', and these are dealt with in chapters entitled 'the international institutions of trade', 'national institutions,' and 'rule implementation and dispute resolution'. By contrast, at 11, he notes that chapters 5–11 take up specific 'regulatory' subjects.

[98] Trachtman (n 32 above).

[99] See, eg, chapter 4 of Jackson, *The World Trading System* (n 3 above) which is entitled 'Rule Implementation and Dispute Resolution'.

with realism about their limitations.[100] Sometimes rules detract from national sovereignty or are wrongheaded, procedurally faulty, or impossible to reform.[101] But a non-rules based system would return us to mere power-based diplomacy, and this would not be a constitutional system; it would be mere politics.[102] Institutional managerial constitutionalization exploits the legitimacy of rules, in conjunction with management techniques, to reinforce the claim that constitutionalization is taking place.

So the management inherent in institutional managerialism is a legalistic form of managerialism. It involves submission to dispute resolution on the basis of rules, and thereby marks a shift from 'realism' in international relations terms to institutional 'legalism'.[103] Legalism is critical to institutional managerialism because binding dispute resolution facilitates compliance, reduces transaction costs, and inspires confidence in the equal application of rules. In the language of regime theory, these methods of enforcement 'discourage defections from the treaty bargain and help solve prisoner's dilemma among trading states'.[104]

The rules-based nature of this form of constitutionalization is best captured in the famous exchange in the *American Journal of International Law* between John Jackson and Judith Hippler Bello, in which Jackson argued that the GATT system of rules was 'binding'[105] while Hippler Bello argued that it was not.[106] According to Hippler Bello, the system was built on a cornerstone of 'flexibility'[107] and that as a result 'compliance...remains elective'.[108] The only 'sacred, inviolable' aspect was preserving the overall balance of rights. If local politics demanded it, Members could still exercise full sovereignty and maintain measures that were inconsistent with the WTO rules.[109] In response, Jackson listed numerous parts of the Dispute Settlement Understanding which reflected the bindingness of WTO law.[110] He argued that WTO law was as

---

[100] In a section entitled 'Do the Rules Work?' John Jackson recalls the ways in which trade diplomats attempt to make the rules work in their favour: ibid 8–9.   [101] ibid 109.

[102] Repeatedly, writers portray Uruguay as a turning point at which Member State negotiators shifted the focus away from politics to law. See, for eg, R Behboodi, 'Legal Reasoning and the International Law of Trade' (1998) 32 *Journal of World Trade* 55, 57 (arguing that the AB stands before 'a fork in the road; it can choose the path well-trodden by the GATT panels before or it can take up the mantle of uniqueness—appellate jurisdiction in international litigation').

[103] Shell (n 84 above).   [104] ibid 856.

[105] JH Bello, 'The WTO Dispute Settlement Understanding: Less is More' (1996) 90 *American Journal of International Law* 416, and JH Jackson, 'The WTO Dispute Settlement Understanding—Misunderstandings on the Nature of Legal Obligation' (1997) 91 *American Journal of International Law* 60.   [106] Bello, ibid 416.

[107] ibid 417.

[108] According to Hippler Bello, states found not to be acting in conformity with the rules have a number of options. They can comply, maintain measures and provide compensatory benefits, or make no change and suffer retaliation: ibid 417.

[109] In Hippler Bello's view, the reason for WTO strength is not its bindingness but the fact that it forces out into the open the costs of economic protectionism: ibid.

[110] Jackson listed eleven DSU clauses indicating that the new system was binding: the objective of dispute settlement is to secure withdrawal of the offending measure; suspension of concessions is only last resort; the Appellate Body can recommend a member bring measure into conformity;

binding as any other type of international law. Even if WTO law was not directly applicable in Member States, it was nevertheless used to exert considerable power over national law.[111] The link between rules, management, and institutions was further strengthened by evidence of the history of WTO law, which was portrayed as a gradual evolution from power-based to rules-oriented diplomacy.[112]

A rule-orientation was reflected also in early GATT jurisprudence about the grounds for bringing a complaint. These cases firmly established the principle that the requirement under the agreement to show harm, or 'nullification or impairment of a benefit'[113] would be presumed where there had been a violation, in the form of a failure to carry out an obligation under the agreement.[114] Moreover, the grip of rules was intensified by the interpretation that accompanied this principle which indicated shift in the burden of proof: once a complainant had adduced *prima facie* evidence of nullification or impairment, the burden shifted to the respondent to rebut that evidence. The combination of this flexible interpretation of nullification or impairment and the shifting of the burden of proof created a rebuttable presumption that nullification or impairment arose whenever there was evidence of breach. The *Oil Fee Case* subsequently confirmed this shift towards a rules-based form of dispute resolution by deciding that even a breach with minimal trade effects would be sufficient to establish nullification or impairment, and therefore a violation.[115] According to one commentator, this case marked the 'high water mark' of a system of rules because the treaty language is virtually turned 'on its head'.[116] These institutional and jurisprudential developments were further evidence of GATT's fealty to a rules-based system.

On the other hand, these are rules with an inbuilt elasticity, again illustrative of the institutional managerial thesis that flexibility is key to constitutionalization.

the language of the provisions refers to 'prompt compliance'; compensation and suspension are only permitted if a ruling is not implemented within a reasonable time; suspension of concessions is temporary; and that for non-violation complaints there is no obligation to withdraw the measure: Jackson (n 105 above) 63.

[111] For example, the interpretation of national law had to be consistent with international law including WTO law, and the WTO was often used both in diplomatic circles and as a means of applying informal pressure on states: ibid 61.

[112] Jackson, *The World Trading System* (n 3 above) 110. Moreover, the development of the GATT as an institution mirrors this trend from power to rules. Institutionally, it began with a simple system in which disputes were decided by the contracting parties; it graduated in the 1950s to a system of working panels in which disinterested parties sat in judgement; and then moved to third party adjudication in the 1960s.   [113] GATT 1947; Art XXIII(1).

[114] GATT Panel Report, *Uruguayan Recourse to Article XXIII* (adopted 16 November 1962) BISD (11th Supp) 95, 100.

[115] GATT Panel Report, *United States—Taxes on Petroleum and Certain Imported Substances*, (adopted 17 June 1987) BISD (34th Supp) 136 (1988).

[116] Jackson, *WTO Constitution* (n 1 above) 70 (arguing that the presumption that nullification or impairment derives from a violation 'almost' discards the notions of nullification or impairment in favour of a finding of violation).

According to GATT (and later WTO)[117] jurisprudence, not only is it possible to bring a case on the basis of a violation, but it is also possible to institute an action for a 'non-violation'.[118] The category of non-violation nullification or impairment was necessary, where, subsequent to the negotiation of market-opening trade concessions, one party imposed another form of trade restriction which may not be subject to a substantive obligation. Thus, non-violation actions were seen as necessary (though rare)[119] in order to protect the reasonable expectations of a party in relation to market access trading concessions.

The flexible nature of WTO rules is illustrated also in the AB's attitude toward regional trade agreements. RTAs require states to eliminate duties on 'substantially all trade' within the union, and to apply 'substantially the same' external duties to non-member states.[120] The AB, reflecting this managerial approach, has said that RTA members should retain a certain 'flexibility' in relation to satisfying these requirements, and has done little to clarify their actual content.[121]

Furthermore, as Tom Franck's work on fairness[122] shows, this is not a strict rule system.[123] Franck argued that international law had entered the 'post-ontological era'[124] in which the fairness and effectiveness of law has superseded questions about law's status. To illustrate his claim, he referred to international trade law, which, he wrote, provided many examples of the new focus on effectiveness and fairness.[125]

In sum, management by rules allows states to balance competing values, maintain the status quo, ensure flexibility in rule-application, deal with trade

---

[117] A description of non-violation and violation nullification and impairments and the difference between them is contained in WTO, Report of the Appellate Body, *India—Patent Protection for Pharmaceutical and Agricultural Chemical Products*, WT/DS50/AB/R (19 December 1997), DSR 1998:I, 9.

[118] GATT 1947 Art XXIII:1(b), DSU Art 26.1. GATT, Report of the Panel, *EEC—Payments and Subsidies Paid to Processors and Producers of Oilseeds and Related Animal-Feed Proteins*, BISD 37S/86 (adopted 25 January 1990), GATT BISD (37th Supp) 86 (1991).

[119] Only 8 have ever been argued: WTO, Report of the Panel, *Japan—Measures Affecting Consumer Photographic Film and Paper*, WT/DS44/R (31 March 1998), DSR 1998:IV, 1179 at para 10.36. A third category of complaint to cover 'any other situation' further extends the flexibility of the GATT–WTO rules: GATT 1947 Art XXIII:1(c), DSU Art 26.2.

[120] GATT 1947, Art XXIV(8)(a).

[121] WTO, Report of the Appellate Body, *Turkey—Restrictions on Imports of Textile and Clothing Products*, WT/DS34/AB/R (22 October 1999), DSR 1998:IV, 1179.

[122] T Franck, *Fairness in International Law and Institutions* (Oxford: Clarendon Press, 1995).

[123] Franck's work is regularly cited by WTO scholars. See, eg, D Steger, 'Review of CE Barfield, *Free Trade, Sovereignty, Democracy: The Future of the World Trade Organization*' (2002) 5 *Journal of International Economic Law* 565; and Behboodi (n 102 above).

[124] Franck (n 122 above) 6 (arguing that the key question is no longer 'what is international law?' but 'is international law effective and fair?').

[125] See ibid, where Franck argues, at p. 7 and in chapters 2 and 3, that fairness is a composite of two variables—procedural fairness and fairness as equity. His composite of equitable fairness is reflected in multilateral aid provision through, for example, the IMF, systems of trade preferences, and market stabilization funds.

disputes in a neutral fashion, and avoid a return to the 'anarchy' of a system managed on a purely diplomatic basis. What is present are some of the elements of the received account of constitutionalization, namely a modified form of deliberative process and a flexible, rules-oriented legitimacy.

Against these claims of balance and neutrality, cushioned by rules, the management element of the approach has been criticized.[126] Howse, for example, argues that the existence of rules in the GATT does not ensure legitimacy of the system: 'The social legitimacy of the rules themselves may depend upon the legitimacy of bureaucratic and judicial power, which is itself not legitimate.'[127] On this view, the trade diplomats, who ran the dispute settlement system of the GATT, developed interpretations of the rules which were largely political in the sense that the overriding goal was to maintain system cohesion, but did not confer any other form of more broadly based social legitimacy.[128]

The concern that the WTO lacks legitimacy is echoed even in work of those who espouse the institutional managerial constitutionalist view. Daniel Esty, for example, argues that, the WTO lacks sufficient processes of effective deliberation, and is undergoing a crisis of legitimacy.[129] He says this crisis has occurred because the old 'club model' of trade relations is perceived today as non-transparent, dominated by special interests, unresponsive to developing country needs, and overly influenced by multinational corporations.[130] According to the internal critics of institutional managerialism then, the legitimacy of the old GATT system, which was derived from the efficacy and rationality of its technocratic decision-making, has been undermined by a new perception that technocracy is undemocratic, and so must be replaced by a form of legitimacy based on democracy.[131] An alternative legitimacy could be achieved, say the critics, if the processes of WTO deliberation were improved. This could happen through a variety of means including national legislative oversight of WTO; a retreat to core trade activities and bequeathing of environmental issues to a global organization; attainment of economic goals with greater sensitivity to other values such as environmental protection and poverty alleviation; improvement of WTO procedural and substantive fairness; and embedding of the organization in a broader system of global governance made up of checks and balances between multi-tiered institutions.[132]

---

[126] See eg, a pragmatic critique of rules as a the sole source of the legitimacy of law arguing that instead judge made law relies on an eclectic balancing of various factors including rules, social science data, and even judicial preference: RA Posner, *The Problematics of Moral and Legal Theory* (1999). See also discussion of the various sources of law's legitimacy in Chapter 2, section 2.4.6.

[127] R Howse, 'The Legitimacy of the World Trade Organization' in J Coicaud and V Heiskanen (eds), *The Legitimacy of International Organizations* (Tokyo; New York: United Nations Press, 2001) (arguing that the GATT panel rulings were often drafted by the Secretariat and that they were based less on rigorous treaty interpretation than on 'intuitions about system maintenance').

[128] R Howse, 'Adjudicative Legitimacy and Treaty Interpretation in International Trade Law: The Early Years of WTO Jurisprudence' in JHH Weiler (ed), *The EU, the WTO and the NAFTA: Towards a Common Law of International Trade* (2000) 38.   [129] Esty (n 16 above) 12.

[130] ibid 11.   [131] ibid 13.   [132] ibid 17–18.

The success of the techniques of management at achieving deliberation of an effective kind is also open to question. Deliberation by 'interface' may leave issues so open-ended that states are barely better off than when there was no agreement. The compulsory licensing and parallel importing provisions of TRIPs are examples of the failure of interface (and indeed of reciprocity) to deliver effective deliberation: for many years the provisions remained effectively dormant because of disagreement over their meaning and even now, some two decades after states had apparently reached agreement on these issues, they still remain subject to heated controversy.[133]

Management, as a technique of supposedly constitutional decision-making, is ill-equipped to achieve the goals of deliberative process noted in Chapter 2. The institution lacks formal structures for deliberation. At the level of states, decision-making is constrained by the need to use either the formal and rigid voting requirements noted in Chapter 1 or to fall back on methods of non-transparent informal decision making. There is no legislative branch capable of providing adequate means of communication and deliberation to test the values of the system. Armin von Bogdandy argues that the legislative function at the WTO is deficient in respect of both democracy and efficiency.[134] There is no public forum in which the views of divergent groups and interests can be debated, and in which citizens can constitute themselves as makers of the law of the WTO. There is insufficient political dialogue about the trade-offs necessary between trade and other values.[135]

Yet despite the absence of formal processes of deliberation, some informal deliberation does occur in the international trade community. Private groups concerned with, for example, the right to trade, or investment, are being linked with the public sphere, through what is loosely referred to as global civil society, and, indirectly, this deliberation is being channelled into institutional decision-making at the WTO. The combined work of developing states concerned about access to medicines, and some international organizations such as Oxfam, influenced the composition of the public health Ministerial Declaration at Doha that inserted some flexibility into interpretation of the TRIPs agreement. Dialogue, of a limited kind, is occurring between NGOs, anti-globalization protestors, and business, thus facilitating civic participation in the law-making process.

Nevertheless, deliberative process, by management, is generally of a poor quality. The adoption of the language of management and neutrality may mask unequal power relations between parties involved in the deliberation, thus undermining the process. As we saw in Chapter 2, the claims of management-based deliberation process may be exaggerated because it ignores defects in

---

[133] See discussion in Chapter 7 n 121.
[134] A von Bogdandy, 'Law and Politics in the WTO—Strategies to Cope with a Deficient Relationship' in JA Frowein and R Wolfrum (eds), *Max Planck Yearbook of United Nations Law*, vol 5 (2001) 609, 625.   [135] Esty (n 16 above) 10–13.

decision-making process related to ignorance, confusion, and unequal bargaining strength.[136] In the institutional managerial constitutionalists' world, 'there is no need to treat governments any differently from firms. They are all transactors, and even regulators may compete in markets.'[137] Institutional managerialism, grounded in institutional economics, is particularly open to this criticism because it treats all actors as equal regardless of economic strength, political function, or political power. An alternative approach would be to adopt the perspective of historical institutionalism, which recognizes that the development of institutions is not the product of freely operating wealth-maximizing states, but is heavily dependent upon pre-existing paths, which may include unequal distributions of power, competition, and coalitions.[138] By omitting power relations from the calculus, institutional managerialism underestimates the need for better processes of deliberation, such as higher levels of civil participation, or a strong public sphere, or even a democratically effective and efficient legislative body.

This masking of inequality has the further effect of undermining the deliberative process because it diminishes the quality and levels of communication and dialogue with, for example, civil society. Daniel Esty argues that 'what is lacking at the WTO is any recognition of the need for more politics—more dialogue and debate, and engagement with civil society—as a way of building the political foundation needed to support the economic structure that is being erected'.[139]

Institutional managerial constitutionalization, according to some, reduces the opportunities for effective deliberation and leads to the 'evisceration of the political'.[140] In relation to compliance, other weaknesses of management, as a technique, are visible.[141] The DSU provides for various options to induce compliance including compensation and suspension of concessions,[142] but each of these is beset by difficulties. Compensation is voluntary;[143] the period to negotiate it is short;[144] no mechanism exists for estimating the amount of compensation to be paid;[145] and, emphasis on compensation rather than retaliation may lead some states to see the former as simply a necessary 'overhead' of doing business. On the other hand, the forms of compensation that can be contemplated are various and flexible, including market-opening compensation and retroactive compensation, and, as a mode of promoting compliance,

---

[136] See criticisms of deliberative process by Richard Posner, Chapter 2, section 2.4.4.
[137] Kennedy (n 57 above) 26.   [138] Nichols (n 7 above) 493.
[139] Esty (n 16 above) 15.   [140] Kennedy (n 57 above) 100.
[141] The following draws, in part, on a report of a working group of which the author was a member: Federal Trust, *Enhancing the WTO's Dispute Settlement Understanding* (2002): <www.fedtrust.co.uk/dsu.htm>.   [142] DSU, Art 22.1
[143] DSU, Art 22.1.   [144] DSU, Art 22.2.
[145] The DSU provides, in Art 22.4, that the level of suspension of concessions shall be equivalent to the level of nullification or impairment and that this level can be subject to arbitration (Art 22.7). No equivalent provision exists to assess the level of compensation payable.

compensation has the advantage of being more attractive to smaller countries which may lack the economic clout to effect substantial retaliation against a larger state by suspending concessions. Retaliation, however, is favoured by others, who perceive it as a necessary 'last resort'.[146] (Alternatively, some argue for the introduction of a system of fines, as this would take the issue of enforcement out of the hands of small states. However, this would bring with it further problems, including the question who is to administer the fines, and whether they would be adequate redress for smaller states, which may prefer the option of cross-retaliation.)[147] So, does institutional managerialism encourage or hinder compliance? It may be that resolution of trade disputes by management does not induce better compliance where states are unequal in terms of economic bargaining power. Management implies neutral techniques, an assumption of power equality, an absence of striving for particular substantive goals, and a disinterested institutional method. However, in view of inequalities of bargaining power between some states, what may be required is a more active means of inducing compliance, the setting of particular substantive goals, and an interested institutional approach. In short, institutional managerialism, when it tries to achieve better compliance, by deliberating through management, lacks sufficient teeth, so to speak, to succeed.

Even where the parties are relatively equal in economic and political power, managerial techniques of deliberation lead to problems with compliance. Both the US and the EU have less than perfect records in relation to implementing recommendations of the WTO dispute resolution body.[148] For example, in the dispute between the US and the EU regarding US special tax treatment for 'foreign sales corporations',[149] it took some four years after the ruling for the US to respond. In addition, the EU had expressed a notable reluctance to pressure the US to comply with the WTO ruling because EU companies with subsidiaries in the US benefited from the WTO-inconsistent FSC rules, and because of fear that EU consumers would protest against any increase in the cost of US goods which would have followed EU retaliation by way of increased tariffs. The EU thus sought to manage the dispute, rather than simply retaliate.

---

[146] DSU, Art 22.2 provides that where negotiations over satisfactory compensation have failed, and the reasonable period of time for implementation has expired, the complaining party may request authorization from the DSB of suspension of concessions. DSU, Art 3.2 refers to this as a right of 'last resort'.

[147] In the *Bananas* litigation Ecuador argued that same-sector retaliation would not be sufficient to address the losses it had incurred because of European protectionism and so argued that it was entitled to cross-retaliation in the form of suspension of patent protection for some European products. For a chronology of the Bananas litigation see M Salas and JH Jackson, 'Procedural Overview of the WTO EC—Banana Dispute' (2000) 3 *Journal of International Economic Law* 145; and JH Jackson and P Grane, 'The Saga Continues: An Update on the Banana Dispute and its Procedural Offspring' (2001) 4 *Journal of International Economic Law* 581.

[148] See, eg, discussion of compliance problems in R Bhala and D Gantz, 'WTO Case Review 2003' (2004) 21 *Arizona Journal of International and Comparative Law* 317, 326–330.

[149] WTO, Report of the Appellate Body, *United States—Tax Treatment for Foreign Sales Corporations*, WT/DS108/AB/R (24 February 2000) DSR 2000:III, 1619.

Thus, it is clear that compliance becomes problematic when states seek to offset the costs and benefits of compliance by managing their effects.

Moreover, some claim that a form of constitutionalization based on an institutional managerialism will fail because of its mechanistic approach. According to this criticism, vast cultural and political differences between states will never be resolved on the basis of an 'interface', which is merely a 'quasi-mechanical and facilitative mechanism focussing on communication and correspondence between systems rather than [a method for] construction of a new international legal order or system. The best we can hope for...is bargained amelioration as the liberal trade spirit becomes more widespread.'[150] Institutional managerial constitutionalization is fascinated with management, and unconcerned with inaugurating a new political order:[151] '[T]he public international policy process has been replaced by decentralized adjustment and bargaining by managers and economic diplomats acting out of an invigorated liberal commercial spirit and vigilant against reassertions of national particularism.'[152]

At the same time, the mechanistic nature of management is, nevertheless, not necessarily neutral: institutional managerialism is informed by specific prescriptions about liberal free trade. In Chapter 2 we saw that critics argued in general that deliberative process, despite its claim to openness, excluded certain norms, and did not adequately take account of difference.[153] In relation to international trade, critics of institutional managerialism claim that it 'internalises unstated assumptions about normal and abnormal trade',[154] excludes some rational first-best solutions,[155] and is 'suffused with a model of sovereign non intervention at the national and international level and in "normal" commercial activity'.[156] Indeed, argues another critic, the WTO under this approach becomes a method for prescribing for a particular type of international liberal trading order in which the values of economic liberalism predominate.[157] According to the critique, the principles of trade liberalization, rather than

---

[150] Kennedy (n 57 above) 95.   [151] ibid 99.   [152] ibid 100.

[153] M Rosenfeld, 'Can Rights, Democracy, and Justice be Reconciled through Discourse Theory? Reflections on Habermas's Proceduralist Paradigm of Law' (1996) 17 *Cardozo Law Review* 791; Chapter 2 above, section 2.4.4.   [154] Kennedy (n 57 above) 10.

[155] Howse (n 127 above) 373 (arguing that the 'network' of trade experts who dominated GATT decision-making prior to 1995 excluded 'as naïve evangelists those who proposed first-best economically rational solutions', such as abolition of anti-dumping duties altogether).

[156] Kennedy (n 57 above) 15.

[157] Howse (n 127 above) 38. In similar vein, it has been argued that private international law has been dominated by a set of liberal concerns, such as facilitation of international commerce, increase of international cooperation, and pursuit of anti-parochialism and non-discrimination between states, and that alternative policy goals of equal importance, such as the need for effective regulation of private relations, protection of broad social interests and legal diversity, are sidelined, ignored, or treated in a negative way as reflecting limited national interests, against international order: R Wai, 'Transnational Liftoff and Juridical Touchdown: The Regulatory Function of Private International Law in an Era of Globalization' (2002) 40 *Columbia Journal of Transnational Law* 209.

the framework of international law, are taken as constitutional norms.[158] '[E]conomic freedom is understood as the *telos* of the WTO' and competing values enter into the picture only as 'narrow and carefully policed exceptions'.[159] As another writer argues, the model of regime maintenance relies heavily on 'normative commitments to economic theory as a foundation for legal interpretation'.[160] Consequently, institutional managerial constitutionalization limits participation and does not take sufficient account of the potentially controversial social and environmental issues which inevitably surround trade.

The absence or skewing of substantive values in the WTO, coupled with the ability of the system to adapt to all manner of trade disputes, has led the institutional form of constitutionalization to become imbued with a sense of omnipotence. This is partly because management, as opposed to a goals-oriented approach, is endlessly flexible; it is imbued with a practical spirit, which is oriented to process and policy, contextual, purposive, and functional.[161] Institutional managerial constitutionalization, according to its critics, perceives itself as being able to resolve any trade dispute. 'All national partisan political programs can be accommodated by an appropriate interface.'[162]

This confidence carries with it dangers, according to the detractors of the approach. Brian Langille infers that an international trade system that makes management its centrepiece may overextend itself and, indirectly, he suggests that the legitimacy of the WTO may be compromised by institutional managerial constitutionalization. He argues that international trade is currently in crisis, because there is no stopping it from extending its reach to new, formerly domestic, regulatory matters.[163] Langille refers to the successful reduction of trade barriers in the past forty years, and points out that this has led inevitably to a focus on non-trade barriers such as subsidies and beyond: matters of 'fair trade' are inevitably free trade's 'destiny'.[164] As a result, '[t]rade theory has found itself unable to limit its concept of what is a trade barrier or distortion, and has found itself sliding down a slippery slope into formerly internal government regulation with no intellectually sustainable stopping point.'[165] Moreover, the normative ambiguity this creates raises questions about the proper relationship between the market and the state: '[O]nce governmental action or nonaction in labor policy (for example) is problematized as a potential subsidy

[158] In Jackson, *The World Trading System* (n 3 above), Jackson describes, at 11, liberal trade, defined as the minimization of government interference in trade flows across national borders, as the 'policy assumption of the international trading system'. At 13, 'other goals' which may be 'partly inconsistent with the central goal' are sectioned off and discussed in a section, at 21, entitled 'competing policy goals and non-economic objectives'.

[159] Howse and Nicolaidis (n 83 above) 229.

[160] Shell (n 84 above) 907 (arguing that issues of stability, distributive fairness and procedural justice are ignored and instead focus is primarily on maximization of economic wealth, such that the system 'under-emphasizes explosive wealth distribution issues that can lead to domestic or even regional political instability'). [161] Kennedy (n 57 above) 23.

[162] ibid 96. [163] Langille (n 74 above) 304–305. [164] ibid 305. [165] ibid 314.

then there is no alternative to engaging in the debate about the appropriate scope of market regulation.'[166] The issue is particularly acute, according to Dan Tarullo, because the WTO has expanded its reach into non-trade barriers which form part of a domestic regulatory regime, and therefore has entered a field where there is no 'normative baseline' according to which the international regime can judge the acceptability or 'normalcy' of domestic regulation.[167]

Accordingly, simple 'management' of disputes may be insufficient to resolve the dilemma of increasing penetration of trade law into the regulatory state. Management implies that it is possible to balance issues about which there is disagreement. But if national control over regulation has been diminished, and trade is stepping behind the state barrier, it may be necessary to do more than manage the issues; it may be necessary to renegotiate the very terms of the bargain—to ask whether or not the issues are even on the table; what is the appropriate role of the state and of the international system?; how should the market function within a state and international system of governance? It is unclear whether the technique of 'interface' is equal to this task, with its mechanistic connotations of providing a space in which states may bargain. What Langille's and Tarullo's arguments do is to point out that, in respect of some issues, (matters deep in the regulatory autonomy of the state) there is not even primary agreement to put them on the table.

If harmonization is one of the prime examples of institutional managerial constitutionalization then perhaps the theory also has consequences for international standardization. In the *EC—Sardines*[168] case, the AB found an EC regulation, which restricted the name 'sardines' to sardine products of a particular genus found mainly in local European waters thereby excluding Peruvian sardines from the European market, inconsistent with the TBT Agreement because it was not based on a relevant international standard. While this is an illustration of the non-discrimination principle, it also shows how harmonization of standards could lead to a drift towards uniformity in products. A sardine, wherever located, is clearly a sardine, but there may be other circumstances in which a state may wish, with good reason, to prevent entry of a product from another state where the latter's product does not meet the internal standards of the importer. Although the TBT agreement provides wide grounds for states to maintain barriers,[169] the case alerts us to the fact that, the techniques of institutional managerial constitutionalization, harmonization in particular,

[166] Langille (n 74 above) 305.
[167] DK Tarullo, 'Logic, Myth and the International Economic Order' (1985) 26 *Harvard International Law Journal* 533; and DK Tarullo, 'Beyond Normalcy in the Regulation of International Trade' (1987) 100 *Harvard Law Review* 546.
[168] WTO, Report of the Appellate Body, *European Communities—Trade Description of Sardines*, WT/DS231/AB/R (26 September 2002).
[169] Exceptions are permitted for reasons of national security; prevention of deceptive practices; protection of human health or safety, animal or plant life or health or the environment; fundamental climatic or other geographical factors; fundamental technological or infrastructural problems: TBT Agreement Article 5.4.

may not always be a fine enough tool with which to address the problem of maintenance of international product standard diversity.

Indeed, institutional managerial constitutionalization contains a tension between maintaining diverse national policies and continuing international trade integration. This tension persists in a number of different guises. Jackson's work, for example, informed, as Kennedy describes,[170] by a committed pluralism, emphasizes the need to protect different cultural and political policies of nation states and to include within the framework of the international trade system different types of economies; the purpose of the 'interface' is as a mechanism to negotiate such differences. At the same time, however, institutional managerialism plays down the effects of constitutionalization on nation states. It conceives sovereignty as 'out of date and archaic', and yet it also considers sovereignty to be a 'great debate' of 'vital and contemporary' importance, which 'turns out to be very complex' because it can be 'decomposed [sic]'.[171] Ultimately, according to institutional managerial constitutionalism, international trade does not threaten sovereignty because the trade treaties lack direct effect and states can withdraw with notice.[172] Nevertheless, although sovereignty may be outmoded, it may be possible to reconceptualize it as a question of the 'allocation of power'.[173] As one of institutional managerialism's critics puts it, the 'specter of a dark national parochialism' constantly threatens the principles of non-discrimination and liberal trade.[174] So, institutional managerial approaches to constitutionalization contain a tension between giving up sovereignty and gripping on to it.

If we examine some of the cases in which sovereignty has been an issue we can see how this tension is played out, and speculate on the adequacy of management as a tool to resolve these problems. The saga over dolphins is a case in point. In contrast to GATT panel decisions in the early 1990s, in the *Tuna—Dolphin* cases,[175] in 1998 the AB in the *US—Shrimp-Turtle* case decided that importing states may condition access to their markets on the basis that the exporter has adopted a policy that is unilaterally prescribed by the importing state, as long as that condition of the importer was non-discriminatory according to the requirements of Article XX.[176] This development in the jurisprudence illustrates precisely the ambivalence present in institutional managerial approaches to constitutionalization, wherein a tension persists between the preservation of national policy difference, and, the right of the international body to intervene. In the earlier case, the GATT panel had come out in favour

---

[170] Kennedy (n 57 above) 23.　　[171] Jackson, *WTO Constitution* (n 1 above) 33.
[172] ibid 34.　　[173] ibid 33.　　[174] Kennedy (n 57 above) 100.
[175] GATT, Report of the Panel, *United States—Restrictions on Imports of Tuna* (not adopted, circulated on 3 September 1991), GATT BISD (39th Supp) (1993) (Tuna Dolphin I) 30 ILM 1594 (1991); GATT, Report of the Panel, *United States—Restrictions on Imports of Tuna* (not adopted, circulated on 16 June 1994), DS 29/R (Tuna Dolphin II) 33 ILM 936 (1994).
[176] WTO, Report of the Appellate Body, *United States—Import Prohibition of Certain Shrimp and Shrimp Products*, WT/DS58/AB/R (12 October 1998), DSR 1998:VII, 2755 at para 121.

of an absolute rule undercutting national sovereignty—states may never uni-laterally impose policies on another state in the name of social goals when those unilateral social policies discriminate in trade. In *Shrimp—Turtle* we see an abandonment of the strict rule and a recognition that GATT Article XX itself embodies the right to derogate from the multilateral trade rules in a manner that preserves full national sovereignty over social policies, even when those policies discriminate in trade. The AB in *Shrimp—Turtle* states that to do otherwise would render 'most, if not all, of the specific exceptions of Article XX inutile'.[177] The world community has recognized 'certain domestic policies as important and legitimate in character'[178] and has thus accepted them as exceptions from general non-discrimination. The same tension between allowing the WTO to 'extend' its scope to environmental issues and permitting states to retain control is present in the important concluding paragraphs of the *Shrimp—Turtle* decision, where the AB felt compelled to explain exactly the boundaries of its findings. After concluding that in this case the US measures were discriminatory, the AB adopted a somewhat self-justificatory tone and stated that it wished to 'underscore' what it had '*not* decided':

We have *not* decided that the sovereign nations that are Members of the WTO cannot adopt effective measures to protect endangered species.... Clearly, they can and should. And we have *not* decided that sovereign states should not act together bilaterally, pluri-laterally or multilaterally, either within the WTO or in other international fora, to protect endangered species or to otherwise protect the environment. Clearly, they should and do.[179]

These statements are clear indication that the AB is aware of profound con-sequences of its decision which seeks to find a middle way between according states complete control over national policy-making and ceding all trade decisions to the trade organization, no matter how much they impinge on other domestic matters. In the face of this tension, it seems unlikely that management will be sufficient to resolve these issues. Strong deliberation including civic and legis-lative participation, dialogue, and communication would instead be necessary, and to this extent managerialism appears inadequate.

Another example of the tension between maintaining national policy diversity and diminishing national economic sovereignty arises in relation to non-violation complaints. As noted above, non-violation complaints occur when a Member State complains that another Member has nullified or impaired benefits accruing to the former Member, but in such a way as not to be otherwise in violation of the GATT. This extremely rare category of cases[180] is believed to safeguard

---

[177] WTO, Report of the Appellate Body, *United States—Import Prohibition of Certain Shrimp and Shrimp Products*, WT/DS58/AB/R (12 October 1998), DSR 1998:VII, 2755, para 121.
[178] ibid.   [179] ibid 2819-1 para 185.
[180] Only 8 have ever been argued: WTO, Report of the Panel, *Japan—Measures Affecting Consumer Photographic Film and Paper*, WT/DS44/R (31 March 1998), DSR 1998:IV, 1179 at para 10.36.

the process of tariff negotiation by ensuring that tariff concessions granted during a negotiation, (and bound under Article II) are not subsequently undermined by the state limiting the concession by some other means, such as the granting of a domestic subsidy to producers of the goods under concession. In the *Oilseeds* Case,[181] it was recognized that improved competitive opportunities legitimately expected from a tariff concession can be frustrated even by measures consistent with the Agreements, and that states have a 'reasonable expectation' that this not occur. Therefore, a right of redress is provided in the form of a non-violation complaint. Non-violation has been confirmed in the WTO context in dicta in the *Japan—Film* Case.[182] Although on the facts of the case the Panel dismissed the US non-violation claim, it confirmed the existence of the cause of action. The US had argued that Japan, through an array of measures, had created a vertically integrated market structure tying in wholesale distribution with locally manufactured products, thereby discriminating against foreign manufacturers of film and photographic paper. The claim was unfounded in this case, but the AB acknowledged that in different circumstances such an arrangement could provide sufficient grounds for complaint. Although most non-violation complaints concerned domestic subsidies, they were not limited to these.

The problem is that non-violation complaints extend the range of matters which a state may be called upon to remedy, and hence raise the spectre of GATT law removing, or at least diminishing, the extent to which states can take economic decisions, judged by them, to be in the national interest. In the *Japan—Film* Case, the panel said that 'a Member's industrial policy, pursuing a goal of increased efficiency in a sector, could in some circumstances upset the competitive relationship in the market place between domestic and imported products in a way that could give rise to an action' [emphasis deleted].[183] This suggests that even insofar as an industrial policy pursues a goal of increased efficiency, which would seem to be quarantined from the usual list of suspected trade discriminations, that policy might be subject to challenge. Thus, the ability of states to set their own economic goals, including industrial policies regarding economic efficiency goals, is potentially conditioned by this broad interpretation of non-violation. Industrial policy is the heartland of national sovereignty. Yet in this case the WTO Panel entertained the possibility that this heartland could be subject to invasion, or at least intrusion. Although, in the institutional management model of constitutionalization, national policy difference must be

---

[181] GATT, Report of the Panel, *EEC—Payments and Subsidies Paid to Processors and Producers of Oilseeds and Related Animal-Feed Proteins*, BISD 37S/86 (adopted 25 January 1990), GATT BISD (37th Supp) 86 (1991) at para 144.

[182] WTO, Report of the Panel, *Japan—Measures Affecting Consumer Photographic Film and Paper*, WT/DS44/R (31 March 1998), DSR 1998:IV, 1179 at para 10.36.

[183] ibid 1649 para 10.38.

respected, in this case the dispute settlement mechanism recognizes that a central tenet of national policy difference—industrial policy—may be challenged.

Finally, there is the problem of culture. The *Canada—Periodicals* decision[184] involved a challenge by the United States to Canadian measures aimed at preserving market share of Canadian-produced periodicals from incursion by US 'split-run' magazines. Canada prohibited imports of such periodicals[185] and imposed a tax on sales on them.[186] On appeal, both measures were found to be inconsistent with WTO rules,[187] highlighting concerns about the ability of the WTO system successfully to negotiate the sovereignty–difference divide when it comes to matters normally within domestic jurisdiction, such as culture.

In reaching its decision, the AB quoted extensively from policy statements by Canadian government officials, which revealed that there was a protectionist impulse behind the measures. These statements included a 'commitment to protect the economic foundations of the Canadian periodical industry', and 'to use policy instruments that encourage the flow of advertising revenues to Canadian magazines and discourage the establishment of split-run... editions'.[188] In Parliament, the Minister of Canadian Heritage was even more blunt: 'the reality of the situation is that we must protect ourselves against split-runs coming from foreign countries and, in particular, from the United States.'[189] As the Appellate Body remarked, 'Canada also admitted that the objective and structure of the tax is to insulate Canadian magazines from competition in the advertising sector, thus leaving significant Canadian advertising revenue for the production of editorial material created for the Canadian market.'[190]

This statement, and the reliance on the policy revelations above, illustrate the difficult balance which WTO rules must maintain between preserving national difference—in this case that represented by Canadian editorial content in magazines—and ensuring that states adhere to a set of uniform multilateral rules about non-discrimination. The case reveals the virtual incapacity of a

---

[184] WTO, Report of the Appellate Body, *Canada—Certain Measures Concerning Periodicals*, WT/DS31/AB/R (30 June 1997), DSR 1997:I, 449.

[185] Tariff Code 9958, Customs Tariff, RSC 1985, c 41 (3rd Supp), s 114.

[186] Excise Tax Act, An Act to Amend the Excise Tax Act and the Income Tax Act, SC 1995, c 46.

[187] A Panel found: the Tariff Code was inconsistent with Art XI GATT 1994 and not justified by Art XX(d); the Excise Act was inconsistent with Art III.2 first sentence but justified within Art III.8(b) as a payment exclusively to domestic producers: WTO Panel Report, *Canada—Certain Measures Concerning Periodicals*, WT/DS31/R, DSR 1997:I para 6.1. On appeal the Appellate Body reversed the Panel's finding in respect of Art III.2 first sentence, but instead found inconsistency with Art III.2 second sentence, and overturned the Panel in relation to Art III.8(b): ibid at 479 para 6.1.

[188] *Task Force Report*, Appendix 5, p 92, ibid at 475–476.

[189] Report of the Panel, para 3.118 cited, ibid at 476.   [190] ibid.

state to foster national editorial content if it does so in a way that conflicts with international trade rules. As a result, one of the key ways in which states encourage national cultural expression has been stymied. Publication of nationally specific editorial material in popular periodicals is a common form of national cultural expression, but any encouragement to national producers which has the effect of discriminating against imports will be inconsistent with GATT.

This is not to say that the decision is unwarranted under WTO rules where national treatment must be accorded to like products. According to previous AB interpretations, this means that products which are directly competitive or substitutable must not be taxed in a dissimilar fashion and must not be afforded protection.[191] Competition within the same segment of the market indicated that in the *Canada—Periodicals* Case the products were in direct competition.[192] The tax was of such a magnitude as to make clear that they were being taxed in a dissimilar fashion, and ministerial statements at the time the tax was introduced, along with its practical effect, indicated that it did afford protection.[193]

But while it may be correct to say that under existing rules Canada has breached their international obligations, it is equally clear that the consequences of the decision for the ability of states to encourage or even permit the manufacture of national cultural products has been severely curtailed. Again, is the institutional management image of a constitutionalized system able to negotiate the dilemma of managing difference in relation to matters such as production of cultural expression, if the rules of non-discrimination are interpreted strictly?

One way out of the conundrum would be to adopt a more nuanced set of criteria for determining what is a 'like product'. In the *France—Asbestos*[194] decision, the AB did just that. In that case, the AB decided that health considerations about carcinogenic inputs in products may be taken into account when assessing the 'likeness' of products, alongside the more conventional factors such as end-use, market, and customer habit. The question therefore arises how far this trend might develop. What other factors might become relevant in determining 'likeness'? Would environmental goals be relevant, for example? If health protection, why not culture? Whatever the answer is, it is clear that a richer definition of 'like product' may allow the AB to avoid or at least minimize, or at least better negotiate, the difference–sovereignty problem.

Related to this issue of balancing integration against diversity is the question of how states may maintain high standards of social regulation in the face

[191] World Trade Organization, Report of the Appellate Body, *Japan—Taxes on Alcoholic Beverages*, WT/DS8/AB/R, WT/DS10/AB/R, WT/DS11/AB/R (4 October 1996) DSR 1996:I, 97.

[192] WTO, Report of the Appellate Body, *Canada—Certain Measures Concerning Periodicals*, WT/DS31/AB/R (30 June 1997), DSR 1997:I, 449 at 473.   [193] ibid 474–475.

[194] WTO, Report of the Appellate Body, *European Communities—Measures Affecting Asbestos and Asbestos-Containing Products*, WT/DS135/ARB/R (12 March 2001) DSR 2001:VII, 3243.

of institutional management constitutionalization. Some argue that pressures on the domestic regulatory field of states by the WTO has led to 'regulatory arbitrage',[195] in which states compete to lower their standards in order to attract investment. Moreover, intensive regulatory competition in combination with globalization of the international economy has undermined classical assumptions underpinning trade theory. Langille says that 'domestic governmental regulatory policy becomes a "factor endowment" and regulatory competition is the norm'.[196] Accordingly, comparative advantage is no longer strictly applicable as production specialization does not take place in particular states. Instead, multinational corporations fragment production by buying materials in one place, manufacturing parts here, processing, distributing, and selling them elsewhere, and transferring capital when their investments are no longer viable. Finally, while capital has the power of 'exit', labour does not.[197] The classical model of economic theory does not any more, according to Langille, realistically describe current trade patterns. If then, the techniques of international trade law are themselves a product of these classical assumptions, then they also may be poorly suited to analysing the current crises. With regulatory competition rife, as Langille suggests, it is rational for states to defect by lowering labour standards.[198] It is rational for a majority of states to refuse to reject inclusion of labour within the WTO. How, then, can institutional managerial techniques resolve matters of trade and labour policy and law if regulatory arbitrage is commonplace? Comparative advantage in labour is, after all, hard to square with transnational corporate separation of the factors of production and the immobility of labour.

In sum, managerialism is supposed to perform the function which deliberation plays in the constitutionalization process by promoting a strong public sphere with high levels of dialogue, communication, and civil participation. In practice, management techniques emphasize the stabilization of expectations, maintenance of the status quo, and a form of neutral decision-making which attempts to cabin the expansion of its competence to narrow trade-related matters. Moreover, we have seen that managerialism can lead to open-ended, formal, mechanistic communication and dialogue, resulting in superficial agreements which nevertheless mask unstated assumptions of classical free-trade theory and can reduce opportunities for dialogue by promoting unequal power relations. Its limitations as a substitute for deliberation are illustrated by the continuing tension within the cases between allowing the international order to fulfil its stated program and ensuring that states retain full decision-making capacity. Moreover, it may not be possible for states to maintain high regulatory standards in the face of this approach, nor for the law generated by it to be naturally corralled.

[195] Langille (n 74 above) 318.   [196] ibid 305.   [197] ibid.   [198] ibid 321.

4.2.3   An empirical, pragmatic method with transformative aspirations

This section will show that the constitutionalization claim of institutional managerialism is based on an uncritical deduction about the factual changes associated with the international trade system. Institutional managerial constitutionalization presents constitutionalization as a naturally occurring phenomenon rather than a controversial result of strongly contested legal and political developments. Moreover, there is a tension between the empirical basis of the approach and its desire to transform the WTO. Therefore, the critique asks, has *Grundnorm* change occurred in the manner assumed necessary under the received account of constitutionalization, or is a new constitutionalized WTO being willed into being, so to speak, by writers and promoters of the approach?

Institutional managerialism represents itself as an empirical approach which has deduced the existence of a process of constitutionalization from factual evidence of change within the WTO. It claims that, through observation of changes that are perceived to be already underway in the international trade system, a new WTO constitution has been discovered. ' "[C]onstitutionalism" or "constitutional evolution"…[is] *what we see* in the historical process that got us to where we are now.' [Emphasis added].[199] Furthermore, the phenomena which give rise to the need for a trade constitution are presented as naturally occurring. For example, we are witnessing what is called 'gallop[ing]'[200] interdependence, a phenomenon which is characterized as a naturally occurring fact which happens when national sovereignty contracts and 'economic forces flow with great rapidity from one country to the next'.[201]

Consistent with this facts-based approach, the institutional managerialism model suggests that the sources of constitutionalization are not only legal. Thus, the leading text draws on international economic 'relations', rather than law. Its method is interdisciplinary; it lacks 'charts and mathematical proofs' and other such tools of conventional economics or law, and relies instead on an 'integrated knowledge of the way the "international trade system" really operates in today's complex and interdependent economic-legal-political environment'.[202] According to this approach, the constitution of institutional managerialism is firmly rooted within an empirical method which derives law from social, political, and economic facts.

This empirical method is combined with a form of pragmatism[203] that bears a resemblance to North American legal pragmatism, a theory that conceives itself as a branch of social science, rather than law.[204] Institutional managerialism,

---

[199] Jackson, *WTO Constitution* (n 1 above).
[200] Jackson, Davey and Sykes, *Legal Problems*, 3rd edn (n 3 above) 1232.   [201] ibid 1.
[202] Jackson, *The World Trading System* (n 3 above) 10.   [203] Kennedy (n 57 above) 102.
[204] Posner (n 126 above). Posner's main target is Ronald Dworkin who has, in Posner's view, at 91, led to the 'infection of legal theory by moral theory'.

like legal pragmatism, adopts a functional analysis.[205] Although, whereas the latter relies on empirical data in the form of history, psychology, sociology, and economics, (plus, where necessary, supplementation by considerations of feasibility, prudence, and institutional capacity),[206] institutional managerialism involves 'pragmatic and empirical analysis of the motivating factors and circumstances of real transactions and government actions'.[207] Like trade law constitutionalization, pragmatism relies heavily on economics, because, according to pragmatism, economics is the most accurate of all explanatory theories, however imperfect, owing to its use of models, natural experiments, and other forms of proof.[208] From this perspective, the new constitutionalization of international trade is the antithesis of an old international law which a critic of institutional managerialism (ironically) refers to as 'mired in foolish formalism'.[209] Instead, a constitutionalized system emerges with an 'enormous burst of inventive energy', pragmatic and institutional and private.[210]

According to this approach then, the constitutionalized WTO has simply evolved and exists for all to see; its sources are based in fact not just law.

In addition to pursuing an empirical method of deducing constitutionalization, institutional managerialism reflects another of the themes of international economic law, a desire to transform world order; institutional managerial constitutionalization comes with normative program. For example, the WTO is portrayed as hidebound by old GATT practices, and so institutional managerialism advocates its reform. It wants to sweep away what it refers to as seven 'mantras'[211] which dominate the organization, including an insistence on consensus decision-making; a 'member-driven' structure; composition by governments to the exclusion of non-state actors; and a reluctance to permit derogations from the package of obligations in the WTO agreements.[212] From the perspective of institutional managerialism the WTO is in a 'constitutional crisis'.[213] It lacks transparency. It has inadequate non-state actor participation. It suffers from institutional decision-making paralysis arising from rules requiring consensus or supermajorities. And the role of the Appellate Body in rule-making, rather than rule-applying, should be scrutinized. Concrete reforms of the internal constitution are therefore proposed, including opening up hearings; establishing a standing committee to assist the Director General; and accrediting non-government organizations to participate in some aspects of the WTO.

---

[205] Posner (n 126 above) at 46.
[206] ibid 129–130. Posner concedes the use of principles but only as instrumental means to achieve social goals, not goods in themselves and characterizes religious toleration and political equality as means to ends not ends in themselves: ibid 111.
[207] Jackson, *The World Trading System* (n 3 above) 6.   [208] Posner (n 126 above) 15, 46.
[209] Kennedy (n 57 above) 19.   [210] ibid.
[211] Jackson, 'Seven Mantras' (n 10 above) 71–73.
[212] Jackson, 'Interesting Times' (n 27 above) 8.
[213] JH Jackson, 'Address at British Institute of International and Comparative Law', WTO Conference, 15 May 2002.

Other institutional managerialists are less sanguine about the possibilities of these sorts of relatively minor technical reforms and advocate more deep-seated reform. For them, the WTO is gripped by a major legitimacy crisis which cannot be reformed by tinkering at the edges. Claude Barfield[214] argues that there is an 'imbalance' between a strong and efficient adjudicatory structure, which has strayed into law-making rather than law-applying, and a weak and inefficient rule-making side, where decisions must generally be made by consensus and the apparatus of legislative process is rudimentary. Barfield's antidote is to return to 'flexible' 'diplomatic' methods of dispute resolution, force states to conciliate and mediate, and even introduce a blocking mechanism whereby the membership could refuse to adopt a decision of the AB objected to by a substantial minority of members.

Other institutionalists respond that Barfield's cure is worse than the disease. The judicial model was developed precisely because the diplomatic model did not work.[215] The answer is not to make the efficient dispute settlement model inefficient, but to make rule-making more efficient,[216] to address the problem of the 'missing legislator',[217] even if this is thought by some to be 'almost impossible'.[218] Instead, the argument goes, greater openness and transparency in the institution as a whole should be promoted, including regular use of *amicus* briefs, and public access to proceedings at both first instance and review stages, with suitable protections for business confidentiality.

The late Robert Hudec[219] was more critical still of the desire to return to the good old days. He insisted that Barfield misconstrued the nature of 'diplomatic' resolution of disputes under GATT, underestimated the problems associated with (re)instituting a political filter for judicial decisions, and failed to prove the existence of any constitutional crisis. 'Diplomatic' in relation to GATT did not mean 'non-legal' at all, according to Hudec; third-party-legalized adjudication existed in fact throughout the period (apart from a brief hiatus during the 1960s).[220] Any political filter of judicial decision-making would create the fear of block votes outweighing Members such as the US and even the EU, and so would not be feasible.[221] Ultimately, Barfield is presented as a naïve critic who does not adequately support his claim[222] because he fails to appreciate the ways in which courts constantly finesse decisions which could

---

[214] CE Barfield, *Free Trade, Sovereignty, Democracy: The Future of the World Trade Organization* (Washington DC: American Enterprise Institute, 2001).

[215] Steger (n 123 above) 566.

[216] ibid 568.   [217] von Bogdandy (n 134 above) 651.   [218] Steger (n 123 above) 565–570.

[219] RE Hudec, 'Free trade, sovereignty, democracy: the future of the World Trade Organization' (2002) 1 *World Trade Review* 211 (reviewing CE Barfield, *Free Trade, Sovereignty, Democracy: The Future of the World Trade Organization* (2001)).

[220] Hudec provides an elegant history of the changes in the meaning of 'diplomatic' within GATT that does not reduce the term to merely decision-making on political grounds: ibid 219–220.

[221] ibid 221–222.   [222] ibid 215–219.

potentially create politically charged situations,[223] and fails to substantiate his arguments in law.[224]

Regardless of the position on reform taken by the various types of institutional managerial constitutionalization, all of the above arguments reflect an enthusiasm for reforming the WTO. They are concerned with making the WTO work better, not with adding a new and radical interpretation of the agreements. Whereas rights-based constitutionalization, discussed in Chapter 5, seeks to alter some of the parameters of the field of international trade law, the model under discussion is not keen to disturb them. Nor are the institutionalist arguments concerned with questioning the very underlying foundations of the entire system of the WTO, which we shall see is the preferred approach of those we label the 'anti-constitutionalization' perspective in Chapter 7.

The other level at which institutional managerial constitutionalists urge reform is in relation to broader international affairs. They claim that old assumptions about the benefits of increased trade have been shown to be flawed, and that, although this does not prove that the old supporting assumptions were wrong, new challenges have arisen. Yet rather than rejecting classical economic free trade theory, institutional managerialism argues that the future is one of 'challenge', a time to 'face up to dilemmas posed by old thinking and institutions, by globalization and technology'.[225] These challenges for the WTO are to develop appropriate safety nets for people affected by adjustment resulting from reduction of trade barriers; balance non-economic goals with economic ones; develop new styles of international decision-making; and even tame weapons of mass destruction.[226] Although institutional managerialism is not suggesting that international trade can single-handedly achieve these goals, the inclusion of a set of far-reaching objectives suggests that the approach has an enormous faith in the transformative capacity of the WTO to contribute to their resolution. The next trade negotiation round is said to 'resemble a Global Constitutional Convention'.[227] The next stage of 'global constitutionalism' will 'involve decades or even centuries of discussions and refinements', and the 'mission' of the organization 'must be understood as fundamentally an exercise in global-scale regime building with profound effects for every person on the planet'.[228]

Similarly, there is optimism about the WTO and its constitutional development, especially in relation to matters beyond its immediate jurisdiction. The *Shrimp-Turtle* decision[229] is a landmark decision because it articulated a

[223] Hudec (n 219 above) 215 (noting that courts possess many legal tools that permit them to deflect pressures to legislate and to avoid head-on collisions with immovable objects).
[224] ibid 215 (questioning why Barfield has to, as Barfield puts it 'plow through' legal arguments which are supposed to support his (Barfield's) views; and chiding Barfield for failing to understand that all judges 'gap-fill' to an extent, as a natural part of legal interpretation).
[225] Jackson, 'Interesting Times' (n 27 above) 10.   [226] ibid 10–11.
[227] Esty (n 16 above) 12.   [228] ibid.
[229] WTO, Report of the Appellate Body, *United States—Import Prohibition of Certain Shrimp and Shrimp Products*, WT/DS58/AB/R (12 October 1998), DSR 1998:VII, 2755 at para 121.

nuanced understanding of the difficult relationship between the WTO agreements and international environmental law. Sovereignty was revealed not to have a binary nature in the sense that states either have all control over an issue or none at all, but rather to be a question of power-allocation, and a question that can be disaggregated into individual issues which can then be addressed separately.

Managerial institutionalism constitutionalization is full of practical solutions and enthusiasm for reform. For example, says Professor Jackson,[230] the answer to the problem of labour–trade linkage being misused by protectionist interests is to mollify poor countries by introducing a special response if a state acts in a protectionist manner in relation to labour. The introduction of incentives for well-performing poorer states would improve labour standards by providing increased tariff-free access or direct aid to assist adjustment. A moratorium on the imposition of anti-dumping duties against poor countries would be worthwhile. Intellectual property royalty payments could be waived in relation to the poorest countries in respect of pharmaceutical and environmental products. The democratic deficit of the World Bank and IMF needs addressing, while consensus decision-making needs to be reformed at the WTO. A constitutionalized system of international trade, in the form of institutional managerialism, can and must meet important challenges posed by globalization, and respond to complex demands of a distributive and democratic nature.

In short, alongside an empirical method for deriving the existence of WTO constitutionalization sits a strong desire to transform the WTO internally through a series of reforms, or, in some guises, to effect a more radical return to its former diplomatic incarnation. Externally, WTO institutional managerial constitutionalization proposes a series of practical solutions to transform a wide range of world political problems, such that this form of constitutionalization positions itself as a universal remedy for international disorder.

The empirical approach to constitutionalization combined, as it is, with aspirational goals presents an interesting dilemma. On the one hand, the institutional managerial model of constitutionalization finds constitutionalization in the social facts of WTO change, and on the other hand it claims that those facts should change in order for the WTO to constitutionalize properly. Moreover, on the one hand the approach claims that constitutionalization just *is*, a modest project on this account; on the other, constitutionalization is presented as a curative for international politics. A series of questions arise. Is it possible to separate the facts upon which the constitutionalized WTO is supposed to have just emerged, almost preformed, so to speak, from the argument about whether the thing itself fits the conception of what a constitution is? What are the consequences of claiming a basis in fact? Can a pragmatic, already existing constitution also be a vehicle for radical transformation of the international economic order? Is there a tension between the stability of

---

[230] Jackson, 'Interesting Times' (n 27 above) 12.

the institutional managerial constitution and its function as a plausible mechanism for inducing worldwide change? These questions lead to a number of criticisms.

First, managerial institutionalism, as we have seen, presents itself as simply deducing a theory about the emergence of a constitution from the existence of pre-existing facts. According to institutional managerialism, the idea of, or desire for, constitutionalization does not precede the construction of a theory around it. There is an inevitability about the pull of history, which is mirrored in John Jackson's famous formulation that the evolution of GATT is, like civilization, the evolution from power-based diplomacy to rules-based diplomacy. It assumes that the story of the international trade system is a linear one, in which any new chapter in the development of trade is positive and progressive, when, in practice, some would cavil at the idea that all changes have been beneficial. Nevertheless, institutional managerialism claims that pre-existing facts took us to where we are now, with a natural momentum, which could not be altered, or indeed stopped.

Not only are the conditions for constitutionalization wholly factual but the thing they create—the constitutionalization process—is factual as well. The fact-based approach to the constitutionalization process leads to the view that the process itself is a factual construct, rather than a conceptual or normative one. In David Kennedy's words, the constitution of the WTO is '[a]n imaginary trade constitution, [which treats] liberal trade ideas, national and international political judgments, a decentralized regime of bargained reciprocity as *facts* rather than commitments'.[231] To this extent Kennedy situates Jackson in the tradition of a post-Second-World-War pragmatism, replacing the idealism of the pre-First-World-War era and the disappointment of the inter-war period. International law and international lawyers of the post-war era are '[i]mbued with new practical spirit, an orientation to process and policy at once contextual, purposive and functional'.[232]

Institutional managerial constitutionalization aims to base itself purely on facts and yet the factual record at the WTO does not necessarily accord with the claim that the WTO has been constitutionalized. If we begin from positivism's approach to the evolution of a new legal system, discussed in Chapter 2, we could assess the claim of constitutionalization by examining whether the new system was effective, according to a series of factors including continuation of business, recognition by governments, economic viability, and collection of taxes. The WTO system is effective because it simply continued the work of the old GATT ('government') in matters of trade liberalization, and dispute resolution. Moreover, it is effective in respect of recognition by government, since 140 or so states signed up immediately to the package of agreements. Neither economic viability nor collection of taxes are relevant yardsticks of

---

[231] Kennedy (n 57 above) 102.   [232] ibid 21.

effectiveness for the WTO because they apply only to a new state and not a new international institution.

However, in key respects, the WTO does not satisfy other criteria of change, set out in the description of the received account in Chapter 2, such as public acceptance; existence of contending rival for power; and abrupt change, beyond the contemplation of the old order, causing destruction of the previous order. Public acceptance of the new system is mixed at the very least; although trade law officials and governments have accepted the new arrangements, large sections of the public seem less willing to do so, as indicated by ongoing large-scale protest against its actions. No contending rival to WTO authority explicitly exists, although a number of specific subject matter organizations have asserted control over these various subject matters at different times.[233] Moreover, the change aspect of *Grundnorm* emergence, arguably, remains unfulfilled. Change was not abrupt but gradual;[234] it did not occur beyond the contemplation of the old system;[235] and it did not cause the destruction of the pre-existing legal order.[236] If anything, the transition between the old GATT 1947 and the new GATT 1994 was mild to some, and invisible to most. Indeed, the non-contentious nature of the change between GATT 1947 and WTO 1995 explains the shock many felt when some commentators began speaking about the new system as if it was constitutionalized. In short, there are insufficient extra-legal facts evidencing the emergence of a new constitutional system, despite the obvious institutional change from the GATT 1947 to the WTO in 1995. On this view, the WTO was a case of continuation of a smooth and unbroken line of legal authority that neither broke with the past system nor established a new differentiated and constitutionalized system of law.

Moreover, the factual evidence upon which institutional managerial constitutionalization is based is incomplete because it excludes some of the key background legal rules which constitute the system upon which WTO constitutionalization is built. So a range of national and international laws that structure the very entities upon which the international trade constitution operates are, with some exceptions, excluded from the ambit of institutional managerial constitutionalization. National laws of contract and property, which

---

[233] The World Intellectual Property Organization (WIPO) was perceived by some as a rival in relation to intellectual property matters. The International Labour Organization retains control over labour issues, even related to trade. Controversy exists over whether environment falls within the ambit of the WTO or multilateral environmental agreements.

[234] The Uruguay Round, which inaugurated the new organization, ran from 1986 to 1994.

[235] Change was contemplated under GATT 1947 Article XXX dealing with amendment, and Article XXV dealing with joint action by contracting parties.

[236] Note that the answer to this question may depend in part on which pre-existing legal order the WTO is said to have broken away from. If the pre-existing legal order is considered to comprise national systems of law, or international law, then the break may be considered less legitimate, than if the pre-existing order consists of GATT, in which case the new order was in the contemplation of the old.

define the entities capable of inhabiting the field, are not considered part of the WTO constitution. International regulation of those rules is excluded too. The rules that form the background to resolution of conflicts between national rules,[237] and between national and international, are not included in the constitutional structure of institutional managerialism. Domestic laws, which directly affect the operation of international trade, such as commercial laws or corporations law, do not form a part of the constitutionalized WTO's ambit. Institutional managerial constitutionalization ignores laws which have indirect but significant impact on international trade, such as attempts to prohibit investment by companies in states which practice serious human rights abuse, or to set standards for multinational companies in relation to conflicts of interest. Institutional managerialism, then, proposes a constitution without its constituting parts. It is a constitution skewed towards a particular set of rules, which, although wide-ranging,[238] are still partial. This approach assumes the prior existence of trading entities, private economic operators, contracting rules between them, and property laws that define their ownership.[239] These things are treated as given facts that no trade constitution can or does affect. Managerial institutionalism is based on an empirical method which is incomplete, inasmuch as it considers only some of the directly affected players and some of the rules within its domain.

Furthermore, in relying on (a partial set of) facts rather than conceptual thinking, as a basis for the constitution of the WTO, some of the arguments of institutional managerialism exhibit a somewhat contradictory stance towards, for example, the role of WTO constitutionalization in relation to problems of national economic planning. On the one hand, interdependence (facilitated by the WTO process of constitutionalization) increases wealth by reducing costs, improving opportunities of choice, facilitating competition, and creating better economies of scale of production.[240] On the other hand, that same interdependence has frustrated states in the implementation of 'worthy' economic policies.[241] It places severe strains on governments. It can, in some situations, lead to financial crisis and potential meltdown.[242] Interest rate fluctuations in developed states can take highly indebted countries to the brink of bankruptcy; oil price changes in the Middle East can affect levels of unemployment, farm income, and living costs in the US.[243] As one critic notes, there is an element of surprise expressed by institutional managerial

---

[237] Wai (n 157 above) (arguing that private international law has a 'regulatory function').

[238] WTO rules extend beyond those aimed specifically at trade between states, such as tariffs, customs, and rules of origin. They extend, for example, to administration of such rules; internal rules relating to sales, distribution, regulation, and even taxation of goods; intellectual property; services, and possibly even competition.   [239] Kennedy (n 57 above) 26.

[240] Jackson, *The World Trading System* (n 3 above) 6.

[241] ibid 1; Jackson, 'Seven Mantras' (n 10 above) 69.

[242] Jackson, 'Interesting Times' (n 27 above) 4.

[243] Jackson, *The World Trading System* (n 3 above) 6.

constitutionalism about the magnitude and complexity of the problems the international trading system faces. 'It has become obvious [to institutional managerialism] that standards questions are much more complex than many thought, with some fundamental policy differences (such as the clash of environmental interests with trade policy goals, and questions about which government institutions should make decisions regarding difficult scientific evidence).'[244] Accompanying this interpretation of events is the view that protectionism is an ever-increasing and uncontrollable natural urge of mankind, which can only be constrained by this type of constitutionalization process. States and individuals are described as 'ingenious' in having endlessly devised new methods of imposing barriers to trade.[245] New mechanisms are required to deal with these ingenious obstacles to international flows of goods and services.[246]

Finally, institutional managerial constitutionalization, in relation to the WTO, underemphasizes the critical interplay between law and fact by failing to acknowledge that creation of a constitution is not a thing in fact, but the result of a 'recursive' interplay between law and politics.[247] The idea that a constitution can be found or identified by adopting a purely empirical method, observing and recording the facts of historical change and legal evolution, is at odds with a constitutive view of the way in which constitutional law and constitutional politics evolve, a view more common amongst European Community scholars. Walker, for example, takes the view that 'constitutional law and politics are mutually constitutive' and hence '[c]onstitutional law and discourse are no mere reflection of a prior political order, but are recursively implicated in the elaboration of that order.'[248] Therefore, he suggests that even the mere use of the language of constitutionalization has a role in creating a constitutional structure. The structure cannot be formed in the absence of the language, and indeed one of Walker's criteria of constitutionalization which he applies in relation to both the EU and the WTO is a 'self-conscious discourse of constitutionalism'[249] or 'discursive maturity'.[250] Quoting Joseph Weiler, who writes that the 'discourse of conceptualisation and imagination' has the capacity to invest the authoritative claims, institutions, and principles associated with the putative polity with polity-affirming, and thus constitutional, status, Walker concludes that this is an 'intensely reflexive process'. Constitutionalization discourse 'is not, or not simply, about observing appropriate types of data "out there [in the] constitutional landscape", but is necessarily itself a constitutive process'.[251]

Similarly, institutional managerialism undervalues the agency which academic lawyers have in contributing to the constitutionalization process, an omission that probably cannot be levelled at positive legal theory. Long ago, Hans Kelsen

---

[244] Jackson, *WTO Constitution* (n 1 above) 3.
[245] Jackson, Davey and Sykes, *Legal Problems*, 3rd edn (n 3 above) 1206.   [246] ibid.
[247] Walker (note 56 above) 39.   [248] ibid.   [249] ibid 38.   [250] ibid 35.
[251] ibid 39.

claimed that positive legal science makes conscious what lawyers already do, an explicit recognition that it is the *lawyers* who are agents in the process of postulating a new foundation.[252] Indeed, Kelsen is read by later writers as saying that a *Grundnorm* changes only when the legal scientist makes a new presupposition, albeit a choice that is heavily constrained by the certain factual preconditions.[253] The important point for present purposes is to note that positive legal theory acknowledges a tension between a desire for factual purity (for any description of law to be stripped back to a description of the law-creating facts which constitute it) and an argument for lawerly action, that legal agents *by their acts of recognizing the existence of new legal systems* can be involved in the creation of law by the imposition of an interpretation upon those law-creating facts. This problem is ignored by institutional managerialism inasmuch as it relies heavily on a fact-based method and denies the role of legal interlocutors in bringing about constitutional change in the WTO.

Ultimately, there is a tension between the factual basis of this approach and its desire to secure transformations in world order. So although this form of constitutionalization is concerned with transformation of the world trade system, and indeed aspires to achieve such, it positions itself outside the transformations, as simply observing and reflecting upon them. While other forms of constitutionalization described in later chapters present themselves as transformative, institutional managerialism presents itself as a neutral recorder of fact. This apparently modest positioning actually confirms the ambitious nature of institutional constitutionalization. 'All national partisan political programs can be accommodated by an appropriate interface.'[254] 'Institutional enhancement'[255] in the form of harmonization, reciprocity, or 'interface' is presented as an almost foolproof device to avoid conflict, resolve difference, and boost institutional strength in the sphere of international trade. The reformist enthusiasm shades into a belief in its own omnipotence.

In sum, this form of constitutionalization displays an incomplete, but adamant, form of fact-derivation which presents the conditions precipitating the approach and the constitution arising from it as essentially factual. Can institutional managerialism observe the facts in order to deduce a constitutionalization process, at the same time as seeking to change those facts? Although adopting a pragmatic social science method, it omits significant elements that structure the constitutionalization process in the first place. Most important of all, it underplays the interrelationship between the political facts,

---

[252] Although Kelsen would see this as a purely *descriptive* act, the agency of lawyering to the finding of a new device is no less active, H Kelsen, *Pure Theory of Law* (trans from the second revised and enlarged German edition edited by Max Knight, University of California Press edn, 1978) (c 1967).

[253] JW Harris, 'When and Why Does the Grundnorm Change?' (1971) 29 *Cambridge Law Journal* 103.   [254] Kennedy (n 57 above) 96.

[255] Jackson, Davey and Sykes, *Legal Problems*, 3rd edn (n 3 above) 1232.

the agency of legal commentators, and the creation of a constitutional system itself, and elides the tension between its factual basis and transformative desires.

4.3 CONCLUSION

To sum up, institutional managerialism, according to its advocates, is about the management of trade disputes, using neutral rules, in order to preserve decision-making flexibility, safeguard national diversity, and exclude a too-rapid extension of WTO law. One purpose of the management techniques of institutional managerialism is to substitute management for diplomacy and politics, and yet the form of deliberation substituted is a weak one. The institutional focus of the approach suggests the system's practices have achieved a level of coherence that signals the emergence of a new *Grundnorm*, and its conflation of institutions with constitutions lends the approach an air of legitimacy. Institutional managerial constitutionalization is factual in its method of derivation, and transformative in its goals. To the critics, however, the deliberative process it promotes is essentially unsatisfactory. Institutional managerialism is suffused with the values of free trade, unable to reconcile an inherent tension between protecting and disturbing national sovereignty, and subject to claims of political influence. Moreover, it is criticized because any legitimacy it finds is based on a conflation of the institution with a constitution. Likewise, any new basic norm is derived from facts which do not necessarily show that constitutionalization has occurred. In respect of the received tradition of constitutionalization defined in the first chapter, this model is focused strongly, though not always successfully, on issues of *Grundnorm* change, legitimacy, and deliberative process. It is cognizant of the problems of modification of relationships between the state and the international entity, but does not address the issue of the nature of the community that authorizes the purported constitutionalization process. In short, the approach does not satisfy the core elements of constitutionalization defined at the outset.

In relation to the appropriateness of the received account in the light of the WTO experience of institutional managerialism, a number of adjustments to traditional theory follow from the WTO experiment. First, it is apparent that assessing whether *Grundnorm* change has occurred is a complex matter of interpretation which may be circular and self-serving: a system is said to have developed a new *Grundnorm* when the facts change, and the facts change when the new *Grundnorm* is apparent. The actual conditions of *Grundnorm* change require further thought when applying the notion to the international legal context. Secondly, it is possible to utilize the legitimacy of the constitutionalization process by reconceiving a simple institution in constitutional terms. The idea of legitimacy needs clarification in the international law context in order to avoid the outcome that any strong institution can be automatically equated with a new constitutional structure. Thirdly, the requirement of deliberative process is inadequately met by the WTO experience of decision-making by management technique. Again, in the international context, a stronger form of deliberation should be assumed. In short, the institutional managerial model of WTO constitutionalization discloses significant gaps in the traditional account of constitutionalization which was, largely, conceived of as a state-centred account. In order to rethink constitutionalization at the international level, the basic requirements would need to be reconfigured in light of the WTO experience.

5

Rights-Based Constitutionalization

5.1 INTRODUCTION

In the last chapter we saw that managerial institutionalism was marked by an emphasis on some of the core elements of constitutionalization, defined in Chapter 2, such as *Grundnorm* change (by its focus on the deduction of constitutionalization from a set of 'facts'), legitimacy (in the way it conflated an institution with a constitution), and deliberation (with the use of management techniques of decision-making). By contrast, the rights-based approach focuses primarily on rights, a non-core element of constitutionalization. Yet the approach shares an interest of that aspect of the received account of constitutionalization which is concerned with recognition of citizens as subjects of a constitutionalized community. However, the theory is less expressive of other key aspects of constitutionalization such as the creation and role of the community itself, deliberation, and *Grundnorm* change. It does, more recently, address itself to another core aspect, namely legitimacy of the constitutionalization process. In general, what this model aspires to—a community of rights-bearing consumer-citizens—is more strongly associated with an elaborated concept of the constitutionalization process, and does not accord with the definition of what constitutes the received account of core constitutionalization. Again questions are raised about the appropriateness of the received account as an ongoing model for post-national constitution building.

The rights-based approach is primarily associated with the work of one writer, Ernst-Ulrich Petersmann, who, over a period of twenty years, has constructed an openly prescriptive, highly controversial theory about what WTO law *should* be, namely a rights-based system for protecting not only states' but individuals' so-called right to trade.[1]

---

[1] Petersmann uses the term 'rights-based' to describe his view of constitutionalism: E-U Petersmann (ed) *International Trade Law and GATT/WTO Dispute Settlement System*, (London: Kluwer, 1997) [hereinafter *Dispute Settlement*] 8. See also: E-U Petersmann, *Constitutional Functions and Constitutional Problems of International Economic Law* (Fribourg, Switz: University Press, 1991) [hereinafter *Constitutional Functions*] and E-U Petersmann, *The GATT/WTO Dispute Settlement System: International Law, International Organizations and Dispute Settlement* (London: Kluwer, 1997) [hereinafter *International Law and Dispute Settlement*].

Briefly, the rights-based approach to constitutionalization is a grand and ambitious theory which is characterized by a number of flaws:

- A disjuncture between a focus on market rights and their direct effect, in the early phase of the theory, and human rights in the current phase. A particular problem here is the attempt to wish away a serious tension between market rights and a different tradition of economic and social rights (to the detriment of the latter).
- A sometimes uncomfortable mix of strategic justifications and normative goals and values.
- A visionary mode informed primarily by a desire to facilitate individual economic goals over social or cultural production. The right to go to market has the potential to overwhelm other forms of human activity as citizens are recast as consumers, and capital smothers demos.

5.2 FEATURES OF RIGHTS-BASED CONSTITUTIONALIZATION

5.2.1 From rights to human rights

The key feature of the rights-based approach to constitutionalization is, obviously, the argument that WTO law consists of rights. In the early phase of the model the claim is that the WTO agreements consist of a series of rights; in the later phase the model claims that they consist of a series of *human* rights. The conceptualization of trade as rights primarily reflects a concern with one of the elements of an elaborated form of constitutionalization (rights), although to a large extent this is in the service of achieving greater legitimacy. Indeed by the time rights-based constitutionalization recasts itself as a theory about the WTO and human rights, the model is almost entirely focused on the legitimacy factor.

The early phase—'rights' to trade

So let us begin with the early phase. In *Constitutional Functions and Constitutional Problems of International Economic Law* (1991), Petersmann argued that international trade law served a 'constitutional function' by restraining governmental action through the conception of WTO rules as rights. This constitutional function was operationalized by construing GATT–WTO law as a system of protection for individual economic rights beyond national borders. Here the rights-based nature of WTO law was said to be evident in the inclusion in the agreements of a range of *private rights*, rights that attach to individuals not just states. These private rights may be substantive, such as intellectual property rights requiring states to recognize particular forms of intellectual property protections recognized in international conventions and incorporated into the TRIPs agreement. Or they may be procedural, such as requiring Member States to maintain procedures, for example, guaranteeing private access to domestic review in certain matter;[2] renewing administration of customs matters;[3] or government procurement;[4] or national subsidy determinations;[5] or allowing enforcement of intellectual property rights.[6] The important point is that the *subjects* of international trade law should be not just Member States (or Contracting Parties as was the case under GATT) but also individuals.[7] 'The numerous special interest rules and protectionist deviations in the domestic laws of government on the implementation of their WTO obligations could be much more effectively limited if the citizens were treated as legal subjects and beneficiaries of the WTO guarantees of freedom and non-discrimination.'[8] The claim to rights amounts both to a claim that the WTO should enforce rights external to the system (TRIPs enforcement of intellectual property rights) and that there is some sort of more generalized 'right to trade' inherent in the system.

This rights-based view oscillates between a claim that the WTO has direct effect[9] and a claim that it could be interpreted as such.[10] Nevertheless, the key purpose of the approach is to stress that a rights-based reading of WTO law would strengthen its overall effectiveness and legitimacy[11] by safeguarding individual rights.

Petersmann's argument for the direct invocability of WTO law in national systems has not been generally accepted. The only explicit expansion of rights of private actors has been to accord then some limited rights of intervention. For example, there has been an ongoing controversy about the ability of private parties to intervene in dispute settlement proceedings, which culminated in the AB affirming both its authority and the authority of panels to receive

---

[2] TRIPS Agreement, Arts 41, 42.   [3] GATT, Art. X:3 (b).
[4] Agreement on Government Procurement, 15 April 1994, WTO Agreement, Annex 4, *The Results of the Uruguay Round of Multilateral Trade Negotiations: The Legal Texts* (1994) [hereinafter GPA Agreement] XX:2.
[5] Agreement on Subsidies and Countervailing Measures, 15 April 1994, WTO Agreement, Annex 1A, *The Results of the Uruguay Round of Multilateral Trade Negotiations: The Legal Texts* (1994) [hereinafter SCM Agreement] Art 23.   [6] TRIPS Agreement, Art 42.
[7] Petersmann, *Dispute Settlement* (n 1 above) 9.   [8] ibid 10.
[9] See, eg, ibid 9 (arguing that the WTO Agreements contain 'numerous precise and unconditional guarantees' including the ones just mentioned in the text above).
[10] See ibid 72 (arguing that WTO provisions '*seem to imply*' 'direct applicability' of WTO law in national courts. See also ibid 120 that there is no requirement on states to incorporate WTO law fully, because in the face of 'diversity of national systems' this would be 'politically unacceptable' but that WTO law is drafted 'enabling' states to incorporate it. Note Petersmann refers to both direct effect and direct applicability).
[11] ibid 73 (likening his approach to the European Union's preliminary procedure, to the extent that citizens become instrumental in enforcing EU law).

submissions from private parties.[12] Yet the rights-based arguments of this model go beyond a claim to rights of representation within WTO proceedings. According to rights-based constitutionalization, WTO agreements have the *potential to be directly invoked by individuals* in national tribunals, and any state attempts to deny that possibility are not legally binding.[13] WTO provisions may be accorded direct effect because, as we have just discussed, some are formulated as private rights, and many are sufficiently precise and unconditional to permit invocation by individuals. Moreover, goes the claim, state practice in Germany and Switzerland allows such a course of action, evidenced by the fact that certain TRIPs rules are directly applicable in domestic courts of those states.[14]

Rights-based constitutionalization would, also, consistent with its central claim, facilitate use of WTO law by domestic courts as an *interpretative guideline* or aid to interpretation in assessing the exercise of executive and legislative foreign policy power thus checking. The effects of this might be quite broad, for example, in extending the classes of participants in national trade-remedy investigative processes. So procedural safeguards, which require safeguard investigations to take account of 'all interested parties', could be interpreted to include the interests of consumers as well as producers.

Moreover, adoption of rights-based constitutionalized WTO law would strengthen domestic rights of *judicial review*.[15] National courts might refer to WTO provisions in assessing whether national measures could be subject to review. Petersmann argues that national courts should subject national legislation to broad grounds of review based on the WTO Agreements. For example, national courts might review national measures in relation to WTO obligations according to the standard administrative grounds such as procedural failure, fact inaccuracy, manifest error, misuse of discretion, inadequate

---

[12] WTO, Report of the Appellate Body, *United States—Import Prohibition of Certain Shrimp and Shrimp Products*, WT/DS58/AB/R (12 October 1998), DSR 1998:VII, 2755 at para 121. For recent affirmation of the principle of private participation through submission of amicus briefs see, WTO, Report of the Appellate Body, *European Communities—Trade Description of Sardines*, WT/DS231/AB/R (26 September 2002) at paras 157–158.

[13] Petersmann, *Dispute Settlement* (n 1 above) 121 (arguing, for example, that the EC Council Decision of 23 December 1994 asserting that WTO law cannot be directly invoked in Community or Member State courts is not legally binding on the European Court of Justice).

[14] Petersmann, *International Law and Dispute Settlement* (n 1 above) 21.

[15] Note that the debate about judicial review has echoes in current US constitutional debate over whether the constitution is just ordinary law or a form of special law. See, eg, LD Kramer, 'The Supreme Court 2000 Term' (2001) 115 *Harvard Law Review* 5, 9, 12 (arguing that the constitution may be ordinary law—and so subject to judicial review—but that this was not the case in the 18th century when it was a 'special form of popular will' and so not subject to interpretation by judges at all). So if WTO law is constitutional law, this does not necessary lead to the conclusion that it must be subject to judicial review; WTO constitutionalized law could simply be a form of what Kramer calls 'popular constitutionalism', ibid 11, falling to be interpreted by the political community from which it is derived.

reasoning, and violation of substantive rules.[16] This also would strengthen 'grass-roots-enforcement' of WTO law.[17]

Finally, rights-based constitutionalization would facilitate interpretation of domestic law by municipal courts in *conformity* with liberal trade rules. This, it is claimed, is consistent with the WTO Agreement itself,[18] and the traditional requirement of domestic law that domestic courts construe domestic law in conformity with international law.[19] Domestic courts should recognize that they have the power to interpret unconditional international obligations contained in GATT–WTO law as conferring corresponding rights on domestic citizens, especially in view of the international law requirement on national agencies (including courts) that they implement international law in good faith.[20]

Although controversial to some extent Petermann's arguments have infiltrated arguments about the WTO obligations and the reception of WTO law in the European legal order. The recent WTO case *EC—Sardines* could be read as a weak expression of the underlying thesis that informs the rights-based view, though not by creating any specific right with direct effect. Here, the AB indirectly strengthened the effect of WTO rules by deciding that the agreement on technical barriers to trade applied to technical regulations adopted prior to 1995 that continued in existence.[21] The EC was therefore required to adjust its product standard prohibiting labelling of Peruvian pilchards as 'sardines'. The result seems to imply that the obligations in the agreements go beyond ordinary international legal obligations, the breach of which gives rise to state responsibility. Instead, the treaty creates the expectation that WTO obligations should be translated into national law, consistent with the conformity requirement in Article XVI of the WTO Agreement. By giving a strong interpretation to the conformity requirement, the AB could be seen as acting consistently with the rights-based approach, to the extent that it indirectly strengthens the effect of WTO rules. This extension is consistent with the rights-based reading of constitutionalization, which argues for a deepening of the effect of WTO law through principles such as 'conformity'.

In relation to EC law, Francis Snyder argues that, despite the absence of direct effect of WTO law in the European legal order,[22] WTO law influences EC law through a variety of means including a presumption of compatibility between EC and WTO law; regular interpretation by European institutions;

---

[16] Petersmann, *Dispute Settlement* (n 1 above) 110.   [17] ibid 119.

[18] ibid 120 (referring to WTO Agreement XVI.4 which provides that Members shall ensure the conformity of its laws, regulations, and administrative procedures with its obligations as provided in the annexed Agreements, and GATT Article X:3 stating that each contracting party shall administer in a uniform, impartial, and reasonable manner all its law, regulations, decisions, or rulings).

[19] ibid 115.   [20] ibid.

[21] WTO, Report of the Appellate Body, *European Communities—Trade Description of Sardines*, WT/DS231/AB/R (26 September 2002) at para 205.

[22] F Snyder, 'The Gatekeepers: The European Courts and WTO Law', (2003) 40 *Common Market Law Review* 313–367 discussing, *inter alia*, Case C–149/96 *Portugal v Council* [1999] ECR I–8395.

as an interpretative aid in European courts; and, importantly, through what have become known as the implementation exceptions. According to these exceptions, WTO law is not a criterion of legality for assessing EC measures except where the Community measure refers to the WTO agreements (the clear reference exception), or where the EC law intended to implement a particular WTO obligation (the transposition exception). Finally, as Snyder points out, there is a growing trend in EC legal argumentation to use the principles of indirect effect or consistent interpretation to bring WTO law to bear on the EC legal order.

In short, the early phase of rights-based constitutionalization suggested that the subjects of WTO law should be extended to include individuals, and a recognition that WTO law contains private rights, invocable by individuals in national courts. One purpose of this was to enhance the legitimacy of WTO law by recognizing that individuals had rights within it. Moreover, even if direct effect of WTO law is not completely accepted, the rights-based view would, it is argued, strengthen domestic judicial review based on WTO obligations; lead domestic courts to construe domestic law using WTO law as an aid to interpretation; and require stronger adherence to the principle of conformity of interpretation.

Current phase—'human rights' to trade

In the current phase, Petersmann has shifted from an emphasis on the language of 'rights' to 'human rights'. In this current form, Petersmann's rights-based constitutionalization expresses three related sets of concerns: linking trade and human rights; responding to the claims of the anti-WTO protest movement without giving up the claims of free trade; and inserting free trade deep into domestic legal arrangements. In this incarnation, the rights-based approach has transformed itself into a human rights model which is primarily concerned with an 'urgent need to clarify the potential synergies and interrelationships between human rights and international economic law'.[23] This transformation has been effected in a number of ways. It builds upon an analogy between human rights and international trade by emphasizing, for example, the relationship between international law's principle of non-discrimination against women and nationalities, and international trade law's emphasis upon discrimination against foreign traders and producers.[24] To emphasize these linkages, Petersmann develops a research agenda for a synthesized human rights–international trade law rights approach.[25] A combined agenda would,

---

[23] E-U Petersmann, 'Human Rights and International Economic Law in the Twenty First Century' (2001) 4 *Journal of International Economic Law* 3, 6 [hereinafter 'Human Rights and International Economic Law']. See, also, E-U Petersmann, 'Time for a United Nations "Global Compact" for Integrating Human Rights into the Law of Worldwide Organizations' (2002) 13 *European Journal of International Law* 621 [hereinafter 'Global Compact'].   [24] ibid 30.
[25] ibid 6–7.

for example, research the relationship between the human right to liberty and the authorization by the WTO of countermeasures including withdrawal of intellectual property rights. It would explore the balancing of a social right to health with intellectual property protection. It would examine ways in which individuals could be made subjects of international trade law and would explore the interpretation of WTO law in the light of human rights law. It might even query WTO rules on non-reparation in the light of state responsibility rules at international law.

The main function for rights-based constitutionalization of a reconceptualization of trade as human rights is to find a way to enhance the legitimacy of WTO law, and, indirectly, of the rights-based model itself. The reinvigorated human rights orientation enables WTO law to further 'benefit from including additional constitutional safeguards such as human rights'.[26] At base, the human-rights emphasis is a means for WTO law, quite simply, to exploit the legitimacy factor of human rights. 'Human rights law offers WTO rules moral, constitutional and democratic legitimacy far beyond the traditional economic and utilitarian justifications.'[27] In this regard, Petersmann has restated his earlier view that a rights approach offers the potential for domestic courts to protect precise and unconditional WTO rules.[28] He again refers to the TRIPs Preamble which explicitly says it creates private rights and state practice in Germany and Switzerland in recognizing the direct effect of TRIPs provisions. He concludes that nothing 'hinders' states from interpreting domestic law in conformity with WTO law, and more strongly, that they could also recognize and apply precise, unconditional rules. So free trade should, according to Petersmann, be protected as a human right because it should be construed as part of the right to liberty encapsulated in the UNDHR, and, like all other such human rights, free trade does not end at national borders. The adoption of a human rights perspective enables rights-based constitutionalization to further its key goal of inserting trade rules into national legal systems as directly effective rights.

There is a quantitative argument about the relative importance of trade to human existence also. According to Petersmann, the vast bulk of human activity is related to free trade. Free trade is therefore necessary for the fulfilment of maximum human liberty and needs. So, according to Petersmann, the classification of free trade as a human right is evidenced by, for example, the overwhelming desire of citizens to use foreign transport, postal, telephone, radio, television, and internet services, and to access foreign markets for 'food, books, school, other goods and services, jobs, information, systems, friends, development assistance abroad'.[29] According to this recent reconceptualization

---

[26] E-U Petersmann, 'The WTO Constitution and Human Rights' (2000) 3 *Journal of International Economic Law* 19, 21 [hereinafter 'WTO Constitution and Human Rights'].   [27] ibid 24.
[28] Petersmann, 'Human Rights and International Economic Law' (n 23 above) 33–34.
[29] ibid 31.

of the model, the use of resources across borders is proof of free trade's being part of the right of liberty, and hence the right to trade across borders is a human right.

In short, the rights-based approach to constitutionalization began its existence focusing on rights as a means to facilitate the direct effect of WTO law into national legal systems, and later developed into a human-rights approach, the function of which was to lend legitimacy, to both the rights-based model and WTO law itself.

There are some serious problems with this approach: an ambivalence about whether the purpose of the theory is to describe WTO law or to change it; a technically flawed structure; and a derivative relationship with human rights which seeks to capitalize on the legitimacy of the latter.

First, there is ambivalence about whether it is the aim of this approach to function as a description of the way WTO is, or as a prescription for what it should be. The theory does not suggest that all WTO provisions necessarily have direct effect, although it implies that this should ultimately be the result. Facially at least, rights-based constitutionalization is consistent with the traditional position of international law whereby the relationship between WTO law (as a subset of international law), and national law, is to be determined by the constitutional system of each state.[30] According to the standard approach—unless the state constitutional system is 'monist', in which case international law can be directly incorporated—most states, which are 'dualist,' require international rules to be transformed by way of legislative, executive, or judicial action, before they have effect in the local state.[31] The theory claims to make no direct challenge to these traditional international law propositions. However, according to rights-based constitutionalization, GATT–WTO provisions are *capable of having direct effect*. Thus, it argues, that although GATT–WTO does not 'requir[e] domestic courts to apply WTO rules and decide on "breaches of WTO law" ',[32] the possibility of direct effect is there. Accordingly, the rights-based constitutionalization models argues that the actions of the United States and the European Union, which have, by various executive, legislative, and judicial means,[33] denied the application of GATT–WTO law within those

[30] Petersmann, *Dispute Settlement* (n 1 above) 120.

[31] For the conventional view see, eg, M Shaw, *International Law* 4th edn (Cambridge: Cambridge University Press, 1997) 99–136.

[32] ibid 115.

[33] Petersmann, *International Law and Dispute Settlement* (n 1 above) (listing the various ways in which the effect of WTO has been diminished. In the US, international trade agreements are ordinarily declared to be non self-executing (18); courts have denied the absence of a vested right to trade between US citizens and foreign nations (18); legislation precludes the application of the Agreements where they are inconsistent with US law (19); the Chevron doctrine allows agencies to deviate from WTO obligations as long as the statutory interpretation they adopt is reasonable (19); and WTO dispute settlement findings will not be incorporated into US law without congressional control and review by a US commission (19). In the EU, an EC Council Decision of December 1994 precludes the Agreements being directly invoked (21); the ECJ has confirmed this denial (22)).

jurisdictions, are inconsistent with a rights-based view of constitutionalization, and therefore undesirable. From this perspective, non-rights-based constitutionalization and the denial of the direct effect of GATT–WTO law undermines the legitimacy of the system; denies individuals rights granted them under WTO law; gives succour to rent-seeking, domestic, protectionist interests; and fails to limit discretionary foreign policy powers of governments.[34] The problem is that, although the theory claims to operate within the constraints of traditional international law argument, its implications are radical; it cannot function simply as a description of the way WTO law is, if it aims to alter the reception of WTO law in national systems. It cannot both provide greater effect for WTO law within national legal systems, and not disturb international law theory in relation to incorporation of international law into municipal law. There is a tension, then, between the descriptive and reformist faces of the theory. Petersmann partly resolves this by arguing that, even if the WTO does not have direct effect, acceptance of the premises of the theory could give WTO law stronger interpretative force within domestic environments where it could be used as an interpretive guideline, or to strengthen judicial review, or to promote the adoption of a principle of conformity. And, as the discussion at page 149–50 above suggests, recent experience in the EC legal order seems to reflect a shift toward some aspects of a rights-based view. Nevertheless, despite these latter trends, it is clear that Petersmann's argument is at odds with the classical international law position as well as with the majority of WTO scholars.

Secondly, there are a set of technical objections to the model. One relates to *definition of rights*. Despite Petersmann's reliance on the language of rights to characterize WTO law, some claim that he neglects to define the attributes and scope of those rights adequately.[35] He refers, variously, to the existence of 'worldwide guarantees of economic freedom in the WTO Agreement'[36] and rules that are 'designed to promote freedom and non-discriminatory conditions of competition for importers, exporters, producers, investors and consumers in international trade with goods and services'.[37] But nowhere are the scope and nature of those rights and worldwide guarantees clearly articulated in the work. Since Petersmann himself concedes that these freedoms are not absolute,[38] how far do the particular rights extend? What sorts of limits are placed on those freedoms? How does one determine the extent of those limits?

---

[34] Petersmann, *Dispute Settlement* (n 1 above) 120–122.

[35] Robert Howse in P Alston, 'Resisting the Merger and Acquisition of Human Rights by Trade Law: A Reply to Petersmann' (2002) 13 *European Journal of International Law* 815.

[36] Petersmann, *Dispute Settlement* (n 1 above) 23.   [37] ibid 18.

[38] Petersmann's 'models of constitutional problems of social order' assumes the need for mechanisms to address 'spontaneous decentralized order (e.g. markets)' and 'market failures and spontaneous disorder (e.g. pollution)': ibid 6, Table 1. See also Petersmann, 'WTO Constitution and Human Rights' (n 26 above) 24.

Moreover, there is a problem with Petersmann's use of the term 'constitutional value'. At times, the term 'value' seems to operate as a synonym for rights, such as the right to non-discrimination, and at other times it seems to signify a broader foundational concept, for example rule of law. This confusion, although not uncommon in legal scholarship on the concept of what is a value,[39] does not assist in clarifying the ambit of rights.

A further problem of uncertainty is that rights-based constitutionalization does not appear to envisage protection for other forms of economic rights, which could arguably be said to be found in the text of the WTO agreements, such as collective rights to development (WTO Agreement Preamble; GATT 1947 Part IV; all special and differential treatment provisions of the covered agreements), or economic self-determination (safeguards protections, balance-of-payments protections). Is the subject matter limited or would rights to permanent sovereignty over natural resources (environmental general exception) be part of the bundle of rights promoted by this form of constitutionalization?

Thirdly, the meaning of an individual 'right to trade' is obscure. No major human rights convention currently includes any individual right to trade. Indeed Steve Peers argues that no such right to trade exists in any international legal instrument and such a right exists only in a much-attenuated form in national constitutions.[40] Furthermore, he continues, from a normative viewpoint it would be anti-democratic to recognize such a right without the proper processes of international treaty-making taking their course, and, in any case, any free-standing right would be subject to uncertainty about how conflicts might be resolved between it and other rights. In short, three substantive problems of indeterminacy related to determining the scope, subject matter, and interpretation of rights have long been the subject of discussion within legal and constitutional theory, but rights-based constitutionalization makes no acknowledgement of these.

The difficulty of conceptualizing WTO law as 'rights' is illustrated in the *US—Shrimp Turtle* decision, where the Appellate Body tried to draw a distinction between *a fundamental premise* of the trading system and a right. The maintenance of the multilateral trading system was a fundamental premise but it was not a right,[41] and so the Panel erred in finding that measures which

---

[39] See, eg, D Coenen, 'A Constitution of Collaboration: Protecting Fundamental Values with Second Look Rules of Interbranch Dialogue' (2001) 42 *William and Mary Law Review* 1575 (suggesting that a number of different concepts such as free speech, free exercise, and federalism are all 'particular substantive constitutional values'); or H Coker, 'Lawyers Must Publicly Promote the Values of the Constitution' (2001) 72 *Florida Bar Journal* 8 (suggesting that self governing democracy is a 'value' of the US constitution); or R Percival, 'Greening the Constitution: Harmonizing Environmental and Constitutional Values' (2002) 32 *Environmental Law* 809 (using the term value interchangeably with environmental 'concerns' and also using it to describe as constitutional values, notions such as state sovereign immunity and regulatory takings doctrine).

[40] S Peers, 'Fundamental Right or Political Whim? WTO Law and the European Court of Justice' in G de Búrca and J Scott (eds), *The EU and the WTO: Legal and Constitutional Issues* (Oxford: Hart Publishing, 2001).

[41] WTO, Report of the Appellate Body, *United States—Import Prohibition of Certain Shrimp and Shrimp Products*, WT/DS58/AB/R (12 October 1998), DSR 1998:VII, 2755 at para 116.

undermined the multilateral trading system were not protected by the exceptional clause in Article XX. The implication is that a right creates a stronger legal obligation than a fundamental premise, which presumably subsists at a higher level of abstraction. However, the AB's distinction and lack of guidance on how it is to be determined alerts us to the uncertainties involved in the claim of rights-based constitutionalization to characterize WTO rules as rights.

In relation to procedure, the rights-based approach also lacks clarity. For example, rights-based constitutionalization does not discuss many crucial issues which have dogged the European Court of Justice, for example, over a period of some thirty years, as it has had to develop an intricate jurisprudence about the circumstances in which EC law has direct effect. How are these rights to be invoked? Is there any difference between 'direct applicability' and 'direct effect'? Does Petersmann's rights-based view imply that WTO law has vertical direct effect, or might it conceivably be interpreted as suggesting horizontal direct effect? Does it apply between citizens? Between citizens and instruments of the state? What are the remedies for failure to give effect?[42] Can individuals challenge actions of another Member State? According to Howse and Nicolaidis, one of the key dangers of the use of the language of constitutionalization is that it encourages the idea that the WTO will ultimately be directly effective within states.[43] Yet, although the rights-based view of constitutionalization extends the classes of participants of international trade from states to citizens, the extent and form of their participation is riddled with uncertainties. It may be that these uncertainties are merely indicative of the textured nature of constitutionalization, particularly in the early days of the project, but if the rights-based constitutionalization model is to be taken seriously these uncertainties must be addressed. In the meantime, their existence weakens the case for the model.

Rights-based constitutionalization also tends to underemphasize the fact that some states object to the notion that private actors should be given greater rights of participation in the WTO dispute settlement system, let alone in national law. The belief that private rights should not be encouraged is illustrated by the ongoing fracas at the WTO related to the use of *amicus* briefs in dispute settlement. After accepting the authority of panels and the AB to receive briefs from friends of the court, both as attachments to state parties'

---

[42] Petersmann, *Dispute Settlement* (n 1 above) 116–117 (arguing that the international law rule whereby local remedies must be exhausted before states may pursue a claim at the international level does not apply to the WTO because, like other treaty arrangements such as ICSID, the WTO agreement does not state that it applies, and in any event state practice indicates that it is not uniformly applicable, particularly as the rule is designed to protect treaty benefits and not individual rights).

[43] R Howse and K Nicolaidis, 'Legitimacy and Global Governance: Why Constitutionalizing the WTO is a Step Too Far' in RB Porter, *et al* (eds), *Efficiency, Equity, and Legitimacy: The Multilateral Trading System at the Millennium* (Washington, DC: Brookings Institution Press, 2001), 228.

submissions, and, in principle, in isolation from party submissions,[44] the AB later agreed to consider briefs from outside interests and set down guidelines for their reception.[45] This perceived willingness to include private parties in the adjudicatory process was met with disapproval and hostility on the part of General Council, especially developing state members who argued that the WTO was a state-to-state system, and that non-government organizations submitting briefs often lined up with Northern state interests.

To this point I have argued that rights-based constitutionalization is ambivalent about its function, and is technically flawed in respect of departure from incorporation theory, definition of rights, procedural issues, and state resistance to increasing private rights. The nature of the rights protected by a rights-based vision of a liberal trading order[46] are, at best, only loosely defined in relation to scope, subject matter, interpretation, and invocation.

A further set of criticisms of the rights-based approach suggest that when it invokes human rights law it misrepresents the nature of the human rights, undermines the effectiveness of the latter, and seeks to capitalize on its legitimacy. The foundational assumptions upon which (human) rights-based constitutionalization is built are weak and, according to one commentator, dangerous from the perspective of human rights law.[47] The dangers, according to the critics, arise because Petersmann seeks to co-opt human rights discourse by linking it with a rights-based approach to the constitutionalization of international trade law. In this form, the model directly engages the key core element of constitutionalization, legitimacy, and tries to harness it to provide a firmer basis for the WTO (and, indeed, indirectly for the model itself). While not disputing the claim that the WTO has already been likened to a constitution in the sense of protecting freedoms, including binding dispute settlement, and containing limited supremacy of law rules, the critique objects to the attempts by rights-based constitutionalization to exploit the standing of human rights, by reconceiving trade as a human right.

These critics argue that the human-rights-based approach should be 'resisted' because it misunderstands the nature of both fields. They argue that the model misrepresents the European Community as a human rights regime, when, in practice, rights were incorporated as an 'afterthought' and only in order to ensure that Member States accepted the supremacy of European law.[48] Moreover, a human-rights-based approach wrongly conflates human rights with market freedoms.[49] Human-rights-based constitutionalization confuses ends (human

---

[44] WTO, Report of the Appellate Body, *United States—Import Prohibition of Certain Shrimp and Shrimp Products*, WT/DS58/AB/R (12 October 1998), DSR 1998:VII, 2755 at paras 108–110.

[45] WTO, Report of the Appellate Body, *European Communities—Measures Affecting Asbestos and Asbestos-Containing Products*, WT/DS135/ARB/R (12 March 2001) DSR 2001:VII, 3243.

[46] Petersmann, *Dispute Settlement* (n 1 above) 7 (stating that the rights-based project is aiming to resolve the question of how a liberal trading order be protected more effectively).

[47] Alston (n 35 above).　　[48] ibid 821.　　[49] ibid 823.

dignity) with means (a right to trade).[50] It fails to recognize that human rights are founded on human dignity whereas 'trade related rights are granted to individuals for instrumentalist reasons.'[51] The approach is also criticized as a form of economic libertarianism that attempts to place law above the political process.[52]

Moreover, in what amounts to a criticism of the bona fides of the approach, the apparent embrace of the *social* aspect of human rights, by human-rights-based constitutionalization, is at complete loggerheads with the economically libertarian sources upon which the model is based.[53] In any case, it might be argued that it is no longer plausible to create a formal legal order in which individual economic rights are inviolate.[54] In this respect, Petersmann's rights-based constitutionalization could be seen as an attempt to return to a neo-liberal vision of rights, which fails to take account of subsequent developments in rights discourse such as rights critiques, or even the effect of globalization on rights. In short, according to the critics, the right to trade is not, and can never be, a human right.[55]

Petersmann's views are underdeveloped in other respects. Potential conflicts between trade rights (whether or not conceptualized as human rights) and conventional human rights are not considered. It is not clear from the rights-based vision of constitutionalization either (a) whether conflicts with other rights systems could occur or (b) how they would be resolved. Moreover, the failure to address the problem of rights conflicts has the tendency to privilege the economic over the social. One strong criticism of the model is that it fails to take this dilemma seriously and has not engaged with these problems which led, in the European example, to a form of rights heavily slanted towards economic over other freedoms.[56] The same approach if adopted for the WTO would lead, so the argument goes, to a legal system in which the constitutional framework is established primarily for the achievement of private law rights such as property and contract.[57]

The failure of the human-rights-based view of constitutionalization to consider its relationship with human rights generally stands in contrast with other discussions of the relationship between WTO law and rights. For example, it has been argued that WTO obligations should be interpreted so as to take into account general international law including human rights law. So, where the objective of TRIPs is to protect intellectual property rights 'in a manner conducive to social and economic welfare'[58] it should be interpreted

---

[50] ibid 828 (arguing that, to this extent, the right to trade is similar to a right to money or a right to the internet because all emphasize a means by which to achieve a goal).   [51] ibid 826.

[52] Howse and Nicolaidis (n 43 above) 228.

[53] Alston (n 35 above) 827 (arguing that the views of writers, such as Hayek and Barnett, on whom the rights model is based, are anathema to any reconciliation of social and economic rights).

[54] J Habermas, 'Paradigms of Law' (1996) 17 *Cardozo Law Review* 771, 777–78.

[55] Alston (n 35 above) 828.   [56] ibid 822.   [57] ibid 842.

[58] TRIPs Agreement, Art 7.

by reference to a range of rights enshrined in human rights covenants, and the UN Charter.[59] Or, developing countries' rights and obligations under the Agreement on Agriculture should be interpreted consistently with the human right to food, drawing again upon human rights conventions.[60] Another state has claimed that its provision of AIDS drugs under its health program, although challenged as infringing intellectual property rights, was actually consistent with its obligation to take full steps for realization of rights to health, housing, work, and education.[61] These examples reveal that the relationship between the fields is hotly contested,[62] and give support to the view that WTO scholars should be addressing these specific questions rather than promoting trade rights as human rights.

Finally, Petersmann's work relies upon a strict opposition between the interests of individuals and the state, an opposition which is inconsistent with mainstream contemporary opinion about the complexity of modern individual–state relationships.[63] Instead, however, rights-based constitutionalization portrays the individual as endlessly struggling against a majoritarian and unresponsive state. For example, when discussing the circumstances of judicial review in relation to a safeguard action, Petersmann argues that a tribunal assessing the imposition of a safeguard should adopt a sceptical approach to any 'public interest' claim put forward by the state. The tribunal should be sceptical because the public interest of the citizens may be different from the public interest of the state.[64] Vivid imagery is used to describe the relationship between a single trader and a powerful government. On the one side is the private citizen, who is motivated by self-interest and liberal trade. With the assistance of courts (not categorized as part of the state for these purposes), the individual can try to achieve market freedoms, by using procedural devices such as 'open and fair procedures, due process of law, and access to justice'.[65] These latter devices are described as the 'important democratic functions' of international trade law.[66] But ranged against notions of the private, liberality, fairness, and freedom are the forces of 'majority politics'[67] and 'strong political pressures,'

---

[59] Richard Elliot in G Marceau, 'WTO Dispute Settlement and Human Rights' (2002) 13 *European Journal of International Law* 753, 786.   [60] Argument of Mauritius, in ibid 788.

[61] Caroline Dommen, in ibid 787.

[62] In relation to compatibility, Marceau argues, at 791, that conflicts between trade rights and human rights would be extremely rare, partly because it must be assumed that states negotiated both sets of obligations in good faith and therefore, at 804, that any interpretation should do its utmost to interpret both sets of rights consistently with each other. She also claims, at 786, that human rights are formulated at such high levels of generality that they would normally not override a more specific treaty obligation. Marceau refers here, at 794–795, to standard international law principles of treaty interpretation including *lex posterior generalis non derogat prior specialis*: ibid. Marceau's argument appears to be a plea for consistency rather than an answer to the question of what to do in the case of conflict.

[63] See discussion Chapter 3 notes 59–69 and accompanying text describing globalization and the relationships between actors as having moved beyond a simple dichotomy between the interests of states and individuals.   [64] Petersmann, *Dispute Settlement* (n 1 above) 114.

[65] ibid 115.   [66] ibid.   [67] ibid.

where ' "rent seeking" interest groups' pressure governments to exercise 'broad discretion' to 'grant subsidies, restrict competition and redistribute income'[68] and to impose other 'protectionist restraints'.[69] It is a battle which ranges fair procedures, law, democracy, and equality against the forces of broad discretion, politics, political favouritism, and redistribution.

So, in sum, this view of constitutionalization is marred by potential inconsistency with standard international law incorporation theory, uncertainty of rights definition and relationships with other fields, and a misappropriation of human rights legitimacy.

However, despite these difficulties, the rights-based view of constitutionalization is more complex than some would give it credit for. In addition to pragmatically promoting international trade by exploiting human rights legitimacy, Petersmann develops an unconventional two-pronged approach whereby he challenges WTO law from the perspective of human rights, and human rights from the perspective of WTO law. First, he addresses WTO law, suggesting that links already exist between international trade and human rights law. He emphasizes the non-economic achievements of the WTO, thereby suggesting that WTO law already includes a human rights perspective. The WTO has achieved many non-economic goals, such as introduction of rule of law and peaceful dispute settlement, and as for its EC counterpart, these achievements are to be celebrated and expanded, for example by establishing an advisory body, similar in nature to the EC Economic and Social Committee, to enhance citizen participation. He also challenges international trade law from the perspective of human rights by imagining ways in which human rights law could be directly implicated in the interpretation of WTO law. Provisions of the covered agreements, where appropriate, such as the GATT General Exceptions, could be interpreted in conformity with 'universally agreed human rights, the 1998 ILO Declaration on Fundamental Principles and Rights at Work, or multilateral environmental agreements accepted by WTO members....'[70] Moreover, according to the theory, the affinity between economic rights and human rights would be further emphasized because rights-based constitutionalization would reduce the domination of international trade rules by a mercantilist agenda, which stresses export interests, and foreign market access. Instead, international trade law would be focused on a right to import, consumer interests, and individual rights of access to challenge trade discrimination.[71] It might be added here that the fundamental freedoms under the EU Treaty arguably have always been, human rights, even if conceptualized in economic terms. There is much more overlap between the two fields than the critics claim, and what is important is the balance between the two, rather than the exclusion of one by the other.

[68] ibid 114.   [69] ibid 115.
[70] Petersmann, 'WTO Constitution and Human Rights' (n 26 above) 21.   [71] ibid 22.

In the second limb of his approach, Petersmann challenges human rights from an international trade-rights perspective. So an emphasis on the individual over corporate interests within trade law could be accompanied by a realignment of the human rights agenda so as to do away with the 'anachron[istic]' approach whereby civil and political rights are considered more important than economic ones.[72] Economic freedom should be understood to be no less important than other fundamental (non-economic) rights.[73] Markets should be seen to be conducive to a range of individual values ordinarily located in human rights discourse, including communication, personal development, autonomy, and responsibility. To this extent, markets perform similar functions to human rights. Markets 'reveal individual preferences, promote dialogues about values, enable individuals to develop and co-ordinate autonomous activities, induce individuals to assume responsibility, and sanction "market failures" '.[74] Moreover, Petersmann's market-based argument is alert to other general concerns, and does not advocate an untrammelled free market. Instead he argues that economic and other rights are inseparable and so economic markets, like political markets, must be controlled against market failure and abuses of political power (for example a lack of separation of powers and a dominant executive), or economic power (for example cartelization). The much-vaunted 'paradox of freedom' according to which absolute freedom may lead to abuse or non-freedom, if uncontrolled, leads Petersmann to the conclusion that there is a need to erect constitutional safeguards against such abuse.[75]

Petersmann's arguments constitute a complex, if unusual, attempt to condition international trade and human rights law from the perspective of each other. Just as he prods international trade diplomats and lawyers into accepting the compatibility and, indeed, commensurability of the two fields, he criticizes human rights activists for their anxieties. Human rights defenders are depicted as 'afraid' that human rights enforcement through WTO mechanisms may lead to a 'new kind of human rights jurisprudence'.[76] Moreover, they are naïve and should be 'help[ed] to understand that *transnational trade* is no less beneficial than *domestic trade*',[77] and, of course, it is 'WTO advocates' who should rescue them.

So, although the critics make strong arguments against human-rights-based constitutionalization, they do not completely address Petersmann's attempt to construct a nuanced, if eccentric, approach to the relationship between trade and rights. For example, Petersmann's claims of affinities between the fields, and his arguments about rights-based constitutionalization being a mechanism

---

[72] Petersmann, 'WTO Constitution and Human Rights' (n 26 above) 23.

[73] ibid (referring to: US Supreme Court dicta to the effect that anti-trust laws are 'a Magna Carta' for free enterprise; Lockean views about private property as a bulwark against government interference in the private sphere; and moral considerations that economic freedom and property rights further human dignity and self-fulfilment).   [74] ibid.

[75] ibid 24.   [76] ibid 22.   [77] ibid 25.

to achieve a social market, may warrant consideration, from a human rights point of view.

Moreover, perhaps, contra the critics, it is not conceptualization of trade as a right that is the problem but a failure to debate the implications of such a position, a failure which could be cured by more and better procedures for communication.[78] On this view, the current level of debate about rights-based constitutionalization is a sign of the health of the system. For example, the debate about access to medicines could be seen as an illustration of constitutionalization in the form of the deliberative process element. From this perspective, an argument that the individual rights of patent holders outweigh the collective rights of peoples to access to medicines necessary to meet emergency public health needs could be met by the response that effective participation by NGOs (Oxfam, Medicins sans Frontières) and national (South African) and international civil society effectively communicated the needs of those affected by individual patent rights, and ultimately an improved solution was developed at Doha. On this reading, right-based constitutionalization does not block human rights, but it shifts the agenda somewhat to include a range of right-holders, some of whom will, and can, include the human rights community.

Finally, it is possible that the very indeterminacy of rights-based constitutionalization is a conscious ploy to engage the international trade community with a different way of thinking about the system, and reflects the deep normative valency of the approach. Rights-based constitutionalization is a visionary, quasi-evangelical argument, an attempt to persuade by argumentative means, rather than an attempt to describe. The absence of any rigid definition of rights is consistent with an approach based not entirely on legal logic and proof but on certain assumptions about the desirability of conceiving of international trade law in rights-based terms. In this sense, the blurriness of definition is related to the proselytizing tones of Petersmann's work referred to above. When Petersmann argues that the legal 'guarantees of economic freedom, non discrimination and rule of law' have 'extended liberal constitutional principles' to 'transnational economic activities of citizens'[79] he is asking the reader not only to accept that the ambit of the law has extended. He is also asking the reader to accept that there is something in the nature of these WTO rules which makes them different from ordinary rules—to assume, for the purposes of the approach, that WTO rules *are* rights. He does, of course, provide certain evidence for that assumption (for example the textual articulation of the rules), but nevertheless the characterization of rules as rights remains, to an extent, an assumption of faith, an assumption that has echoes in the faith-based

---

[78] Habermas (n 54 above) 783 (arguing that some of the problems with rights could be cured if a procedural approach to law was adopted whereby those affected by rights decisions have sufficient opportunity to communicate their concerns).

[79] Petersmann, *Dispute Settlement* (n 1 above) 26.

approach to building a constitutional community described in the received account in Chapter 2. At some deep, conceptual level one must assume the rule to be a right in order to proceed on the basis that rights-based constitutionalization makes sense. So, on one interpretation, Petersmann's work lacks definition; viewed more closely, this very definitional ambiguity is critical to his rights-based theory.

The next aspect of Petersmann's theory I want to discuss is the way in which it is justified by a combination of strategic and normative rationales.

5.2.2 Mixed strategic justifications and normative goals

Rights-based constitutionalization is characterized by a distinctive combination of strategic justifications and normative goals. First, rights-based constitutionalization is justified by the text of the agreements. Just as institutional managerial constitutionalization sought to invoke the terms of the 'WTO charter' as evidence of its form of constitutionalization, so too does rights-based constitutionalization.[80]

Similarly, just as institutional managerial constitutionalization was necessary to overcome the 'ingenious' methods for imposing protectionist barriers to trade,[81] so too rights-based constitutionalization sees itself as performing the function of metaphorically tying the hands of government so that it cannot act in a protectionist manner. It, however, adopts the potent image of Odysseus defying the sirens' call by chaining himself to the mast of his ship, in order to explain how rights-based constitutionalization helps national governments chain themselves to the mast of international trade rules in order to repress their uncontrollable urge to protect.[82] Rights-based constitutionalization is therefore justified because it checks national governments from succumbing to pressure from domestic interests calling for protectionism over liberal trade. A 'constitutional function' would thus be served if WTO law were interpreted according to the rights-based model because it would limit abuses of national foreign policy power.[83] We can see here how the denominator 'constitutional'

---

[80] For evidence that the text of agreements contain rights, Petersmann refers, *inter alia*, to the protection of intellectual property rights in the TRIPs agreement; various guarantees of access to domestic courts such as those contained in Article X of GATT; Article 14 of the Agreement on Implementation of Article VI of the General Agreement on Tariffs and Trade 1994, [hereinafter the Anti-Dumping Agreement], and Article 42 of the TRIPs Agreement. He concludes: 'The text, context and objective of many WTO provisions are thus not confined to rights and obligations of governments but aim at the protection of the rights and obligations of traders and other citizens engaged in international trade': ibid 9. He further states that other provisions imply that WTO law is directly applicable in domestic court proceedings: ibid 72.

[81] See Chapter 4 above note 245.

[82] For a discussion of constitutionalism as an aid to defeat fears of corporatism, or government, see A Sajó, *Limiting Government: An Introduction to Constitutionalism* (English edition 1999) (New York: Central European University Press, 1995) in a chapter entitled 'Ulysses Binds Himself to the Mast' 7 (claiming that the Homeric metaphor was first used by Jon Elster).

[83] Petersmann, *Dispute Settlement* (n 1 above) 8.

when used in relation to rights-based constitutionalization also stands for a particular image of that term, namely a version of liberal constitutionalism, defined as limitation of government intervention in the market. To this extent then, the human rights critics discussed above are correct in arguing that Petersmann's vision of rights is a limited one.

Moreover, like the earlier model, rights-based constitutionalization is justified also on the basis that it will make international trade law more *effective*. To this extent the rights-based approach shares the institutional managerial constitutionalization concern with improving the effectiveness of the WTO. But whereas institutional managerialism was concerned to show the existence of a new *Grundnorm* by pointing to the effectiveness of the system,[84] rights-based constitutionalization focuses on effectiveness in respect of achieving liberal market based goals, and effectiveness in commanding assent of the relevant constitutional community. So, according to the advocates of rights-based constitutionalization, WTO law effectiveness would be enhanced by a rights-based approach because it would inaugurate a decentralized system of checks and balances in which individuals could initiate actions within states, and so a greater number of stakeholders would share an interest in compliance.[85] As evidence for this contention, the example is given of the European Union in which a combination of ECJ rulings stating that EU law had direct effect, and the reference procedure allowing national courts to refer matters of EU law to the ECJ for a preliminary opinion, improved the overall compliance and effectiveness of EC law.[86]

Allied to both the effectiveness argument and the prevention of abuse justification, rights-based constitutionalization contends that it is *politically necessary* to hold to this model because of the propensity of governments to adopt less than optimal policy instruments to correct market failures.[87] The absence of restraints in the area of foreign executive power, pressure from rent-seeking interest groups, and the tendency towards mercantilism in the WTO system[88] could lead governments into making sub-optimal decisions in relation to trade. Some other factor, such as direct applicability of WTO law, must perform the function which domestic constitutional restraints perform in the domestic arena.

---

[84] See discussion in Chapter 2 at section 2.4.2.

[85] This claim is made at two levels: interstate, and intrastate. At the interstate level, again Europe is the example of strong enforcement supported by decentralized control, and political science literature is referred to for the view that individual rights enforcement increases stakeholders' personal interest in maintenance of the system: Petersmann, *Dispute Settlement* (n 1 above) 73. At the intrastate level, he makes this argument more specific and argues, for example, that the SCM procedural requirements in relation to investigation would be 'enforced more effectively' if various individual interests could rely on such a provision in domestic proceedings: ibid 10.

[86] ibid 73.

[87] So for example, governments impose an import tariff which leads to higher prices, fewer products, less freedom of choice for domestic consumers, and perhaps also redistribute income in a way which avoids domestic legal constraints: see ibid 20, Table 4.   [88] ibid 120.

So rights-based constitutionalization shares many of the strategic justifications of institutional managerialism in respect of textual justification, government restraint, effectiveness, and political necessity. However, rights-based constitutionalization is justified on the basis also of a series of normative goals and values, which are not explicitly present in the earlier model.

First, rights-based constitutionalization relies upon higher-order concepts sometimes referred to as *values*. WTO law includes 'constitutional values',[89] 'international guarantees',[90] and 'long term *constitutional rules* of a higher legal rank' (emphasis in original).[91] So, whereas institutional managerialism might refer to non-discrimination as a rule or principle, rights-based constitutionalization refers to the same idea as a value. The rights-based model of constitutionalization is much thicker and includes internally a panoply of constitutional concepts and values, rather than just a set of institutional structures and rules. This is not to say that institutional managerialism was merely a descriptive theory: as we discussed above, it too was normatively loaded, but it did not explicitly claim to be a set of prescriptions in the way rights-based constitutionalization does. The rights-based model's inclusion substantive rights, and things it describes as 'values', (although the concept is not defined),[92] focuses on 'world-wide legal guarantees of freedom, non-discrimination and rule of law'.[93] It includes constitutional attributes and concepts such as rule of law, separation of powers, fundamental rights, necessity and proportionality of governmental restraints, democracy, and social justice.[94] Moreover, reflections of each and every one of these constitutional indicia are carefully articulated.[95] So, for example, rule of law is exemplified by principles of non-discrimination and transparency; separation of powers by Article III; necessity and proportionality by prohibition of 'unnecessary' trade restrictions in the TBT Agreement.[96] The thicker,[97] internal constitutional aspect of rights-based

---

[89] See, eg, ibid 23 (arguing that the GATT/WTO agreements were 'brought about at the initiative of constitutional democracies and focus on constitutional values').   [90] ibid 8.

[91] ibid 5.   [92] See notes 98–100 below and accompanying text.

[93] Petersmann, *Dispute Settlement* (n 1 above) 18.

[94] Petersmann, *International Law and Dispute Settlement* (n 1 above) 30–31.   [95] ibid 28–29.

[96] ibid.

[97] In other respects, the theory of rights-based constitutionalization is underinclusive. Strangely, Petersmann's *internal description* of the constitutionalization of the WTO excludes a number of functions that would ordinarily be classified as constitutional. For example, Petersmann's description of the 'constitutional' functions does not include matters of 'rule-making' and 'executive, surveillance and dispute settlement': Petersmann, *Dispute Settlement* (n 1 above) 11. These are dealt with in a separate section, at page 21, not about constitutionalization, entitled 'Executive, Surveillance and Dispute Settlement Functions of the WTO Agreement'. This leads to a classificatory anomaly whereby 'constitutional', as a description of the internal structure of the WTO, refers only to certain characteristics of a system such as its integratedness, independence, hierarchical nature, effectiveness, and rights-based content. Constitutional, in this mode, does not include two key constitutional functions, namely rule-making rules and dispute settlement rules. No explanation is given as to why rule-making and dispute settlement are not included, but it does appear to be an oversight in the construction of a coherent constitutionalization theory. In short, Petersmann's descriptive use of the term constitutional is narrow in some important respects.

constitutionalization reflects a thicker normative stance as well. Whereas institutional managerial constitutionalization positions itself as largely descriptive, relatively value-neutral, and free of too many constitutional concepts, rights-based constitutionalization is prescriptive, dense with constitutional concepts, and, as we shall discuss below, (Section 5.2.3) comprised of a particular value set.

These values are carefully tabulated and the approach is compared favourably with other theories of international order.[98] Whereas states are key actors in realist theory, individual liberty, dignity, and legal equality are the 'highest sources of values' for 'constitutional theories'.[99] Whereas functionalism conceives of legal change as a result of functional interdependences or spillovers, constitutionalists theorize change on the basis of the application of general, long-term rules of a higher legal rank.[100] Petersmann is a constitutionalist where constitutionalization implies a more desirable, ethically rich method of conceiving of international law.

Moreover, these higher-order concepts are presented as natural extensions of the foundational values of international law, interpreted from a Kantian perspective,[101] in which citizens are treated 'as legal subjects, rather than as mere objects of "paternal government" '.[102] The approach thereby automatically links its interpretation of WTO law with a wider tapestry of international legal values. Petersmann's invokes the *nature* of international trade law which, he argues, predisposes it toward rights-based constitutionalization because WTO law already includes these values.[103] The normative tendency of the model is apparent, and, again, its relationship with liberal values is visible.

The model is infused with a concern for morality rather than strict law: traditional realism should be rejected in favour of a more 'democratic claim' because the latter does not deny that 'moral requirements apply to international behaviour.'[104] It is based on a cosmopolitan ethic in which the international

---

[98] Petersmann, *Dispute Settlement* (n 1 above) 14 Table 3.   [99] ibid.   [100] ibid.

[101] Petersmann's work is heavily influenced by Immanuel Kant, the work of whom Petersmann interprets as emphasizing that international law, no less than national law, derives its legitimacy from protecting the rights and interests of the citizens rather than those of their governments: ibid 8.

[102] ibid 10. Petersmann's approach has affinities with other commentators but the outcomes promoted are different. See, eg, S Charnovitz, 'WTO Cosmopolitics' (2002) 34 *New York University Journal of International Law and Politics* 299 (arguing for a WTO 'cosmopolitics' grounded in theories of cosmopolitanism, defined as the individual, rather than the state, being the basic unit of the state system (311) and a programme of 'global political action transcending a strict state-to-state, or multilateral basis' (299). But whereas cosmopolitanism for Petersmann directs him to promote a right to trade, for Charnovitz it is the basis for arguing for formal NGO participation in the WTO constitutional structure).

[103] Petersmann, *Dispute Settlement* (n 1 above) (arguing, at 9 and 18, that international trade law includes these values, but, at 10, that states have interpreted them in a manner far removed from Kant's perspective).

[104] AB Zampetti, 'Democratic Legitimacy in the World Trade Organization: The Justice Dimension' (2003) 37 *Journal of World Trade* 105, 111.

community is 'bound together as a single moral community'.[105] The WTO should 'aid "burdened societies" '[106] and integrate human rights because they 'represent a moral connecting tissue' between individuals across national boundaries.[107]

This strong normative quality is seen most starkly in the call for an interpretation of WTO law which accords with what it calls Kant's 'moral imperative'.[108] In this respect, rights-based constitutionalization also therefore displays an affinity with the discussions in Chapter 2 about legitimacy, and about the importance to constitutionalization of a shared faith in the processes of constitutionalization and the outcome. For example, Petersmann constantly uses the denominator 'constitutional' to make a *prescriptive* argument that international trade law *should* protect the rights of individuals as well as states.[109] In the introduction to *International Trade Law and the GATT/WTO Dispute Settlement System*, Petersmann argues forcefully that international trade law should move from its 'statist orientation', according to which trading rights operate between states, to a 'democratic interpretation', according to which citizens themselves are granted rights of non-discrimination and freedom of trade directly.[110] In this guise then, Petersmann advocates constitutionalization a strategy to improve citizens' rights and enhance international order.

The advocacy role is reinforced in the other set of normative justifications for rights-based constitutionalization. These are the promotion of *equality and citizenship* of all international actors including individuals. The purpose of rights-based constitutionalization is to oppose the inherent mercantilism of the system of trade law,[111] which privileges interests of exporters over importers, and consumers, and fails to treat all citizens (including consumers) substantively equally.[112] Again citing Kant, Petersmann advocates an image of international order, inclusive of an international civil society, as the foundation for rights-based constitutionalization. International law, and its subset international trade law, will only achieve legitimacy when constitutionalism is recognized at three levels: between citizens and their state, between states, and between citizens and states on the cosmopolitan plane.[113] The very *legitimacy* of international trade law is derived from this 'moral imperative'.[114]

---

[105] AB Zampetti, 'Democratic Legitimacy in the World Trade Organization: The Justice Dimension' (2003) 37 *Journal of World Trade* 105, 113.

[106] ibid 112 quoting John Rawls, *The Law of Peoples* (Cambridge, Mass: Harvard University Press, 1999).   [107] ibid 115.

[108] Petersmann, *Dispute Settlement* (n 1 above) 9.

[109] ibid 8–10, noting, however, that both the EC and the US have legislated to preclude that result: ibid 9 notes 12 and 13.   [110] ibid 10.

[111] ibid 120.   [112] ibid 121.   [113] ibid 8.

[114] See also WTO, Report of the Panel, *United States–Sections 301–310 of the Trade Act of 1974*, WT/DS152/R (22 December 1999) DSR 2000:II, 815 for an interesting discussion, at Panel level, of the way in which individual economic operators are conceived of the 'beneficiaries' of the WTO legal system. This position is far from Petersmann's vision in which individuals are subjects of the WTO, but it does confirm that individuals, at the least, not just states, are objects of the WTO system.

However, the nature of citizenship within the rights-based view is quite different from the emphasis on citizenship in the received account of constitutionalization, or the implied emphasis of the human rights critics. The rights-based view is about vesting the citizen with more trade rights, specifically of an economic nature, in order that they be directly invocable in the state, and, indirectly making the system more effective and legitimate. The concern of traditional constitutionalization theorists is that more economic rights will not make for a more active citizenry, and it is the failure of the citizenry to act and constitute the community, politically, which most undermines the claim of constitutionalization of Europe.[115] From the perspective of the received account on the human rights critics, an increase in economic rights does not mean stronger citizenship, and so more economic rights will not naturally lead to constitutionalization, defined in those terms. Until the members of the community conceive of themselves as more than economic citizens, and instead see themselves as political citizens, constitutionalization cannot be said to have occurred, according to the received model. Petersmann, by contrast, views humankind from an economic perspective and the citizen as a market actor, and on this basis economic citizenship could ground constitutionalism, albeit of a narrow kind.

In short, rights-based constitutionalization is justified on the strategic grounds involving political necessity, effectiveness of law, and restraint of governmental power. Legitimacy of the WTO system therefore becomes a focus. In addition, rights-based constitutionalization is justified according to a series of normative goals: the values of non-discrimination and rights must be extended from international law into international trade law; the statist orientation of the latter discarded; and equality and citizenship promoted, although the focus of that citizenship is narrowly economic. Furthermore, whereas institutional managerial constitutionalization takes states as its subject, rights-based constitutionalization accords primacy to the individual. In relation to the normative justifications, rights-based constitutionalization displays more of a concern with a form of elaborated constitutionalization than does the earlier model, although legitimacy and community feature to some extent.

5.2.3 A visionary mode informed by individual economic goals

Rights-based constitutionalization wants to use constitutionalization to transform, in the first place, the WTO, and, ultimately, the broader world order. However, rights-based constitutionalization has a much more elaborately articulated vision of change than institutional managerialism. And although the vision of rights-based constitutionalization leans heavily toward a desire to facilitate the realization of individual economic freedom, it is informed by a somewhat odd

---

[115] Recall Joseph Weiler's call for a political community to authorize Europe (see discussion above in Chapter 2 at 2.4.3) and his dismissal of the Maastricht Treaty's notion of citizenship as 'banal' (see Chapter 2 n 71).

human rights orientation, discussed in Section 5.2.1. Individual economic freedom is not an aspect of constitutionalization as defined in Chapter 2, and so, to this extent, the rights-based view of constitutionalization is not about constitutionalization in general, but about achievement of a particular vision of the constitutionalization process. However, that vision is not inherent in the rights-based view which could be, and to some extent is, informed by other social, civil, and political goals.

Rights-based constitutionalization's visionary mode is expressed in three ways discussed below. It would make the WTO legal system more open, transparent, and therefore more legitimate. It would make the system itself useful as a model for other systems of international law. Finally, rights-based constitutionalization would transform the system into a higher state of law in which individual economic freedom, markets, and democracy are realizable.

The first of these modes encompasses the claim that rights-based constitutionalization can improve the very structures of WTO law by improving transparency and participation.[116] So Petersmann argues that participatory and representative mechanisms would be improved because, as well as providing individuals with directly enforceable rights, adoption of the approach would lead to other changes such as creating advisory committees or parliamentary bodies on a permanent basis; opening dispute settlement proceedings; and allowing individual parties advisory standing in cases where their interests are affected.[117] These changes would follow because national governments do not necessarily represent all interests, are not always democratically legitimate, rarely supervise confidential trade rule-making by executives, and because the WTO itself has a democratic deficit in the absence of weighted voting.

In the second mode, rights-based constitutionalization becomes a model for the constitutionalization of other international legal systems such as the United Nations.[118] Petersmann uses a series of indicators drawn from the WTO model to argue that the UN could constitutionalize in a manner similar to international trade. United Nations law could follow the Uruguay Round model and replace the current ad hoc system of agreements with a new set of unified rules. Human rights could be linked to the UN Charter just as the WTO Agreement was linked to intellectual property protection. Compulsory dispute settlement could be introduced and even cross-retaliation could be introduced between, say, the Security Council and the World Bank (as contemplated under the WTO agreements). Regional human rights agreements could be disciplined in the same way in which Article XXIV of the GATT operates in relation to regional trade agreements.[119] International economic law could incorporate

---

[116] Petersmann, 'Human Rights and International Economic Law' (n 23 above) 35.

[117] ibid 36.

[118] Petersmann, *Dispute Settlement* (n 1 above) 23 and Petersmann, *International Law and Dispute Settlement* (n 1 above) 57.

[119] Petersmann, *Dispute Settlement* (n 1 above) 24; and Petersmann, *International Law and Dispute Settlement* (n 1 above) 57–65.

matters such as environmental law and become a template for World Economic Order, if it only could resolve its problems of legitimacy.[120] The aspirational character of the project is again clear in the enthusiasm for reproduction of the WTO model in other international arenas. All elements of the right-based constitutionalized model of international trade law deserve to be transplanted to other systems of international law.

But rights-based constitutionalization has even stronger, long-term aspirations. In the third visionary mode, constitutionalization of the WTO is portrayed as a step towards world peace.[121] The introduction of direct effect of trade law rights-based constitutionalization fulfils the Kantian mission of international relations by extending the reach of WTO law into national legal systems. Rights-based constitutionalization, therefore, describes the most advanced state of law. History, according to Petersmann, goes like this. It began with simple rules governing decentralized transactions. These were the lowest forms of law, and were developed in response to problems of coordination between traders, producers, and consumers. Later, as problems such as market failures and other abuses of power occurred, the need for organizational law arose in which some institutional structures were centralized and these institutions intervened to ensure supply of public goods such as peace, security, human rights, and open markets. (GATT–WTO law is currently at this second stage). Finally in the third, as yet unrealized, stage, in the international sphere individual rights are protected, and government abuse such as trade protectionism is regulated.[122] Rights-based constitutionalization, then, is the highest form of law and is a natural step in the development of legal systems.

In this mode, individual economic goals are paramount, and they are linked, inevitably, with the realization of free markets and also democracy: 'international economic law has...become one of the most important foreign policy instruments for promoting not only economic welfare, but also rule of law and democracy'.[123] And again: 'The worldwide trend towards deregulation, market economies, protection of human rights and democracies reflects also an increasing recognition that individual freedom, non-discrimination and rule of law are the best conditions for promoting individual and collective self-determination and social welfare.'[124]

The benefits which will flow from liberal trade are many, including 'enhance[d] consumer welfare, individual freedom of choice, competition, efficiency, productivity, innovation and monetary stability'.[125] Rights-based constitutionalization brooks no opposition to these claims emphasizing that these benefits are the

---

[120] M Bronckers, 'More Power to the WTO?' (2001) 4 *Journal of International Economic Law* 41.

[121] HL Schloemann and S Ohlhoff, ' "Constitutionalization" and Dispute Settlement in the WTO: National Security as an Issue of Competence' (1999) 93 *American Journal of International Law* 424, 451.   [122] Petersmann, *Dispute Settlement* (n 1 above) 5.

[123] Petersmann, *International Law and Dispute Settlement* (n 1 above) 2.   [124] ibid 1.

[125] ibid 9.

subject of 'worldwide consensus'.[126] Moreover, there are strong causal links, in Petersmann's view, between constitutionalization of international trade and the achievement of world peace.[127] Constitutionalization is about transforming international society because constitutionalization will lead to the extension of the free market and the free market is a key component of democracy. International economic law has the potential to transform anarchy into peace.[128]

The historical pedigree of the view that a freer market is directly associated with democracy, and that trade leads to improvements in global welfare, and, ultimately, improvements in security, is impeccable:

This empirical fact is in line with a long tradition in political philosophy (e.g. of I. Kant and D. Hume) and economic theory (e.g. of D. Ricardo and A. Smith) which emphasizes that the mutual gains from voluntary international trade, and from an international division of labour based on liberal rules, are the most important means to overcome the 'Hobbesian war of everybody against everybody else' through peaceful cooperation, even if people and governments act as self-interested utility-maximizers.[129]

The confidence of the theory in the transformative possibilities for international trade law leads to a crusade against non-believers. In this economically focused visionary mode, rights-based constitutionalization is a confirmation of Noreena Hertz's claim that arguments (for globalization) have become suffused with a confusion of democracy with capitalism, and the citizen with the consumer.[130]

Moreover, Petersmann expresses frustration with what is seen as the myopia of general international lawyers towards international economic law. General international lawyers have 'fail[ed] to understand the economic logic and moral foundations of international economic law and its systemic significance for a peaceful international order'.[131] They are castigated for their failure to understand that the market is 'an indispensable complement'[132] to human rights. Market institutions promote 'individual autonomy and human well-being in a vital part of everybody's life (e.g. as student, producer and consumer)'.[133]

This frustration with public international lawyers is linked to a wider disciplinary complaint about the place of international trade law within that field. Like an unhappy sibling, rights-based constitutionalization contends that international trade law should no longer be content to sit back and play second fiddle to general international law, especially in view of the more highly developed effectiveness of the former. There is 'no reason for neglecting international

[126] Petersmann, *International Law and Dispute Settlement* (n 1 above) 2.   [127] ibid 1.
[128] ibid 2.   [129] ibid.
[130] N Hertz, *The Silent Takeover* (London: Heinemann, 2001) (arguing, at 99, that there has been a conflation of democracy with capitalism. At 99–100, she claims that US intervention in Iran in 1953 and Guatemala in 1964, in the name of democracy, had the purpose of safeguarding US corporate interests.)
[131] Petersmann, *International Law and Dispute Settlement* (n 1 above) 2.   [132] ibid.
[133] ibid.

economic law as an immature specialization', since individual rights and dispute settlement are more effective in international economic law 'than in many traditional areas of international law'.[134]

In short, Petersmann adopts a visionary style and promotes the approach as a template for particular legal systems, and for a better world order, the highest stage of legal development.

Rights-based modelling for other forms of international order, a belief in rights-based constitutionalization as the highest state of law, and confidence in the values it imparts, take Petersmann's model beyond the simple transformative urge of institutional managerialism. Whereas institutional managerialism was relatively modest in tone, arguing that its vision of the WTO might lead to improvements in international trade law and international economic policy, (albeit while not revealing a more vigorous reformism), rights-based constitutionalization exhibits an almost messianic tone at times. Rights-based constitutionalization is not just a theory of how constitutionalization could improve international order, or a description of how it is; rights-based constitutionalization represents a vision of the way the world could be made better for all, more democratic, fairer, and, importantly, more liberal. Constitutionalization is presented as a means of transforming the international order and even achieving lasting peace.[135] In a tone reminiscent of the idealism of the pre-League-of-Nations international scholarship, Petersmann emphasizes the reformative possibilities of a liberal international trade order. It could be a template for international organizations[136] and adjudication[137] because it represents some sort of apotheosis for world order. The extension of liberal constitutional principles to benefit citizens in the areas of 'economic policy-making of governments and the transnational economic activities of citizens', combined with 'a highly developed case law', a shift from power to law, and a focus on international economic relations could lead to 'important new developments in international law'.[138] The field of international economic law 'has moved to the centre of foreign policy making'.[139] The WTO Agreement is a 'milestone...on the long and winding road to world-wide economic freedom, consumer welfare and democratic peace'.[140]

The visionary mode of rights-based constitutionalization echoes the understandings of constitutionalization, discussed in Chapter 2, which emphasized the importance of faith in the constitutionalization project[141] and the belief that it is a way to achieve what Phillip Allott referred to, in his discussion of international constitutionalism, as 'good social order'.[142]

---

[134] ibid 3.   [135] Petersmann, *Dispute Settlement* (n 1 above) 7–8.   [136] ibid 23.
[137] ibid 25.   [138] ibid 26.
[139] Petersmann, *International Law and Dispute Settlement* (n 1 above) 2.   [140] ibid 4.
[141] See discussion above Chapter 2 at section 2.4.3.
[142] P Allott, *Eunomia: New Order for a New World* (Oxford: Oxford University Press, paperback edn, 2001, first published 1990), xxvi–xxvii.

Yet in relation to this vision most critics argue that rights-based constitutionalization is an incomplete recipe for the achievement of particular individual economic goals. The rights, which this model seeks to protect, are rights taken very specifically from classical economic theory, and indeed these rights are elevated, even valorized, over other rights. Critics point out that, in order for the model to be an accurate reflection of international affairs, the right to trade would have to be recognized internationally as it is domestically, when in fact only a limited number of countries protect such a right internally. Worse, the rights-based view is not consistent with a human rights approach grounded in human dignity, only instrumental goals are valued, and it is fixated on only one category of human rights, namely individual economic rights.[143]

Moreover, say the critics, the text of the GATT preamble has changed from its strictly economic early emphasis on 'full use of world's resources' to a later incarnation which includes 'sustainable development' in order to argue that the goal of wealth maximization is not primary to the WTO. Others argue that liberal free trade should not, in any case, dominate the system and, hence, that environmental and other social matters should be accorded weight similar to that of economic matters. Moreover, there is no necessary match between 'trade' and 'economic' as opposed to 'trade' and 'law', or indeed 'trade' and 'social', and the current system relies too heavily on economic theory.[144]

Others contend that, in any event, the European Union is an inappropriate model for rights-based constitutionalization to draw upon, because economic rights in that regime are not justified on their own merit but as a by-product of the pursuit of a common goal—the single market—which has never been a good pursued by the WTO.[145] Moreover, the model does not answer the question how rights conflicts will be resolved. As noted above, how will a right to trade of a producer of one state be balanced, for example, against the right to work of another citizen of an importing state when that work may be displaced as a result of an increase in imports? What of the balance between individual rights (right to invest) with collective rights (permanent sovereignty over natural resources)? Could it ever be argued that an unrestrained application of the non-discrimination principle in trade which resulted in complete lowering of all tariff barriers, and now non-tariff barriers as well, could jeopardize the economic self-determination rights[146] of importing developing states.

---

[143] Alston (n 35 above).

[144] GR Shell, 'Trade Legalism and International Relations Theory: An Analysis of the World Trade Organization' (1995) 44 *Duke Law Journal* 829. See also ibid 906 (arguing that the current system relies too heavily on a normative commitment to economic theory, drawing parallels with the notorious US Supreme Court judgment in *Lochner*, and comments that economic theories do not determine the meaning of the constitution).   [145] Howse and Nicolaidis (n 43 above) 238.

[146] Joint Article 1 of the human rights covenants provides for a right to self-determination which includes a right of economic self determination: International Covenant on Civil and Political Rights 1966, 99 UNTS 171; and International Covenant on Economic, Social and Cultural Rights 1966, 993 UNTS 3.

In short, non-economic, cultural, and social goals are elided while economic imperatives dominate.[147] This is illustrated in the decision in *Canada— Periodicals*[148] in which the Appellate Body decided that measures designed to limit and prohibit import and distribution of split-run periodicals in Canada were discriminatory. Culture, long perceived as the last bastion of competences belonging to the state, was thus subjugated to free trade considerations through a straightforward interpretation of 'like product' for the purposes of the national treatment provision.

But despite the explicit promotion of a particular vision of liberal economic order focusing on economic efficiency, rights-based constitutionalization is not entirely accurately categorized as promoting only economic goals, at the expense of other social goals. The emphasis on expanding trade beyond simple trade goals, and a desire to increase the WTO stakeholders, are also features of the current phase of human-rights-based constitutionalization. For example, according to Petersmann, the extension of trade into issues beyond its conventional border, such as health, telecommunications, and intellectual property, necessitates new approaches to constitutional restraint on the WTO,[149] and is indicative of rights-based constitutionalization. The old fast-tracking methods for ratification of trade agreements appropriate in 1947 (to combat circumvention of democracy by log-rolling leading to introduction of destructive high tariffs) must be replaced by new methods taking into account interests in the new fields.[150]

The rights-based approach is, also, in some respects, consistent with two models drawn from Richard Shell's typologizing of the WTO into Regime Management, Efficient Market Mechanism, and Trade Stakeholders.[151] Regime Management, which we discussed in relation to institutional managerial constitutionalization, emphasizes regime stability, rule maintenance, and rule enforcement. Efficient Market Mechanism stresses rigorous competition under conditions of comparative advantage, and elimination of government interference with market efficiency. Trade Stakeholders focuses on legitimacy, and contends that it will not be achievable until the WTO includes greater participation of non-state actors, collective deliberation, and contextual decision making.[152] But while Regime Management, and hence institutional managerial constitutionalization, emphasizes the role of states as autonomous self-maximizing actors, both of the latter models place the individual at the fore. In Shell's view, they share liberalism's classic emphasis on the idea that

---

[147] Alston (n 35 above) 816. Petersmann has responded by arguing that he favours the 'social market' model in which both the economic and social are recognized: E-U Petersmann, 'Taking Human Dignity, Poverty and Empowerment of Individuals More Seriously: Rejoinder to Alston' (2002) 13 *European Journal of International Law* 845, 847.

[148] WTO, Report of the Appellate Body, *Canada—Certain Measures Concerning Periodicals*, WT/DS31/AB/R (30 June 1997), DSR 1997:I, 449.

[149] Petersmann, 'Human Rights and International Economic Law' (n 23 above) 25.

[150] ibid 27.   [151] Shell (n 144 above) 834–838.   [152] ibid 914–915.

international law is, ultimately, not for the benefit of states alone but for individuals. This vision of international citizenship strikes a chord with Petersmann's work.

Moreover, Petersmann is critical of the domination of international trade law by producer interests, and trade bureaucrats. Rights-based constitutionalization favours stronger competition rules to combat producer bias, and market failures such as monopolization and cartelization. He claims that domination can lead to 'one-sided protection of producer rights' in agreements concerning antidumping, textiles, and intellectual property. The sheer length and complexity of international trade agreements reduces the ability of national parliaments to understand the consequences of the agreements sufficiently before they ratify them.[153] Legitimacy concerns affect judicial decision-making, which has led to conflicting interpretations; moreover it is non-transparent; dominated by a trade orientation; and not sufficiently controlled by the membership.[154]

The later phase of human-rights-based constitutionalization also displays a partial reversal from a former absolutism about the inefficiency of linking social concerns with trade issues, evident in a shift between his 1997 work and his 2000 work on the WTO and human rights. In 1997, Petersmann states that discriminatory trade policies (including restriction of imports and subsidization of exports) for social reasons are not 'optimal policy instruments for the efficient correction of "market failures" directly at their source'.[155] This is a standard liberal trade justification for rejecting corrections of social problems such as failing domestic employment by the introduction of trade policies. The social aspect of trade is severable from its economic aspect, on this view. However, by 2000 Petersmann's views have altered. In his work on the 'WTO Constitution and Human Rights' Petersmann refutes the efficiency arguments of economists who claim that 'social...problems should be dealt with directly by means of social.... law, without restricting the welfare gains made possible by international trade'.[156] Instead he concedes that, although 'sub-optimal', 'issue linkages'—between trade and human rights, or trade and social rights— could be valid, although it must be noted that in the case of the earlier argument the aim of the social measures was to protect domestic interests, whereas in the later argument the aim is to protect interests in foreign states from rights abuse. Nevertheless, a small but critical shift has been effected because Petersmann is now recognizing the utility, and indeed legitimacy, of a link between the economic sphere and non-economic spheres such as those represented by human rights.

This suggests that the rights-based model could be a vehicle for pursuing two rather different goals, one of which may be aimed at particular free-market objectives and the other of which has a more procedural end related

---

[153] Petersmann, 'Human Rights and International Economic Law' (n 23 above) 27–30.
[154] ibid 28.   [155] Petersmann, *International Law and Dispute Settlement* (n 1 above) 10.
[156] Petersmann, 'WTO Constitution and Human Rights' (n 26 above) 20.

to inclusiveness. This paradox is largely ignored by the critics of the rights-based constitutionalization approach. Briefly put, the rights-based model could, if other changes were made, be about the politics of economic liberalism or it could be about the politics of participation, where the latter may or may not be directed towards free-market goals. This is not to suggest that the participation and procedural emphasis of rights-based constitutionalization would necessarily lead to outcomes other than those promoted by Petersmann. The procedural route to legitimacy is not necessarily a path to inclusion of non-economic goals; to the contrary, the procedural route may be a path to more, and stricter, economics.[157]

Nevertheless, signs of a shifting emphasis away from a strictly classical economic theory may also be detected in some work of the AB. The *Shrimp—Turtle* case[158] is recognition of the need to balance environment and other values against the free-trade goals of the WTO. In the *France—Asbestos* case, one member of the AB, concurring in the decision, went so far as to imply, in dicta, that principles other than economic ones might inform interpretation of key provisions.[159] In that case, health considerations were be taken into account in interpretation of 'like product' for the purposes of deciding whether asbestos-containing products were 'like' non-asbestos products that otherwise had the same function and markets. The result of the AB's inclusion of health in the analysis was that France was entitled to prohibit import of carcinogenic products. Within the WTO system, there is increasing recognition that economic goals may not, in all circumstances, be paramount over other social goals.

In sum, most critics of the rights-based approach claim that it tends towards protection of particular liberal economic goals over other competing values. This is illustrated by the way the approach associates its brand of economic freedoms with democracy, finds the roots for that view in history, expresses frustration with the myopia of international law about the benefits of economic freedom, and is frustrated about its subordinate position within the disciplinary hierarchy. However, there may be no necessary correlation between rights-based constitutionalization and classical economic theory. Emphasis on the role of the individual over the state, and a concern to include all actors on an equal

---

[157] Recent European case law has moved from an emphasis on anti-protectionism alone, to a consideration of the extent to which the disputed measure has trade effects: *compare* Joined Cases C–267 and C–268/91, *Keck and Mithouard* [1993] ECR 1–6097 and Case C–189/95, *Franzen* [1997] ECR I–5909.

[158] WTO, Report of the Appellate Body, *United States—Import Prohibition of Certain Shrimp and Shrimp Products*, WT/DS58/AB/R (12 October 1998), DSR 1998:VIII, 2755.

[159] WTO, Report of the Appellate Body, *European Communities—Measures Affecting Asbestos and Asbestos-Containing Products*, WT/DS135/ARB/R (12 March 2001) DSR 2001:VII, 3243. The member stated that 'the necessity or appropriateness of adopting a "fundamentally" economic interpretation of the "likeness" of products under Article III:4 of the GATT 1994 does not appear to me to be free from substantial doubt'.

level, may lead to inclusion of non-economic values into rights-based constitutionalization, although the procedural solution is no sure route to inclusion of social values either. Finally, in its most recent form, human-rights-based constitutionalization promotes extension of forms and subjects of participation, moving away from domination by producers and bureaucrats, and even contemplates inclusion of social values in the calculus of international trade.

5.3 CONCLUSION

To sum up, rights-based constitutionalization is a strongly prescriptive argument for the constitutionalization of the WTO, the main element of which is a focus on rights (not one of the core elements of the constitutionalization process outlined in Chapter 2). Rights-based constitutionalization promotes recognition of trade rules as rights that can be invoked by individuals directly within national legal systems, and other forms of increasing the law's effect. In recent times the approach has attempted to acquire the gloss of human rights legitimacy, but it is less interested in other core constitutional elements such as deliberation, community, or *Grundnorm* change. The transformation of rights-based constitutionalization into a human-rights conceptualization has led to strong criticism from some quarters. To be sure, the approach contains significant technical problems (for example, related to its effect in national systems) and it seeks to capitalize on the authority of human rights law. Critics suggest, too, that rights-based constitutionalization is nothing but a mask for a radically economically libertarian free-trade agenda. Nevertheless, we cannot ignore some interesting tendencies within rights-based constitutionalization towards equality and participation.

In relation to the core elements of constitutionalization defined in the first chapter, this model is fairly weak. Although it promises to nurture the legitimacy of the constitutionalization project and, to some extent, pays lip-service to the need for a wider trade community, and an effective participatory, deliberative process, the latter two issues are not major concerns for the approach. The rights-based constitutional community is constituted by consumers not citizens. The primary focus is, of course, rights, not a matter considered essential to constitutionalization in the received tradition of constitutionalization defined in Chapter 2. The questions when and how the *Grundnorm* of international trade changed is barely addressed.

6
Judicial Norm-Generation

6.1 INTRODUCTION

This chapter will set out another understanding of WTO constitutionalization, one that emphasizes the way an international adjudicatory body might contribute to the creation of a new legal system. This approach will be labelled constitutionalization by *judicial norm generation*. According to this understanding, which I have outlined elsewhere,[1] the WTO appellate review tribunal is the dynamic force or engine behind constitution-building, by virtue of its capacity to generate norms and structures of a constitutional type in the WTO. The judicial norm-generation approach to constitutionalization of the WTO is, of course, an adaptation of standard US constitutional law argument, as applied in other national,[2] and supranational[3] jurisdictions, which holds that the process of judicial interpretation of a set of basic laws can be constitutive as well as reflective of constitutional law. The methodology of the approach is, therefore, an explicitly common law, constitutional methodology[4] in which cases generate constitutional norms.[5]

---

[1] DZ Cass, 'The "Constitutionalization" of International Trade Law: Judicial Norm-Generation as the Engine of Constitutional Development in International trade' (2001) 12 *European Journal of International Law* 39.

[2] For a survey of national jurisdictions and the role of judicial interpretation in the constitutionalizing process see, eg, VC Jackson and M Tushnet, *Comparative Constitutional Law* (New York: Foundation Press, 1999).

[3] One of the seminal arguments about the constitutionalization of European Community law documented the emergence of a quasi-constitutional framework from the body of judgments of the European Court of Justice. According to this view, the growth of doctrine facilitated a progression within the EC from a set of institutions to oversee interstate relations in specific fields, to the development of a constitutional structure by a central adjudicatory body which defined legal principles akin to those which operate in federal constitutional systems such as direct effect, supremacy, and judicial review: JHH Weiler, 'The Transformation of Europe' (1991) 100 *Yale Law Journal* 2403.

[4] See LD Kramer, 'The Supreme Court 2000 Term (2001) 115 *Harvard Law Review* 4, 19 (commenting that methodologically fundamental law (constitutional law) and common law are 'siblings' because they are both formed by a similar method of constructing arguments based on analogy, principle, and forensic history).

[5] This position is in accord with the view of Joseph Weiler (discussing the European Union): '[I]n the beginning there was doctrine', because it is the first 'substratum' of the 'geology' of constitutionalism; it is 'concrete', 'foundational', and it is ultimately the 'gold seam' without which the process cannot occur, JHH Weiler, 'The Reformation of European Constitutionalism' in JHH Weiler, *The Constitution of Europe* (Cambridge: Cambridge University Press, 1999), 224–225.

In summary, this account[6] claims that the WTO is undergoing a process of constitutionalization to the extent that the Appellate Body (AB) generates norms and structures of a constitutional type using three techniques. First, the AB contributes to the constitutionalization process when it *amalgamates constitutional doctrines*, such as those relating to jurisdictional competence and substantive discrimination, and, arguably, rational relationship testing. The effect of the amalgamation of these techniques, in terms of the received account of constitutionalization, can be to realign the internal relationships between the members and the central entity, and enhance the legitimacy of the WTO by creating a constitutional system. Secondly, the AB engages in *system making* when it makes decisions about, amongst other matters, fact-finding methods, and the relationship between WTO law and other legal regimes. Thirdly, the AB *incorporates domestic subject matters* such as health and environment within its jurisdiction, and thus further realigns the internal relationships of power by contributing to the constitution of a new international trade system. The sum of these techniques is a form of incomplete constitutionalization because, applying the received image of constitutionalization defined in Chapter 2, the approach known as constitutionalization by judicial norm-generation focuses attention upon legitimacy, realignment of relationships, and *Grundnorm* change.

In this chapter, I will approach the discussion somewhat differently to the earlier models, as readers may be less familiar with the judicial norm-generation model. The chapter will, therefore, begin by showing the various ways in which judicial activity has facilitated the constitutionalization process, and will discuss the relationship between this approach and the received definition of constitutionalization given in Chapter 2. I will then identify some general examples of judicial norm-generation theory from the literature, and their critiques, before going on to articulate some specific examples of judicial norm-generation practice, the results of which show that, as well as producing legitimacy, this practice contributes to a realignment of relationships between states and the international entity, and *Grundnorm* change. It will be shown that other elements, such as deliberative process and community, are weak or absent from this model, and so the chapter concludes that, although judicial practice generates constitutional formations in the WTO, the approach does not qualify as constitutionalization by the measure of the standard definition. I will conclude, contrary to my earlier work, that the judicial norm-generation argument claims too much in respect of constitutionalization; pays insufficient attention to the equation between legitimacy and constitutionalization; and underestimates the role of politics in the consitutionalization process.

The key feature of this approach, then, is the idea that the process of adjudication itself can constitute a new system of law. This view has roots in

---

[6] These arguments are based on Cass (n 1 above).

positive theory that held that the judicial act was constitutive[7] because legal instruments were merely 'semi-manufactured products finished in the judicial decision'.[8] The contemporary literature on supranational constitutionalization by judicial norm-generation has its most compelling advocate in Joseph Weiler. Weiler's early work on the constitutionalization of the European Community argued convincingly that the activities of the European Court of Justice had led to transformation of the European Community from an international system of law to a constitutionalized system.[9] This transformation occurred as a result of the court's generation of a series of doctrines which had the effect of developing a structure of a constitutional type for Europe: direct effect, supremacy, implied powers, human rights, and (contested) *kompetenz-kompetenz*.[10] Complementing these judicially inspired doctrines, which Weiler referred to collectively as the 'constitutionalization' process, were treaty mechanisms that reinforced the latter, such as the establishment of judicial review of Community actions, and Member State actions both at the Community level and at the Member State level.[11] Although the judicial norm-generation argument does not operate in precisely the same way in relation to the WTO (because the EU has a different institutional structure from the WTO[12] and equivalent doctrines have not developed),[13] I have argued previously that the contours of the argument are similar.[14] Armin von Bogdandy also, for example, refers to the 'autonomous' nature of the judicial function and its ability to generate new substantive law.[15] In an article discussing judicial interpretation of a GATT general exception Schloemann and Ohlhoff state that, '[c]onstitutional structures are developing much faster in international trade law than in any other area of international law',[16] and the authors explicitly link this phenomenon to

---

[7] H Kelsen, *General Theory of Law and State*, trans Anders Wedberg (Russell and Russell edn, 1961) (c 1945) 132–136. Kelsen argued that the judicial act is constitutive, rather than declaratory. The judicial act creates a new individual norm, by applying a higher level norm, and, in order to do this, the judge must establish the presence of the conditions in the general norm which are present in the concrete situation, ascertain the facts that condition the sanction, and stipulate the sanction.   [8] ibid 135.

[9] Weiler (n 3 above).   [10] ibid 2414–2417.

[11] ibid (arguing at 2419–2420, that an 'integrated unitary system of judicial review' (2420) arose from the existence of a mandatory exclusive forum for adjudicating disputes; an independent central body to invoke central law against a Member State; and a reference procedure whereby Member States could refer national measures to the European level to assess compliance with European rules).

[12] For a comparison of the EU and the WTO institutions in a constitutional context see P Holmes, 'The WTO and the EU: Some Constitutional Comparisons' in G de Búrca and J Scott (eds), *The EU and the WTO: Legal and Constitutional Issues* (2001) 70 Table 2. See also discussion at p. 50 above.

[13] WTO jurisprudence lacks the doctrinal foundations of, for example, direct effect and supremacy, and the system of judicial remedies and enforcement is rudimentary at best.

[14] Cass (n 1 above).

[15] A von Bogdandy, 'Law and Politics in the WTO—Strategies to Cope with a Deficient Relationship' in JA Frowein and R Wolfrum (eds), *Max Planck Yearbook of United Nations Law* Vol 5 (2001) 625.

[16] HL Schloemann and S Ohlhoff, ' "Constitutionalization" and Dispute Settlement in the WTO: National Security as an Issue of Competence' (1999) 93 *American Journal of International Law* 424.

judicial activity by stating that 'the limits of the dispute settlement mechanism...
are...the limits of the constitutionalization of the organization as a whole'.[17]
Alee Stone Sweet anticipates judicialized dispute resolution leading to even
grander goals such as the 'construction of governance',[18] or even 'international
society's peacetime order'.[19] Robert Howse suggests not that the WTO is constitutionalizing, as such, but that the judicial process is creating greater legitimacy both for the adjudicatory body and for the WTO itself.[20]

The argument therefore comes in various forms. The dispute settlement system is said to be increasingly popular.[21] The introduction of judicial power,
over and above bureaucratic power,[22] has the potential to increase the legitimacy of the system,[23] defined as fair procedure, coherence, and institutional
sensitivity.[24] Or it is claimed that adjudication is a route toward legitimacy,
because courts are perceived as a mechanism to balance competing values.[25]

[17] HL Schloemann and S Ohlhoff, ' "Constitutionalization" and Dispute Settlement in the WTO:
National Security as an Issue of Competence' (1999) 93 *American Journal of International Law* 424.
[18] AS Sweet, 'Judicialization and the Construction of Governance' (1999) 32 *Comparative
Political Studies* 147.   [19] Schloemann and Ohlhoff (n 16 above) 451.
[20] PM Nichols, 'GATT Doctrine' (1996) 36 *Virginia Journal of International Law* 379.
[21] Schloemann and Ohlhoff (n 16 above) 424 n 1.
[22] R Howse, 'The Legitimacy of the World Trade Organization' in J Coicaud and V Heiskanen
(eds), *The Legitimacy of International Organizations* (Tokyo; New York: United Nations Press,
2001) 358–359 and 371–374 (arguing that the GATT decision-making was controlled by a group
of trade experts whose main aim was to maintain the system. Moreover, in an atmosphere of 'explicit
normative ambiguity' about what constituted acceptable domestic regulation and what constituted
protectionist cheating, this elite wielded enormous power, based on 'an intuitive sense of what the
system could bear', and displayed 'greater political subtlety than intellectual or juridical clarity').
[23] ibid (arguing that although GATT maintained a measure of procedural legitimacy derived
from bureaucratic power, defined in the previous note, it was short on what Joseph Weiler has
called substantive, or social, legitimacy).
[24] ibid 376. Legitimacy by fair procedure was to be found in the new WTO in the dispute settlement system's complex procedures and institutional disciplines which required more openness,
defined participation rights, and established formal requirements to produce written requests and
standardized terms of reference. Coherence was enhanced because the AB was explicitly required
to refer to international law rules of treaty interpretation. Institutional sensitivity was bolstered by
the AB's increasing tendency to take account of other legal regimes such as international health,
and environment. Compare with R Howse and K Nicolaidis, 'Legitimacy and Global Governance:
Why Constitutionalizing the WTO is a Step Too Far' in RB Porter, *et al* (eds), *Efficiency, Equity,
and Legitimacy: The Multilateral Trading System at the Millennium* (Washington DC: Brookings
Institution Press, 2001) [hereinafter, 'A Step Too Far'] 228, later work, in which Howse (and his
co-author) appear to lose faith in the potential of judicial power to provide the necessary legitimacy to the WTO, and instead advocate what is referred to, at 249, as a 'non-constitutional' route.
What is interesting here is that some of the factors, which were indicative, in the earlier work, of
a new-found WTO legitimacy, reappear as necessary ingredients of the preferred non-constitutional
route. So, for example, rights of participation and other procedural aspects of fairness, which, in the
early work, feature as part of a bundle of indices of growing social legitimacy, reappear, in the non-
constitutional model, as part of a the non-constitutional route. This would suggest that a tension
exists within Howse's work as to whether these elements can vest legitimacy and hence lead to
constitutionalization, or whether they are representative of 'non-constitutionalization'. For non-
constitutionalization: see Chapter 7 below.
[25] R Howse, 'Adjudicative Legitimacy and Treaty Interpretation in International Trade Law: The
Early Years of WTO Jurisprudence' in JHH Weiler (ed), *The EU, the WTO and the NAFTA:
Towards a Common Law of International Trade* (Oxford: Hart Publishing, 2000) 41.

This is reminiscent of Weiler's claim that increased judicial activity of this nature inculcates a habit of obedience in members of the system and so has the potential to increase the system's social acceptance.[26]

Sometimes the link between legitimacy and constitutionalization is presented in a strong form resembling a claim that a new rule of customary international law has emerged, from dispute settlement, suggesting that international trade law is, indeed, a constitution.[27] Without using the usual labels of custom, Schloemann and Ohlhoff argue that 'overwhelming acceptance' (*opinio juris*) and 'use of the dispute settlement mechanism' (state practice) have 'pushed the multilateral trade system' to develop into what they call 'a proto-supranational structure'.[28] While the term 'proto-supranational' is not equivalent to constitutional, the implication—in an article entitled ' "Constitutionalization" and Dispute Settlement in the WTO'—is that the two concepts are closely related. Indeed in this work, constitutionalization resembles a new system-structure and that structure itself has become a rule of custom. The same authors go on to claim that WTO can be said to have 'constitutionalized' because it has achieved a new 'independent third party' status within the international community, which 'displays elements of a new social contract'.[29] On this bold view, the WTO now possesses the necessary symbolic and political legitimacy to call itself constitutionalized.

A more cautious form of legitimacy analysis is found in Robert Howse's early work referred to above.[30] While not suggesting that the WTO had attained the necessary legitimacy to be constitutionalized, Howse argued that the introduction of judicial power into the system in 1995 could have the effect of enhancing the institution's legitimacy. Howse suggested that, although the WTO had formerly included a measure of procedural legitimacy derived from bureaucratic power, it was short on substantive or social legitimacy, and so he argued that this gap would be partly filled[31] by the introduction of judicial power to supplement the existing power of rules and of the bureaucracy. The reason for the enhancement of legitimacy via judicial means was that judicial decision-making enabled decisions to be based on contests between competing values, rather than purely on political considerations. On this view then,

---

[26] 'The combination of "constitutionalization" and the system of judicial remedies...introduced on the Community level the *habit of obedience* and the respect for the rule of law which traditionally is less associated with international obligations than national ones': Weiler (n 3 above) 2421. See discussion above in Chapter 2 notes 124–126 and accompanying text.

[27] Schloemann and Ohlhoff (n 16 above) and accompanying text.   [28] ibid 1.

[29] ibid.   [30] Note 25 above and accompanying text.

[31] Howse (n 22 above) (arguing that even if judicial power functioned to enhance WTO legitimacy, further legitimacy gaps remained. For example, the WTO did not include domestic procedures for consultation over new rules; it maintained a practice of secrecy of drafts in relation to negotiating rounds; and the package deal approach adopted in negotiation militated against outcomes with a high level of national legitimacy. Moreover, he argued, even if the defects of democratic control of rule-creation process could be resolved by Shell's stakeholder model, or by international civil society, inequalities in access, participation, power, and accountability would remain.)

the legitimacy deficit of constitutionalization could be potentially addressed by substantive or social legitimacy derived from adjudication, as opposed to the GATT model in which legitimacy had to be based on bureaucratic power.

A further variant of this argument is Rambod Behboodi's claim that the WTO's increased legitimacy by judicial means arises through a process of adjudication whereby the texts of the agreements are clarified in an ongoing 'conversation' between adjudicators and the legal community to whom they speak.[32] As evidence, reference is made to a series of cases which have, respectively, increased WTO legitimacy by building confidence in the AB and in the WTO system,[33] established the WTO as a separate legal framework,[34] brought in the developing countries,[35] and, finally, given effect to certain compromises necessary in a legal order between national sovereignty and integration.[36] This process of clarification of text by interpretation legitimizes the new system of law, moves it further away from an earlier diplomatic demeanour, and vests it with the 'mantle of uniqueness'—appellate jurisdiction in international law.[37] Moreover, the newly acquired legitimacy arises precisely because members dispensed with the old diplomatic mode of operating and chose the route of law, legalism, and formalism, over diplomacy, pragmatism, and realism.[38]

Further evidence for this claim that legitimacy arises from ongoing conversations between actors in a given political–legal community might be found in the events surrounding the *Shrimp—Turtle* decision. In this case, a robust dialogue developed over the use of *amicus* briefs, and involved various groups of actors including, non-government organizations who wished to submit briefs, states which variously supported and rejected their use, judicial bodies which were charged with deciding the issue, and a General Council which

---

[32] R Behboodi, 'Legal Reasoning and the International Law of Trade' (1998) 32 *Journal of World Trade* 55, 98. Compare Behboodi's discussion of legitimacy with Deborah Steger above, Chapter 4 note 123. While Behboodi argues that legitimacy arises from a dialectic between the interpreters and the community with the former seeking to persuade the latter of certain legal meanings, Steger portrays legitimacy as a simple matter of 'clarification' of text. This difference explains why I have classified Steger with the institutional managerialists and Behboodi with judicial norm-generation constitutionalists. For Steger, the process of legitimizing a system is a mechanical matter: it requires good management, good powers of persuasion, and ultimately the meaning of the text will be clarified and legitimacy will then result. For Behboodi the process is more complex, even somewhat mysterious, and is best represented by a conversation between interpreters and community. Something deeper than management is going on here.

[33] ibid 69 (referring to WTO, Report of the Appellate Body, *United States—Standards for Reformulated and Conventional Gasoline*, WT/DS2/AB/R (29 April 1996), DSR 1996:I, 3).

[34] ibid 75.

[35] ibid 76 (referring to WTO, Report of the Appellate Body, *United States—Restrictions on Imports of Cotton and Man-made Fibre Underwear*, WT/DS24/AB/R (10 February 1997) DSR 1997:I, 11.

[36] ibid 84 (referring to WTO, Report of the Appellate Body, *Japan—Taxes on Alcoholic Beverages*, WT/DS8/AB/R, WT/DS10/AB/R, WT/DS11/AB/R (4 October 1996) DSR 1996:I, 97.

[37] ibid 57.

[38] ibid 57–62 (arguing that the law versus diplomacy debate within the WTO is a reflection of the legalist versus pragmatist debate in legal theory, and the formalist versus realist debate in international relations).

then clarified the membership's position on the use of briefs. The vigorous conversation that ensued clearly had the effect of influencing the debate about the WTO's legitimacy, although to some its legitimacy was strengthened and to others it was weakened. Either way, the very fact that the debate took place, that it involved so many disparate groups, and that it was resolved in accordance with the procedures of the organization suggest that the conversation served a legitimating function.

However, at this point in the discussion about legitimacy it is worth pausing in order to consider what exactly is being claimed. One of the problems with an account that directly links increased legitimacy by judicial norm-generation to constitutionalization is that it risks reducing the relationship into a simple cause and effect model, when, in practice, constitutionalization and legitimacy stand in a complex relationship to each other. Increased legitimacy is, as we have argued throughout, a necessary condition for constitutionalization but it is not sufficient to achieve that outcome. Increased legitimacy of an institution could occur without stepping up the process of constitutionalization. For example, the legitimacy of international institutions such as the United Nations, the World Bank, or the International Monetary Fund waxes and wanes without necessarily leading to constitutionalization of these organizations. Of course, one difference may be that the legitimacy that WTO authors refer to is one generated by judicial activity, and so this form of legitimacy generation may have a greater likelihood of influencing the process of constitutionalization. But putting that difference aside for moment, it seems that any thesis linking legitimacy with constitutionalization would require further problematization before it could be claimed that there is a cause and effect relationship between the two.

Secondly, does judicial activity of itself lead directly to legitimacy, or do the results of judicial activity foster legitimacy (and, ultimately, constitutionalization) in a more indirect sense? In the European Union, it was argued that judicial activity of the court created constitutional norms, but also that a secondary process of legitimization occurred. There are two distinct processes here, and, of the two, the second is more significant. An adjudicatory body cannot build a constitution on its own, but it can create an environment in which its decisions are accorded a level of respect and legitimacy that allows constitutionalization to flourish.[39] In relation to the WTO, some judicial norm-generation theorists pay insufficient attention to discussion of the second, more indirect phenomenon.

Some critics make the normative argument that a judicial body should not have sole responsibility for the interpretation of a constitution. In one of the foremost examples of constitution building by judicial means, the United States,

---

[39] LR Helfer and A-M Slaughter, 'Toward a Theory of Effective Supranational Adjudication' (1997) 107 *Yale Law Journal* 273, 310 (arguing that effective supranational adjudication occurs when conversations take place between national and international adjudicatory bodies).

there is a long tradition of constructing and interpreting a constitution by popular means.[40] This 'popular constitutionalism', extant in the eighteenth century, and still encoded in an accommodation about the respective interpretive power of the political and judicial branches of the US in the twentieth century,[41] held that the constitution was not just 'ordinary law' subject to judicial interpretation, but a 'special form of popular law, law made by the people to bind their governors'.[42] According to this argument, constitutional norms can and should be generated by non-judicial interpretation as well. Therefore, these critics argue, a balance between judicial and non-judicial means of interpretation and constitution-making is essential to constitutional democracy.[43] Given that the WTO does not possess a written constitution equivalent to the US version (although the WTO Agreement and covered agreements might constitute such), that the WTO lacks a proper legislative arm to correct any over-reaching of the judicial branch, and that the AB is not asserting its authority of constitution-making for the purpose of protecting individual rights, the political constitutionalization argument has resonance. The underlying concern of the critique remains to 'balance' the role of the judiciary against other political institutions'[44] means of constitution-making and interpretation. Constitutionalization can occur in many different ways at the WTO, too, for example, through popular forms of constitutional norm-generation including discussion, argument, and debate in the various other institutions of the WTO, and beyond, in international civil society.

Indeed the WTO system contains a set of political institutions, formal and informal, which can and occasionally do function as sites of constitutionalization. The membership of the WTO, through the General Council and Ministerial Conference, has the power to produce authoritative interpretations of the agreement. Either body can in theory therefore overrule the DSB in matters of interpretation of the agreements. These bodies have, therefore, ultimate constitutional authority, which could be exercised in response to judicial norm-generation.

The political institutions of the WTO are, however, not equipped to act in a manner consistent with a branch of government with a full complement of constitutional power. Armin von Bogdandy argues that the legislative function of the WTO is seriously deficient in comparison to its adjudicative function in terms of both democracy and efficiency.[45] There is a 'serious mismatch between the cumbersome political institutions and procedures on the one hand and the WTO's often far-reaching rules applied by compulsory adjudication

---

[40] Kramer (n 4 above).

[41] ibid 14–15 (arguing that a reconciliation between popular constitutionalism and judicial review was effected in the 'New Deal accommodation', encapsulated by Carolene Products footnote 4 recognition of the power of the judiciary to protect individual rights, but that this accommodation began to give way in the 1990s under the pressure of the Rehnquist Court's claim to be the authoritative interpreters of the Constitution.)   [42] ibid 10.

[43] ibid 15.   [44] ibid.   [45] von Bogdandy (n 15 above) 609.

on the other'.[46] Democracy is compromised by, for example, an absence of a forum for open discussion of rule creation; a powerful and autonomous WTO bureaucracy; national parliamentary deference to governmental measures issuing from international treaties; and deficiencies of information in national arenas about the WTO.[47] Efficiency is compromised by slow and cumbersome treaty-making procedures; inadequate amendment procedures; and protection of economic sovereignty in cases where amendment alters the rights and obligations of members, by the provision that a member must agree to the particular amendment before it becomes obligatory for that member.[48] While similar criticisms could be made about international treaty-making generally, von Bogdandy suggests that the problem is particularly acute in the WTO because the social and economic conditions to which WTO law applies change at a rapid pace,[49] and the adjudicatory function is compulsory, autonomous,[50] and law-generating.[51] The WTO's 'missing legislator'[52] cannot be adequately replaced by functional equivalents for legislative efficiency or democracy because the alternatives are inadequate. Rule-making by WTO organs has been weakened in the 1995 WTO Agreement as compared to the 1947 GATT, and 'out-sourcing' of rule-making by, for example, international standard-setting bodies, risks capture by private interests,[53] while science is not a foolproof way of resolving economic and political controversy.[54] As a result, the relationship between law and politics in the WTO is awry and there is no self-correcting political mechanism to act as a counterweight to judicial activity.

The incapacity of the WTO political arm to correct judicial rule-making is all the more critical, according to the critics, not only because of the dynamic nature of the field, and the compulsory, autonomous character of WTO dispute resolution, but because the legal process is not attuned to deciding complex economic disputes.

There are inherent limits to any adjudicative process convincingly drawing the line between political intervention and economic freedom: regulatory problems can only exceptionally be settled through litigation. In general, adjudicative organs lack the expertise for such policies; their information is dependent on those who participate in the adjudicative process and issues may be decided without hearing affected interests which do not participate.[55]

Despite the superficial appeal of the judicial norm-generation argument because of its resemblance to the approach taken in relation to European constitutionalization, ultimately it fails to convince. In its strong from, as claim for a grand vision of a constitutional structure, the argument overstates its case, and in its more moderate form—where it merely claims increased legitimacy— it fails sufficiently to problematize the relationship between judicial activity,

---

[46] ibid 612.   [47] ibid 619–620.   [48] ibid 623, discussing WTO Art X.   [49] ibid.
[50] ibid 614.   [51] ibid 625.   [52] ibid 651.   [53] ibid 637.   [54] ibid 643–44.
[55] ibid 656.

legitimacy, and constitutionalization. In any event, constitutionalization solely by judicial means, and in the absence of sufficient avenues for political constitutionalization, is illegitimate: it skews the relationship between politics and law, and leads to complex economic regulatory decisions being made on the basis of inadequate information, expertise, and interest input. From a normative viewpoint, then, constitutionalization by judicial norm-generation is undesirable. Nevertheless it is important to understand the way in which the argument works and to consider the effects judicial activity may have on the constitutionalization process. The remainder of the chapter will describe in more detail the judicial norm-generation model, and discuss its relationship with aspects of the received account of constitutionalization including legitimacy, realignment of constituent relationships, and *Grundnorm* change. To the extent that this model reflects these elements, constitutionalization by judicial norm-generation can be a powerful tool in the armoury of constitutionalization promotion.

6.2 FEATURES OF JUDICIAL NORM-GENERATION CONSTITUTIONALIZATION

6.2.1 Amalgamation of constitutional doctrine

One method of constitutional norm-generation, detailed below, occurs through the amalgamation of doctrines from domestic and supranational constitutional law, which have a constitutional bearing, with two results. First, the WTO adjudicatory system begins to resemble a system of a constitutional type, and this has the effect of legitimizing the adjudication system. Secondly, constitutional doctrine has the effect of realigning relationships between the members and the centre, thereby fashioning a constitutional system.

The use of adjudication in the service of legitimacy and realignment of constitutional relationships is illustrated by the tribunal's amalgamation into its reasoning of doctrines such as jurisdictional competence.

Jurisdictional competence

Before any decision-maker can decide how to apply the law to particular facts, the decision-maker must understand (and sometimes decide) the boundaries of its own power. The question is constitutional because it affects, in a literal sense, the constitution or the making of the system at hand. It is constitutional also in a normative sense because the power of a decision-maker to decide this issue is one indicator of the autonomy and legitimacy of the decision-maker.[56] This section will highlight the way the AB's doctrine of jurisdictional

---

[56] JHH Weiler, 'The Autonomy of the Community Legal Order' in Weiler (n 5 above) 303–304 (arguing that the conventional position, at international law, is that states cannot, by

competence has influenced the conceptualization of relationships between the states and the international entity.

The *Hormones* case[57] introduces a major preoccupation of constitutional law—jurisdictional competence—into the case law of the WTO, and this doctrine one of the sites for renegotiation of the relationship between the states and the international entity. This constitutionalizing process occurs at two levels, one of which concerns the specific rule Panels are to apply in reviewing Member State acts. The other level concerns the justification for the rule. First to the rule context.

The rule: the standard of review by Panels of national state decisions should be 'objective assessment'

In the *Hormones* case, at first instance, a Panel found that an EC ban upon the importation of meat produced with growth hormones was inconsistent with provisions of the Sanitary and Phytosanitary Agreement (the SPS Agreement).[58] On appeal, the EC argued, *inter alia*, that the Panel had applied an incorrect standard of review to the EC's decision. Essentially, it argued that the Panel should have deferred to the decision of the Member State about whether or not the ban was warranted on scientific grounds. It claimed the Panel should not have applied full *de novo* review, but instead should have respected the EC judgment,[59] a standard often referred to, in constitutional law, as deferential or reasonableness review.[60]

On appeal, the AB rejected the EC's argument. The AB noted that, although the SPS Agreement was silent on the issue of the standard of review, Article 11 of the DSU[61] supported a finding that the standard required of a Panel was

'autointerpretation', determine the competence of a central, international adjudicatory body created under treaty; international tribunals have jurisdiction to determine this themselves. See also Helfer and Slaughter (n 39 above) 310 (arguing that a conversation about competences between the European courts and national courts within the European Community led those entities to develop a relationship of 'partnership').

[57] WTO, Report of the Appellate Body, *European Communities—Measures Concerning Meat and Meat Products (Hormones)*, WT/DS26/AB/R, WT/DS48/AB/R (16 January 1998), DSR 1998:I, 135.

[58] Agreement on the Application of Sanitary and Phytosanitary Measures, 15 April 1994, Annex 1A, Marrakesh Agreement Establishing the World Trade Organization, Annex 2, *The Results of the Uruguay Round of Multilateral Trade Negotiations: The Legal Texts* (1994) [hereinafter SPS Agreement] Arts 3.3 and 5.1.

[59] WTO, Report of the Appellate Body, *European Communities—Measures Concerning Meat and Meat Products (Hormones)*, WT/DS26/AB/R, WT/DS48/AB/R (16 January 1998), DSR 1998:I, 135 at para 111.

[60] Briefly, in national systems, the term 'deference' signals that a judicial body should defer to the opinion of a legislative or executive one, and 'reasonableness' means that the reviewing tribunal should not review the merits of a legislative or executive decision but only ask whether the decision was made in a reasonable fashion.

[61] Understanding on Rules and Procedures Governing the Settlement of Disputes, Marrakesh Agreement Establishing the World Trade Organization, Annex 2, *The Results of the Uruguay Round of Multilateral Trade Negotiations: The Legal Texts* [hereinafter DSU Agreement]. Art 11 requires Panels to make an 'objective assessment of the matter before it, including an objective assessment of the facts of the case and the applicability of and conformity with the relevant covered agreements'.

neither *de novo* nor deferential review but 'objective assessment'.[62] The AB indicated that the WTO will adopt a standard that steers a middle course between full review on the merits, and the far less intrusive standard of procedural or reasonableness review. Nevertheless, a Member State cannot simply assert that it has satisfied the requirements of the SPS Agreement without being prepared to justify that decision before an interstate adjudicatory body with the power to make an objective assessment of it. The constitutional significance of this seemingly practical issue is obvious. Because legal outcomes turn, at least in part, on factual assessments, the sort of review power possessed by an international tribunal becomes important. And the review power of the tribunal will, in turn, affect the scope and manner of national (or in this case supranational) decision-making. Member States will not be able to make risk assessments based on scientific data that fails to meet the objective assessment standard. This result prefigures a long process whereby the AB will have to negotiate the difficult constitutional waters of international judicial deference to Member State decisions.

An interpretation which no longer leaves factual decisions with trade effects entirely to the state modifies relationships between entities within the new system. The result has constitutional implications to the extent that it affects the extent of Member State power within the WTO legal system, and the relationship between the two levels of control. This modification is particularly acute given that although no legislative power or executive has been *explicitly* transferred to the WTO, and the classic all-encompassing autonomy of national jurisdictional competence remains intact, a significant alteration has been effected in the relationships between the entities which comprise the system. Importantly, for our purposes, the change has occurred via the adjudication process. By generating a rule relating to jurisdictional competence in the process of ordinary judicial interpretation, the AB has decided that national authorities can no longer make decisions without those decisions being subject to international judicial oversight by WTO Panels. Deference is no longer the order of the day, so, even if the actual scope of national power remains the same, its exercise is forever affected. Grafted on to the national systems of Member States of the WTO is a limit, however minimal, which qualifies their previous full complement of regulatory authority, and the distribution of power between central and peripheral entities of the WTO legal system has been adjusted. The review standard rule struck by the AB perfectly illustrates the implications of adoption of an understanding of constitutionalization based on judicial

---

[62] WTO, Report of the Appellate Body, *European Communities—Measures Concerning Meat and Meat Products (Hormones)*, WT/DS26/AB/R, WT/DS48/AB/R (16 January 1998), DSR 1998:I, 135 at para 117. (At para 118, the AB relied in part on customary international law interpretation rules, the general interpretative approach of which pointed to this reading of Article 11).

norm-generation. By amalgamating a technique of a standard constitutional type, regarding the difference between deferential and *de novo* review, the Tribunal has contributed to a closer resemblance between WTO law and constitutional law, and has realigned the relationships between parts of the system in a manner typical of constitutional arrangements.

Moreover, the constitutionalizing significance of the dispute is clearly visible. Although the tribunal finesses a conflict between national and national institutional authority, through the genteel language of standards of review, any audience interested in constitutional disputation would recognize the fragile compromises that lie underneath.

Once the debate moves out of the confines of a national setting, and where the actors are a review tribunal established under international treaty and executive bodies of national states, then the question of standard of review leaves the domain of national constitutional organization and becomes imbued with international constitutional meaning.

The justification: the division of power

The deep constitutional significance of the decision is made more explicit when one moves from the level of rule articulation to rule justification. Here, the AB links the problem of what is the appropriate level of review to a standard constitutional value which it expresses as being about the problem of 'balance' of jurisdictional competence within a non-unitary legal system.[63] It is clear from this language alone that the AB itself believes that the standard of review is not a mere technical rule. 'The standard of review appropriately applicable in proceedings under the *SPS Agreement*, of course, must reflect the balance established in that Agreement between the jurisdictional competences conceded by the Members to the WTO and the jurisdictional competences retained by the Members for themselves.'[64]

This statement contains an explicit recognition that nested within questions of review—which may appear somewhat bland on their surface—are critical constitutional indicators about the way relationships are to be defined within the WTO structure, and, even about the integration process itself. If the AB had settled upon full *de novo* review of members' decisions by Panels then the WTO agreements would have represented a much deeper level of integration between Member States than many had formerly expected. In the event, however, the AB instead adopted a less intrusive approach to the questions of review, jurisdictional competence, and its own role within the WTO system.

---

[63] WTO, Report of the Appellate Body, *European Communities—Measures Concerning Meat and Meat Products (Hormones)*, WT/DS26/AB/R, WT/DS48/AB/R (16 January 1998), [1998] 1 DSR 135 at para 115.
[64] ibid at para 114.

Moreover, the language of the tribunal suggests that the AB was acutely aware of the sensitivities raised by the decision. It was aware, for example, that the question raised the problem of the appropriate alignment of relationships between Member States and the WTO. In portraying the question as one of balance, and in effectively discounting the suggestion that Panels might review national authorities' decisions for substance as well as for process, the AB indicated that the Panels' constitutional role is one of oversight review rather than full-blooded review.

In addition to the constitutionalizing effects of judicial norm-generation, the case is constitutionalizing because it suggests that, even in the exercise of mere treaty interpretation by a central tribunal, the legal system under interpretation can be constructed in a particular way. Here, adoption of the doctrine of jurisdictional competence, and its application in relation to standard of review, has created a system in which the scope of legislative power of the Member States has been subtly altered, or perhaps even 'lost',[65] without an explicit transfer of power occurring. Even taking account of the important qualification that states have not transferred regulatory power to any centralized body, an alteration in the national–international relationship has occurred, and largely by way of judicial intervention. Secondly, this construction of a particular constellation of relationships between national and central entities of the WTO legal system by way of judicial intervention has been done without explicit authorization of the Member States of the organization (or indeed the political communities they represent), and thus the legitimacy of the change may be open to question. Thirdly, the decision has constitutionalizing effects because it suggests that the AB has begun to act as though the legal systems subject to its jurisdiction were not only singular systems of law in their own right but a part of a broader system of law, thus enhancing the coherence of that system and lending it a constitutional gloss.

The problem of the relationship between the states and the international entity is cast as a matter of deference in another case, and overlaps with the question of the relationship between international and municipal law. In *India— Pharmaceuticals*,[66] the AB rejects a Member's assertions that a particular mode of implementing a TRIPs obligation, by the issuance of 'administrative instructions', is satisfactory, particularly in view of the continuing existence of mandatory legislation which did not conform with TRIPs.[67] Despite the Indian government's assertion to the contrary, the AB is 'not persuaded that

---

[65] For a discussion, in the European context, of the phenomenon of 'lost' sovereignty see: N MacCormick, 'The Maastricht—Urteil: Sovereignty Now' (1995) 1 *European Law Journal* 259.

[66] WTO, Report of the Appellate Body, *India—Patent Protection for Pharmaceutical and Agricultural Chemical Products*, WT/DS50/AB/R (19 December 1997), DSR 1998:I, 9.

[67] The Indian Patents Act provided that food, medicine, and drug substances were not patentable, and required the relevant official to refuse any such patent applications: ibid.

administrative instructions would prevail over contradictory mandatory provisions' of an Act.[68] They point also to the Indian government's failure to provide any text of its 'administrative instructions' to the WTO bodies,[69] and note that the government had initially considered it would have to enact legislation[70] to implement the obligation.[71] They refer also to public international law rules on the relationship between municipal and international law, stating that, although the international tribunal may not interpret the local law, it can assess whether the national government, in applying the law, is conforming with the international obligation.[72] By refusing to defer to a state's claim that it has implemented the WTO obligation by way of administrative means, the AB reduces the capacity of states to claim complete autonomy in respect of decisions about implementation. In short, both examples illustrate an awareness, on the part of the AB, that it is fashioning a system of law by realigning relationships between a central body and its constituent parts.

Substantive discrimination

A second example of doctrine amalgamation, and resulting enhanced legitimacy, concerns the AB's refinement of a sophisticated doctrine of substantive discrimination.[73] In including discrimination doctrine as one of the indicators of an adjudication system of a constitutional type, it is true that this type of doctrine is as common to labour law as it is to constitutional settings. However, the experience of mature constitutional systems, for example in the United States, Canada, and Australia, has been that a proportion of constitutional adjudication is taken up with deciding questions of discrimination, between individuals, among individuals residing in different parts of the constitutional system, and between the different constituent parts themselves.[74] To this extent, the increasing refinement of discrimination doctrine in the WTO can be

---

[68] WTO, Report of the Appellate Body, *India—Patent Protection for Pharmaceutical and Agricultural Chemical Products*, WT/DS50/AB/R (19 December 1997), DSR 1998:I, 9 at para 69.

[69] ibid at para 61.   [70] ibid at para 61.   [71] ibid at para 62.   [72] ibid at para 62.

[73] Although WTO law has refined the substantive approach, it has its historical roots in GATT jurisprudence: see, eg, GATT, Report of the Panel, *Italy—Discrimination Against Imported Agricultural Machinery*, BISD 3S/77 (adopted 23 October 1958), GATT BISD (7th Supp) 60 (1959), in which the provision of favourable credit facilities to Italian producers of agricultural machinery infringed the national treatment rule; and GATT, Report of the Panel, *United States—Section 337 of the Tariff Act 1930*, BISD 36S/345 (adopted 7 November 1989), GATT BISD (36th Supp) 345 (1990), in which procedural advantages accorded to US patent holders, in relation to having a choice of forum in which to assert their patent rights, was considered to infringe the national treatment rule.

[74] For some examples in the Australian context, see the different approaches towards discrimination in *James v Commonwealth* (1928) 41 CLR 442 (formal), and *Street v Queensland Bar Association* (1989) 163 CLR 461 (substantive), and discrimination doctrine developed in relation to section 92 of the Australian Constitution which states that interstate trade and commerce shall be 'absolutely free'.

interpreted as enhancing the resemblance between it and a constitutional system of adjudication. In addition, the legitimacy of the adjudication process, and indirectly of the constitutionalization process of which it forms a part, is strengthened by the tribunal's indication that it will investigate behind a state's claim of pure facial or formal equality of treatment and examine actual outcomes, effects, or results of a measure, as applied, to ensure that no discrimination between parties has occurred.

How, then, has this augmentation of discrimination doctrine been manifest in WTO caselaw? First, the AB has indicated that it will assess discrimination historically, and in context. As a consequence, facially non-discriminatory measures may, upon historical and contextual examination, prove to be discriminatory.[75] Moreover, by adopting an effects-based approach to interpretation, the AB rejected formal equality as the goal of the non-discrimination principle, specifically where competitive disadvantage continues.[76] Finally, mere equalization of opportunities may be found insufficient to overcome past discrimination, and what may be required is a form of positive discrimination favouring those who have previously been discriminated against.[77] In short, the AB's interpretation of non-discrimination rules displays an acute awareness of the ways in which facially neutral measures can nevertheless have discriminatory effects in practice. A similar emphasis characterizes the *Shrimp—Turtle* decision in which provisions, which were facially valid, were, in their application, regarded

---

[75] In WTO, Report of the Panel, *European Communities—Regime for the Importation, Sale and Distribution of Bananas*, (Decision by the Arbitrators under Art 22.6) WT/DS27/ARB (9 April 1999), DSR 1999:II, 725 at paras 5.26 and 5.32, the arbitrators adopted a definition of discrimination that took into account the ongoing effects of past disadvantage upon the then current arrangements for allocation of quotas under GATT Article XII.2 and licensing under the GATS. They also stated that where 'de facto discrimination has been found in the past, and where reliance on license usage may result in a prolongation of the results of a violation of GATS rules' it is only logical that the EU's current choices may be limited.

[76] ibid. For evidence of continuing competitive disadvantage signalling a discriminatory regime, the AB referred to the European Commission 'freeze' on any new allocations, and to the fact that the previous representative period is one in which allocations were GATS inconsistent. Similar conclusions about the meaning of discrimination were reached in relation to aspects of the licensing regime dealing with 'single pot' allocations. Although the AB accepted the theoretical possibility that treating all operators similarly could achieve a level of equality, it found that this would be merely formal. It said, at para 5.88 'when a single pot solution relies on skewed reference period...the de facto less favourable conditions of competition for US service suppliers are aggravated through the carry-on effects of the previous regime'. Newcomers faced the obstacles also, the tribunal said at 5.94. For example, they had to show an ongoing relationship with EC trade during the period in which it was harder for them to obtain licences.

[77] ibid. In relation to the revised licensing allocation procedures the outcome was similar. At para 5.70 the Arbitrators decided that the basis of the licence allocations continued a previous discrimination, because the reference quantities upon which the allocations were based referred to amounts imported between 1994 and 1996 by traditional operators who had to import a certain minimum quantity during the period. Therefore, an increase in non-EU licence allocations would not have levelled the field, because they simply have redressed the most egregiously discriminatory aspects of the previous regime.

as discriminatory.[78] A substantive approach to discrimination is displayed also in *Japan—Alcoholic Beverages*, which sets out a three-step process for determining whether discrimination has occurred, a process which recognizes the existence of forms of indirect as well as direct discrimination.[79] And this same approach is reflected also in decisions that recognize that formally different treatment is not necessarily less favourable treatment; difference is permitted as long as it does not amount to less favourable treatment;[80] and that substantive equality requires the matters that are being compared to be determined within a like group.[81] This nuanced understanding was further refined in *EC—Tariff Preferences*, where the AB reversed a Panel's finding that all developing states were to be treated identically in relation to preference schemes. Instead the tribunal, after noting the difference between formal equality and differential equality, found that as developing states may have different development needs it was possible to treat those states differently, as long as all similarly situated states were treated in a like manner.[82] In all cases, a substantive discrimination approach is being refined, in relation to different parts of the legal system, in a manner which echoes constitutional doctrine in national legal systems.

Rational relationship doctrine

Our final example of a constitutional device is the use of the language of rational connection when testing state measures for conformity with WTO

---

[78] WTO, Report of the Appellate Body, *United States—Import Prohibition of Certain Shrimp and Shrimp Products*, WT/DS58/AB/R (12 October 1998), DSR 1998:VII, 2755 at para 121. Despite a holding, at para 141, that it was not discriminatory for the US to ban the importation of shrimps caught with fishing technology that could harm turtles, these measures, as applied, constituted unjustifiable or arbitrary discrimination on trade. Certification was available only to countries using technology identical to the US's despite the existence of protective techniques elsewhere (paras 162, 163, 165); countries whose technology had not been certified lacked information about the process of certification (paras 73–175, 181); countries with whom the US had not conducted bilateral agreements were subject to tighter time periods than others (para 172); and the US had not made use of multilateral channels to achieve an accommodation of the trade and environment conflict involved here (paras 166–171). Moreover, the discrimination was unjust because the policy was unilaterally shaped without participation of the shrimp exporters (para 72).

[79] WTO, Report of the Appellate Body, *Japan—Taxes on Alcoholic Beverages*, WT/DS8/AB/R, WT/DS10/AB/R, WT/DS11/AB/R (4 October 1996) DSR 1996:I, 97.

[80] WTO, Report of the Appellate Body, *Korea—Measures affecting Imports of Fresh, Chilled and Frozen Beef*, WT/DS161/AB/R, WT/DS169/AB/R (11 December 2000) DSR 2001:I, 5 at paras 135, 137, 138, and 144.

[81] WTO, Report of the Appellate Body, *United States—Tax Treatment for Foreign Sales Corporations*, WT/DS108/AB/R (24 February 2000) DSR 2000: III, 1619: Member States are not required to tax foreign source income, but once they decide to tax a category of it (namely that income that is connected with US trade or business) then they cannot carve out an exception for a particular type of corporation.

[82] WTO, Report of the Appellate Body, *European Communities—Conditions for Granting of Tariff Preferences to Developing Countries*, WT/DS246/AB/R (7 April 2004), esp paras 149, 160, 162, and 173.

requirements. This possibility arose when the tribunal in the *Hormones* Case[83] had to examine the SPS agreement in order to determine whether a state had complied with the requirement that any health protection measures with trade effects were to be supported by risk assessment based on scientific justification. In this case, although the AB does not use the precise language of rational relationship testing, the approach it does use—rational connection—is reminiscent of rational relationship tests in constitutional doctrine.[84] According to the WTO tribunal, the problem for the state imposing the import ban was that, despite the legitimacy of its public health concern, its non-discriminatory purpose, and the absence of arbitrary differential regulation, the measure failed because there was no rational connection between the measure and the risk posed. Articles 5.1 and 3.3 of the SPS Agreement required national standards to be based on a risk assessment supported by scientific justification. In rejecting the EU's argument that its risk assessment was scientifically justified, the AB agreed with the Panel at first instance, which had concluded that 'the scientific reports...do not rationally support the EC import prohibition.'[85] Studies which did show the existence of a risk were addressed more to the use of hormones in general, and not to the use of the specific growth hormones in question, and the studies were not conducted on meat products specifically.[86] So despite the legitimacy of the purpose, the measures violated the SPS Agreement because there was no rational link between the reports, the manifestation of which was the import prohibition (means) and the safeguarding of health (purpose). In this way, the AB spoke in terms that echo constitutional doctrine in other legal systems.

What these examples illustrate is the growing propensity of the WTO judicial body to use, refer to, or, indeed directly amalgamate into its reasoning processes, doctrines which are commonly associated, in domestic and supranational adjudication, with constitutional law. All of this vests the WTO with the hallmarks of a maturing, constitutionalizing legal system. The appearance of such a strongly substantive approach also fits squarely with the thesis that international law is increasingly informed by notions of fairness, which are not only procedural

---

[83] WTO, Report of the Appellate Body, *European Communities—Measures Concerning Meat and Meat Products (Hormones)*, WT/DS26/AB/R, WT/DS48/AB/R (16 January 1998), DSR 1998:I, 135.

[84] The AB may simply be interpreting the text without the aid of any constitutional devices such as rational relationship testing. However, in the context in which it occurs, in which sensitive questions of the correct balance between Member State capacity and central decision-making competence are in play, I would argue that even the use of language of rational connection takes on the gloss of a constitutionalizing technique. See also discussion above in Chapter 2 note 123 about whether these matters are 'procedural' or 'constitutional'.

[85] WTO, Report of the Appellate Body, *European Communities—Measures Concerning Meat and Meat Products (Hormones)*, WT/DS26/AB/R, WT/DS48/AB/R (16 January 1998), DSR 1998: I, 135 at para 197.

[86] ibid at para 199.

but also equitable in nature.[87] The WTO, by virtue of its judicial activities, seems, then, to exhibit two of the core features of the received account of constitutionalization, legitimacy, and internal relationship realignment.

6.2.2 System making

The second example of the way that judicial norm-generation constitutionalizes the WTO occurs in the making of a system of law by the AB. First, the choice of fact-finding method suggests the emergence of a new basic norm, or *Grundnorm*, for international trade. Secondly, the fact-finding method chosen has further enhanced the legitimacy of the new system.

Fact-finding method

The choice of an expansive method of fact-finding for the WTO legal system contributes to the making of a system of law. To this extent, this decision reflects the autonomy of the legal order and illustrates the thesis that a new *Grundnorm* has developed. A simple procedural question about the right to seek information therefore carries with it connotations of constitutionalizing because fact-finding rules can code for one form of system rather than another.

As a result, the AB finds in the agreements a procedurally, informal system whereby information can be elicited from a variety of sources, and the tribunal is not hemmed in by strict rules of evidence and procedure. In *Hormones*, the AB decided that the first instance Panel had not violated any provisions of the DSU when it selected and used its own experts rather than establishing an experts review group. It said that the DSU enabled a Panel to 'seek information and advice as it deem[ed] appropriate in a particular case'.[88] Moreover, the United States and Canada, who were separate complainants in the action, were entitled to exchange information.[89] And the Panel itself could rely on its own arguments in making its decision, although it could not raise new claims.[90]

This type of fact-finding method, which might be loosely defined as inquisitorial, was confirmed and elaborated in *Shrimp—Turtle* when the AB described

---

[87] T Franck, *Fairness in International Law and Institutions* (Oxford: Clarendon Press, 1995) 7–10, and see discussion above in Chapter 2 note 53, and Chapter 4 notes 122–124. For a counterpoint to Franck's argument in the trade context see R Bhala, 'Preference for its Former Colonies', *Legal Times*, 8 Feb 1999 (arguing that the *Bananas* cases do not reflect concepts of justice and efficiency).

[88] WTO, Report of the Appellate Body, *European Communities—Measures Concerning Meat and Meat Products (Hormones)*, WT/DS26/AB/R, WT/DS48/AB/R (16 January 1998), DSR 1998: I, 135 at para 147.

[89] ibid at paras 152–154.   [90] ibid at para 156.

the Panel as having a broad discretionary authority to accept information from a range of sources including non-parties[91] (at least when attached to a party submission). Contrary to the Panel's finding therefore, the Panel was entitled to receive submissions from environmental organizations on the specific questions before it.[92] While the Panel was not obliged to receive such information, it certainly possessed the discretionary authority to seek further information, including information from non-members' environmental groups.[93]

The effects of these cases are worth emphasizing. Potentially, they expand the range of actors and sources of information within the WTO legal system. They imply that the tribunal can take judicial notice of information provided by non-WTO members. Moreover, the nice distinction between obligation and authorization gives the Panels a broad mandate to seek and receive information relevant to its determinations from a wide range of sources: government, non-government, private and public, commercial and non-commercial.

These results lend weight to the constitutionalization thesis in two senses. First, the outcomes are constitutional because they are expressive of the autonomy of the WTO legal order. In this sense, the cases give rise to an implication that a new, and assertive, system of law is developing. It is not a continuation of the old GATT system but a new, more openly inquisitorial system of law. Secondly, the cases suggest an increased legitimacy for the WTO because non-state actors are able to contribute to the decision-making processes. Access to international fora is normally quite restricted. But under these interpretations a wide range of groups can become involved in the judicial process: corporations, unions, and environmental and health organizations. Despite strict rules of standing, the development of flexible rules regulating fact-gathering opens up international trade to a variety of non-traditional sources of influence. Moreover, in view of the importance of facts in conditioning legal rules, this expansion could shape the types of rules that are ultimately formulated. This has the further effect of enhancing the social legitimacy of the international trade law decision-making process, a feature which has not been overwhelmingly prominent in previous incarnations of the regime. It is therefore part of the constitutionalizing process because it enhances the legitimacy of the system by introducing

---

[91] WTO, Report of the Appellate Body, *United States—Import Prohibition of Certain Shrimp and Shrimp Products*, WT/DS58/AB/R (12 October 1998), DSR 1998:VII, 2755 at para 102.

[92] This liberal attitude toward the fact-finding power of the Panel (and intervention by third parties) is particularly noteworthy because only Members of the WTO (ie states) have a sufficient legal interest in the matters before a Panel to be accorded standing: ibid at para 101.

[93] ibid at para 110.

greater 'fairness',[94] notwithstanding the lack of formal standing for non-state entities.[95]

In sum, the choice of fact-finding method affects the constitution of the WTO legal system because it makes the system in a particular way, suggestive of the emergence of a new *Grundnorm*, and broadens participation in the rule-making apparatus; so potentially enhancing its legitimacy.

Relationship with other regimes

Other examples of system-making by judicial norm-generation arise in decisions about the relationship between international trade law and other legal regimes. These decisions suggest that a new system of law with its own coherence and unity, and a new *Grundnorm*, has developed. For example, the tribunal has concluded, on the basis of the agreement on dispute settlement,[96] that customary international law principles of interpretation require the WTO body to consider those rules of international treaty construction as codified in the Vienna Convention on the Law of Treaties. In so doing, the tribunal has had to identify the boundaries of the WTO legal system and has thus engaged in a process of making the system, which is akin to a function of a constitutional type. Similarly, the tribunal has reflected upon the relationship between trade law and environmental law and found that non-trade international standards, such as those drawn from environmental law, may affect WTO law, especially where the WTO treaty anticipates their influence.[97] Accordingly, said the tribunal, exceptions to general trade disciplines ought to be interpreted in the light of contemporary standards of international environmental law, especially since the preamble of the new GATT 1994 explicitly recognized a change in the relationship between international trade and international environmental law.

These decisions are constitutionalizing because they determine the nature of the relationships between WTO law and other systems of law; they are thus system-making in nature. Many questions remain open for the AB in drawing the parameters of these relationships. It remains to be seen what is the relationship between the trade agreements and fields not specifically contemplated by the actual instruments. If developments in a field we might designate 'international health law' were potentially to affect the interpretation of international trade, should they be relevant to WTO interpretation given their absence from the GATT 1994 preamble? How important to the *Shrimp—Turtle* opinion is

---

[94] For an argument about the relationship between procedural fairness and justice to legitimacy of international institutions see Franck (n 87 above).

[95] DSU Agreement, Art 3.7 (stating that 'Members' may exercise their judgement as to bringing a case). [96] DSU Agreement, Art 3.2

[97] WTO, Report of the Appellate Body, *United States—Import Prohibition of Certain Shrimp and Shrimp Products*, WT/DS58/AB/R (12 October 1998), DSR 1998:VII, 2755 at paras 129 and 153.

the fact that an interrelationship between international trade and international environmental law was within the intention of the contracting parties? Is the international trade law regime hermetically sealed from outside legal regime influence; is it within the power of international trade to decide when and how other bodies of law will impinge upon its legal territory?

Furthermore, how will other international law and international trade treaty conflicts be resolved? Although the *Hormones* decision disposes of a conflict between custom and treaty, it does not address the problem of competing interpretations of the supposedly 'higher' rules of international law or rules of *jus cogens*[98] and international trade law. For example, if the international law regime were specifically to recognize a rule of *jus cogens* which designated that states had permanent sovereignty over their natural resources,[99] how would this interact with treaty rules concerning foreign investment? In the constitution of a system of international trade law, conflicts with pre-existing customary norms, some of which may be non-derogable, may arise. This is essentially the same question which arises in a non-trade context, but it has added piquancy here partly because the particular treaty provisions in question are being enforced with greater enthusiasm than is the case in other treaty regimes. One solution would be to adopt the position articulated by Joost Pauwelyn, who argues that WTO law is part of general international law and must be interpreted so as to take account of other norms of international law where they represent the common intentions of all WTO members. In the case of conflict, WTO rules may have to give way to other international legal rules especially where 'inherent normative conflict' occurs between obligations of an 'integral' type such as human rights or environment and WTO treaty obligations of a 'reciprocal' type.[100]

Whatever the outcome of the ongoing examination of the relationship between WTO law and other general international law, it is clear that the AB's decisions on how to negotiate those boundaries demonstrate that the setting of the parameters of a system facilitates the conceptualization of WTO law as a set of laws with coherence and unity. This is consistent with the classic emergence of a new *Grundnorm*, and ultimately, a separate legal system.

6.2.3   Subject matter incorporation

The final example of judicial norm-generation that will be discussed is the incorporation of subject matters into the WTO jurisprudential system that

---

[98] For the principle of *jus cogens* see, eg, *Oppenheim's International Law*, extracted in L Henkin, RC Pugh, O Schachter, and H Smit, *International Law*, 3rd edn (1993) 91.

[99] Resolution on Permanent Sovereignty over Natural Resources, GA Res 1803 (XVII), UN GAOR, 17th Session, Supp 17, p. 15, A/5217 (1962), 2:1 ILM 223 (1963). See also discussion in *Texaco v Libyan Government* (1978) 17 ILM 1.

[100] J Pauwelyn, *Conflict of Norms in Public International Law: How WTO Law Relates to other Rules of International Law* (Cambridge: Cambridge University Press, 2003) 490–491.

were formerly beyond its ambit. The important point about subject matter incorporation is that, in accordance with the received account of constitutionalization, it modifies the relationships between the states and the international entity.

The example chosen to illustrate how judicial norm-generation modifies and constitutes relationships between entities within a system, occurs in relation to national legislative competence in non-trade standard setting. One of the vexing issues for WTO analysis is the continuing scope of national authorities to set standards for issues which fall within traditional state sovereignty and yet have an impact upon free trade: issues at the border of international trade law and national law.[101] Health and environmental standards are two prominent examples, as well as so-called 'new' or 'Singapore' issues of competition and investment. Decisions on these matters are a part of the constitutionalizing process, conceptualized as judicial norm-generation, because they focus attention upon the way in which subject matters, formerly within the domain of the state, may be incorporated into the ambit of WTO adjudicatory jurisdiction.

Hormones again provides an example. Here, the case indicates that the WTO appellate tribunal will tread lightly upon national legislative competence in relation to non-trade standard setting but nevertheless shows that the WTO considers it within its competence to answer such questions.

The rule: national health measures do not have to correspond precisely with international standards in order to be in conformity with international trade disciplines

The SPS Agreement sets down a range of rules and principles which seek to discipline the use of sanitary and phytosanitary measures as disguised restrictions upon trade. In the *Hormones* decision, the AB rejected the US claim that in order for a national standard to be 'based on' international standards, as required by Article 3 of the SPS Agreement, the national standard had to correspond precisely with the international standard. Beginning from the ordinary rules of statutory construction, the AB said that the ordinary meaning of the words 'based on' was different from the words 'conforming to'; a national measure did not have to be exactly the same as the international standard in order to be consistent with the Agreement.[102] The words 'based on' did not suggest uniformity of standards but harmonization.[103] Countries may continue to set health standards that are different to the prevailing international standard,

---

[101] This subject is sometimes referred to as the 'trade and' debate or the 'linkages' problem: see Chapter 3 notes 119–122 and accompanying text.

[102] WTO, Report of the Appellate Body, *European Communities—Measures Concerning Meat and Meat Products (Hormones)*, WT/DS26/AB/R, WT/DS48/AB/R (16 January 1998), DSR 1998: I, 135 at para 163.   [103] ibid at para 165.

without violating the SPS Agreement as long as those different standards are set in accordance with other provisions of the Agreement. For example, Article 3 of the Agreement requires standards set higher than the international level to be scientifically justified, and this scientific justification is to take place through a risk assessment conducted in accordance with Article 5.1. To this extent, the AB was not prepared to modify the control that national bodies had over standard setting.

The justifications: state sovereignty, obligations and non-obligations, judicial prudence

The reluctance of the tribunal to step on national legal competence was evident in its justifications for its stance. According to the decision, states do not easily relinquish their control over issues of health policy and hence the AB, 'cannot lightly assume that sovereign states intended to impose upon themselves the more onerous, rather than the less burdensome, obligation by mandating conformity or compliance with such standards guidelines and recommendations [AB's emphasis omitted]'. In support of this conclusion, the tribunal relied upon two other arguments: first it stated that a distinction existed between provisions in international agreements which are obligatory and those which are not, (in this instance the wording of the relevant article indicated that it was not obligatory); secondly, the tribunal took care not to assume more than was absolutely necessary in order to give effect to the Agreement, indirectly invoking principles of effectiveness in treaty interpretation and judicial prudence.[104]

So once again, underlying a simple question of treaty interpretation were a host of deeper constitutional concerns, all concerned with the modification of relationships between the state and the international entity. First, all three justifications relied upon by the tribunal had echoes in the constitutional jurisprudence of national and supranational constitutionalism, thus confirming a resemblance between the WTO and a constitutionalized system. The invocation of sovereignty reflects other international tribunals' attempts to traverse the tricky divide between intergovernmentalism and supranationalism;[105] the obligation–non-obligation distinction is a recurring theme of domestic constitutional law;[106] and notions of judicial economy or prudence are staple tools

---

[104] For another example of judicial economy see: WTO, Report of the Appellate Body, *United States—Measures Affecting Imports of Woven Wool Shirts and Blouses from India*, WT/DS33/AB/R (25 April 1997) DSR 1997:I, 323, stating that the DSU did not require Panels to examine all legal claims put before them, but only to resolve the particular dispute.

[105] The sovereignty rationale has resonance in ECJ jurisprudence, although with different results. The ECJ used the inverse of the argument relied upon by the AB to deepen European integration when it said that signature to the Treaty of Rome, being an exercise of state sovereignty which transferred regulatory power to the centre, was an act that should not be taken lightly: Case 6/64, *Costa v Enel* [1964] ECR 585. This argument founded a range of doctrinal devices which weakened a strong form of sovereignty although at the same time Member States retained regulatory control in the legislative/executive body of the Community, the Council: Weiler (n 3 above) 2403.

[106] For an example see the Australian case of *Victoria v Commonwealth* (1996) 187 CLR 416, 486 (Australia).

of constitutional interpretation.[107] The language of constitutional decision-making has been used in relation to matters of policy-making power between national and central bodies.

Secondly, the very fact that the AB considers itself competent to decide the question who has the authority to make such decisions indicated a shift in relations between states and the international trade law system. Things formerly deemed domestic because they automatically fell within national legislative jurisdiction now appeared upon the international trade judicial agenda, even if only for consideration of whether they belonged there. Constitutionalization in this context means the consideration by the international trade mechanisms of matters within state jurisdiction.

Thirdly, underlying the interpretation was perhaps the key concern of constitutional governance, namely the level of integration[108] between constituent parts of a legal system. When the AB interpreted these provisions of the SPS Agreement as requiring harmonization but not uniformity, it is also flagged the level of legal system integration the WTO embodies. According to that interpretation, parties retain a substantial measure of national legislative competence upon trade-related health issues, but must be mindful of their international obligations.[109]

In short, decisions about national legislative competence over enactment of non-trade standards raise the problem of subject matter incorporation by the AB and affect relationships between the state and the WTO, in a manner reminiscent of the constitutionalization process defined in Chapter 2. Again, while the parties did not specifically give up any legislative authority over these matters by signing the WTO Agreements, their authority has been subsequently conditioned by the introduction of various doctrines by the AB such that, from the point of view of national governance, they no longer possessed *absolute*

---

[107] The AB's prudence recalls Weiler's argument that the ECJ's introduction of review of national measures for violation of fundamental human rights had the 'hallmarks of deepest jurists' prudence' with the result that Member States were more receptive to profound changes wrought by direct effect and supremacy: Weiler (n 3 above) 2417. Notions of judicial economy permeate domestic constitutional theory. For example, see Cass Sunstein's argument for judicial 'minimalism' in CR Sunstein, *One Case at a Time: Judicial Minimalism at the Supreme Court* (Cambridge, Mass: Harvard University Press, 1999).

[108] Various levels of economic integration are possible, ranging from, at the lowest level, complete diversity of laws, through mutual recognition of laws, harmonization, to unification of laws. Each level represents a different level of constitutional integration of a legal system. At the lowest level, the separate parts of a system, or parts of different systems, have complete independence to decide how to regulate. At the highest level of unification, that independence has gone and has been transferred to the central decision-making body, and, at the different points in between, are variations of regulatory competence. For a typology of levels of integration see: B Balassa, *The Theory of Economic Integration* (Homewood, Ill: RD Irwin, 1961).

[109] Some commentators were disappointed by the result because they believe it weakened not only the SPS Agreement but also the WTO itself: DE McNeil, 'The First Case under the WTO's Sanitary and Phyto-Sanitary Agreement: The European Union's Hormone Ban' (1998) 39 *Virginia Journal of International Law* 89 (arguing that interpreting the Agreement as only mandating harmonization of standards weakens the Agreement and the WTO).

autonomy to decide on measures with trade consequences. The increased use of such constitutional devices constrains the ability of states to argue that non-trade-related measures, facially permissible under international trade law, will necessarily be valid, and contributes to the constitution of a new system in which national regulatory power is closely monitored.

6.2.4 Summary

This particular articulation of the theory of judicial norm-generation constitutionalization can now be summarized in simple tabular form (see Table 1). It is clear, therefore, that although legitimacy is one of key elements reflected in the approach of judicial-norm-generation constitutionalization it is by no means the only one. *Grundnorm* change and realignment of relationships between the Member States and central entity also occur as a result of judicial norm-generation. To this extent, then, the model promotes constitutionalization. It has the potential to readjust decision-making capacities of the states, and to signal the emergence of a new system of law, at the same time as doing so in a manner that legitimizes the processes that are occurring.

Nevertheless, judicial norm-generation constitutionalization only weakly, if at all, addresses two other core elements of constitutionalization. The creation of a viable constitutional community is not addressed, although arguably the inclusion of non-trade interests in sources of information might have the effect of broadening the basis of any such community. But, in general, judicial norm-generation does not speak directly to the problem of the need for a constitution to be authorized by a community of members who share a similar set of goals and faith in the institution of such a structure. Similarly, and relatedly, the processes of deliberation used in the community to make law are not of concern to judicial norm-generation. Few mentions are made of any of the tools of deliberative process, such as participation, communication, and transparency.

TABLE 1 Constitutional outcomes of judicial norm-generation

Technique	Example	Outcome in relation to received account of constitutionalization
Doctrine amalgamation	Jurisdictional competence	Relationship realignment Legitimacy
System making	Fact-finding method	*Grundnorm* change Legitimacy
	Relationship with other legal systems	*Grundnorm* change
Subject matter incorporation	New subject matters	Relationship realignment

6.3 CONCLUSION

This chapter has argued that a further understanding exists as to the meaning of WTO constitutionalization, one in which constitutionalization can be seen in WTO law as the generation of constitutional norms and structures by judicial decision-making. By amalgamating constitutional techniques from other constitutional systems; by making a new system of law; and incorporating issues formerly within national constitutional domains, the Appellate Body is contributing to constitutionalization of the system. This definition emphasizes judicial dispute resolution not merely as an institution of a new constitutional structure, as it was in both of the previous models, but also as an engine of constitutional creation. Although appealing in some respects, most notably its similarity to European Community models of constitutionalization, ultimately the model is not convincing. It claims too much—that a proto-constitutional structure is being formed—or its claims are not clearly enunciated to the extent that the relationship between judicial work, legitimacy, and constitutionalization is unclear. Importantly, the judicial norm-generation constitutionalization models undervalues the political aspects of a constitutionalization process.

In the light of the received account of constitutionalization outlined in Chapter 2, judicial norm-generation constitutionalization focuses attention upon three aspects of the constitutionalization process, legitimacy, modification of relationships between entities within the new system, and *Grundnorm* change. In relation to these elements, judicial norm-generation has the effect of generating some legitimacy when it amalgamates constitutional doctrine within it, thereby creating resemblances between WTO law and a domestic constitutional system and developing sophisticated doctrines of a constitutional type such as substantive discrimination. It modifies relationships between entities in the putative constitutionalized sphere, using the doctrine of judicial competence, and it shows some of the signs of *Grundnorm* change in the delineation of a particular fact-finding method consistent with discovery of a new system of law. However, the approach is notable for its absence of discussion of other key features of constitutionalization. There is no engagement with the idea that a deliberative, law-making constitutional community might be required in order to authorize the creation of a new constitutionalized structure. By the measure of the received account, then, judicial norm-generation constitutionalization provides only partial evidence for the constitutionalization thesis.

PART III

AGAINST CONSTITUTIONALIZATION

7

Anti-Constitutionalization

7.1 INTRODUCTION

To this point I have argued that there is a standard, received definition of constitutionalization contained in the domestic and international literature (Chapter 2), and that this definition emerged from, and therefore shares some of the themes of, international economic law and international relations literature generally (Chapter 3). The received account of constitutionalization comprises six core elements, and a number of other elaborations, the latter of which are 'variables' in the sense that they do not feature in every account of constitutionalization. The core features of constitutionalization are a set of social practices that constrain political and economic behaviour; a higher-order device that functions as a way of recognizing the validity and membership of the rules and practices that form part of the system; a community of members authorizing the constitution; a realignment of relationships between constituent members and the central entity; and social acceptance conferring legitimacy upon the constitutional system.

In Chapters 4–6, I discussed the WTO constitutionalization literature in terms of three models, and argued that, to an extent, these models satisfy some elements of the received account. However, I also demonstrated that, in a variety of respects, the models do not match the received account of constitutionalization. Institutional managerialism addresses the problem of *Grundnorm* change, and to some extent legitimacy, deliberative process, and realignment of relationships, but it ignores the need for a community to authorize the constitution-making process. Rights-based constitutionalization was strong only in relation to an element which was not essential to the core definition, namely rights, although, in passing, it did address problems of the nature of the community and its deliberative processes. Judicial norm-generation addressed the realignment of relationships issue, some legitimacy and *Grundnorm* change aspects, but did not seem sensitive to the requirements of community or deliberative process to any extent. In short, the WTO constitutionalization literature has not shown that the WTO is constitutionalized.

Nevertheless, the failure of each of the models to meet the criteria of the received definition of constitutionalization, in any substantial way, is not the end of the enquiry. The question we have been asking—is the WTO constitutionalized?—turns out to be more complex than it might at first appear and cannot be addressed simply by attempting to measure each formulation against an established model. First, at the risk of repetition it depends on what one means by constitutionalization. As I have shown, the term is used to describe three quite different processes. Secondly, if the standard way of thinking about constitutionalization at the international level is not convincing in its various incarnations in respect of the WTO, then perhaps a radical rethinking of the language and structures of constitutionalization is necessary. On the one hand is a failure to come up with a scholarly account which meets the standard criteria for constitutionalization. On the other is the extent to which we might want to consider whether the WTO is moving towards constitutionalization, but of a kind which is less familiar, less received, so to speak. Transnational constitutionalization may be, by contrast to state-based constitutionalization, a transformed constitutionalization which challenges our current perceptions of that phenomenon. This transformed vision of constitutionalization is the missing dimension from the WTO models so far discussed, and will be explored below in Chapter 8. Thirdly, as noted in the earlier chapters, even if the WTO were to be constitutionalizing, some would still object. In this chapter I will begin to explore more deeply the normative concerns that lie behind the objection to the constitutionalization project, again with reference to the template of the received account of constitutionalization.

This critique, or indeed series of related critiques, which I will label the 'anti-constitutionalization' critique, is underpinned by the view that constitutionalization is a misnomer when applied to the WTO. To this extent the discussion in this chapter does more than simply synthesize arguments made in Part II, although it does, necessarily, draw upon them. The anti-constitutionalization critique does not claim definitively that the WTO is not constitutionalized and should not be constitutionalized. Nor does it necessarily state that it is happening and should be restrained. Instead, the anti-constitutionalization critique, in its strong form at least, objects to the very terms on which the debate is taking place. It says that it is not possible to answer either the 'is-or-is-not', or the 'should-or-should-not' question, because the terms of the discussion already presuppose the existence of the phenomenon. This makes it virtually impossible to escape from the terms of the assumption in order to try to answer the constitutionalizing question. Instead, the three styles of anti-constitutionalization critique described below begin to explain why the constitutionalization question cannot be adequately answered, and suggest ways in which the entire project requires rethinking.

The anti-constitutional normative critique comes in three forms, which correspond to the three sections below: weak, moderate, and strong[1] anti-constitutionalization. *Weak* anti-constitutionalists accept that a realignment of

---

[1] The appellations 'strong', 'moderate', and 'weak' do not denote any evaluation of the arguments. A strongly anti-constitutional argument may not be convincing and a weak one may be more so. Rather, the terms are meant to measure the position's respective weight, or resonance, so to speak, against constitutionalization.

the relationship between members and a central entity consistent with the received account of constitutionalization is occurring, but claim that this realignment is too severe and needs to be readjusted. It is weak, therefore, only to the extent that it accepts, descriptively, that the WTO is moving in the direction of constitutionalization, but objects to this in normative terms. Specifically, those weakly against constitutionalization for normative reasons claim that it contracts the decisional capacity of states in such a way as to cause an excessive realignment of power away from states towards the central entity. In terms of the constitutional question above, the point here is that constitutionalization is happening, but should be curbed.

Moderate anti-constitutionalists do not accept that constitutionalization should proceed unless its basic premises are challenged, because, again referring back to the received account, deliberation, participation, and accountability are poor and constraints on social, economic, and political behaviour unevenly applied. The moderate critics decry the failure of deliberative process in the WTO and claim that constitutionalization, in its current form, provides inadequate guarantees of transparency, participation, and accountability in international trade decision-making. In addition, in terms of constraints on social behaviour, the moderate critics assert that the scope of WTO decision-making privileges economic concerns, and restricts the types of economic choices available, while at the same time paying insufficient regard to the economic effects of its decisions, thus constraining some types of social behaviour more than others. This form of the critique is thus oriented towards rejecting the argument that constitutionalization has happened, while acknowledging that some of the processes of constitutionalization are taking place.

Strong anti-constitutionalists argue that constitutionalization should not proceed, and, indeed, has not occurred. The strongest critique comes from those who claim that the disciplines on socio-political behaviour provided by the WTO are incomplete in an even more extensive sense than the moderate critics allow, in that the role of private law in generating, creating, and maintaining constraints of a constitutional type on socio-political behaviour is ignored. Then there are those who claim that constitutionalization should not take place, and has not taken place, because its social legitimacy is being artificially constructed by repeated use of the language of constitutionalization.

Before I begin to outline the critique, some important caveats should be noted. First, the anti-constitutionalization critique argues against the WTO constitutionalization thesis. But it should be emphasized that the point of this critique is not to suggest another model, but to criticize existing models. In this sense, the critique is 'anti' the entire notion of constitutionalization, rather than 'for' any particular improvement of the process. So although some elements of the critique are drawn from writings setting out alternative and better understandings of WTO constitutionalization, in general the critique positions itself in opposition to the three models discussed in earlier chapters, including their reformist tendencies.

Secondly, the anti-constitutionalization critique seems, at times, to be targeted at three different problems: the constitutionalization of the WTO, constitutionalization accounts in general, and the international economic legal order. The reason for this is that there is no bright line between these three fields. Indeed, the chapter progression of this study is structured in such a way as to make the overlapping relationship between them explicit: Chapter 1 begins with a description of constitutionalization in general, which leads, naturally, in Chapter 2 to an account of how this definition grew out of international economic law arguments, and then Chapters 4–6 describe the growth of specific WTO constitutionalization models from the culture provided by international economic law and general constitutionalization accounts. Therefore, it should be clear that, however variable the targets of anti-constitutionalization critique might seem, this does not preclude their being combined in the manner of this chapter. In fact, it is precisely because of this variability that it is crucial to a full appreciation of the problem of WTO constitutionalization to consider the anti-constitutionalization critique in the broadest sense possible.

Thirdly, in targeting constitutionalization literature, the anti-constitutionalization position does not specifically distinguish between the particular model of constitutionalization responsible for the deficiencies identified. So, for example, a general charge is made against constitutionalization on the grounds of undermining state decisional capacity. It is probably true that each of the various models discussed in this work could be identified with this failure. The strength of the institution of the WTO, and the AB in particular, and the eliding of its capacities with that of a constitution (institutional managerialism) clearly make it possible, for example, for the WTO to see itself as the appropriate conduit for a rule proclaiming the correctness of international product-standard setting. The deepening effect of WTO law through re-characterization of the legal obligations as 'rights' rather than mere rules (the rights-based view) encourages the tribunal to take a strong view of its role in reviewing national legislation for conformity with WTO law, especially in respect of intellectual property rules, which were, after all, the first body of specific rules positively incorporated into national legal systems. And, of course, the robust attitude of the tribunal to its role in generating norms of a constitutional type for the system could lead inevitably to the tribunal believing that it has mandate to determine formerly 'political' questions concerning a state's balance-of-payments, or its control of the environment and health. Whichever model is relied upon to prove the proposition that state decisional capacity has been diminished, the important point, for the purposes of the anti-constitutionalization critique, is that constitutionalization modelling has been a trigger for such a change.

Fourthly, it is important to note that the so-called 'anti-constitutionalization' position is not homogeneous. Different motives may drive what one writer called 'constitutional denial'[2] even when the arguments invoked are shared. Some critiques are motivated by concern that constitutionalization would encroach upon their interests,[3] or lead to an increase in another entity's power.[4] Others are motivated by fear of the ideological connotations of the term and the fact that it carries with it significant 'symbolic capital'.[5] To others still, the use of the term dictates a particular form of ideology which privileges economic rights over other social values.[6] Moreover, anti-constitutionalization as a descriptive term does not necessarily refer to particular writers, although there are indeed some who would warrant that label. Instead, anti-constitutionalization is used here to describe a type of argument that appears in many works, both for and against WTO change. What binds the arguments discussed in this chapter is then, first, a deep-seated scepticism, both in tone and in content, about whether it is possible to reform the constitutionalization process simply by eradicating the deficiencies of, say, legitimacy and community, which have already been problematized by critiques of the earlier models, and secondly, a belief that deeper foundational principles are at stake as a result of the transformations in the WTO and the tendency to describe them as constitutionalized.

7.2 ANTI-CONSTITUTIONALIZATION CRITIQUE

7.2.1 Weak anti-constitutionalization

The first type of argument comes in the form of a claim that one of the core elements of constitutionalization—the realignment of the relationships between members of the constitutional structure and the central entity—has been too severe because the decisional capacity of states has been drastically reduced. It is only weakly anti-constitutional in nature, because it neither sets itself against the project in its entirety nor denies that it is in train but rather seeks to restrain the excesses of constitutionalization so that the process does not severely constrain state autonomy.

[2] N Walker, 'The EU and the WTO: Constitutionalism in a New Key' in G de Búrca and J Scott (eds), *The EU and the WTO: Legal and Constitutional Issues* (Oxford; Portland, Oregon: Hart Publishing, 2001) 52.
[3] ibid (arguing that this form of denial is 'self-serving' and cynical).
[4] ibid (arguing that denial might 'increase the relative advantage accruing to rival polities in overlapping domains' and might therefore be 'every bit as ideologically motivated and contestable as those they seek to deny').
[5] ibid (arguing that constitutional discourse has a 'strong and pervasive ideological currency').
[6] See discussion above at Chapter 5.2.3.

Contraction of the decisional capacities of states

This argument asserts that the constitutionalization process has contracted the decisional capacities or 'sovereignty'[7] of states.[8] From this perspective, the instantiation of constitutionalization in the form of broadly worded international agreements containing many (necessarily) vague interpretive 'gaps' is problematic because it intrudes upon domestic governance.[9] The 'monolithic mandate' of the WTO eschews consideration of matters such as national sovereignty.[10] The WTO undermines decisions of democratically authorized national constituencies.[11] The Uruguay agreements have ushered in a new era of positive integration in which states became obliged to incorporate particular standards into their legal systems in areas such as intellectual property (rather than just an interdiction against discrimination), and has therefore impeded national regulatory choice.[12]

The diminished capacity argument appears also in the guise of a concern about increased judicial power. The dispute resolution system impinges on national sovereignty in relation to environmental protection.[13] A caution is sounded against the AB acting in an overly legalistic manner and ignoring the diplomatic ethos[14] of a GATT dispute settlement approach more respectful of national autonomy. The proportionality doctrine, developed in the constitutionalization process, is not a neutral device and could force WTO tribunals into making complex, political choices 'imposing [their] values on the level of

---

[7] For a discussion of the effects of different types of trading rules on national sovereignty see P Holmes, 'The WTO and the EU: Some Constitutional Comparisons' in G de Búrca and J Scott (n 2 above) 70 Table 2.

[8] These arguments have echoes in the claim that developments in private international law threaten the ability of states to regulate transnational business: R Wai, 'Transnational Liftoff and Juridical Touchdown: The Regulatory Function of Private International Law in an Era of Globalization' (2002) 40 *Columbia Journal of Transnational Law* 209.

[9] LA DiMatteo, K Dosanjh, PL Frantz, P Bowal and C Stoltenberg, 'The Doha Declaration and Beyond: Giving a Voice to Non-Trade Concerns within the WTO Trade Regime' (2003) 36 *Vanderbilt Journal of Transnational Law* 95, 98.

[10] ibid. See also JW Head, 'Throwing Eggs at Windows: Legal and Institutional Globalization in the 21st Century Economy' (2002) 50 *University of Kansas Law Review* 731, 776 (arguing that the WTO has 'shattered the anachronistic concept of absolute state sovereignty').

[11] R Howse, 'From Politics to Technocracy—and Back Again: The Fate of the Multilateral Trading Regime' (2002) 96 *American Journal of International Law* 94, 112 (discussing the principle of 'global subsidiarity' as a means to address this democratic issue. The author also advocates procedural solutions to the problems of interference, such as better transparency and public justificatory processes.)

[12] MJ Trebilcock and R Howse, *The Regulation of International Trade*, 2nd edn (London; New York: Routledge, 1999) 54, 56, 58 (arguing national regulatory choice is constrained by provisions of the TRIPs and TBT Agreements because these agreements extend beyond a basic requirement of non-discrimination and prescribe positive standards of non-discrimination which national authorities must meet).

[13] DiMatteo, Dosanjh, Frantz, Bowal and Stoltenberg (n 9 above) 99.

[14] JHH Weiler, 'The Rule of Lawyers and the Ethos of Diplomats: Reflections on WTO Dispute Settlement' in RB Porter, *et al* (eds), *Efficiency, Equity, and Legitimacy: The Multilateral Trading System at the Millennium* (Washington, DC: Brookings Institution Press, 2001).

tolerable risk allocation in society'.[15] State decisional capacity will be seriously undermined as a result of an 'institutional imbalance' within the WTO system caused by the judicial arm acting in an activist fashion, instead of adopting a policy of judicial prudence, combined with the existence of a weaker rule-making arm.[16] In the absence of a legislative body to decide common standards, it will be left to a quasi-judicial body to decide which regulatory barriers are trade restrictive or not.[17]

To others, constitutionalization, in the form of increased judicial power, may not be malign for sovereignty, but it nevertheless has negative implications for state decisional capacity because it may result in the transfer of political questions about risk allocation into the judicial arena. One experienced EC commentator observes that the WTO tribunals have, perhaps unwittingly, extended their reach into areas of national regulatory control and thereby reduced national regulatory choice.[18] This will lead the WTO tribunals into a more complex interpretative terrain where they will have to pronounce on the wisdom or otherwise of policy choices formerly excluded from WTO law.[19] As a result, tribunals will be forced to confront problems about the correct boundary of state and supranational competence. Likewise, difficult questions of the correctness of justificatory arguments about health and the environment, for example, will challenge the WTO tribunals.

Statue autonomy may be further undermined because constitutionalization may lead to a shift in the underlying philosophy of the WTO away from the 'embedded liberalism' of the past towards a unified market approach. This shift, is characterized as a move away from a 'discrimination approach' to an 'obstacle' approach.[20] In turn, this heralds a move away from the GATT principle of market 'fragmentation', whereby the market was conceived of as a 'transnational market place'[21] and the 'balance between free trade and very broad national regulatory autonomy'[22] was maintained, towards a potentially unified market, similar to Europe. The inevitable result will be to limit Member

---

[15] Weiler sounds this caution in the light of the experience of the European Court of Justice: JHH Weiler, 'Epilogue: Towards a Common Law of International Trade' in JHH Weiler (ed), *The EU, the WTO and the NAFTA: Towards a Common Law of International Trade* (Oxford: Oxford University Press, 2000) 222.

[16] CE Barfield, *Free Trade, Sovereignty, Democracy: The Future of the World Trade Organization* (Washington, DC: American Enterprise Institute, 2001).   [17] Holmes (n 7 above) 70.

[18] Weiler (n 15 above) 202, 214 (predicting that a decisive shift will occur as a by-product of the AB's more generous reading of Article XI taken in the *Hormones* decision, a reading which amplified non-discrimination from one which caught purely protectionist measures, to one which was directed to prohibiting all obstacles to trade. Joseph Weiler likens this to a similar shift in the European Community marked by the ECJ cases 8/74, *Procureur du Roi v Benoît and Gustave Dassonville* [1994] ECR 837, and 120/78, *Rewe-Zentral AG v Bundesmonopolverwaltung für Branntwein* (*Cassis de Dijon*) [1979] ECR 649).   [19] ibid 222.

[20] Weiler claims that, formerly, GATT took a discrimination or national treatment approach to internal regulation whereby only protectionist measures were prohibited, but has since moved to an obstacle approach to both internal regulation and market access: ibid 211.   [21] ibid 215.

[22] ibid 210.

States' 'liberty of social and economic regulatory choice'.[23] According to the anti-constitutional position, once the tribunal pierces the veil, so to speak, of national regulatory control, very few areas of social ordering will be excluded. Trade policy, industrial policy, labour market reform, and even social services can be removed from domestic jurisdiction and placed within WTO competence. Policy areas traditionally conceived as within the domestic domain, such as health, education, and culture, may be next.[24]

In sum, one form of anti-constitutionalization argument contends that the constituent relationship realignment which is a part of the constitutionalization process has been too severe, when judged in the light of the reduced decisional capacity of the states. State decisional capacity is being undermined by the posture and role of the WTO tribunals, the positive integration encapsulated in the WTO agreements, and the increasingly expansive 'free trade' interpretations given to key provisions by the tribunal.

However, it is important to note that this critique is not generally calling for wholesale retraction of the WTO from the ambit of state policy-making. Robert Howse, for examples, argues as follows: '[W]e must recognize in the first instance that the trading regime *should interfere with substantive regulatory choices* made by institutions and actors with greater democratic legitimacy *only to the extent needed* to maintain a bargain that can avoid reversion into beggar-thy-neighbour protectionism.'[25]

Similarly, Joseph Weiler does not argue for the dismantling of WTO adjudicatory power; he merely sounds a cautionary note to the AB, in particular that it should be aware of the delicate regulatory terrain it is about to enter upon. The focus of this form of anti-constitutionalization is not on stopping the realignment of Member State and central entity relationship, but on making it more legitimate. 'Rather than attempt once again to decide what is "in" or "out" of the WTO, we should try to mold the rules and their interpretation to structure the interaction of the trading regime with other powers and authorities, both domestic and international, in a legitimate manner.'[26]

The tempered nature of the claim is reflected also in Howse's nice point that, whether or not strong critics of the WTO understand it, they are contributing to a process of legitimizing AB interpretations which reduce state autonomy.[27] To this extent, even strong critics concerned with drawing a

---

[23] Weiler (n 15 above).

[24] BA Langille, 'General Reflections on the Relationship of Trade and Labor (Or: Fair Trade is Free Trade's Destiny)' in J Bhagwati and R Hudec (eds), *Fair Trade and Harmonization: Prerequisites for Free Trade? Vol 2: Legal Analysis* (Cambridge, Mass: MIT Press, 1996) (arguing, logically, in principle, there is nothing to stop any state from arguing that almost any regulatory measure—such as the provision or absence of another state's maternity leave policies—is an impediment to export and thus a potentially discriminatory trade barrier).

[25] Howse (n 11 above) 112 (emphasis added and footnote omitted).   [26] ibid.

[27] R Howse, 'Adjudicative Legitimacy and Treaty Interpretation in International Trade Law: The Early Years of WTO Jurisprudence' in JHH Weiler (ed), *The EU, the WTO and the NAFTA: Towards a Common Law of International Trade* (Oxford: Oxford University Press, 2000) 69 and

brighter, and thicker, line between the state and the WTO in relation to the realignment of constitutional relationships are, nevertheless, making an argument that has the potential to bolster, rather than undermine, the very process they are intent upon criticizing.

The limited nature of the argument is apparent from a brief survey of WTO cases, which indicates that in practice the line demarcating the relationships between the centre and the Members is constantly moving. For example, a number of concrete case examples can be found to support the claim that state power is being reduced vis-à-vis the international institution. Since the *Sardines* case, the decisional capacity of states is subject to increasing pressure to adopt international standards in relation to technical regulations and product standards. While the SPS and TBT Agreements encouraged states to take account of international standards in relation to products,[28] it was not until recently that the obligations were interpreted with any 'bite'. In this case, the AB decided that states should, where a relevant standard exists, base their technical regulations on international standards,[29] except where the latter is ineffective or inappropriate to fulfill a legitimate objective.[30] Moreover, the preference for international standards rule was applied retrospectively so that pre-existing standards, adopted prior to the introduction of the Technical Standards Agreement, but continuing to exist, must also now be based on international standards.[31] This trend toward international standardization of product standards and technical regulations is one example of the way in which generation of constitutional norms by judicial means has the potential to diminish the extent to which states can maintain national standards, and thus impinges on their decisional capacity.

A similar trend can be perceived in relation to environment and health regulation generally. The SPS Agreement provides that states may maintain health

---

51–52 note 46 (arguing that the legitimacy of WTO constitutionalization, is, paradoxically perhaps, facilitated both by questioning of the extent of WTO intrusion into state matters by 'economic globalization's "liberal" friends', and by critical legal scholars attempting to 'open[...] up new spaces for critique and contestation').

[28] See, eg, Agreement on the Application of Sanitary and Phytosanitary Measures, 15 April 1994, Marrakesh Agreement Establishing the World Trade Organization [hereinafter WTO Agreement] Annex 1A, *The Results of the Uruguay Round of Multilateral Trade Negotiations: The Legal Texts*, (1994) [hereinafter SPS Agreement] Art 3: 'To harmonize sanitary and phytosanitary measures on as wide a basis as possible, Members shall base their sanitary or phytosanitary measures on international standards....' and Agreement on Technical Barriers to Trade, WTO Agreement, Annex 1A, *The Results of the Uruguay Round of Multilateral Trade Negotiations: The Legal Texts*, (1994) [TBT Agreement] Art 2.4: 'Where technical regulations are required and relevant international standards exist or their completion is imminent, Members shall use them...as a basis for their technical regulations except when such international standards...would be an ineffective or inappropriate means for fulfilment of the legitimate objectives pursued....'

[29] WTO, Report of the Appellate Body, *European Communities—Trade Description of Sardines*, WT/DS231/AB/R (26 September 2002).   [30] TBT Agreement, Arts 2.2 and 2.4.

[31] WTO, Report of the Appellate Body, *European Communities—Trade Description of Sardines*, WT/DS231/AB/R (26 September 2002).

standards,[32] but only under a series of conditions concerning necessity, scientific justification, and non-discrimination.[33] The interpretation of these provisions has, according to one view, reduced the capacity of states to decide matters of health policy in two respects. First, the AB has rejected arguments based on the precautionary principle in favour of the clear words of the treaty text,[34] (although it accepted that the principle infused the meaning of the text), and, secondly, it did not accept the state's assertion that its risk assessment provided scientific justification for the particular measure in issue.[35] Hence judicial interpretation has further restricted state capacity to make health policy decisions.

Furthermore, state control is compromised by an inherent tension between the claim that states retain complete autonomy to set the level of risk they wish to be subject to, and the subjection of states' determinations of risk to judicial oversight. Although states can choose the level of protection from risk they wish to bear, this choice itself must be clearly justifiable by scientific evidence. These justifications must be made in circumstances where a judicial body with jurisdiction over trade matters has the final say on whether or not the scientific evidence is sufficient, and where there is widespread acceptance that the interpretation of science, and indeed science itself, has embedded within it important political and social choices about the level of risk that scientists (and policy-makers) are prepared to countenance.[36] The result is that a WTO tribunal may now decide questions which formerly lay within the purview of political debate within the state.

---

[32] SPS Agreement, Art 2.1.

[33] The measure may be maintained to the extent that it is necessary to protect life or health, it must be based on scientific principles and sufficient scientific evidence, and must not unjustifiably or arbitrarily discriminate between Members where similar conditions prevail: SPS Agreement, Arts 2.2 and 2.3.

[34] WTO, Report of the Appellate Body, *European Communities—Measures Concerning Meat and Meat Products (Hormones)*, WT/DS26/AB/R, WT/DS48/AB/R (16 January 1998), DSR 1998:I, 135 at para 124. The precautionary principle was interpreted to mean that in the absence of conclusive scientific evidence about the health implications of a situation, states were entitled to regulate in a precautionary manner.   [35] ibid at para 197.

[36] For discussion of the relationship between trade, science, and law see, eg, Armin Bogdandy, 'Law and Politics in the WTO—Strategies to Cope with a Deficient Relationship' in JA Frowein and R Wolfrum (eds), *Max Planck Yearbook of United Nations Law* Vol 5 (2001) 612, 643–644 (arguing that although science should inform legislative decision-making it cannot 'provide the answer to what constitutes an (un)acceptable risk'; this decision should be left to the political process); and, VR Walker, 'Keeping the WTO from Becoming the "World Trans-science Organization": Scientific Uncertainty, Science Policy, and Fact Finding in the Growth Hormones Dispute' (1998) 31 *Cornell International Law Journal* 251, 252 (stating that it has been long recognized that the relationship between science and regulation is 'part fact, part policy and part decision-making', and, at 259, that there will always be several plausible scientific conclusions with wide disagreement about them. Science policy, he concludes, at 260, is not made on only scientific grounds). See also J Pauwelyn, 'The WTO Agreement on Sanitary and Phytosanitary (SPS) Measures As Applied in the First Three SPS Disputes' (1999) 2 *Journal of International Economic Law* 641.

Although there are conflicting readings of these cases which are discussed further below,[37] some have suggested that judicial deference towards national agencies' determinations has been reduced in a series of trade remedies cases where the AB has shown increasing unwillingness to accept national agency determinations.[38] Control over other social goods such as consumer protection has also been weakened in conformity with an anti-constitutional reading of case law. States may not separate the sale of foreign and domestic products, on the grounds of protecting consumers from the risk of buying foreign products when they want to buy local, if less trade-restrictive means of achieving the same goal are available.[39]

Wider questions of state macroeconomic policy are also said to be threatened by constitutionalization. National autonomy over the imposition of trade restrictions for balance-of-payments reasons has been effectively reduced by taking such questions away from the sole province of the political organs of the WTO and including them within the jurisdiction of the adjudicative body.[40] Decisions about national development policy may now be subject to WTO supervision since the AB decided that it has the competence to confirm whether the IMF has the right to require adjustments to macroeconomic policy.[41]

A similar contraction of state power has apparently occurred in respect of state implementation of WTO obligations by administrative means. The traditional position of international law is to permit a wide margin of deference to the manner in which individual states choose to implement an international obligation. In the WTO context however, the conservatism of the international adjudicative process has been modified by the view, for example, that the AB will not defer to a Member's claim that its method of implementation was satisfactory and will investigate that claim carefully, as part of the tribunal's

---

[37] See pp. 218–220.

[38] For critical comments on the AB's approach to trade remedies see, eg, J Greenwald, 'WTO Dispute Settlement: an Exercise in Trade Law Legislation?' (2003) 6 *Journal of International Economic Law* 113 (arguing, at 113, that WTO decision-making on trade remedies cases is 'an exercise in policy making' because the AB reads language in or out of the agreements in order to reach a particular policy, which coincidentally all have, at 115, a 'pro-complainant' outcome. As evidence he cites, at 116, a reading in of a requirement in relation to safeguards that any injury to domestic industry be the result of a 'sudden' or 'sharp' or 'significant' increase in imports.)

[39] WTO, Report of the Appellate Body, *Korea—Measures Affecting Imports of Fresh, Chilled and Frozen Beef*, WT/DS161/AB/R, WT/DS169/AB/R (11 December 2000) DSR 2001: I, 5.

[40] WTO, Report of the Appellate Body, *India—Quantitative Restrictions on Imports of Agricultural, Textile and Industrial Products*, WT/DS90/AB/R (23 August 1999), [1999] 4 DSR 1763. For a critique of overburdening adjudicative bodies, see F Roessler 'Are the Judicial Organs of the World Trade Organization Overburdened?' in RB Porter, *et al* (eds), *Efficiency, Equity, and Legitimacy: The Multilateral Trading System at the Millennium* (Washington, DC: Brookings Institution Press, 2001).

[41] WTO, Report of the Appellate Body, *India—Quantitative Restrictions on Imports of Agricultural, Textile and Industrial Products*, WT/DS90/AB/R (23 August 1999) DSR 1999:IV, 1763.

duty to make an objective assessment of the matter before it.[42] Where a Member maintains legislation inconsistent with the WTO obligation, and the Member issues administrative instructions to implement the obligation, the WTO may still find implementation to be inadequate.[43] Moreover, when deciding whether the state has implemented the international obligation in its national law, the WTO will examine whether the national measure conforms to the trade obligation, an examination which takes the tribunal closer to interpreting national legislation.[44]

In sum, a sample of cases indicate that state decisional capacity has been reduced or conditioned in a number of ways, including in relation to pressure towards international harmonization of product standards; diminution of control over achievement of social goods such as environment, health, and consumer protection; questioning of the state's singular role in the attainment of economic policies concerning balance-of-payments and development; and a reduced deference towards Member State implementation of obligations through administrative means, and towards national agency determinations in trade remedies. The curtailing of state sovereignty in these respects provides some evidence of the anti-constitutionalization argument that constitutionalization is causing a realignment of the relationships of members of the constitutional system. But the ledger, so to speak, on state decisional capacity, is not one-sided. Other evidence suggests that the claim may be exaggerated.

Standard of review doctrine is one example. In relation to reviewing decisions of Member States for conformity with the agreements, WTO tribunals must neither defer outright, nor conduct a completely new review, but instead must adopt a middle course which is consistent with objectively assessing the situation.[45] This suggests that constitutionalization, rather than detracting from state sovereignty, has maintained the capacity of states to decide matters of policy, and that judicially generated constitutional norms expressly recognize that capacity.

---

[42] Understanding on Rules and Procedures Governing the Settlement of Disputes, Annex 2, WTO Agreement, *The Results of the Uruguay Round of Multilateral Trade Negotiations: The Legal Texts*, 404 [hereinafter DSU] Art 11.

[43] WTO, Report of the Appellate Body, *India—Patent Protection for Pharmaceutical and Agricultural Chemical Products*, WT/DS50/AB/R (19 December 1997), DSR 1998:I, 9 at paras 56–62.

[44] ibid at para 66. In this respect the WTO applies a fine, but well-recognized, distinction between interpreting national law (a power the WTO, along with all international tribunals, lacks) and the power, consistent with general international law, to determine whether the Member State is applying the law in conformity with WTO obligations, a result which is often quite close to a power of interpretation.

[45] WTO, Report of the Appellate Body, *European Communities—Measures Concerning Meat and Meat Products (Hormones)*, WT/DS26/AB/R, WT/DS48/AB/R (16 January 1998), DSR 1998:I, 135 at para 117; WTO, Report of the Appellate Body, *United States—Restrictions on Imports of Cotton and Man-made Fibre Underwear*, WT/DS24/AB/R (10 February 1997) DSR 1997:I, 11; and WTO, Report of the Appellate Body, *Argentina—Safeguard Measures on Imports of Footwear*, WT/DS121/AB/R (14 December 1999) DSR 2000:I, 215.

In addition to respecting state decision-making power generally, when conducting the objective assessment, the Panel must put itself in the place of the Member when it made the relevant decision and not consider facts which subsequently came to light.[46] So while a Member must exercise due diligence in making a safeguard determination, a Panel will exceed its authority if it takes into account evidence that did not exist at the time the competent Member authority made its determination, because it thereby conducts *de novo* review.

In relation to assessing whether a state has conformed with WTO obligations, the case law also indicates a margin of appreciation belonging to states. Although a WTO tribunal is not bound to accept the domestic authorities' interpretation of domestic legislation it is mindful of that interpretation and how it was reached; a Panel decision suggests it should take account of wide-ranging diversity in legal systems and the 'multi-layered character' of the national law under consideration including not just statutory language but also other relevant administrative elements.[47]

Key agreements in health and other social issues provide a degree of discretion for states to take trade restrictive measures. States may retain different, nationally appropriate standards through the let-out clauses in the Agreements relating to matters including national security, consumer protection, health, and environment.[48] Moreover, proportionality doctrine remains a brake on WTO competence because states are permitted to set aside an international technical standard if that standard is an inefficient or inappropriate means of achieving a legitimate objective.[49] And potentially most far-reaching of all in respect of state power over matters of health, the AB will take account of health risk in assessing the meaning of 'like product' for the purposes of deciding whether a state was justified in regulating the product in a manner different to other, facially similar, products.[50]

It might also be argued that, rather than diminishing state capacity, WTO constitutionalization promotes international order, and this in turn strengthens sovereignty. International standard-setting is promoted through particular agreements, such as the SPS and TBT Agreements, and as a result of judicial interpretation which encourages states to rely on international standards, or, at the very least, have very good reasons for departing from them.[51] This has

---

[46] WTO, Report of the Appellate Body, *United States—Transitional Safeguard Measure on Combed Cotton Yarn from Pakistan*, WT/DS192/AB/R (8 October 2001) DSR 2001:XII, 6067 at paras 77–78.

[47] WTO, Report of the Panel, *United States—Sections 301–310 of the Trade Act of 1974*, WT/DS152/R (22 December 1999) DSR 2000:II, 815 at para 7.24–7.26.

[48] See, eg, GATT Arts XX, XXI; SPS Agreement, Arts 3.1 and 3.3 and TBT Agreement, Arts 2.2 and 2.4.

[49] TBT Agreement, Art 2.4. See WTO, Report of the Appellate Body, *European Communities—Trade Description of Sardines*, WT/DS231/AB/R (26 September 2002).

[50] WTO, Report of the Appellate Body, *European Communities—Measures Affecting Asbestos and Asbestos-Containing Products*, WT/DS135/ARB/R (12 March 2001) DSR 2001:VII, 3243.

[51] Where a relevant international standard exists, states must use it as a basis for national measures: WTO, Report of the Appellate Body, *European Communities—Trade Description of Sardines*, WT/DS231/AB/R (26 September 2002).

the added effect of encouraging harmonization of standards at an international level, and of creating momentum for states to become involved in standard-setting, even if with a view to protecting their national interests. In an analogy with Europe, it has been argued that the adoption by the European Court of an approach which banned all obstacles to trade, (not just discriminatory ones), led directly to a political response in the form of the New Approach to Harmonization and alterations to the Single European Act whereby majority voting was introduced for harmonization of proposals.[52] Counter-intuitively perhaps, Weiler suggests that this led to *more rather than less* regulatory autonomy because a) the EC took a minimalist approach to harmonization, calling for it in relation only to what was necessary for the common market, and b) it set only the overall standards, and left it to national standard-setting bodies to establish their own specifications. Transposing this result to the WTO field would not be easy, as the WTO lacks a legislative procedure equivalent to that of the European Union comprising joint decision-making between the Commission, the Council, and the Parliament. However, the essential point remains that increased pressure to harmonize might, given the right political conditions, deepen, rather than lessen, national autonomy. In the WTO context, where the internal political function is relatively weak, this outcome could instead take place in the international standard-setting organizations, where pressure might be exerted to strengthen national autonomy. However, this could depend on the operations of the organizations, especially where international standard-setting organizations confer a strong role on private actors, rather than states. In the longer term, reform of the WTO institutional structure and the introduction of a legislative equivalent to that of the EU could also lead to a similar result, though one would need to have a fairly positive outlook[53] to believe that either option was at all likely. More plausibly some suggest that the obstacle approach initiated in *Hormones*, combined with pressure to conform to international standards as illustrated in *Sardines*, will undercut national standard-setting autonomy. Nevertheless, the Member States remain 'masters' of the treaty, retaining the ultimate authority in General Council to interpret the agreement, and so this outcome can still be avoided.

In sum, the cases indicate that there is some support for the anti-constitutionalization position on the decisional capacity of states, to the extent that WTO decisions have indeed undercut state control in matters relating to international product standards, social goods, some aspects of economic

---

[52] Weiler (n 15 above) 224.

[53] ibid (arguing that the notification requirements of the new approach to harmonization introduced in the EC in 1986 were 'recognition that in the setting of socio-economic values and the mix of regulation and market, it is the Member States and the organic societies they represent that are the long term repositories of wisdom and legitimacy').

policy, implementation of WTO obligations, and deference to state agency decisions. However, state decisional capacity has also been protected by interpretations on standard of review and conformity doctrine which provide a margin of appreciation to states; the incorporation of health risk in interpretation of the nature and quality of 'like product'; let-outs in agreements available to states in respect of health, environment, national security, and safety rules; and even interpretations which promote the harmonization of such standards.

So our brief survey of WTO cases indicates that evidence exists both to support and to contradict the claim that dispute settlement leads to reallocation of power by contracting state decisional capacity. In short, the line demarcating the relationships between the centre and the Members is in constant flux. Dispute settlement has indeed generated a set of outcomes in which contraction of state capacity vis-à-vis the international institution has occurred, but not in any simple or unidirectional manner. As is so often the case with international institution building, dispute settlement bodies can play a complex, and even perhaps contradictory, role in allocating powers between the international institution and Member States.

The important point is that, although some realignment of the relationship between the central entity and the Member States has occurred, the extent of it is unclear. So the critique based on a claim of excessive realignment infringing on state capacity is a limited one only, both because the evidence is unclear and because, in any event, the goal of the critique is to make that process of realignment more legitimate, not to abolish it altogether.

7.2.2 Moderate anti-constitutionalization

The *moderate*, or contingent, critique of constitutionalization has both a descriptive and a normative component. It contends that the process should not proceed unless its basic premises are challenged in three ways. First, it claims that the deliberative requirement of constitutionalization is not being met because the WTO provides inadequate guarantees of participation, representativeness, transparency, and accountability in international trade decision-making. Secondly, constraints on social, economic, and political behaviour, another element of the received account of constitutionalization, are unevenly applied, to the extent that economic *goals* are privileged over other social concerns in WTO decision-making. Paradoxically, and thirdly, the economic *effects* of its decisions are not taken fully into account. I begin by considering the first aspect of the moderate critique, namely that the deliberative process is inadequate, insofar as there exist poor mechanisms for participation, representation, accountability, and transparency.

Participation, representativeness, accountability, and transparency

One of the key claims of the anti-constitutionalization position, and indeed a view also of some promoting constitutionalization,[54] is that the WTO should be more participatory, representative, and accountable.[55]

The deliberative aspect of constitutionalization could be enhanced, according to the critique, by introducing new forms of participation. This could occur with the inclusion of more stakeholders in WTO decision-making, including state and non-state, business and non-business orientated interests, in order to improve participation and collective deliberation.[56] It could take the form of a cosmopolitan approach[57] in which 'a vocal, public politics'[58] is encouraged, and public debate on trade is transferred from the national to international level,[59] with corresponding improvements in expertise, political support,[60] and the level of public debate.[61] Better communication and civic participation should be introduced in the form of national parliamentary oversight of the organization and connection to publics through NGOs.[62] Moreover, it is argued, in the absence of diverse participation there will be continued problems of legitimacy,[63] as well as a perceived reduction in the range of choices available to consumers, while all the while the WTO masquerades as a vehicle for increasing choice.[64]

In a critique of existing 'visions' of constitutionalization, Peter Gerhardt[65] argues that WTO enthusiasts should abandon their 'internal, economic vision',[66] which focuses on the WTO as an organization to help domestic governments overcome special interest protectionist lobbying, and focus instead on its 'external, participatory'[67] role. According to this latter vision, the WTO would facilitate dialogue between states. Drawing on US dormant Commerce

[54] See, eg, discussion in Chapter 5 in relation to widening participation to include non-producer interests at notes 116–117, 153–154, and accompanying text, and indeed the argument for allowing individuals to invoke WTO law in national courts at Section 5.3.

[55] J Atik, 'Democratizing the WTO' (2001) 33 *George Washington International Law Review* 451 (canvassing a range of proposals to 'democratize' the WTO including: requiring democratic practice within states as a condition of WTO membership; introducing a WTO parliament; creating a new law-making body removed from the negotiating rounds; and allocating votes according to various methods to distribute power). A variant of this approach in domestic constitutional theory is the idea that the judicial body should not have sole authority over constitutional interpretation. See LD Kramer, 'The Supreme Court 2000 Term' (2001) 115 *Harvard Law Review* 4, 15 (arguing that 'nothing can vouchsafe the rights of what these [judicial] institutions do, nothing can save them from partiality and blindness, other than democratic challenge, scrutiny, and revision').

[56] GR Shell, 'Trade Legalism and International Relations Theory: An Analysis of the World Trade Organization' (1995) 44 *Duke Law Journal* 829.   [57] See Chapter 2.4.3, and Chapter 5.

[58] S Charnovitz, 'WTO Cosmopolitics' (2002) 34 *New York University Journal of International Law and Politics* 299 (canvassing various strategies of 'cosmopolitics' including, at 329–344: better market orientation, greater publicity and transparency, stronger persuasion and debate, issue-based alliances, parliamentary participation, broadening official delegations, NGOs speaking for themselves).   [59] ibid 300.

[60] ibid 318.   [61] ibid 325.

[62] DC Esty, 'The World Trade Organization's legitimacy crisis' (2002) 1 *World Trade Review* 7, 16–19.   [63] ibid.

[64] See Chapter 3 at nn 101–108 and accompanying text.

[65] PM Gerhart, 'The Two Constitutional Visions of the World Trade Organization' (2003) *University of Pennsylvania Journal of International Economic Law* 1.   [66] ibid 5.

[67] ibid 72.

Clause case law,[68] the author argues that, in a period in which issues in one state increasingly affect interests in another (globalization), and economic efficiency is recognized as only one basis upon which social policy should rest,[69] the 'external, participatory' vision of the WTO would enhance its legitimacy, be consistent with values of democracy, sovereignty, and federalism and forestall further criticism of the constitutionalization process.

Transparency and accountability cause another set of problems, because the WTO is opaque in its operations.[70] According to its critics, the WTO is '[a]ccountable to no one, [it] has restricted our choice over what we can eat, overridden laws passed by our democratically elected governments, started or sanctioned trade wars, and put our health at risk'.[71] So, it is argued by the critics that constitutionalization has gone 'too far'.[72]

One solution to the related problems of transparency, participation, accountability, and deliberation generally would be for the WTO to follow the route of 'non-constitutionalization',[73] and revert to a model of 'embedded liberalism', the name given to the bargain struck after the Second World War in which states agreed to constrain the worst excesses of protectionism, while at the same time retaining a substantial degree of economic and political control necessary for internal stability.[74] A return to such a model would be accompanied by the benefits of deliberative process by introducing into the WTO stronger principles of participation, transparency, and accountability. In a carefully articulated programme, the proponents of this idea promote global subsidiarity[75] which could be promoted by the introduction of 'institutional sensitivity',[76] 'political inclusiveness',[77] and 'top-down empowerment'.[78] On this definition, all three notions of accountability, transparency, and participation would be enhanced: institutional sensitivity would lead the WTO to adopt a policy of deference in relation to other states, institutional regimes, political negotiations, and interpretation of norms of international law. Politically, WTO decision-making would include national citizens, groups, or parliaments in trade policy decision-making at domestic level.[79] Top-down empowerment would require enactment of limits on 'extreme' instances of social or environmental dumping or tax competition, although these would be applied differentially depending on the level of development or type of actor involved.[80]

---

[68] ibid 32–45.   [69] ibid 70.   [70] Head (n 10 above) 764.

[71] N Hertz, *The Silent Takeover* (London: Heinemann, 2002), 105. See also Wai (n 8 above) (arguing that similar accountability issues arise in relation to private international law where there has been a privatization of legal processes such that they are clothed in confidentiality and do not recognize the importance of the principle of open justice).

[72] R Howse and K Nicolaidis, 'Legitimacy and Global Governance: Why Constitutionalizing the WTO is a Step Too Far' in RB Porter, *et al* (eds), *Efficiency, Equity, and Legitimacy: The Multilateral Trading System at the Millennium* (Washington, DC: Brookings Institution Press, 2001).

[73] ibid 249.

[74] ibid. For discussion of embedded liberalism see Chapter 3 nn 152–155.   [75] ibid 243.

[76] ibid.   [77] ibid 245.   [78] ibid 246.   [79] ibid 245.

[80] ibid 247 (arguing, for example, that system legitimacy would be enhanced by requiring MNCs to apply minimum social standards before local producers).

Others deride what is referred to as a 'mismatch' between the 'cumbersome political institutions and procedures' of the WTO and its 'far-reaching' compulsory adjudication function, which has skewed the proper relationship between law and politics and made it virtually impossible for political processes to act as a brake on developments of law.[81] In response, practical reforms are suggested such as curtailing the consensus requirement for General Council amendments of the agreements[82] so that the political branch could act more swiftly and efficiently in response to legal change or alterations in the social conditions in which WTO law operates. More importantly, the WTO should follow an approach labelled 'co-ordinated interdependence',[83] the key to which is to adopt a 'procedural conception of substantive law'[84] which forces members to take into account outside interests when making economic decisions which affect those interests.

In short, this aspect of the anti-constitutionalization thesis criticizes the WTO on the ground that it does not provide for sufficient levels of participation, transparency, and accountability, and suggests a number of concrete, procedural reforms in order to create a deliberative process consistent with the received account of constitutionalization.

A further way in which the WTO is criticized, in this moderate register, involves claiming that the constraints which the WTO places upon socio-political behaviour are skewed towards valuing economic over non-economic goals, and free trade over other legitimate economic choices.

Narrowly focused economic goals and limited economic choices

This aspect of the moderate critique targets the scope of WTO decision-making and argues that its focus is too narrowly economic and free-trade orientated, and that non-economic goals that are linked with trade should be taken into account in WTO decision-making. So the relative absence of social and cultural concerns from the WTO is criticized.[85] 'Contextual' decision-making is promoted because, it is said, this would emphasize values other than maintenance of the trade regime, or efficiency of the market.[86] As with the participatory critique, it is said that the WTO should adopt a decision-making model in which a wider range of stakeholders' interests are taken into account, thereby 'eschew[ing] reliance on any ideology such as free trade theory to define an

[81] A von Bogdandy, 'Law and Politics in the WTO—Strategies to Cope with a Deficient Relationship' in JA Frowein and R Wolfrum (eds), *Max Planck Yearbook of United Nations Law* Vol 5 (2001) 612. [82] ibid 632.
[83] ibid 658. [84] ibid 666.
[85] Hertz (n 71 above) 112 (arguing that non-economic concerns are absent at the WTO, and that national finance ministries, the IMF, and the WTO make decisions on purely economic criteria even when their implications stretch beyond the economic domain). See also Phillip Trimble in JH Jackson, WJ Davey and AO Sykes, *Legal Problems of International Economic Relations*, 3rd edn (St Paul Minn: West, 1995) 1224 (arguing that emphasizing economic over political goals is 'undesirable' because although 'free trade is an important goal', it 'is not the only one'). [86] Shell (n 56 above) 911.

objective "good" for global society' because 'the priorities for global society are open-ended and subject to deliberation by those whose lives will be affected by economic decisions'.[87] At the very least, when economic decisions are taken, they should be taken with 'greater sensitivity' to other goals such as environmental protection and poverty alleviation.[88]

Taking this argument further, it is suggested that assumptions about any necessary link between an international trading system and free trade should be discarded. The critics point out that the terms 'free trade' and 'market integration' 'do not appear anywhere as a WTO objective'.[89] The WTO should therefore reject free trade, market integration, or even regulatory competition, as necessary goals of the system and focus instead on the goal that is set out in the text of the agreements, the more 'limited' objective of prevention of national discrimination.[90]

The textual reason for rejecting free trade as an monolithic objective of the WTO is supported by other normative justifications. Law is simply an inappropriate method for deciding essentially political questions: 'legal research should be careful: neither constitutional theory nor legal theory possess the tools to decide the involved controversies'.[91] More importantly, however, reasonable people might decide, reasonably, to disagree about the sorts of economic arrangements under which they live, and choose to reject the free-trade thesis as a necessary component of their society: '...under domestic constitutional law, it is quite legitimate for a political community to opt for less wealth and less integration in the global market and give preference to other values to be realized through economically sub-optimal instruments'.[92] None of these options should be excluded in the transnational constitutionalization experiment at the WTO.

Others argue that the WTO should move beyond the confines of classical economic theory by taking other fields of international law, such as human rights, into account. Sometimes this argument is put in a strong form in which it is said that WTO legal instruments should be interpreted in the light of general human rights law. For example, it has been suggested that an obligation under the International Covenant on Economic and Social Rights to take steps for the full realization of the right of health could be invoked as an aid to interpretation of WTO obligations should a state with strong intellectual property interests wish to challenge another state's provision of medicines in contradiction of patent rights.[93] Likewise, it has been argued that the human right to food, derived from various provisions of the human rights covenants, could be relevant in interpreting the scope of the Agreement on Agriculture. Others

---

[87] ibid.   [88] Esty (n 62 above) 12.   [89] von Bogdandy (n 36 above) 659.
[90] ibid 662–663. See also Weiler (above n 15) and Howse (above n 11).
[91] von Bogdandy (n 36 above) 656.   [92] ibid.
[93] G Marceau, 'WTO Dispute Settlement and Human Rights' (2002) 13 *European Journal of International Law* 753, 786–787.

make the weaker claim that, although WTO adjudicating bodies lack jurisdiction to interpret or apply human rights law, it can be assumed that states negotiated their human rights and trade obligations in good faith,[94] and a good faith interpretation of WTO treaties should normally result in no conflict between the fields.[95] By contrast, the more comprehensive argument is made that WTO law is, simply, part of a broader framework of general international law and should be interpreted and applied as such. 'The WTO treaty must be construed and applied in the context of all other international law. This other law may fill gaps or provide interpretative material. But it may also overrule WTO norms. WTO law must thus be united with other public international law, through a process of both vertical integration (that is, in its relationship to other sub-systems) and horizontal integration (that is, vis-à-vis general international law).'[96]

Whatever approach is adopted, either in relation to general international law or specifically to human rights, the key point is that the WTO should not focus exclusively upon economic issues, should not be restricted to a free-trade objective, and should, where relevant, take account of related social and cultural issues. It is only by taking such issues into account that WTO rules can constrain socio-political behaviour in all its forms.

Sometimes this aspect of anti-constitutionalization critique, which attacks the WTO for having too narrow a focus on economic issues, revisits the 'fair' trade debate of the 1980s, although the discussion is now framed in terms of 'linkage' rather than fairness.

All methods of argument seek to find a plausible way to determine which issues, which are characterized as non-trade and therefore beyond the ambit of the WTO, can be included.[97] Indeed, some critics of the alleged narrowness of WTO decision-making claim that so-called 'social' issues such as labour will have to be recharacterized to fit within the trade sphere if constitutionalization is to proceed.[98] Whichever way it is put, this argument is consonant with the idea of the progress of constitutionalization in the European sphere, the trajectory of which is recounted as developing from a mere economic community in 1957, through a more constitutionalized phase reflected in the Treaty on Economic Union, to open discussion today of a constitutional treaty, inclusive of social issues explicitly provided for in a Charter of Fundamental Rights.

Others take an optimistic perspective about the current structure, arguing that the WTO is not a 'mono-culture'[99] and so it should move 'from trade to economic

---

[94] G Marceau, 'WTO Dispute Settlement and Human Rights' (2002) 13 *European Journal of International Law* 753, 804.   [95] ibid 767.

[96] J Pauwelyn, *Conflict of Norms in Public International Law: How WTO Law Relates to other Rules of International Law* (Cambridge: CUP, 2003) 492.

[97] See discussion above Chapter 3 at section 3.2.5 especially at notes 156–159 and accompanying text.

[98] JT Gathii, 'Re-Characterizing the Social in the Constitutionalization of the WTO: A Preliminary Analysis' (2001) 7 *Widener Law Symposium Journal* 137.

[99] M Bronckers, 'More Power to the WTO?' (2001) 4 *Journal of International Economic Law* 41, 44.

policy' and become a 'meeting place for different communities', including trade, intellectual property, environment, and labour.[100] If it recognized trade and other societal values as 'equals' and excluded a liberal trade bias in interpretation,[101] the WTO could, on this view, become a 'vehicle for global governance'.[102]

The global governance argument has been taken up enthusiastically by some who see the WTO's institutional structure as holding out possibilities for a new form of more inclusive international economic decision-making. The WTO's 'impressive institutional framework of councils and committees' could 'become the laboratory for . . . international governance' and so 'help to meet the challenges of globalization'.[103] Although not fully articulated, the suggestion seems to be that the cross-sectoral, transnational, setting of the WTO allows conversations between civil, business, governmental, and other groups which could facilitate changes in the way decisions are taken that affect multiple states and plural interests.

In sum, the moderate critique implies that constitutionalization is to be rejected until the WTO conforms better with the received account's requirement of deliberation by enhancing its mechanisms for participation, transparency, and accountability, and, takes fuller account of its constraints on economic, social, and political behaviour, by extending the range of its decision-making practices to include social, as well as economic, goals.

Omission of economic effects and distributive consequences

Relatedly, the moderate anti-constitutionalization critique also challenges constitutionalization on the basis of constraints on socio-political behaviour when it suggests that the WTO pays insufficient heed to the economic *effects*[104] or distributive consequences of its decisions. Unlike the previous argument, which stressed the need for consideration of more than economics when decisions were being taken, this argument stresses the need for attention to effects as well as goals.

The effects/distributive consequences argument is made by both those concerned with freeing up the market and those concerned with distributive justice. From the perspective of freeing up the market, it is said that the WTO should seek to achieve a form of fairness defined as respect for conditions of fair competition, and that it is this principle which should be the basic constitutional principle of international trade law.[105] Indeed, the underlying theme of most trade law scholarship is to encourage greater attention to the economic effects of trade protection.[106]

---

[100] ibid 53.   [101] ibid 41.   [102] ibid 56.   [103] von Bogdandy (n 36 above) 632.

[104] 'The constitutionalist . . . seeks to include all relevant constraints within the analysis': G Brennan and JM Buchanan, *The Reasons of Rules: Constitutional Political Economy* (Cambridge: Cambridge University Press, 1985).

[105] AB Zampetti, 'The Notion of "Fairness" in International Trade Relations and the US Perspective' (1995) (unpublished manuscript, on file with the author).

[106] The *raison d'être* of the national treatment provision is to make more competitive existing market conditions of competition. See discussion Chapter 3 n 36.

From the perspective of distributive justice, it is argued at a general level that the distributive effects of WTO decisions[107] should be openly acknowledged,[108] or that fairness, defined in both procedural and substantive terms, should be the key to the legitimacy of international law, including international trade law.[109] More specifically, the effect of WTO decisions on domestic labour markets in developed states should be monitored.[110] Unskilled workers, particularly in flexible labour markets such as that in the US, stand to lose the most in terms of 'greater insecurity and a more precarious existence'.[111]

In relation to developing states, it is said that WTO rules produce 'disastrous global disparities in income and welfare'.[112] WTO constitutionalization discourse ignores the negative welfare effects of the non-discrimination principle, whereby, for example, tariff liberalization and pressure to privatize and deregulate reduce the revenue of states and have a differential impact upon citizens, with those in the least privileged socio-economic position bearing the harsher consequences of these policies.[113] The implications of WTO law for developing states should be confronted, especially where tariff reductions lead to local producers being unable to compete with cheap, subsidized imports from developed states.[114] The stalemate which many less-developed and developing states face must be examined. Southern states are stymied in their attempts to escape from poverty because any expansion in production will lead to a contraction in Northern sectors of the same industry, usually hitting lowest paid workers, and inevitably leading to protectionist pressure in the North, thus denying the South critical market access growth.[115]

The distributive consequences of the WTO should not be ignored in relation to specific sectors either. The WTO inevitably creates 'benefits and burden,

[107] All decisions have distributive effects to the extent that each decision must necessarily prefer one interest over another. For example, in WTO law, decisions may favour producer interests over consumers, or consumers over workers, or importers over exporters, or exporters over government. See also, JL Dunoff and JP Trachtman, 'Economic Analysis of International Law' (1999) 24 *Yale Journal of International Law* 1, 23 (arguing that the design of international rules of prescriptive jurisdiction in international trade affect assignments of property rights).

[108] D Kennedy, 'The International Style in Postwar Law and Policy' (1994) 1 *Utah Law Review* 7.

[109] T Franck, *Fairness in International Law and Institutions* (Oxford: Clarendon Press, 1995).

[110] A Sapir, 'Who's Afraid of Globalization? Domestic Adjustment in Europe and America' in RB Porter, *et al* (eds), *Efficiency, Equity, and Legitimacy: The Multilateral Trading System at the Millennium* (Washington, DC: Brookings Institution Press, 2001) (noting that European and American critics of globalization claim that trade, rather than technological change, has led to deterioration of economic and social conditions).   [111] Dani Rodrik (1997) in Sapir ibid 180.

[112] MH Davis and D Neacsu, 'Legitimacy, Globally: The Incoherence of Free Trade Practice, Global Economics and their Governing Principles of Political Economy' (2001) 69 *UMKC Law Review* 733, 734.

[113] JT Gathii, 'Good Governance as a Counter Insurgency Agenda to Oppositional and Transformative Social Projects in International Law' (1999) 5 *Buffalo Human Rights Law Review* 107.

[114] *Life and Debt* (film) (Directed by Stephanie Black 2002) (presenting Jamaica as caught in an endless cycle of poverty due, in part, to pressures resulting from tariff liberalization).

[115] A Deardorff, 'Market Access for Developing Countries' in RB Porter, *et al* (eds), *Efficiency, Equity, and Legitimacy: The Multilateral Trading System at the Millennium* (Washington, DC: Brookings Institution Press, 2001) (illustrating the cyclic nature of the problem for Southern and Northern states).

such as market access opportunities in various sectors'.[116] The benefits of enforcing standardized intellectual property protection worldwide accrue to a small number of pharmaceutical and industrial chemical manufacturers, and, through them, to the states in which they are incorporated.[117] Thus WTO decisions promoting trade-linked intellectual property standards have led to a net transfer of resources from the South to the North.[118] Others elaborate the way that the economic effects of comparative advantage are undermined by the TRIPs agreement because it contains obligations on states to incorporate strong intellectual property protection standards into domestic regimes regardless of whether those states' comparative strength is in innovation (in which case protection would be to their advantage) or imitation and adaptation (in which case increased protection may not increase domestic welfare).[119] Moreover, states are required to introduce considerable administrative and judicial reform, including new remedies, tightening of procedures, and enactment of judicial review, thereby increasing compliance costs for many.[120]

These obligations will have a negative economic impact upon states that lack the resources to introduce such reforms, again exacerbating the inequality of the obligations. Exacerbating inequality is the virtual dormancy of compulsory licensing and parallel importing provisions which were designed to assist those states without the technical and financial capacity to produce their own pharmaceuticals.[121]

[116] AB Zampetti, 'Democratic Legitimacy in The World Trade Organization: The Justice Dimension' (2003) 37 *Journal of World Trade* 105, 118.

[117] See eg, P Drahos, 'Global Property Rights in Information: The Story of TRIPS at the GATT' (1995) 13 *Prometheus* 6 (arguing that the United States, prompted by US corporations with large intellectual property portfolios, used economic coercion to achieve agreement to TRIPs by Member States, the majority of whom are net importers of intellectual property); and P McCalman, 'Reaping What You Sow: An Empirical Analysis of International Patent Hamonization' (2001) 55 *Journal of International Economics* 161 (arguing that TRIPs redistributed economic rents from poor countries to rich countries).

[118] World Bank, *Global Economic Prospects and Developing Countries 2002: Making Trade Work for the World's Poor* (estimating that full implementation of TRIPs would generate a transfer of US$20billion from poor to rich countries).

[119] Trebilcock and Howse (n 12 above) Chapter 10 *passim*.   [120] Zampetti (n 116 above).

[121] Member States are entitled to authorize the making of certain drugs without authorization of the patent right holder subject to certain conditions including the requirement that production be primarily for the supply of the domestic market: TRIPs Agreement, Art 31(f). In states which either lack the capacity to produce, or where it would be inefficient to do so only for domestic supply, the operationalization of this provision has been difficult. The Doha Declaration on Public Health was designed to overcome these problems: Declaration on the TRIPs Agreement and Public Health, WT/MIN(01)DEC/W/2. It provided *inter alia* in paragraph 6 that: 'We recognize that WTO Members with insufficient or no manufacturing capacities in the pharmaceutical sector could face difficulties in making effective use of compulsory licensing under the TRIPs Agreement. We instruct the Council for TRIPs to find an expeditious solution to this problem and to report to the General Council before the end of 2002.' However, progress on paragraph 6 has been slow and controversial. One deadline for agreement on interpretation passed in December 2002 because the United States, the leading pharmaceutical manufacturer, argued that it was necessary to limit the eligibility of countries entitled to use compulsory licensing, and to limit the number of diseases which would be covered. For a description of the stalemate in the current negotiations see Bridges Weekly

Neglect of the economic effects of WTO law is also criticized in respect of substantive issues such as agriculture, where negotiations are now largely stalled,[122] and in relation to trade remedies,[123] and in respect of the now-failed attempts to introduce into the system 'new issues' of environment, investment, and competition.[124] Finally, economic effects are not sufficiently taken into account in relation to procedural matters such as implementation, lack of technical assistance, capacity-building, and the use of *amicus* briefs in tribunal proceedings insofar as briefs are often submitted by non-governmental organizations reflecting Northern interests in, say, environment.

To some extent, the argument that the economic effects and distributive consequences of the WTO should be accorded more prominence echoes the NIEO argument of the 1960s and 1970s by seeking to question the underlying premises of the way in which the field was constituted. It revisits, in a new context, the problems of Western dominated law-making (TRIPs), of failure to reflect non-Western interests (Agreement on Agriculture), and a general claim of bias (the single-package deal required developing states to sign up to services and intellectual property protection in return for improvements in market access in agriculture and textiles and clothing, the latter of which have been slow arriving or have barely materialized).

In its contemporary form, the economic effects argument is sometimes also associated with the human rights argument. One critic wants to 'resist' the rights-based view of constitutionalization, which he derides as the 'merger and acquisition' of human rights law by trade law,[125] claiming that it would 'hijack' the human rights project and turn it into a largely economic libertarian project.[126] The rights approach to constitutionalization is dangerous because it would 'detach' human rights from its goal of achieving dignity and make it purely instrumental to economic purposes turning individuals into 'economic agents acting to uphold the WTO agenda'.[127] Moreover, powerful economic

Trade News Digest, Vol 7, Number 5, 12 February 2003, Last-Minute Attempt To Save TRIPs & Health Discussions, <www.ictds.org>.

[122] For a description of the current negotiations see, eg, Agriculture Modalities: Deadline Missed, Eyes Now On Cancun, Bridges Weekly Trade News Digest, Vol 7, Number 12, 2 April 2003 available at <www.ictsd.org>.

[123] Anti-dumping has been long argued to be anti-competitive in nature and antithetical to the underlying philosophy of the free trade system, but nevertheless is a frequent source of response to 'unfair' trade. For a discussion of theoretical rationales for anti-dumping law see, eg, Trebilcock and Howse (n 12 above) chapter 7.

[124] In August 2004 the General Council decided that investment, competition, and transparency in government procurement would not form part of the Work Programme set out in the Doha and that no work towards negotiations on any of these issues would take place within the WTO during the Doha Round: Decision Adopted by General Council on 1 August 2004, WT/L/579 2 August 2004: <http://www.wto.org/english/tratop_e/dda_e/draft_text_gc_dg_31july04_e.htm>.

[125] P Alston, 'Resisting the Merger and Acquisition of Human Rights by Trade Law: A Reply to Petersmann' (2002) 13 *European Journal of International Law* 815.   [126] ibid 816.

[127] ibid 843.

actors such as corporations would be further empowered and non-economic human rights would languish in the ordinary institutions of general international law. This would have the added effect of further entrenching the domination of international governance by corporations.[128]

In short, from the perspective of either freeing up the market or promoting distributive concerns, the economic effects and distributive consequences of WTO law should be acknowledged in respect of the internal markets of developing and developed states, particular sectors, and WTO procedures. Again, implicit in this critique is the view that in a constitutionalized entity, economic behaviour, like other forms of social life, should be negotiated or constrained.[129] This is not equivalent to a claim that constitutionalization must include economic equality or distributive justice, although some desire this.[130] Rather, this is a more moderate claim that a constitutionalized WTO ought to take better account of its economic effects. If some of those effects are ignored, or left out of the equation, then the constitutional requirement of constraint is at best unevenly applied across the sectors of economic, social, and political life, and at worst, it is discriminating.

7.2.3 Strong anti-constitutionalization

The *strong* anti-constitutionalization critique comes in two forms, one of which is a descriptive attack on the construction of a WTO constitution because it excludes private law, and therefore leaves out one of the major constraining influences on behaviour; the second makes the normative claim that the social legitimacy of WTO constitutionalization should not be being artificially constructed.

---

[128] Hertz (n 71 above) 112 (arguing that governments and 'supposedly neutral global governance systems' are increasingly 'dancing to the corporate tune').

[129] For example, when the Australian federal constitution was enacted in 1901, in addition to providing that interstate trade and commerce should be absolutely free (s 91), and vesting the central government with power to levy taxes (s 51(ii)) the constitution encapsulated a series of fiscal provisions providing for, *inter alia*, abolition of the capacity of constituent states to levy customs, duties, or excises and vesting of central government with exclusive power to impose such (s 90); vesting central government with power to impose a uniform tariff (s 88); redistribution of tariffs back to the states; vesting the central government power to make conditional grants to the states (s 96); and prohibiting central government from discriminating between the states (s 117): for discussion see, P Hanks and D Cass, *Australian Constitutional Law: Materials and Commentary* 6th edn (Sydney: Butterworths, 1999) chapter 9.

[130] See, eg, T Pogge, *World Poverty and Human Rights: Cosmopolitan Responsibilities and Reforms* (London: Polity Press, 2002) (arguing that the global economic order is, in part, responsible for making it appear that wealthy states and individuals are disconnected from the poor); J Trachtman, 'Legal Aspects of a Poverty Agenda at the WTO: Trade Law and "Global Apartheid"' (2003) 6 *Journal of International Economic Law* 3, 21 (arguing that although the WTO has contributed to poverty reduction by encouraging trade liberalization, further redistribution of wealth is needed, and the WTO should ensure that it does not block any such redistribution); and Zampetti (n 116 above) 116 (arguing that 'democratic legitimacy requires addressing distributive and justice-related problems').

The absence of private law

One strong form of anti-constitutionalization attacks the constitutionalization process again on the basis that it does not take sufficient account of all the various types of constraint on socio-political behaviour. The strong challenge says that WTO constitutionalization ignores the role that private law has in constituting the terms upon which international trade operates. A constitutionalization thesis focused solely on the public law between states is incomplete because it ignores key constitutive mechanisms of economic life. According to this view, private law, at the national and international level, does more than merely set the background rules upon which economic activities, including trade, are then transacted.[131] Private law is not merely facilitative. Rather, according to Robert Wai, it regulates economic activities in the same way that public law does by deterring socially harmful or wasteful conduct.[132] The critique argues that domestic private law regulates economic activities by, for example, providing triple damages remedies in anti-trust law, or by specifying in tort law that compensation will be paid to a person who is not in a contractual relation with the tortfeasor, or by voiding a contract on public policy grounds in contract law.[133] So private law has a regulatory function in constructing economic actors, giving them rights, and regulating their conduct. It therefore contributes to the creation of the conditions in which trade operates domestically, in much the same way as do governmental restrictions and permissions for trade—classic instances of public law. Accordingly, any analysis of the international constitution of the WTO which focuses primarily, as do current models, on national public law measures such as tariffs, quotas, and subsidies, but neglects to address national private laws concerning contract, tort, and property, is underinclusive, and overlooks a key element of the international trade constitutional system.

Furthermore, the same authors argue that private law at the international level has a regulatory function which is also significant for the constitution of a system of transnational economic governance and should not be ignored. Private international law or conflicts law regulates relations between states, and between state and non-state parties, by virtue of rules of jurisdiction, choice of law, and arbitration clauses. These rules regulate the extent to which parties damaged by transnational activities of private economic actors can pursue claims in national courts.[134] Transposing this argument to the WTO context, it could be argued that these rules are a crucial part of the international trade constitution. By ignoring the critical role of private international

---

[131] Jackson, Davey, and Sykes, (n 85 above) 2–3 (referring to the rules of private national law as the 'transactional rules', as opposed to the constitutional rules of the WTO proper).

[132] Wai (n 8 above) 235.   [133] ibid 235–236.   [134] ibid 238, 253.

law, the constitutionalization models undervalue its regulative and constitutive functions in the international trading system.

Furthermore, even if private international law is included in the constitutional equation, it has, Wai claims, become dominated by liberal concerns about the facilitation of international commerce, increase of international cooperation, and pursuit of anti-parochialism and non-discrimination, at the expense of other social goals. So, just as we saw the critics of deliberative process arguing that it excluded certain norms,[135] so, too, it is argued that private international law, and indeed WTO law itself, has excluded other equally important policies concerned, for example, with the need for effective regulation of private relations, the protection of broad social interests, and legal diversity.[136] There is no reason, according to the critique, that any constitution of world trade should omit these latter concerns.

One result of the omission of private law rules from the constitutionalization thesis is that the potential for states to exercise control over transnational business has been reduced.[137] If this is correct, then the focus of WTO constitutional law on the public law aspects of the problem, namely, the structure and function of WTO laws and state measures specifically related to trade relations, is misconceived. It is misconceived because it leaves out equally important ways in which the behaviour of members of the constitutional system is regulated, namely, through the application of private laws of the state, international private law, and conflicts law.

Nevertheless, national constitutions are not made up of *all* the laws that bear upon economic relations, including private ones, but they still bear the name 'constitutional'. And yet there is something compelling to the argument. To the extent that the term constitutional functions as a label for government measures with public policy implications that make up a legal system, the argument points out that the description of what is inside the WTO constitutional box is partial. In this aspect, the claim mirrors the position taken by some US legal scholars that private law rules (property, tort, corporations, commercial etc), far from being neutral in the market, were constitutive of it, and, like public law, had an effect on the operations of the market.[138] Similarly, the international trade critique would suggest that the constitutional sphere of international trade (which currently includes only public laws within the nomination constitutional) cannot be fully understood without considering the effect that private law has had, for example, in regulating the types of entities that can form as companies and so participate in trade; in determining which bodies can sue and in what forum; or in deciding which parties could

---

[135] M Rosenfeld, 'Can Rights, Democracy, and Justice be Reconciled through Discourse Theory? Reflections on Habermas's Proceduralist Paradigm of Law' (1996) 17 *Cardozo Law Review* 791, 812; see discussion at Chapter 2 note 85.   [136] Wai (n 8 above).
[137] ibid.   [138] Wai relies on Cass Sunstein's summary of this point: (n 8 above).

participate in the making of international standards, which WTO Member States are then required, under the agreements, to respect. Like the US critical legal studies argument before it, this aspect of the WTO anti-constitutionalization critique succeeds in spotlighting the constructed nature of the boundary of constitutionalization, and forces into the open the question of what is being left out of the description that might have had some, or even significant, influence on the character of a purportedly constitutionalized system.

Legitimization by constitutional language

A final version of the strong critique questions the use of constitutional language to describe transformations in the WTO, which might otherwise be simply matters of (non-constitutionalized) international law. On this view, the language of constitutionalization should not be used to legitimize the changes occurring within the WTO, because this artificially constructs another of the core elements of constitutionalization, social acceptance by a constitutional community. This critique comes in a robust form, and in one that is more ambivalent.[139] Those who strenuously reject the use of constitutional language in the WTO display a deep scepticism towards promoting the term constitutionalization in relation to the WTO, claiming that the constitutionalization project is 'mischievous and fanciful'[140] or even 'misguided'.[141] It marks the organization out as untouchable,[142] in the sense that its decisions are not open to contestation in the manner of an unconstitutionalized body. Or, these writers object to the use of the denominator 'constitutional' to describe the transformations on the basis that discussing change in terms of constitutionalization prejudges the existence of the phenomenon of constitutionalization, because it 'presupposes the very conditions of legitimacy that [the constitutionalizers] want to create'.[143] Moreover, goes the claim, the point of using the term constitutionalization is not to describe a change in trade governance, but to make a strategic, political intervention into a debate about the proper ambit of the WTO. For example,

---

[139] For another strong critique of the WTO questioning the legitimacy of the WTO but on the basis of the use of comparative advantage rather than constitutionalization as a technique of legitimization, see Davis and Neacsu (n 112 above) (arguing, at 756, that comparative advantage operates to legitimize WTO effected globalization in the same way that the rule of law operates to legitimize Western legal systems. Comparative advantage, which the authors claim is operationalized only to the extent that it benefits industrialized interests and is abandoned as soon as it does not (766–773), is presented as a rule, or a 'law', and so legitimizes the practices of the WTO, when in reality comparative advantage has been shown not to have been predictive, at 761, and, at 757, 'not a scientific rule but a rationalization designed to support a political goal', namely, at 766, a 'massive fraudulent tilt in favour of the first world').

[140] JHH Weiler, 'Cain and Abel—Convergence and Divergence in International Trade Law' in Weiler (n 27 above) 4.   [141] ibid 2.

[142] Davis and Neacsu (n 112 above) 747 (arguing that legitimacy 'asserts at a level immune from debate that all parties are autonomous and competent').

[143] Robert Howse in Walker (n 2 above) 51.

Robert Howse and Kalypso Nicolaidis have suggested that constitutionalization was introduced in order to plug a gap left in the wake of legitimacy crises which arose after the Second World War, when the informal deal between states, known as embedded liberalism, collapsed under the strain of the abandonment of the gold standard, the demise of macroeconomic management, and the rise of internal subsidies.[144] When this collapse occurred, the WTO system expanded to take in some issues such as intellectual property but not others, such as labour. As a result, a legitimacy crisis emerged, and it was only in response to that crisis of legitimacy that people began to use the language of constitutionalization in relation to the WTO.[145] The constitutionalization thesis, according to this critique, serves to authorize and legitimize changes in the WTO, which might otherwise be open to deep criticism. According to the anti-constitutionalist critique, the terms of the debate operate to shield the WTO from criticism by importing into the discussion a term which carries strong overtones of normative authority.

Moreover, these critics, borrowing from the EU literature, might argue that the attempt to import moral authority into WTO law could fail because the language of constitutionalization cannot do what is asked of it by the constitutional enthusiasts. It cannot clothe an international organization with the authority and legitimacy because it cannot solve the organization's deep, internal paradoxes.

On closer scrutiny, the . . . constitutional question carries a heavier political baggage than that in the overhead compartment, because it tries, not always easily, to straddle the mutually exclusive concepts of 'state' and 'international entity' and to solve the problems of legitimate authority and social integration with reference to conflicting principles such as democracy and intergovernmental co-operation, unity/centrality and subsidiarity, integration/homogeneity and diversity/heterogeneity.[146]

Other WTO anti-constitutionalization critics remain merely ambivalent about the use of constitutional language to describe the WTO. While it would be wrong to classify this latter group as constitutional enthusiasts in the manner of institutional managerialism, rights, or judicial norm-generation constitutionalists described in Chapters 4–6, these critics want to use the language of constitutionalization to criticize the WTO, but not to discard it altogether. Heightened judicial activity engenders both 'new possibilities for legitimation' and 'new spaces for critique and contestation', and could ultimately lead to enhanced social legitimacy.[147] Constitutionalization need not be an 'enemy' of

---

[144] Howse and Nicolaidis (n 72 above); and Howse (n 11 above) 105.

[145] Howse and Nicolaidis (n 72 above).

[146] G Frankenberg, 'The Return of the Contract: Problems and Pitfalls of European Constitutionalism' (2000) 6 *European Law Journal* 257, 258 (arguing that European constitutionalism cannot sustain the many contradictory urges that are invested in it).

[147] Howse (n 27 above) 69.

legitimacy.[148] If the right conditions exist, defined as greater institutional sensitivity, top-down empowerment, and political inclusiveness, constitution-alization might be possible, and even desirable.[149] Nevertheless, constitu-tionalization is not a project which will ever be neatly 'finished'[150] in the sense implied by the institutional, rights-based, or judicial approaches. Yet remains the 'best stocked normative reservoir of values'[151] which could be imported into the WTO, and if this occurred, the concept would lend the organization much-needed authority. '[It] is not the enemy of a normative discourse of responsible self-government but rather its necessary accompaniment. The idea of constitutionalism is linked in a powerful and resilient chain of signification to a whole series of polity-constitutive values, such as democracy, separation of powers and rule of law.'[152]

This approach is reminiscent of European Union literature which emphasizes not constitutionalization by ECJ doctrinal development,[153] but a more flexible form consisting of, for example, the creative use of substitutes for traditional forms of evaluation, legitimation, and accountability,[154] and revitalization of a procedural approach to law-making which emphasizes proceduralism's capa-city for moving beyond fixed positions, exploring new relations between par-ties, and establishing new forms of dialogue.[155]

Neither wholly enthusiastic nor wholly sceptical, this recent anti-constitutionalization literature contains glimpses of an ambivalence which char-acterizes the idea of constitutionalization as a fluid concept, one that carries with it risks but also conveys strong connotations of democracy, rule of law, certainty, and protection from abuse of power. According to this more ambiva-lent scepticism, constitutional language could be used to criticize the WTO, and to promote changes within the system. Constitutionalization language could be embraced, albeit within the context of a vigorous debate over meaning.

---

[148] DK Tarullo, (2002) 5 *Journal of International Economic Law* 941 (reviewing G de Búrca and J Scott (eds), *The EU and the WTO: Legal and Constitutional Issues* (2001).

[149] See Howse and Nicolaidis (n 72 above) 248 (arguing that their particular guidelines—institutional sensitivity, political inclusiveness, and top-down empowerment—might help 'creat[e] some of the conditions for Constitutionalism in the long run').   [150] Tarullo (n 148 above).

[151] Walker (n 2 above) 57 (arguing that constitutionalization is not the 'enemy of.... responsible relational politics' and instead is the 'the most persuasive medium in which it may be articulated').   [152] ibid 53.

[153] See JHH Weiler, 'The Transformation of Europe' (1991) 100 *Yale Law Journal* 2403.

[154] D Chalmers, 'Post-nationalism and the Quest for Constitutional Substitutes' (2000) 27 *Journal of Law and Society* 178, (arguing that 'the post-national condition ... is characterised by increased legal pluralism, ... and ... by ... political disordering, leading to the emergence of new political arenas and a reflexive awareness by traditional political actors of their own limitations').

[155] J Shaw, 'Relating Constitutionalism and Flexibility' in G de Búrca and J Scott (eds), *Constitutional Change in the EU: From Uniformity to Flexibility* (2000) (arguing for a linking of the concepts of flexibility through differentiated integration, with constitutionalism, so that the lat-ter is transformed from, at 339 a 'static, concept' to one which is, at 347, non-linear, non-static, and non-fixed. She proposes conceiving of constitutionalization as 'dialogic, and conversational rather than contractual providing fixed outcomes.')

7.3 CONCLUSION

The anti-constitutionalization critique contends that the WTO constitutional-ization thesis is flawed in a number of different respects. The weak form of the critique is against constitutionalization because it has resulted in a realignment of the relationship between the Member States and the central entity which to some is excessive (although others believe that the defect could be cured if the contraction of state decisional capacity by the AB was vested with greater legitimacy). The moderate form of anti-constitutionalization challenges basic premises of the WTO concerning rights of participation, transparency, and accountability; the range of economic and social goals it takes into account; and the economic effects of its decisions. Moderate anti-constitutionalization seeks to reform the deliberative process requirement of constitutionalization and ensure that the constraints which constitutionalization places on social, economic, and political behaviour are evenly applied. A stronger form of the anti-constitutionalization critique claims that the whole system of constraint is fundamentally skewed and incomplete because it ignores the role of private law in constructing the framework of any constitutionalized WTO, and because social legitimacy is being artificially constructed through the use of constitu-tional language.

Finally, these various anti-constitutionalization critiques have different implications for the WTO and constitutionalization literature generally. Some appear to suggest that the process of WTO constitutionalization can be reformed, while others imply that it should be abandoned altogether. Still others force us to rethink the project both in relation to the WTO and in general.

8

Conclusion: Trading Democracy

[T]he 'constitution' of the WTO will clearly shape world economics for decades
to come, and can also have important influences on many non-economic
goals, including vital issues of maintaining peace in the world.[1]

This study has examined the idea of constitutionalization as it is applied to
the World Trade Organization. It began, in Part I, by establishing a series of
propositions about what constitutionalization is, propositions which together
combined to create what I have called a 'received account' of constitutionalization processes beyond the nation state. While this account is not fixed, or
indeed the only one possible, it provided us with a stationary focal point
according to which we could examine the claims of WTO constitutionalization.
Essentially, the received account held that constitutionalization is associated
with the emergence of a foundational device signalling a new, coherent system
of constraining social practices. The authority of the system is legitimized by a
political community whose views are represented, and which, in turn, uses
a deliberative process to make law and which has the effect of realigning
traditional sovereign relations among constituent entities, and between itself
and those sub-parts.

The study then broadened to think about where that concept of constitutionalization came from, and focused on the context provided by international
economic law. For example, the apparently natural link between the idea of
an institution and the idea of a constitution, which informed international
economic law scholarship, opened up the possibility for thinking about the WTO
as constitutionalized, as did the anxiety within that discipline to be a force
for transformation of public international order. Chapter 3 was therefore both
background to the debate and an opportunity to understand the relationship
between this quite specific question of WTO constitutionalization and broader
questions concerning the international economic order as a whole. (The content
of the chapter, with its shifting emphasis between arguments within international
economic law, arguments within economic literature, and arguments within
WTO literature, foreshadowed the critiques in Chapter 7 which move between
these fields in the same fashion.) Importantly, Chapter 3 argued that the trends

---

[1] JH Jackson, *The World Trade Organization: Constitution and Jurisprudence* (London: Royal
Institute of International Affairs, 1998).

in international economic law scholarship provided a fertile culture in which WTO constitutionalization, and, more pertinently, talk of it, could grow.

The finding that WTO constitutionalization, both in practice, and in conceptualization, grew out of international economic law's more general concerns set the ground for a discussion of the specific contours of WTO constitutionalization. The central chapters, in Part II of the study, explored those contours and distinguished three main schools of constitutionalization: institutional managerialism, rights-based constitutionalization, and judicial-norm generation.

Each of these three models of constitutionalization was analysed (and found wanting) against the template provided by the received account of constitutionalization. For example, while institutional managerialism was strong in relation to behavioural constraints, and to some extent deliberation, it was weaker in relation to legitimacy. While rights-based constitutionalization emphasized legitimacy, it failed to confront the requirements of community or deliberation. And, although judicial norm-generation addressed problems of legitimacy and realignment of constitutional relationships, it was less amenable to discussions of community or deliberative process. The point of the discussion was both to explore the models in order to show the ways in which they managed to meet the requirements of the received account, and also to examine how their particular configurations raised for discussion, and put in question, one or another of the core elements of the received account.

At this point in the argument, therefore, it would appear that if the WTO were reformed to accord more closely to the received account then it would meet our criteria of constitutionalization. However, a further set of questions remained. It seemed prudent, alongside the question whether the WTO could be constitutionalized, perhaps by some general tinkering with its structures and rules, to ask a further question: *should* it in fact be so? And, here, the study explored the various arguments *against* WTO constitutionalization. I recounted the challenges of those who argue, for example, that constitutionalization threatened the decisional capacity of states; insufficiently addressed problems of deliberation, participation, and dialogue; skewed decision-making towards economic goals while ignoring their economic effects; marginalized private law; and claimed to be authoritative without going through the ordinary processes of legitimization. In the view of the anti-constitutionalist argument then, WTO constitutionalization should be resisted because the constitution it produces is democratically deficient, harmful to sovereignty and states' redistributive capacities or welfarist tendencies, and self-legitimating.

These various anti-constitutionalization critiques have different implications for the WTO and constitutionalization literature generally. Some appear to suggest that the process of WTO constitutionalization can be reformed, while others imply that it should be abandoned altogether. Still others force us to rethink the project both in relation to the WTO and in general. So while the received account of constitutionalization formed the focal point against which to conduct this study (both in respect of the question whether the WTO is constitutionalized and in respect of the question whether it could be constitutionalized), the implication of some of these criticisms is that the very conception of constitutionalization that animates our discussion requires rethinking.

The received account of constitutionalization described in this study or something like it, clearly no longer functions as an adequate analytical tool, or operational model, to describe the changes occurring at the international level in relation to constitutionalization generally,[2] or more specifically within the WTO context. Conceived in an intrastate or statist positivist tradition, the received account has been revealed as neither descriptively adequate, nor normatively appealing. The necessity for transformation of the constitutionalization thesis is therefore one underlying theme of this study, along with the finding of the inadequacy of its WTO manifestations. In this respect, Cottier and Hertig have argued for a new model of constitutionalization for the twenty-first century, claiming that 'an exclusive focus of constitutionalism on the Nation State cannot be maintained'.[3] Neil Walker notes the 'genuine difficulties of translating the received wisdom of state polity building to the supranational context', and the 'unprecedented problems of institutional design' faced by non-state constitutionalization processes.[4] Instead, he advocates transforming the idea of constitutionalization into 'a graduated approach, which views constitutionalism as a process, extending constitutional structures to fora and layers of governance other than nations'.[5] These commentators, whom I will call the constitutional transformationists, want to critique the received account but nevertheless harness it in transformed fashion to the job of transnational constitution-building. They promote a constitutionalization capable of 'mastering the interaction and the interface of the different layers of national, regional and international governance, whatever their constitutional nature and quality'.[6] The transformation thesis is therefore characterized by a strong, although somewhat vaguely defined, desire to alter transnational constitutionalization. In part, this alteration is about how the process should be imagined: constitutionalization should adopt the model of a 'five-storey house'[7] with each storey representing one of the layers of governance from sub-local to international, through local, national, and regional. EU constitutionalism should not be a 'closed book' but an 'open-textured and provisional affair' with the potential to 'address . . . deep-rooted and urgent tensions over institutional design and fundamental values'.[8] Moreover,

---

[2] N Walker, 'Constitutionalising Enlargement, Enlarging Constitutionalism' (2003) 9 *European Law Journal* 365, 373.

[3] T Cottier and M Hertig, 'The Prospects of 21st Century Constitutionalism' in AV Bogdandy and R Wolfrum (eds), *Max Planck Yearbook of United Nations Law*, vol 7 (2004) 264.

[4] Walker (n 2 above) 373.   [5] Cottier and Hertig (n 3 above).   [6] ibid.

[7] ibid 299–300.   [8] Walker (n 2 above) 365.

according to this view, change is inevitable because the proposed, transformed, transnational approach will be more functional,[9] less dogmatic, and have greater flexibility[10] than its statist counterpart. Constitutionalization, in this transformed mode, will be practical, recognizing the 'entanglement' of powers that often govern a particular issue such as the environment, or culture.[11] It will be relational, focusing on 'communication and interaction'[12] rather than maintaining strict boundaries of power division. And, all the while, it will hold to an unswerving belief in a presumption of hierarchy of the international over the domestic.[13] The importance of the WTO, according to this vision, is not as an institution for economic reform, but as a site for politics. This is true for those with a free trade agenda who argue, for example, that, 'the legitimacy and importance of the WTO lies not in its role in opening markets or in helping countries suppress "special interest" legislation. Its importance lies in the success that it has had in moving globalization toward new forms of transnational participation and thus new forms of global democracy.'[14] And for those who reject the potential of free trade to achieve economic growth, politics is again the key. 'Despite these criticisms, [that global welfare has been reduced by trade] there is substantial evidence that international trade institutions are effective in reducing conflict, coordinating trade policy and stabilizing governments. As economic engines institutions like the WTO and the NAFTA may be abject failures, but as political policymaking institutions, they have succeeded brilliantly.'[15]

Constitutional transformation theory is, in short, optimistic.[16] To the extent that the WTO models in Chapters 3–6 were anchored in an increasingly inappropriate state-based form, emphasized the economic over the political role of the WTO, or privileged judicial activity over other forms of constitutional change, constitutional transformationism departs from these models and opens up arguments about constitutionalization itself.

Yet, in my view, there is something indecisive and unsatisfactory about the transformation argument also. Although appealing in its openness, it runs the

---

[9] On this view multi-layered constitutionalism is simply a function of the fact that disputes cross national and international boundaries. See, for example, the decade long dispute about the EU's import regime for bananas which has held the attention of various levels of courts including the European Court of Justice, the German Constitutional Court, and the GATT/WTO: ibid 302–303.

[10] According to Cottier and Hertig (n 3 above) twenty-first century constitutionalism must accommodate, for example, at 293–296 the absence of clear political communities, at 318 the difficulty of allocating power strictly between levels of government, at 296 the absence of the big-bang theory of *Grundnorm* change.   [11] ibid 318.

[12] ibid 313.   [13] ibid 307, 309.

[14] PM Gerhart, 'The Two Constitutional Visions of the World Trade Organization' (2003) *University of Pennsylvania Journal of International Economic Law* 1, 73.

[15] JR Paul, 'Do International Trade Institutions Contribute to Economic Growth and Development' (2003) 44 *Virginia Journal of International Law* 285, 339.

[16] Walker (above n 2) 383.

risk of repeating the error identified in relation to the existing models, of being endlessly flexible and neutral in their aspirations, and, at the same time, reflecting, perhaps on a subliminal level only, an unchanged agenda for free trade. And yet, there are other agendas and other choices. There is an agenda which questions a system, purportedly based on non-discrimination in trade, in which developed countries maintain protection by granting, in the form of export subsidies and trade-distorting domestic support, twice the amount they give in foreign aid to developing countries.[17] There is an agenda that permits domestic polities, legitimately, to choose to adopt sub-optimal solutions to the problem of trade discrimination, to choose, for example, environmental or health values over trade.[18] There is an agenda which questions the necessary assumption of free trade over other forms of managed or strategic trade, in a context in which the former is not mandated by the text or context of the WTO Agreements. In conclusion, I would propose not only the rethinking of current WTO constitutional models, and the adoption of a constitutional transformationist mindset, but also a merging of the latter with democratic arguments about economic development taken from the anti-constitutionalizationist thesis—those arguments, for example, that focus on the distributive consequences of constitutionalization, the omission of non-economic values from the calculus of WTO decision-making, and the constructed nature of the playing field upon which international trade operates. A constitutionalization process is warranted that sanctions the possibility that asymmetries of economic power may become less significant in the transformed system.[19] In short, I argue for what I call 'trading democracy'. WTO constitutional theory, to be relevant, cannot afford to be either so endlessly flexible in its goals, or dogmatically oriented to free trade, as to leave these critical issues out of the constitutionalization equation. Trading democracy, not merely trading constitutionalization, should be the key to WTO constitutionalization in this century.

The trading democracy argument, therefore, has two parts. First, WTO constitutionalization should be procedurally transformed so as to take account of the conditions of contemporary international society including, for example, the decline of the state as the sole necessary locus of constitutionalization, the changed nature of interstate relations in an era of globalization, and the increased forms and varieties of techniques of governance (the transformationist argument). Secondly, in addition to these procedural (democratic) transformations, trading democracy would entail reorienting the WTO towards its primary

[17] S Cho, 'A Bridge Too Far: The Fall of the Fifth WTO Ministerial Conference in Cancun and the Future of the Trade Constitution' (2004) 7 *Journal of International Economic Law* 219 citing *Globalization, Growth, and Poverty: Building an Inclusive World Economy* (Washington, DC: World Bank, 2002) 9, 53.

[18] A Von Bogdandy, 'Law and Politics in the WTO—Strategies to Cope with a Deficient Relationship' in JA Frowein and R Wolfrum (eds), *Max Planck Yearbook of United Nations Law*, Vol 5 (The Hague; London; New York: Kluwer, 2001) 609, 656.

[19] Walker (n 2 above) 368.

goal, development, a concept which has, for so long, existed at the periphery of the international trade system[20] but which has rarely had explicit impact on international economic institutions.[21]

This is not to say that development could be applied in the WTO context uncontroversially. As with free trade, the meaning, status, and fungibility of economic development remains contested,[22] with some focusing on environmental sustainability, others on distribution of social goods and opportunities, and others still, on participation. To some, development is about enlarging the size of the economic cake. To others, it is about creating conditions for a more equitable, fairer distribution of the cake. In the view of one critic, trade does not, in any case, enhance economic growth or development,[23] and, according to another, the particular combination of the export of economic globalization with free-market democracy breeds ethnic resentment and global violence.[24] For Amaryta Sen, development is about freedom itself. I do not claim to have the answer to these dilemmas about the meaning of development, but argue instead for placing them at the centre of the WTO constitutionalization project. Putting trading democracy, emphasizing development, at the heart of the WTO is necessary, in my view, in order to reflect the authentic desires of the putative international trade community,[25] to be faithful to the intentions of treaty framers,[26] and, to force into the open the relationship between trade and development, which is key to any effective, democratic, and lasting resolution of the problems of international economic order.

Making trading democracy, in the form of a focus on development, central to the WTO constitutionalization project would necessarily require altering some long-standing and tenacious assumptions about the international trading system. It would involve, for example, openly acknowledging, as many already have,[27] that free trade is not an explicit objective of the system.[28] Moreover, the only plausible reconciliation of the tension in the agreements between the principles of non-discrimination, multilateralism, liberalization,[29] and

---

[20] JT Gathii, 'Re-Characterizing the Social in the Constitutionalization of the WTO: A Preliminary Analysis' (2001) 7 *Widener Law Symposium Journal* 137.

[21] S Marks and A Clapham, 'Development' in *International Human Rights Lexicon* (Oxford University Press, forthcoming) citing Anne Orford, 'Globalization and the Right to Development', in P Alston, *People's Rights* (2001).

[22] The following paragraph draws on the summary of economic development scholarship in S Marks and A Clapham, ibid.   [23] Paul (n 15 above).

[24] Amy Chua, *World on Fire* (London, Heinemann, 2003).

[25] To an extent, this argument for a reading of constitutionalization as trading democracy and focusing on economic development is, simply, an application of constitutional political economy, which provides that purposes or goals do not form part of a constitution, but they can be chosen by members of the constitutional community. See Section 2.2 above.

[26] A treaty should be interpreted according to the intention of the contracting parties, as indicated by the ordinary meaning of the terms, in context and in light of the objective and purpose of the treaty: Vienna Convention on the Law of Treaties (1969), Art 31. See Addendum below (a) and (b).

[27] See Chapter 3, nn 150–155.   [28] von Bogdandy (n 18 above) 659.

[29] Jackson (n 1 above) 23.

transparency in trade, and the numerous departures from, and indeed contradictions with, them[30] both within the terms of the agreement[31] and its contextual interpretive background[32], is that the overriding *telos* of the WTO is economic development through non-discriminatory trade.[33] Once explicit agreement is reached that the principles of non-discrimination and the like exist to serve the goal of development, then it might be possible to construct a better constitutionalization project capable of accounting for this. How that would influence practices at the WTO would, of course, be a matter of debate. Perhaps, for example, the judicial bodies would interpret the agreements in the light of the treaty intention as described. Non-discrimination might be interpreted with development needs of states in the forefront of the dispute resolution bodies' consideration, an approach which is sometimes visible.[34] Balance of payments requirements, safeguards, and anti-dumping provisions might all be viewed in a different light. Interpretation of intellectual property provisions might explicitly take into account social and welfare concerns rather than relegate them to some vaguely defined, higher status norms of irrelevant effect. In the non-judicial arena we might witness increased market access for developing states, more labour mobility, institutional reform enabling a redistribution of resources to developing states such that they can participate and integrate into the world economy, redirection of tariff revenue (including anti-dumping and counter-vailing duties) by developed states towards a redistributive mechanism, and, establishment of a development policy review body.[35] While reasonable states may disagree as to exactly what development means or how to attain it, the recognition that it is the organizing principle of the system would lead, at the very least, to a more explicit, argumentative, substantive form of constitutionalization than is currently the case.

This study has shown that the dominant models of WTO constitutionalization are deeply unsatisfying, a finding of some importance in view of the connections made between constitutionalization, economics, and world order in the quotation at the beginning of this chapter by one of constitutionalization's

---

[30] Paul (above n 15), 320–333 arguing, at 333, that this leads to a largely 'incoherent' system of 'protectionism, preferences and anti-competitive rules' which inhibits power of states to address market distortions and correct market failure.   [31] See Addendum, p. 247 para (a).

[32] ibid, p. 248 para (b).

[33] cf JH Jackson, *The World Trading System: Law and Policy of International Economic Relations*, 2nd edn (Cambridge, Mass; London: MIT Press, 1997) 13–14, describing economic development as a WTO goal which 'may be partly inconsistent' with its 'central goal' of liberal or free trade.

[34] See, eg, a Panel decision in October 2004 that the EC had subsidized exports of sugar in excess of its commitments under the Agriculture Agreement, coupled with the suggestion by the Panel that Europe 'consider measures to bring its production of sugar more into line with domestic consumption whilst fully respecting its international commitments with respect to imports, including its commitments to developing countries': WTO, Panel Report, *European Communities—Export Subsidies on Sugar* (complaint by Australia) WT/DS265/R (15 October 2004).

[35] J Trachtman, 'Legal Aspects of a Poverty Agenda at the WTO: Trade Law and "Global Apartheid" ' (2003) 6 *Journal of International Economic Law* 3, 17–20.

key scholars. If WTO constitutionalization is a force capable of transforming not only trade, economics, and law, but also world politics in general, then it is important that a number of conclusions raised by this study are addressed. First, and obviously, asking the question 'is the WTO constitutionalized?' requires some clarification before it can be answered, both in relation to what constitutionalization means in the abstract, and how it is conceived of within the WTO literature. Secondly, measuring the WTO according to the received account of supranational constitutionalization leads to the conclusion that the WTO may not be constitutionalized, although this still leaves the normative dimension unexplored. Thirdly, even if it were possible to reform the WTO, or models of WTO constitutionalization, so that the match between the organization and the criteria was more appealing, the outcome is undesirable because, according to the anti-constitutionalization critique, the current forms of WTO constitutionalization are weakly deliberative, pay insufficient attention to non-economic goals, and have a self-legitimizing agenda. Fourthly, the problem of constitutionalization is not only one of descriptive inaccuracy, or even a prescriptive undesirability. When one looks at the WTO models, and at the context from which WTO constitutionalization was derived, it is clear that there are some common trends. In both WTO and general international economic law, politics, law, and economics are being mixed, if not confused; things formerly called institutional are being legitimized with the mantle of constitutionalization; and the very notion of what is a constraint has been broadened to take in non-legal, non-state sources of regulation, while at the same time, those constraints are applied in an uneven fashion to economic and social behaviour. The result has been the emergence of similar critiques of WTO constitutionalization and general international economic law, a situation that suggests that the ascendancy of these particular models of constitutionalization is related to these perceived deformities of democracy, sovereignty, and economic and political organization in the international order. Fifthly, any attempt to address these deformities must begin by revisiting the constitutionalization thesis, which originated with the experience of the nation state, and adjusting it in the light of contemporary conditions of, for example, state boundary permeability, and, ongoing economic underdevelopment. Importantly, the constitutional thesis requires transformation, in a manner that addresses not only the question of form—what and how should the WTO take into account the various interests involved in international trade decision-making—but also the question of substance—what are the aims that a democratic trading system should be directed towards achieving. In my view then, WTO constitutionalization should become both procedurally transformed, and democratically informed, with development as its key goal.

In sum, the dominance in WTO constitutionalization scholarship, of three models' has sometimes inhibited thinking about WTO constitutionalization in principle and its place within international economic law. In consequence, constitutionalization has been presented as a *fait accompli* rather than as an argument about what should or should not occur in relation to international trade. This study has been an attempt to create some space to think about this question more clearly. While the WTO experiment has provided a hospitable environment in which to consider the transformation of non-state constitutionalism, the international trade 'constitutionalization project' should take more seriously the powerful and insistent claims of legitimacy, democracy (of both substance and form) and community.

Addendum

Consistent with international law rules guiding treaty interpretation contained in the Vienna Convention on the Law of Treaties, this addendum lists evidence for the argument made at 243–244 that the WTO covered agreements contain a tension between principles of non-discrimination, multilateralism, liberalization, and transparency on the one hand, and departures from those principles.

(a) Text: Reconciling the goals of free trade with departures from those goals

In addition to the principles of non-discrimination, multilateralism, liberalization, and transparency expressed in GATT 1947 in, for example, the national treatment provision (Article III), most-favoured-nation treatment (Article 1), liberalization (Article II), and abolition of quotas (Article XI), the covered agreements contain a number of significant departures from those principles. A non-exhaustive list of departures from the goals associated with free trade would include the following. All states may impose safeguards when import surges injure or threaten domestic industry: Article XIX GATT and Agreement on Safeguards; or duties against states which subsidize industry contrary to GATT principles or dump goods at less than market value: GATT 1947 Article VI, Agreement on Implementation of Article VI of the General Agreement on Tariffs and Trade 1994, and Agreement on Subsidies and Countervailing Measures; they may form customs unions and free trade arrangements which discriminate against non-members: GATT 1947 Article XXIV, Understanding on the Interpretation of Article XXIV of the General Agreement on Tariffs and Trade 1994; they may protect intellectual property rights in a 'manner conducive to social and economic welfare': TRIPS Article 7; and, they may erect barriers to freely traded goods and services for reasons of health and environment: GATT 1947 Article XX, Agreement on the Application of Sanitary and Phytosanitary Measures, and Agreement on Technical Barriers to Trade. In relation to developing states the *telos* of economic development, rather than free trade, is even more explicit. The WTO Guide to the Uruguay Agreements, <http://www.wto.org/english/docs_e/legal_e/guide_ur_deving_country_e.pdf> notes the following departures from the principle of non-discrimination. The text of various agreements targets the needs of developing countries and less-developed countries by permitting flexibility in the use of trade measures by developing countries to protect their infant industries, and in the use of quantities restrictions to alleviate balance-of-payments problems: GATT 1947 Article XVIII. It modifies the general rules in favour of those states by facilitation of increased market access by developing countries and modification of the requirement of reciprocity in relation to the negotiation of trading concessions: GATT 1947 Part IV. It encourages developed states to adjust their obligations by licensing them to maintain preferential trading arrangements with developing states: the Enabling Clause (Decision on Differential and More Favourable Treatment, Reciprocity and Fuller Participation of Developing Countries), 28 November 1979 L/4903. Particular agreements also contain numerous let-outs and modifications of the strict rules by, for example, recognizing least-developed and developing country interests, easing the rules and obligations they must meet, providing longer time-frames for implementation, and providing for technical assistance. See, for example, specific developing country provisions in WTO Agreement; Decision on Measures in Favour of Least-Developed Countries; Decision on Notification Procedures; Understanding on Rules and Procedures Governing the Settlement of Disputes; Understanding on Balance of Payments Provision of GATT

1994; Agreement on Agriculture; Decision on Measures Concerning the Possible Negative Effects of the Reform Programme on Least Developed and Net Food-Importing Developed Countries; Agreement on the Application of Sanitary and Phytosanitary Measures; Agreement on Textiles and Clothing; Agreement on Technical Barriers to Trade; Agreement on Trade-Related Investment Measures (TRIMs); Agreement on Implementation of Article VI of the GATT; Agreement on Subsidies and Countervailing Measures; Agreement on Safeguards; Agreement on Implementation of Article VII of GATT 1994; Agreement on Preshipment Inspection; Agreement on Import Licensing Procedures; General Agreement on Trade in Services; and Agreement on Trade Related Aspects of Intellectual Property Rights.

(b) Context: An emphasis on development rather than free trade

The context of the covered agreements emphasizes that economic development, rather than free trade, is the overriding goal informing their interpretation. Alterations to the preamble to the agreements in 1994 now focus, not purely on free trade, but on different developmental needs of states and the need for positive efforts in relation to addressing those differences. Whereas economic development as growth was emphasized in the preamble to GATT 1947 which stated that trade be conducted 'with a view to raising standards of living, ensuring full employment and a large and steadily growing volume of real income and effective demand' this has since changed. Economic development interpreted as environmental sustainability, and economic development in the form of recognition of economic inequality are added to the expanded preamble in 1994, which states that trade must be pursued with an eye to environmental preservation, and 'different levels of economic development'. The later agreement also recognizes the redistributive aspect of economic development when it calls for 'positive efforts' to ensure that developing countries 'secure a share in the growth in international trade' and that this should be commensurate with their particular economic needs. Further evidence of the changing context for interpretation of the agreements is provided by the expansion of GATT into two sectors of vital interest to developing and less-developed states, agriculture and textiles, and the central importance placed on ongoing efforts to strengthen these disciplines. Equally, the current round of negotiations was christened the Development Round, and focuses on the important role of international trade in the promotion of economic development and places the alleviation of poverty and the needs and interests of developing countries 'at the heart of the Work Programme': Ministerial Declaration, WT/MIN(O1)DEC/1, <http://www.wto.org/english/thewto_e/minist_e/min01_e/mindecl_e.htm>. The new positioning of development as the key to international trade, rather than an inferior or ancillary goal, is confirmed in the 2000 United Nation Millenium Declaration (GA Res 55/2, GAOR, 55th Sess (2000)) the aims of which are to eradicate poverty; achieve universal education; promote gender equality; reduce child mortality; improve maternal health; combat HIV–Aids and other diseases; ensure environmental sustainability, and develop a global partnership for development. Finally, plans for implementation of these goals achieved increasing support in 2005 with the announcement by the British Chancellor for a new Marshall Plan targeting health, education, and infant mortality; continuing trade rule reform; and debt forgiveness (see, eg, speech by the Chancellor of the Exchequer Gordon Brown at a conference on 'Making Globalisation Work For All—The Challenge Of Delivering The Monterrey Consensus', 16 February 2004, <http://www.hm-treasury.gov.uk/newsroom_and_speeches/press/2004/press_12_04.cfm>).

Select Bibliography

P Allott, *Eunomia: New Order for a New World* (Oxford: Oxford University Press, 2001)

P Alston, 'Resisting the Merger and Acquisition of Human Rights by Trade Law: A Reply to Petersmann' (2002) 13 *European Journal of International Law* 815

JE Alvarez, 'Symposium: The Boundaries of the WTO' (2002) 96 *American Journal of International Law* 1

—— and R Howse, 'From Politics to Technocracy—and Back Again: The Fate of the Multilateral Trading Regime' (2002) 96 *American Journal of International Law* 94

A Appadurai, 'Disjuncture and Difference in the Global Cultural Economy' (1990) 2 *Public Culture* 1

J Atik, 'Democratizing the WTO' (2001) 33 *George Washington International Law Review* 451

I Ayres and J Braithwaite, *Responsive Regulation: Transcending the Deregulation Debate* (New York: Oxford University Press, 1992)

B Balassa, *The Theory of Economic Integration* (Homewood, Ill: RD Irwin, 1961)

VN Balasubramanyam (ed), *Jagdish Bhagwati—Writings on International Economics* (Delhi: Oxford University Press, 1997)

CE Barfield, *Free Trade, Sovereignty, Democracy: The Future of the World Trade Organization* (Washington, DC: American Enterprise Institute, 2001)

M Bedjaoui, *Towards a New International Economic Order* (New York: Holmes & Meier, 1979)

R Behboodi, 'Legal Reasoning and the International Law of Trade' (1998) 32 *Journal of World Trade* 55

JH Bello, 'The WTO Dispute Settlement Understanding: Less is More' (1996) 90 *American Journal of International Law* 416

JN Bhagwati and RE Hudec (eds), *Fair Trade and Harmonization: Prerequisites for Free Trade? Vol 2: Legal Analysis* (Cambridge, Mass: MIT Press, 1996)

R Bhala and D Gantz, 'WTO Case Review 2003' (2004) 21 *Arizona Journal of International and Comparative Law* 317

A von Bogdandy, 'Law and Politics in the WTO—Strategies to Cope with a Deficient Relationship' in JA Frowein and R Wolfrum (eds), *Max Planck Yearbook of United Nations Law*, Vol 5 (The Hague, London and New York: Kluwer Law International, 2001) 609

J Braithwaite and P Drahos, *Global Business Regulation* (Cambridge: Cambridge University Press, 2000)

G Brennan and JM Buchanan, *The Reason of Rules: Constitutional Political Economy* (Cambridge: Cambridge University Press, 1985)

M Bronckers, 'More Power to the WTO?' (2001) 4 *Journal of International Economic Law* 41

G de Búrca and J Scott (eds), *The EU and the WTO: Legal and Constitutional Issues* (Oxford and Portland, Oregon: Hart Publishing, 2001)

—— *Constitutional Change in the EU: From Uniformity to Flexibility* (Oxford: Hart Publishing, 2000)

C Carmody, 'Remedies and Conformity under the WTO Agreement' (2002) 5 *Journal of International Economic Law* 307

DZ Cass, 'The "Constitutionalization" of International Trade Law: Judicial Norm-Generation as the Engine of Constitutional Development in International Trade' (2001) 12 *European Journal of International Law* 39

—— 'International Business and Commerce' in P Cane and M Tushnet (eds), *The Oxford Handbook of Legal Studies* (Oxford: Oxford University Press, 2003)

D Chalmers, 'Post-nationalism and the Quest for Constitutional Substitutes' (2000) 27 *Journal of Law and Society* 178

S Charnovitz, 'WTO Cosmopolitics' (2002) 34 *New York University Journal of International Law and Politics* 299

Sunjoon Cho, 'A Bridge Too Far: The Fall of the Fifth WTO Ministerial Conference in Cancun and the Future of the Trade Constitution' (2004) 7 *Journal of International Economic Law* 219

Amy Chua, *World on Fire* (London: William Heinemann, 2003)

J Coicaud and V Heiskanen (eds), *The Legitimacy of International Organizations* (Tokyo; New York: United Nations Press, 2001)

M Coper, *Encounters with the Australian Constitution* (North Ryde, NSW: CCH Publishing, 1987)

T Cottier and M Hertig, 'The Prospects of 21st Century Constitutionalism' in AV Bogdandy and R Wolfrum (eds), *Max Planck Yearbook of United Nations Law*, Vol 7 (2004) 261

J Crawford, *The Creation of States in International Law* (Oxford: Clarendon Press, 1979)

MH Davis and D Neacsu, 'Legitimacy, Globally: The Incoherence of Free Trade Practice, Global Economics and their Governing Principles of Political Economy' (2001) 69 *UMKC Law Review* 733

LA DiMatteo, K Dosanjh, PL Frantz, P Bowal, and C Stoltenberg, 'The Doha Declaration and Beyond: Giving a Voice to Non-Trade Concerns within the WTO Trade Regime' (2003) 36 *Vanderbilt Journal of Transnational Law* 95

J Dunoff and J Trachtman, 'Economic Analysis of International Law' (1999) 24 *Yale Journal of International Law* 1

S Esserman and R Howse, 'The WTO on Trial' (2003) 82 *Foreign Affairs* 130

D Esty, 'The World Trade Organization's Legitimacy Crisis' (2002) 1 *World Trade Review* 7

IF Fletcher, L Mistelis, and M Cremona (eds), *Foundations and Perspectives of International Trade Law* (London: Sweet and Maxwell, 2001)

T Franck, *Fairness in International Law and Institutions* (Oxford: Clarendon Press, 1995)

G Frankenberg, 'Tocqueville's Question—The Role of a Constitution in the Process of Integration' (2000) 13 *Ratio Juris* 1

—— 'The Return of the Contract: Problems and Pitfalls of European Constitutionalism' (2000) 6 *European Law Journal* 257

JT Gathii, 'Good Governance as a Counter Insurgency Agenda to Oppositional and Transformative Social Projects in International Law' (1999) 5 *Buffalo Human Rights Law Review* 107

—— 'Re-Characterizing the Social in the Constitutionalization of the WTO: A Preliminary Analysis' (2001) 7 *Widener Law Symposium Journal* 137

S George, 'Corporate Globalisation' in E Bircham and J Charlton (eds), *Anti-Capitalism: A Guide to the Movement* (London: Bookmarks, 2001)

PM Gerhart, 'The Two Constitutional Visions of the World Trade Organization' (2003) *University of Pennsylvania Journal of International Economic Law* 1

J Greenwald, 'WTO Dispute Settlement: an Exercise in Trade Law Legislation?' (2003) 6 *Journal Of International Economic Law* 113

J Habermas, 'Paradigms of Law' (1996) 17 *Cardoza Law Review* 771

—— 'A Constitution for Europe?' (2001) 11 *New Left Review* 5

M Hardt and A Negri, *Empire* (Cambridge, Mass: Harvard University Press, 2000)

DJ Harris, *Cases and Materials on International Law*, 4th edn (London: Sweet and Maxwell, 1991)

JW Head, 'Throwing Eggs at Windows: Legal and Institutional Globalization in the 21st Century Economy' (2002) 50 *University of Kansas Law Review* 731

LR Helfer and A-M Slaughter, 'Toward a Theory of Effective Supranational Adjudication' (1997) 107 *Yale Law Journal* 273, 310

N Hertz, *The Silent Takeover* (London: Heinemann, 2001)

BM Hoekman and MM Kostecki (eds), *The Political Economy of the World Trading System*, 2nd edn (Oxford: Oxford University Press, 2001)

P Holmes, 'The WTO and the EU: Some Constitutional Comparisons' in G de Búrca and J Scott (eds), *The EU and the WTO: Legal and Constitutional Issues* (Oxford and Portland, Oregon: Hart Publishing, 2001)

R Howse (ed), *The World Trading System: Critical Perspectives on The World Economy* (London: Routledge, 1998)

—— 'Tribute—The House that Jackson Built: Restructuring the GATT' (1999) 20 *Michigan Journal of International Law* 107

—— 'Adjudicative Legitimacy and Treaty Interpretation in International Trade Law: The Early Years of WTO Jurisprudence' in JHH Weiler (ed), *the EU, the WTO, and the NAFTA: Towards a Common Law of International Trade* (Oxford: Oxford University Press, 2000)

—— 'The Legitimacy of the World Trade Organization' in J Coicaud and V Heiskanen (eds), *The Legitimacy Of International Organizations* (Tokyo: United Nations Press, 2001)

—— and K Nicolaidis, 'Legitimacy and Global Governance: Why Constitutionalizing the WTO is a Step Too Far' in RB Porter, *et al* (eds), *Efficiency, Equity, and Legitimacy: The Multilateral Trading System at the Millennium* (Washington, DC: Brookings Institution Press, 2001)

RE Hudec, *Developing Countries in the GATT Legal System* (London: Gower Publishing Co, 1987)

—— *Enforcing International Trade Law: The Evolution of the Modern GATT Legal System* (Salem, NH: Butterworth Legal Publishers, 1993)

—— *Essays on the Nature of International Trade Law* (London: Cameron May, 1999)

—— and JD Southwick, 'Regionalism and WTO Rules: Problems in the Fine Art of Discriminating Fairly' in M Mendoza, P Low, B Kotschar (eds), *Trade Rules in the Making: Challenges in Regional and Multilateral Negotiations* (1999)

JH Jackson, 'The WTO Dispute Settlement Understanding—Misunderstandings on the Nature of Legal Obligation' (1997) 91 *American Journal of International Law* 60

JH Jackson, *The World Trading System: Law and Policy of International Economic Relations*, 2nd edn (Cambridge, Mass, and London, England: MIT Press, 1997)

—— *The World Trade Organization: Constitution and Jurisprudence* (London: Royal Institute of International Affairs, 1998)

—— 'Fragmentation or Unification Among International Institutions: the WTO' (1999) 31 *New York Journal of Law and Politics* 823

—— *The Jurisprudence of GATT and the WTO: Insights on Treaty Law and Economic Relations* (Cambridge: Cambridge University Press, 2000)

—— 'International Economic Law in Times that are Interesting' (2000) 3 *Journal of International Economic Law* 3

—— 'The WTO "Constitution" and Proposed Reforms: Seven "Mantras" Revisited' (2001) 4 *Journal of International Economic Law* 67

——, WJ Davey and AO Sykes, *Legal Problems of International Economic Relations*, 3rd edn (St Paul, Minn: West Publishing Co, 1995)

——, —— and —— *Legal Problems of International Economic Relations*, 4th edn (St Paul, Minn: West Publishing Co, 2002)

VC Jackson and M Tushnet, *Comparative Constitutional Law* (New York: Foundation Press, 1999)

I Jennings and CM Young, *Constitutional Laws of the British Empire* (Oxford: Clarendon Press, 1938)

CR Kelly, 'The Value Vacuum: Self-Enforcing Regimes and the Dilution of the Normative Feedback Loop' (2001) 22 *Michigan Journal of International Law* 673

H Kelsen, *General Theory of Law and State* (Cambridge, Mass: Harvard University Press, 1945)

—— *Pure Theory of Law* (Berkeley: University of California Press, 1967)

D Kennedy, 'The International Style in Postwar Law and Policy' (1994) 1 *Utah Law Review* 7

P Kennedy, *The Rise and Fall of the Great Powers* (New York: Vintage Books, 1987)

R Keohane and J Nye, 'The Club Model of Multilateral Cooperation and Problems of Democratic Legitimacy' in RB Porter, *et al*, (eds), *Efficiency, Equity, and Legitimacy: The Multilateral Trading System at the Millennium* (Washington, DC: Brookings Institution Press, 2001)

N Klein, *No Logo* (London, Flamingo, 2000)

B Langille, 'General Reflections on the Relationship of Trade and Labor (Or: Fair Trade is Free Trade's Destiny)' in J Bhagwati and R Hudec (eds) *Fair Trade and Harmonization: Prerequisites for free Trade? Vol 2: Legal Analysis* (Cambridge, Mass: MIT Press, 1996)

K Leitner and S Lester, 'WTO Dispute Settlement 1995–2002: A Statistical Analysis' (2003) 6 *Journal of International Economic Law* 251

MA Levy, OR Young and M Zurn, 'The Study of International Regimes' (1995) 1 *European Journal of International Relations* 267

M Loughlin, 'Ten Tenets of Sovereignty' in N Walker (ed), *Sovereignty in Transition* (Oxford: Hart Publishing, 2003)

MP Maduro, 'Reforming the Market or the State? Article 30 and the European Constitution: Economic Freedom and Political Rights' (1997) 3 *European Law Journal* 55

G Marceau, 'WTO Dispute Settlement and Human Rights' (2002) 13 *European Journal of International Law* 753

S Marks and A Clapham, 'Development' in *International Human Rights Lexicon* (Oxford University Press, forthcoming)

P Nichols, 'GATT Doctrine' (1996) 36 *Virginia Journal of International Law* 379

PM Nichols, 'Forgotten Linkages—Historical Institutionalism and Sociological Institutionalism and Analysis of the World Trade Organization' (1998) 19 *University of Pennsylvania Journal of International Economic Law* 461

DC North, *Institutions, Institutional Change and Economic Performance* (Cambridge: Cambridge University Press, 1990)

PM North and JJ Fawcett, *Cheshire and North's Private International Law*, 13th edn (London: Butterworths, 1999)

JR Paul, 'Do International Trade Institutions Contribute to Economic Growth and Development' (2003) 44 *Virginia Journal of International Law* 285

Steve Peers, 'Fundamental Right or Political Whim? WTO Law and the European Court of Justice,' in Grainne de Burca and Joanne Scott (eds), *The EU and the WTO, Legal and Constitutional Issues* 111 (Oxford and Portland, Oregon: Hart Publishing, 2001)

E-U Petersmann, *Constitutional Functions and Constitutional Problems of International Economic Law* (Fribourg, Switzerland: University Press, 1991)

—— *The GATT/WTO Dispute Settlement System: International Law, International Organizations and Dispute Settlement* (London: Kluwer, 1997)

—— (ed), *International Trade Law and the GATT/WTO Dispute Settlement System* (London: Kluwer, 1997)

—— 'How to Constitutionalize International Law and Foreign Policy for the Benefit of Civil Society?' (1998) 20 *Michigan Journal of International Law* 1

—— 'Constitutionalism and International Adjudication: How to Constitutionalize the UN Dispute Settlement System?' (1999) 31 *New York Journal of International Law and Politics* 753

—— 'The WTO Constitution and Human Rights' (2000) 3 *Journal of International Economic Law* 19

—— 'Human Rights and International Economic Law in the Twenty First Century' (2001) 4 *Journal of International Economic Law* 3

—— 'Time for a United Nations "Global Compact" for Integrating Human Rights into the Law of Worldwide Organizations' (2002) 13 *European Journal of International Law* 621

S Picciotto and R Mayne (eds), *Regulating International Business: Beyond Liberalization* (Basingstoke: Macmillan, 1999)

T Pogge, *World Poverty And Human Rights: Cosmopolitan Responsibilities and Reforms* (London: Polity Press, 2002)

RB Porter, *et al* (eds), *Efficiency, Equity, and Legitimacy: The Multilateral Trading System at the Millennium* (Washington, DC: Brookings Institution Press, 2001)

RA Posner, *The Problematics of Moral and Legal Theory* (Cambridge: Belknap Press, 1999)

B Rajagopal, 'Corruption, Legitimacy and Human Rights: The Dialectic of the Relationship' (1999) 14 *Connecticut Journal of International Law* 495

—— 'From Resistance to Renewal: The Third World, Social Movements and, the Expansion of International Institutions' (2000) 41 *Harvard International Law Journal* 529

D Rodrik, *Has Globalisation Gone Too Far?* (Washington DC: Institute for International Economics, c 1997)

M Rosenfeld, 'Can Rights, Democracy, and Justice be Reconciled through Discourse Theory? Reflections on Habermas's Proceduralist Paradigm of Law' (1996) 17 *Cardozo Law Review* 791

E Rothschild, *Economic Sentiments: Adam Smith, Condorcet and the Enlightenment*, (Cambridge, Mass. and London, England: Harvard University Press, 2001)

M Salas and JH Jackson 'Procedural Overview of the WTO EC—Bananas Dispute' (2000) 3 *Journal of International Economic Law* 145

F Schauer, *Playing By The Rules: A Philosophical Examination of Rule-based Decision Making in Law and in Life* (Oxford, England: Clarendon Press, New York: Oxford University Press (1991)

HL Schloemann and S Ohlhoff, ' "Constitutionalization" and Dispute Settlement in the WTO: National Security as an Issue of Competence' (1999) 93 *American Journal of International Law* 424

I Seidl-Hohenveldern, *International Economic Law*, 3rd edn (The Hague: Kluwer, 1999)

J Shaw, 'Relating Constitutionalism and Flexibility' in G de Búrca and J Scott (eds), *Constitutional Change in the EU: From Uniformity to Flexibility* (Oxford: Hart Publishing, 2000)

M Shaw, *International Law*, 4th edn (Cambridge: Cambridge University Press, 1997)

GR Shell, 'Trade Legalism and International Relations Theory: An Analysis of the World Trade Organization' (1995) 44 *Duke Law Journal* 829

R Skidelsky, *John Maynard Keynes, Volume 3: Fighting for Britain 1937–1946* (London: Macmillan, 2000, Papermac 2001)

F Snyder, 'Governing Economic Globalisation: Global Legal Pluralism and European Law' (1999) 5 *European Law Journal* 334

D Steger, 'Review of Claude E Barfield, *Free Trade, Sovereignty, Democracy: The Future of the World Trade Organization*' (2002) 5 *Journal of International Economic Law* 565

JE Stiglitz, *Globalization and its Discontents* (London: Penguin Books, 2002)

GR Stone *et al* (eds), *Constitutional Law*, 2nd edn (Boston: Little Brown, 1991)

AS Sweet, 'Judicialization and the Construction of Governance' (1999) 32 *Comparative Political Studies* 147

DK Tarullo, 'Beyond Normalcy in the Regulation of International Trade' (1987) 100 *Harvard Law Review* 546

—— 'Book Review—The EU and the WTO: Legal and Constitutional Issues' (2002) 5 *Journal of International Economic Law* 941

G Teubner, *Global Law without a State* (Aldershot: Dartmouth Publishing Co, 1997)

JP Trachtman, 'The Theory of the Firm and the Theory of the International Economic Organization: Toward Comparative Institutional Analysis' (1997) 17 *Northwestern Journal of International Law and Business* 470

—— 'The Domain of WTO Dispute Resolution' (1999) 40 *Harvard International Law Journal* 333

—— 'Legal Aspects of a Poverty Agenda at the WTO: Trade Law and "Global Apartheid" ' (2003) 6 *Journal of International Economic Law* 3

MJ Trebilcock and R Howse, *The Regulation of International Trade*, 2nd edn (London and New York: Routledge, 1999)

R Wai, 'Transnational Liftoff and Juridical Touchdown: The Regulatory Function of Private International Law in an Era of Globalization' (2002) 40 *Columbia Journal of Transnational Law* 209

N Walker, 'Flexibility within a Metaconstitutional Frame: Reflections on the Future of Legal Authority in Europe' in G de Búrca and J Scott (eds), *Constitutional Change in the EU: From Uniformity to Flexibility* (Oxford: Hart Publishing, 2000)

—— 'The EU and the WTO: Constitutionalism in a New Key' in G de Búrca and J Scott (eds), *The EU and the WTO: Legal and Constitutional Issues* (Oxford and Portland, Oregon: Hart Publishing, 2001)

—— 'Constitutionalising Enlargement, Enlarging Constitutionalism' (2003) 9 *European Law Journal* 365

VR Walker, 'Keeping the WTO from Becoming the "World Trans-science Organization": Scientific Uncertainty, Science Policy, and Fact Finding in the Growth Hormones Dispute' (1998) 31 *Cornell International Law Journal* 251

C Weeramantry, *Nauru: Environmental Damage under International Trusteeship*, (Oxford University Press, 1992)

JHH Weiler, *The Constitution of Europe* (Cambridge: Cambridge University Press, 1999)

—— 'The Constitution of the Common Market Place: Text and Context in the Evolution of the Free Movement of Goods' in P Craig and G de Búrca (eds), *The Evolution of European Union Law* (Oxford: Oxford University Press, 1999)

—— 'Cain and Abel—Convergence and Divergence in International Trade Law' in JHH Weiler (ed), *The EU, the WTO, and the NAFTA: Towards a Common Law of International Trade* (Oxford: Oxford University Press, 2000)

—— 'The Rule of Lawyers and the Ethos of Diplomats: Reflections on WTO Dispute Settlement' in RB Porter, *et al* (eds), *Efficiency, Equity, and Legitimacy: The Multilateral Trading System at the Millennium* (Washington, DC: Brookings Institution Press, 2001)

—— and JP Trachtman, 'European Constitutionalism and its Discontents' (1997) 17 *Northwestern Journal of International Law and Business* 354

M Williams and B MacDonald, *The Phosphateers: A History of the British Phosphate Commissioners and the Christmas Island Phosphate Commission* (Melbourne: Melbourne University Press, 1985)

AB Zampetti, 'The Notion of "Fairness" in International Trade Relations and the US Perspective,' (1995) (unpublished manuscript, on file with author)

—— 'Democratic Legitimacy in the World Trade Organization: The Justice Dimension' (2003) 37 *Journal of World Trade* 105

Index